JUDO, THE AVENGERS & ME

CYD CHILD / CHRIS GALLIE 7th Dan

DEDICATION

I dedicate this book to my long-suffering husband, Peter, who has had to put up with a lifetime of me ruining the illusion of all the action films he likes to watch. Without his help and encouragement, this book would never have been written.

First published in 2021 by Fantom Publishing, an imprint of Fantom Films
www.fantompublishing.co.uk

A catalogue record for this book is available from the British Library.

First edition ISBN: 978-1-78196-379-1

Printed and bound by Instant Print (UK)
Typeset and Designed by Dexter O'Neill

With thanks to:
Phil Reynolds Media Services, Leamington Spa, Paul W.T. Ballard & Jason Clifford

Contents

Preface

Be yourself; everyone else is already taken.
Oscar Wilde

It had never occurred to me that anyone might be interested in reading my story. However, over the years I have been made aware that many people want to know all about the behind-the-scenes stories of life in the film industry. When I was working as a stunt girl, we were not acknowledged. The general public were encouraged to believe that their idols did all their own stunts. To this end, we were not given credits, and expected not to tell anyone about our work.

Consequently, it is difficult to find a photographic record of stunts performed – unless you took your own camera and persuaded a friend to take photos for you, which was not always possible. There are also a great many people who find it hard to appreciate just how unbelievably difficult it was for women to gain equal opportunity to take part in competitive judo, and how long it took for us ladies to rectify this. So, I have been persuaded to tell all (that I remember...). I hope you find it interesting.

INTRODUCTION

Brian Jacks

Many times international judo champion and Superstars champion.
B.J.A. 8th Dan WMAC 10th Dan

What a privilege it is for me to write an introduction for Christine Gallie (a.k.a. Cyd Child), an amazing pioneer for British judo. She helped to change the shape of the sport in this country, particularly for women, and there is no doubt that she's been an inspiration to many women who followed her, such as Karen Briggs MBE.

In 1971, at the first British Women's Open Individual Championship in Bracknell, Chris won the heavyweight title and picked up a bronze in the open weight. Not happy with the bronze, Chris had to look for ways to 'up her game' and came up with a plan that, I have to say, put the Budokwai in a bit of a spin. Upping her game meant that she had to find taller and better opponents; and there were not a lot of British women who could help with that, apart from Christine Wildman.

So Chris decided that she wanted to train with men; and she came to see me about joining the British men-only elite Olympic training class, at the Budokwai. Although I ran this, I felt Syd Hoare, the manager and senior to me, should make the decision. But Syd pushed it back to me and, as much as I wanted to allow Chris in, there were many people who might have been upset with this. For a woman to train with the men-only elite class was totally unheard of in those days, and a lot of questions were asked. Eventually we agreed, with a few guidelines put in place to stop this becoming the norm, and Chris came in. I never gave her any special privileges, and she did very well. I think in most training sessions we had between sixty and seventy people training, and she held her own with most of the men.

In the early days, I might even have pushed her harder than many of the men, and she responded positively. She took everything I threw at her. Did I take my belt off to her? Well, in jest I might have done, but I knew her mission and I wanted to help. I took great pleasure in lifting her onto my shoulders so that she could see another way forward – a way to become the best – and she never let me or herself down.

Did her plan work? Well, she won the British Open, in her weight category, five times in a row between 1971 and 1975. In 1973 she also won the open weight category. In 1974 Chris won gold at the women's test European Championships in Genoa, and she followed that up the next year with gold again in the Official European Championships in Munich; this made her the first British woman to win a European Championship gold medal. So, the answer to the question is a definite yes – her plan worked; plus she also became the first woman in Britain to reach Fifth and Sixth Dan status.

I talk and write a lot about my four Ds, and she had all of these in abundance and some more: Dedication, Determination, Desire and Discipline. She also developed a superb Uchi-Mata, which gave me great pleasure as it was my favourite throw and I think it became her favourite as well.

Chris raised her own bar, but she also wanted to elevate the status of women's judo in Great Britain. She went on a crusade to introduce more Dan gradings, and I helped with that by agreeing to be one of the examiners. As a result, the numbers of women participating in British judo began to grow.

I remember, at one point, Chris and I were engaged in some special training for a kata presentation. Chris had become a real kata expert. Unfortunately, I sustained an injury that meant I couldn't take part in the presentation. This might have been a blessing in disguise as I'm sure that Chris's parrot knew more about the katas than I did!

Outside of judo, Chris became 'The *Avengers* Girl' and I know she helped many of the star women on the show. She stunt-doubled for Diana Rigg and Linda Thorson, while for Joanna Lumley ('yes darling') she became her personal trainer. She helped get Joanna in such amazing shape that I'm sure it meant a lot more people tuned into *The New Avengers*. The Avengers, old and new, were a big success and cult viewing.

In much the same way that I helped to inspire people to take up judo with my appearances on *Superstars*, Chris did the same with *The Avengers*.

Chris Gallie, the first British woman to make an impact in world judo, I salute you.

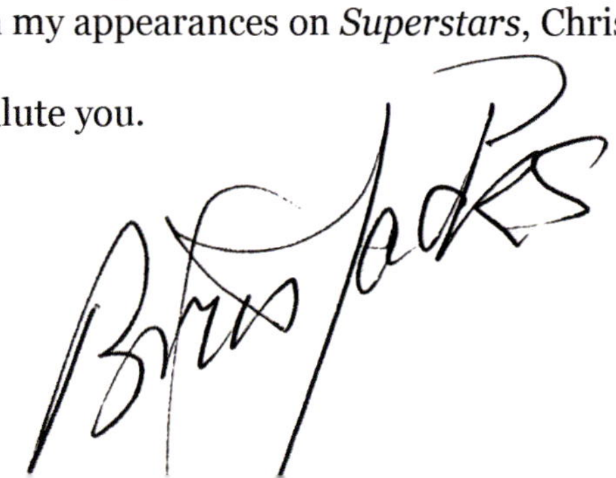

FOREWORD
Elizabeth Viney MBE

BJA Women's Team Manager 1972-74
& BJA Hon. National Coach 1975-85

It is a great honour and privilege to write the foreword to Chris's book.

It is one thing to have talent, but it is another to use it and to take it to exceptional levels. Chris's skill, effort and incredible determination enabled her to achieve what many would consider impossible.

Her dedication to our sport helped to put Great Britain at the forefront of international women's judo, leading us ultimately on to both world and Olympic participation.

Chris's record as a member of the first British Judo Association National Women's Squad and beyond is breathtaking, and I have pleasure in recording it here:

Gold medallist in all of the following international judo events:

- Gelsenkirchen, West Germany 1972
- Italian International 1972
- Swiss International 1973
- Italian International 1973
- German Open, Munich, West Germany 1973
- Dutch Open Championships 1974 and 1975.

Plus golds in the BJA Women's National Individual (Open) Championships – from the first event in 1971 onwards to 1975 – and actually taking two golds in this event in 1973!

Chris crowned her outstanding success by taking further golds for Great Britain in both the first European Women's Judo Tournament in Genoa, Italy – December 1974 (a trial event) and the first Women's European Judo Championships in Munich – December, 1975.

Chris received the Dame Enid Russell-Smith Trophy in 1974, as the person who had done the most to promote women's judo, and the Vic Terry 'Personality of the Year' Silver Cup in 1975.

The British Judo Association awarded Chris her Sixth Dan (black belt) in May 1983 and her Seventh Dan in January 1998.

Chris was also mentioned in the 1974 Guinness Book of Records for the most consecutive British wins.

This remained unchallenged for seventeen years until the record was removed from the book in favour of international records.

Warmest congratulations, Chris, on your remarkable story and your fantastic judo achievements, from me, Liz.

FOREWORD

Joanna Lumley

Well known and much-loved actress and TV presenter.
Purdey from *The New Avengers*

I knew her as Cyd, but she already had legendary status as heavyweight judo champion and glorious stunt double to my two predecessors in The Avengers. But we were the New Avengers, and things were going to be slightly different. Cyd was to oversee fights and stunts and only double for me whenever necessary; but first she put Gareth Hunt and me through a training regime which nearly broke my shabby, unfit, weedy body.

She was superb: she was a sort of goddess, not too strong a word, strong, lethally unforgiving, beautiful and as kind as the morning sun. All I did and learned I achieved through trying to please Cyd; never in my adult life have I worked so hard.

She was selfless: she knew flesh would be deeply cut by putting an arm through a car window, and although I feebly piped up that I would have a go, she carried the can, was cut to ribbons and never said a word.

She fought in the dark water of a flooded cellar, throwing herself backwards into the filthy slush in a move that would have snapped my spine; she prepared every stunt, no matter how challenging or easy (for her), with meticulous attention to detail. She was The Business: and yet how little of her I really knew!

Reading this extraordinarily gripping book I realise that it is her life that should be made into a film; she is the heroine we all secretly swoon to see: secretly, because often we cannot tell she was there on screen, making the actresses look brilliant; secretly, because her dedication to judo and astonishing achievements in that field are the stuff of legend and should be shouted from the rooftops.

Everything shines and gleams in this wonderful account of a dazzling life. I kneel before her (and half-hear her voice quietly coaxing me to get my leg a bit higher, just past the ear... 'Go on Jo! You can do it!').

If I did, it was because of you, Cyd Child. Thanks, you amazing woman, for having me in your life.

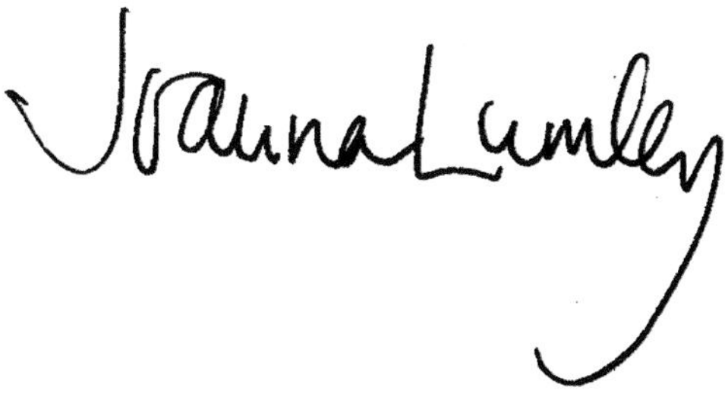

CHAPTER ONE
In the Beginning

If there is effort, there is always accomplishment.
Jigoro Kano (The Father of Judo)

Now it's the M4, all tarmac and rushing traffic... but when I was a child, it was a paradise. Green fields filled with buttercups, daisies, lady's slippers, wild orchids and innumerable wild flowers; trees to climb and ditches to jump over. It was just after the war; adults appeared always to be preoccupied with important things to do, and we kids used to run wild. It seems that whenever you remember your childhood, the sun is always shining, the grass around your feet is always lush and full of flowers. You remember that there was snow, but you can't remember the feel of the chill.

I was born in Collinswood Maternity Home near Slough towards the end of World War Two. My mother told me that a doodlebug (V1 rocket) flew over while I was being born. I'm not sure if that was an omen... As I was born at Christmas, my parents decided to call me Christine Carol (as I was a little Christmas Carol). I had a brother who was eleven years older than me and I idolised him. His name was Tony.

We lived in a council house in Cippenham, near Slough. My Dad was a master welder, and during the war he had helped to make the flail tanks and the Mulberry harbours that were used in the D-Day invasion of Normandy. He worked in the maintenance department at the Mars factory in Slough, which was great for our family. I can remember when I was small I took a dislike to bread and butter and my Dad made me sandwiches made from a sliced Mars Bar to encourage me to eat bread. Another time he brought home what looked like giant chunks of Kryptonite, which were the result of the machine that made Spangles breaking down – absolutely delicious! We just hacked bits off. This was just after the war and sweets were in short supply; they would continue to be rationed until 1953.

I was a terrible tomboy; in fact I was probably a great cause of worry to my mother. I was always coming home scratched, bruised and grubby. My father didn't seem to mind. He would much rather have had another son than a daughter. My mother told me that when I was born he had been a bit disappointed that I was a girl, but had said that at least I had blue eyes and blonde hair. Unfortunately that didn't last long; my eyes turned brown and eventually my hair became dark as well.

We always seemed to have a dog, and sometimes cats too; at one time we had a wonderful German Shepherd dog. I called him Rinty (after the famous dog Rin Tin Tin). We loved each other. I probably gave him a bit of a hard time. I was only a child and he was so big (to me), and I would try to ride him.

He dealt with this by just walking under the table so that I had to get off. He never hurt me. He wanted to be with me all the time and would follow me out to play.

This worried my mother as he would sit watching us (the children) playing and, if anyone pushed me, the corner of his mouth would lift to show his teeth and he would give a low growl. Because of this she took to bolting the kitchen door in an attempt to keep him indoors when I went out, but he learned to unbolt it with his teeth and would go out to find me.

One day I went out with my brother and Rinty. I was skipping along the pavement on the way to the fields where we played. My brother was following behind with Rinty on a lead. We had to go into a small close to get to the entrance to the footpath. Unbeknown to me, living in one of the houses in the close was a dog that made a habit of trying to bite the back of people's legs. Suddenly there was the most almighty commotion behind me. I had been totally unaware that the dog was sneaking up on me; but Rinty, realising what was about to happen, had ripped his lead out of my brother's hand, charged the other dog and rolled him down the road. He was my hero!

Unfortunately, the adults in my life were not so impressed with him. In those days, there was no television, and people would visit each other in the evening and sit around chatting. If anyone came to visit us, Rinty had to be locked in the bathroom because everyone was frightened of him. I didn't see the problem. I adored him.

Then one day, I came home from school and he wasn't there. I asked where he was and was given some lame excuse which I didn't understand. He wasn't there the next day either... or the next. By this time I wasn't believing anything I was being told, and demanded to know where he was. Eventually, I found out that my father had taken him to be put down as he was so worried that he would hurt a child. I didn't speak to my father for weeks, and I couldn't forgive him. Now, I understand his dilemma, but I wish he had just found Rinty another home.

My mother told me that, as I was obviously going to be tall, I needed to learn 'deportment'. I was duly enrolled in ballet classes. I was four years old. Maybe this was her way of trying to make me more ladylike.

I did actually enjoy these classes. I made friends and we had fun, learning the basics of ballet and tap dancing. The lady who ran the classes put on shows from time to time, so we got to wear costumes and make-up, which is very exciting when you are young. Unfortunately, as I was tall, if there was a boy in the story it was usually me... Little Boy Blue springs to mind!

This is me with my brother, Tony.

There were four of us who became firm friends. There was me, Renee, Diane and Lesley. We all went to the same classes and progressed through the grades together. We were usually around the same level. I loved ballet and dreamed of being a ballerina. However, there came a time when things began to change.

Our teacher introduced us to 'pointwork', where you dance on your toes. I found myself struggling as my ankles just weren't strong enough. I was lagging behind and my friends began to progress without me. As if this wasn't depressing enough, it was also being pointed out to me that I was really a bit too tall to do well in the ballet world. My partners would struggle to lift me...

I had reached a point where I was questioning whether or not I should continue. I was at a crossroads really and, without realising it, was looking for something else. I had been going to ballet classes regularly and needed another interest.

Aged 5.

My parents were now running a small pub, 'The Crooked Billet', out in the sticks in Buckinghamshire.

We lived in a small hamlet called Sheepridge. It was composed of six cottages, a farm and our pub. There was nothing around us except fields and woods. When we first moved in we had oil lamps upstairs and no proper plumbing. Our water was pumped down from the farm. On one occasion the farmer went on holiday and forgot to make arrangements for the supply of water. All of a sudden nobody had any water, and my Dad and the other locals had to go up to the farm to work out how to restart the supply. They managed it, which was fortunate for us as the farmer wasn't due to return for another week.

There were no shops nearby. There was a mobile shop, a converted removal van, which sold mainly fruit and vegetables and would call by once a week. In fact my first Saturday job was riding on this vehicle as a helper.

I wanted to continue at the same school that I had been at before we moved, which was in Slough, so I had a lengthy trek every day. Besides having to catch two buses, I needed a lift to the nearest village to start my journey. Sometimes, when I returned, my Dad would be too busy to fetch me and I would have to walk, which was miles! If I was lucky, though, my brother would pick me up on his motorbike.

This is Rinty with my brother and I.

My Dad had been a farrier in the Royal Horse Guards and had trained as a blacksmith. He got himself a portable forge and used to shoe the horses for the local gypsies who would frequently camp near us.

That's me far right
on the end...
in one of our shows.

Me on the left as Little
Boy Blue with Diane.

This time far left - with
Renee far right and Lesley
in the middle.

November 1951. Aged 6.
I'm on the far right, again!

The Crooked Billet, Sheepridge.

This is my Mum and she has just been 'shopping' from the van...

My Dad changing horse shoes.

Dad with the forge that the brewery built for him.

My brother on his motorbike .

They used to pay him with 'things' such as copper kettles, antique furniture and, on one occasion, a brass milk-skimmer. Dad made the lamps to go on the wall when we 'went electric', and also a fire basket for the lounge. The brewery were so impressed that they built him a proper forge behind the pub!

Dad was concerned that sometimes he would have to leave my Mum and me on our own at the pub, while he took the darts team to other pubs. He decided to solve this problem by getting a German Shepherd dog for my mother. We found the ideal dog. Her name was Karan and she was being sold by a gamekeeper who had tried to 'attack-train' her. He had been attacked himself by poachers and wanted a vicious dog to protect him, but his methods had failed dismally with her. He had only succeeded in making her afraid of men. She would hide in terror if my Dad so much as picked up a newspaper. She took to my mother immediately, and accepted me as another friend. It took her a bit longer to realise that Dad wouldn't hurt her either. Like all German Shepherds she was very intelligent, and she also had a very lovely nature. Eventually Mum bred a litter of puppies from her. They all went to good homes and people were constantly asking Mum to let her have some more; but it was such hard work and Mum had enough to do with running the pub, so she declined.

One day, one of our customers came in and was telling us about a new club in the next village, where they were doing something called 'judo'. This piqued my interest. I had no idea what judo was; nobody I spoke to seemed to know either. Judo was not well known at this time; it was something mysterious to do with self-defence... and foreign. So I decided to find out about it, and went for a visit.

The club was in a small village hall. The people there were very friendly and made me feel welcome. I was invited to join in, and they loaned me a jacket. I discovered that judo is a bit like a kind of physical chess: you are trying to outwit your opponent and score points off them before they can score off you.

That first evening I had so much fun that I wanted to go again... and again... I was fifteen. I became a regular, and gradually worked my way through the grades. The only bit I didn't like was the walk home, in the dark with no lights or houses. It was approximately two miles and very creepy.

The club was called the Veraloy Judo Club. It was named after a company in High Wycombe that had sponsored it. The main instructor was a man called Dil Bowen. He was very helpful and encouraging.

The club outgrew the village hall, and we moved closer to High Wycombe, renting an upstairs room in an old pub. This didn't last long. I arrived one evening for my regular practice and was told that we weren't allowed in! I eventually found out that the landlord didn't want us any more because our sessions had been making the plaster fall off the ceilings downstairs...

We then moved into an old manor house even closer to the town, and settled in there. The only annoying thing was that we had to store our mats in a large cupboard halfway up the staircase. These were thick horsehair mats, held together with a wooden frame and covered with a laced-up canvas sheet, and were very heavy. Nobody enjoyed bringing the mats down, or taking them back again, but it had to be done.

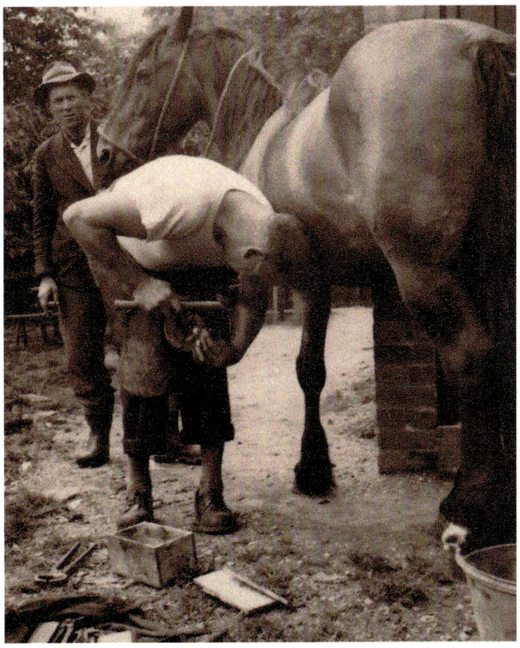

Our guard dog, and her litter...

Puppies with mum.

Certain people devised various subterfuges to avoid this chore; however, my bus timetable meant that I was always there when the mats had to be moved, so I couldn't get out of it.

There were hurdles for me to cross, though. At that time judo was really dominated by men; there were not very many women involved, and that was often a problem when it came to gradings. To be graded, you need someone to compete against, but there were only ever a few girls at the gradings and very often they would all be different grades. Occasionally the examiner would suggest using some of the men for the ladies' grading; but nobody liked that idea – neither men nor women. This meant that sometimes you would make the effort to travel to a grading but have to return home with nothing because there had been nobody for you to compete against. Another problem I faced was that my schoolteachers were not happy with the bruises that I would sometimes appear with and tried to forbid me from continuing with judo. I quickly learned to give a different reason for any bumps and scrapes, although I'm not sure that they believed me.

After our GCE 'O' level examinations were over and we had our results, I told my parents that I would really like to go to the art college at Maidenhead. However, my father had other ideas. He said to me, 'It's time you earned your own living!' So that was that. At the time I was rather resentful that I wasn't allowed to go, but I didn't realise how hard life was for my parents. Now I can understand.

The summer holiday after I left school was spent studying the newspapers for 'situations vacant', desperately trying to find some kind of job that I might like to do. My father wanted me to be an engineering draftsman. I went along with it for a while because I didn't know what that was! I discovered that this was a job for men. Apparently the training took quite a long time and no one wanted to train females as they would probably leave to have babies! I did find one eminent company in London who were willing to take me on; but after I had gone for an interview (and they did offer me a job), I found that the amount of pay I would receive would hardly cover me for my travel to work. So I declined.

I really liked the idea of joining the Navy. I wanted to go to sea! Then I was told that women in the Royal Navy didn't go to sea. The prospect of a position on land didn't appeal, so I applied for jobs working as a 'purserette' with various shipping companies such as P&O, but they wouldn't take me on until I was 24 years old. It seemed to be a distinct disadvantage to be female...

Eventually I started work as a lab assistant for Monsanto earning £2 ten shillings a week (£45 in current money). I wasn't mad about the job but I did my best. There was a resident lady photographer there; I was fascinated with her job and decided that that was more like something I could enjoy, so I left and joined a small photographic business in High Wycombe. I joined the local college going to night school in photography and ended up working as a photographer for the Ministry of Aviation. However, I managed to keep up my judo studies.

The Red Lion.

I remember going to Beaconsfield for a grading that was to be held in a local school. Geoff Gleeson, the National Coach, was the examiner, and he arrived late. We were all waiting and wondering if he was going to turn up. When he arrived, the organiser gushingly welcomed him and then desperately looked around for someone to provide His Eminence with some refreshment. His eyes lit up when he saw a female (me), and I was told to go and make Mr Gleeson a cup of tea. I remember being most put out, thinking, 'I've paid to come here for the grading, not to make tea... and I don't even know where the kettle is!' But, at the time, that was the attitude of a lot of the men – women in judo were not really to be taken seriously.

Although we loved living out in the countryside, Dad had an offer of a better pub in a neighbouring village, and we moved to the Red Lion in Wooburn Green. Dad was particularly attracted to it because it used to be an old coaching inn and still had the original forge. The forge hadn't been used for a long time, and I was not so keen as Dad coerced me into cleaning it up for him. The windows were very dirty so it was dark in there, and the whole place seemed to be covered in a thick layer of black soot – and there were the biggest spiders I had ever seen!

The advantage, though, was that we were now in a village with local shops, a village green in front of us, and a bus service. On the May bank holiday we would have a visit from the Morris dancers which used to draw sightseers. They always danced in front of the pub, one reason being that they got free beer for doing it! There was also, at that time (before Dr Beeching's cuts), a small branch line of the railway which ran behind our garden, with a tiny railway station. My brother was now living in Wales and I could travel on the train to visit him. My ticket was a written receipt which would carry me all the way from Wooburn Green to Bridgend, even though I had to change at Maidenhead and Reading.

CHAPTER TWO
The Budokwai

In skill opposed, in spirit united.
Budokwai motto

I persevered at my judo and eventually won my brown belt. As usual, I immediately turned to my teacher and said, 'What do I have to do now for my next grade?'

He looked at me rather blankly and told me, 'I can't help you any more. You'll have to go to London.'

That was a huge step for me. I had no idea how to go about it.

One of the men at the club also used to practise at the Budokwai in South Kensington, London. I had no idea where it was, so he offered to take me there to show me how to find it (I was such a country bumpkin!). Of course, on the day we went it was a men-only training session so I was not allowed to join in, but at least I found out the timetable, where it was and, most importantly, how to get there; so the next evening, I came for the ladies' session.

I knew nothing about the Budokwai when I first went there, but eventually I came to learn that at that time it was the premier judo club in Europe, and the oldest. It was founded in 1918 by Gunji Koizumi, who was still a presence there when I joined. He used to appear in the doorway of the ladies' dojo to see what we were doing. The Budokwai is also closely linked to the Kodokan which was, and still is, the most important judo club in Japan. I found the Budokwai amazing. It had two dojos (judo training rooms): a large one that took up the whole first floor, and a smaller one on the ground floor. The mats were permanently in place which meant there was no more worrying about getting them out or putting them away. It seemed to be full of black belts, which were a rare commodity where I came from. It also had a ladies' section, something I had never seen before, and had a few lady black belts (or Dan grades to give them the correct term).

The chief instructor was Charles Palmer (5th Dan) and he taught the ladies. Charles had his own impressive history. He was a former international competitor who was known as a formidable opponent. He had studied under Gunji Koizumi (who founded the Budokwai) and Trevor Leggett, who both were – and still are – respected as the most influential teachers in British judo. Charles himself was a colourful character who was thoroughly steeped in judo. He eventually became Chairman of the Budokwai, and Chairman (and later President) of the British Judo Association. He was also the first non-Japanese President of the International Judo Federation. He persuaded the International Olympic Committee to give judo a regular place on the Games programme, and was awarded an OBE for his services to international judo. He became a member of the British Olympic Association in 1983, and in 1997 he was given his Tenth Dan. For those of you who don't know what this means, it is the highest grade possible in judo and at that time they were a very rare species. All this was to come, but I tell you this to give you an idea of how much respect he was held in. He was also a bit of a rarity in that he encouraged women's judo.

Charles was a good sensei (teacher) and he would push you as far as he could. On one occasion he had me in a strangle, and I tapped: the normal sign of submission, upon which the winner is expected to release the loser. This time, Charles said, 'Oh no, you can go further than that' – and he carried on! I was rather frightened by this, and fought back as hard as I could; and he was actually quite right – I could go on longer. It's important to hold on as long as you can because it might make the difference between winning and losing.

I admired the judo of another lady in the class – Iris Dehnel. She was a 2nd Dan, much older, more experienced than me and her judo was superb. She had fantastic ashi-waza (leg techniques). Iris could sweep you off your feet before you realised it was happening. I practised with her as much as possible because I wanted to learn her secrets.

Eventually I would get somewhere near to performing a foot sweep on her, but she would whisk

The Budokwai.

Entrance to the Budokwai.

The main dojo of the Budokwai.

her foot out and around again and it would be me sailing through the air! However, all this practice with Iris must have helped because one day, while having randori (free practice) with Charles, I threw him with a foot sweep! He went down with an almighty crash, flat on his back! It had been an instinctive thing. I had thrown him before I even realised that I had done it. I was horrified! I thought he would be angry with me, but he just lay there laughing. 'I made a mistake!' he cried, in between laughing.

The Budokwai became my club and I practised there regularly, catching the train up to London after work and then, after training, the last train back. My Dad would meet me at Beaconsfield Station to take me home, as by that time it was getting late and there were no buses around. I used to nod off on the train and was always worried that I would miss my stop. Eventually, my aunt and uncle, who lived just outside London, came to the rescue and allowed me to sleep over at their place after training. This helped a lot as the last tube train to Hillingdon left later than the last mainline train to Beaconsfield and I now didn't need to rush quite so much, although there was still a last train and a two-mile walk to their home.

They would be asleep by the time I got there and I would have to hunt for the key which would be under a rock (usually with my legs crossed because I was desperate for the loo!). Once in my bed, feeling sleep drift over me, I would become aware of the results of that evening's session on my body – the mat burns, bruises, fingerprints and bits of skin missing... but it was all worth it.

During the time I had been with my original club, things had been tough. I had had to practise with men and they didn't like the idea of a girl throwing them; so they made sure that I couldn't by using lots of strength and resistance, which is why I favoured ne-waza (ground technique). The men didn't do much work on that, and if they made a mistake and ended up on the ground, then I had a chance. So I became known as someone who was good on the ground.

It is actually an advantage to not be frightened of ground work. It means that you don't have to hold back when you are doing throwing techniques – because you don't care if you end up on the ground!

It was a refreshing change to be part of a club that actually had a thriving ladies' section. We had to train in the downstairs dojo, which is quite small, and no men other than our teacher were allowed to train with us, except towards the end of the class when it was randori (free practice). Then, certain Dan grade men could wait by the door and, if one of the ladies bowed to him, this was an invitation to come and join in. It was often Tony Sweeney, Syd Hoare or Tony Reay. Tony Sweeney was the first British judoka to get his Fourth Dan without having to travel to Japan to train, and he was selected to be part of the British team that went to Japan for the 1964 Olympics – the first time that judo was included in the Games. He was also three times a bronze medallist in the European Championships, and would eventually gain his Ninth Dan.

Syd Hoare and Tony Reay had only recently returned from training in Japan. Like Tony Sweeney, Syd was selected for the 1964 Olympic team, and he also won a silver medal in the 1965 European Championships in the Open category (although he himself was a middleweight). His opponent in that final was six feet seven inches tall, much bigger than Syd. He also eventually became a Chief Instructor at the Budokwai, British National Coach and, at one time, Chairman of the British Judo Association. He was a hard practise. Tony Reay was, for a while, manager of the Budokwai. He went on to be General Secretary of the British Judo Association, and also became its Development Officer. He eventually wrote many books on judo, as did Syd.

I managed to become a Dan grade on 8 September 1964 at the Budokwai. I was nineteen. The examination took hours. I had to win contests, take a line-up, demonstrate techniques and perform kata (formal techniques). My examiners were Charles Palmer and Tony Sweeney – both, as I've described, eminent senior judoka who were held in huge respect. In those days, if you had done all that was necessary for a Dan grade, then your licence was kept by the examiners. They, in turn, passed it on to be ratified, and you couldn't actually say that you had achieved the grade until your licence was back in your hand and you knew that the result had been accepted. I remember sitting on the platform of the tube station waiting for my train at the end of a very exhausting day, physically and mentally. All I could think was, 'I might be a black belt... I might be a black belt,' and then another voice in my head was saying, 'Don't think about it, they might not accept it...' It was a really big deal, and I was so excited I couldn't wait to get my results. There were no competitions or championships for ladies at this time, so bettering your grade was your main focus.

Tony Sweeney.

For a period of time, we ladies were forced to put a white stripe down the middle of our belts to denote to anyone with bad eyesight that we were female. We had managed fine with the same belts as the men and we were using the same syllabus, so when this directive was received it was not accepted easily; we couldn't understand why it was needed. But there was no escape – we had to have the white line, and it was necessary to stitch white ribbon down the middle of any belt you had. Without the line, you could not take part in any event and you would be disqualified if you tried. We all found this very offensive, as we had fought hard for our grades and this idea seemed to be degrading them. However, the order came from the Kodokan so it had to be done. The ladies in Japan had a harder time of it – their jackets were shaped so that they had a 'waist' and their trousers were pulled in around the bottom of the leg so that they didn't rise up and show the knee. The white line order lasted for some years, and we kept pestering for it to be rescinded. One fine day, when Charlie arrived to take our class, he announced, with a smile on his face, that we no longer had to wear it. When we realised that he wasn't joking, we whooped with joy and had a ritual 'line stripping' session before the class started while Charlie looked on, laughing.

Syd Hoare.

The Budokwai became a very important part of my life. In a way it was home. I went there as often as I could and joined in as many courses as I could, particularly those run by Kisaburo Watanabe who was the resident Japanese instructor and former Asian Games champion. He was amazing. His graceful, sinuous style earned him the nickname 'The Cat', and he could throw equally well on his left as on his right. We all respected him very much. He was a Fifth Dan which at that time was a very high grade.

His standard put him in a different league to the rest of us. The only person with a higher grade was T. P. Leggett who was the only Sixth Dan in Britain. Watanabe was very friendly and, although we were all in awe of him, we would chat with him whenever we had a chance. He didn't have much English when he first arrived, and he attended regular English language classes. We would talk to him afterwards to ask him what he had been learning. One day he said, 'Today, I learned that there are sixteen different meanings for the word "have",' which stumped us; as you can imagine, we were all trying to work out the sixteen meanings!

Charles Palmer & Tony Reay sharing a joke at one of the Crystal Palace events.

I learned that judo is not just a sport; it is a way of life. You learn discipline and respect, and you learn a lot about yourself; Mr Koizumi famously said, 'You come to judo to learn how to throw, and the first thing you learn is how to fall.' Jigoro Kano (the Father of Judo)

Kisaburo Watanabe 5th Dan.

Trevor Pryce Leggett.

Charles Palmer.

advised his students to aspire to a three-sided body-mind relationship goal: namely, to perfect themselves physically, intellectually and morally so that they were not just good at judo, they aspired to be good at everything life threw at them. It didn't matter how advanced you became, there was always someone who could beat you.

This was made very plain one day. I was on one of Watanabe's courses, and at the time I was a brown belt. At the end of each session we used to do a randori (free practice) which was organised as two lines opposite each other. After each two-minute practice, one side would move up one place so that everyone would get a new partner who was not of their choosing. I found at one point that my next partner was a tall Second Dan man. I was, at this time, still a First Kyu (brown belt) so he was two grades higher than me. Randori is not a contest. It is supposed to be a relatively relaxed practice when you can practise techniques that you have learned; higher grades should be encouraging lower grades. This particular man decided to practise his techniques in such a way that he smashed me all over the mat. He didn't even give me a chance to get properly back on my feet before he threw me again... and again... and again. I could feel tears starting in my eyes from sheer frustration that I couldn't do anything to stop this. Anyway, the call came for the end of the two minutes, so we bowed to each other and went back to our places in the lines. One person moved up and we had our next partner in front of us. I noticed something happening next to me and then realised that, very discreetly and quietly, Mr Leggett (who was a Sixth Dan at the time) had gently pushed the person next to me out of the line and taken his place.

This put him in front of the Second Dan I had just practised with. When we began again, Mr Leggett gave my tormentor the same treatment that he had just given me. He very elegantly wiped the floor with this man. When the session ended and we were back in line, Mr Leggett swapped back again with the chap who had been there originally. No words were spoken, but a lesson was learned.

Trevor Leggett was regarded with something like reverence by everybody (including Watanabe). He was a Sixth Dan, the highest grade in Britain. A well-educated man who spoke fluent Japanese. He had lived in Japan and had been interned during World War Two as he was attached to the British Embassy in Tokyo when war broke out. He returned to England as part of an exchange with London-based Japanese embassy staff. While he was interned, he had continued his judo training by practising with his guards. During the war he worked for the Ministry of Information, and afterwards he spent twenty-four years with the BBC as Head of the Japanese Service. He joined the Budokwai in 1932 and had achieved Third Dan before going to Japan in 1938, reaching the grade of Sixth Dan at the Kodokan. In 1945 he began teaching judo at the Budokwai, and in 1954 became the senior instructor. At one time he held Sunday classes at the Budokwai, which were by invitation only. Leggett's intense teaching methods were both respected and feared. In 1984 the Japanese Government awarded him the Order of the Sacred Treasure for his services in introducing Japanese culture to the UK.

The Budokwai used to put on an annual display at the Royal Albert Hall. This was a very important event. All members taking part would get very stressed worrying that their contribution should be perfect. People would travel from miles away to see the show. I remember going to see it when I was a low grade at my previous club. I was very excited when I was included and allowed to take a small part in the forty-eighth and forty-ninth displays.

PROGRAMME

1. METROPOLITAN POLICE CHAMPIONSHIP DAN GRADE Semi-finals
2. PRINCIPLES — S. HOARE, 4th dan
3. WOMEN'S SECTION — M. SATHAYE, 3rd dan; I. DEHNEL, 2nd dan; M. JENNINGS, 2nd dan; C. CHILD, 2nd dan; P. TILLETT, 1st dan; A. SWINTON, 1st dan
4. INTERNATIONAL JUDO FEDERATION CONTEST RULES — K. WATANABE, 5th dan; A. SWEENEY, 4th dan
5. METROPOLITAN POLICE CHAMPIONSHIP KYU GRADE Final
6. JUDO IN CONTEST — B. JACKS, 3rd dan; K. SORENSEN, 1st dan; L. RALPH, 1st dan; R. BARRETT, 1st dan
7. TRAINING METHODS — K. WATANABE, 5th dan
8. TEAM MATCH — Affiliated Clubs v. Budokwai

INTERVAL

9. JUNIORS — B. JACKS, 3rd dan
10. METROPOLITAN POLICE CHAMPIONSHIP Dan grade final
11. DEFENSIVE METHODS — The techniques of Judo, Karate and Aikido in use against the same attack — C. MACK, 5th dan Judo, 2nd dan Karate, 1st dan Aikido; J. CORNISH, 4th dan Judo, 1st dan Aikido
12. TEAM MATCH — Scottish Selection v. Budokwai
13. NEWAZA VARIATIONS — Modification of standard holds on the ground due to difference in physique — A. REAY, 3rd dan; T. BROADBENT, 1st dan; L. RALPH, 1st dan; R. BARRETT, 1st dan
14. KARATE — H. KANAZAWA, 5th dan; K. ENOEDA, 5th dan
15. TOKUIWAZA — Favourite techniques and their associated physical factors — K. WATANABE, 5th dan; A. SWEENEY, 4th dan; S. YASUMOTO, 4th dan; A. REAY, 3rd dan
16. ONE v. SEVEN — S. YASUMOTO, 4th dan

THE QUEEN

Timekeeper: D. BURR, 3rd dan. Commentary: J. H. DRESLER, J. NEWMAN, T. P. LEGGETT, K. WATANABE, J. GOODBODY.
Judo Information, Books, Literature, etc., available at Information Stalls adjoining Main Door, Door 4 and Door 9.

12 13

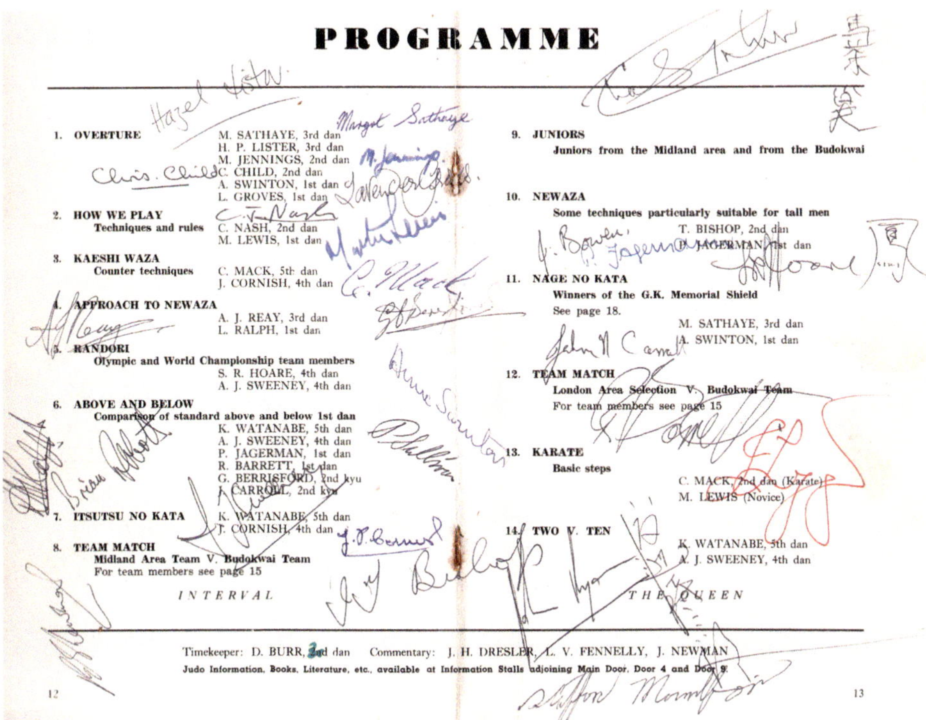

PROGRAMME

1. OVERTURE — M. SATHAYE, 3rd dan; H. P. LISTER, 3rd dan; M. JENNINGS, 2nd dan; C. CHILD, 2nd dan; A. SWINTON, 1st dan; L. GROVES, 1st dan
2. HOW WE PLAY — Techniques and rules — C. NASH, 2nd dan; M. LEWIS, 1st dan
3. KAESHI WAZA — Counter techniques — C. MACK, 5th dan; J. CORNISH, 4th dan
4. APPROACH TO NEWAZA — A. J. REAY, 3rd dan; L. RALPH, 1st dan
5. RANDORI — Olympic and World Championship team members — S. R. HOARE, 4th dan; A. J. SWEENEY, 4th dan
6. ABOVE AND BELOW — Comparison of standard above and below 1st dan — K. WATANABE, 5th dan; A. J. SWEENEY, 4th dan; P. JAGERMAN, 1st dan; R. BARRETT, 1st dan; G. BERRISFORD, 2nd kyu; J. CARROLL, 2nd kyu
7. ITSUTSU NO KATA — K. WATANABE, 5th dan; J. CORNISH, 4th dan
8. TEAM MATCH — Midland Area Team V. Budokwai Team — For team members see page 15

INTERVAL

9. JUNIORS — Juniors from the Midland area and from the Budokwai
10. NEWAZA — Some techniques particularly suitable for tall men — T. BISHOP, 2nd dan; P. JAGERMAN, 1st dan
11. NAGE NO KATA — Winners of the G.K. Memorial Shield — See page 18. — M. SATHAYE, 3rd dan; A. SWINTON, 1st dan
12. TEAM MATCH — London Area Selection V. Budokwai Team — For team members see page 15
13. KARATE — Basic steps — C. MACK, 2nd dan (Karate); M. LEWIS (Novice)
14. TWO V. TEN — K. WATANABE, 5th dan; A. J. SWEENEY, 4th dan

THE QUEEN

Timekeeper: D. BURR, 3rd dan. Commentary: J. H. DRESLER, L. V. FENNELLY, J. NEWMAN
Judo Information, Books, Literature, etc. available at Information Stalls adjoining Main Door, Door 4 and Door 9.

12 13

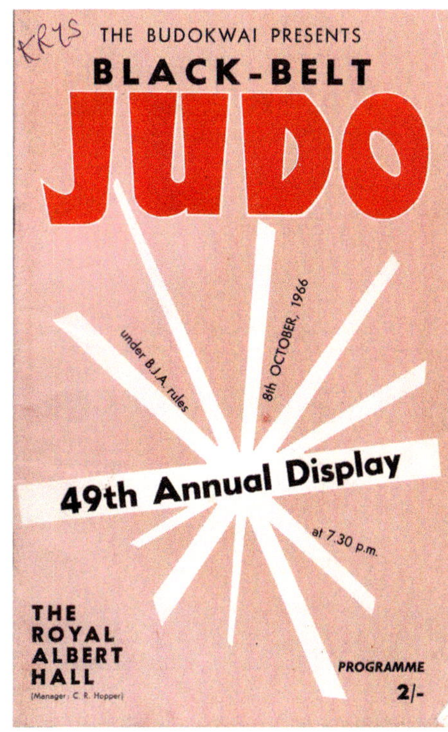

I achieved my Second Dan, a year on from my first Dan, on 7 September 1965 at the Budokwai. My examiners this time were Charles Palmer, the ladies' instructor, and Kisaburo Watanabe. Again, it was an exhausting day involving contests, line-ups, demonstrations of techniques and kata. I remember being incredibly nervous performing kata with my friend Christine Wildman and hearing Charles and Watanabe, who were judging us, talking to each other: about Charles's latest passion – flying...

As I've already mentioned, Charles was quite a character. He was a bit of a disciplinarian in that he wanted everything to be correct. One day, a Dan grade lady in our class announced that, regardless of Charlie's unarguable judo talent, she had the idea that if he was subjected to a surprise attack by a group of people all at the same time, he would be overcome. She proceeded to plot this, saying, 'You grab his right leg, you grab his left, I'll grab his right arm,' and so on. I was given instructions on what she wanted me to do, but I didn't like this idea at all! I thought to myself, 'This is going to end very badly...' As it happened, the attack was planned for the end of class, and I always needed to leave a few minutes before the very end in order to catch my last train home. So I, rather thankfully, left the class and got changed.

As I was making my way out through the lobby, I heard an almighty racket start in the ladies' dojo, ending with several loud thumps and crashes, followed by a very irate Charlie throwing the door

My photographic work on the cover of Judo Bulletin.

open and stamping out of the dojo leaving limp regretful bodies scattered around… I was *so* glad that I hadn't joined in!

Charlie was like Marmite; you either liked him or you didn't. He had a very strong personality which upset some people, but he was actually a very thoughtful and kind man. I was working as a photographer and studying for my exams in photography at Ealing College. Our class was given a project – 'Motorway Driving' – and we were asked to prepare photographs for it. I was rather stumped, unsure how to go about this. I even went to the entry slip road for the M4 at the Chiswick Flyover and climbed up the outside to get some photos… then I realised just how dangerous this was and yet the photographs were nothing special, so I gave that idea up. I was looking for inspiration. Anne Swinton, one of the high-grade ladies, had promised to clean Charlie's new car – an E-type Jaguar – and a group of us had followed her around to Charlie's flat to see it. I wondered if it would be a possible subject for my 'Motorway Driving' project. I asked Charlie if he would mind me taking photographs of it, and he was very interested in what I was trying to do. 'Would you like me to take you down the motorway in it?' he said. 'Wow!' I thought… and there we were, hurtling down the M4, and he was throwing ideas at me – culminating in me hanging out of the back of the car with my camera, and Charlie holding on to my coat to stop me falling out!

The Budokwai had a quarterly magazine called *Judo Bulletin* and a piece of my college photographic work was used on the front cover of the January 1966 edition.

Eventually a National Championships for women was held in 1966. It was a team competition, so in order to participate I had to return to my Northern Home Counties roots and qualify for their team.

The championship was a 'closed' event, meaning that it was an invitation-only affair held behind closed doors; the general public were not allowed in to watch as the organisers considered it inappropriate for women to be seen 'fighting'. This silly reasoning lasted for several years; and when, due to growing popularity, the event was moved to the Crystal Palace in 1969, a curtain was drawn to hide the contest area from general view… At these first championships, which were held in Liverpool, we discovered that we would be using a different scoring system. The normal accepted system was that if you managed to score an 'ippon' (one full point, worth ten points) then the contest ended and you had won. Any lower scores and the contest continued. For some unknown reason it had been decided that women needed a different scoring system to the men. I've no idea why, but here we were and we would have to go along with it. It was called the CKI system and meant that every contest would go the full time, and all your scores would be added together and multiplied by your 'style' mark (which changed every contest). The highest total score won. It was not a fair system and was open to manipulation; the style marks varied wildly.

I had been nominated as team captain, and eventually a rather worried lady came up to me and said, 'They are trying to get your team disqualified!'

'What?' I replied anxiously. 'How d'you know?'

She said, 'I heard them talking…' The story she told me was that she had heard Geoff Gleeson (the National Coach) tell the ladies in charge, 'Northern Home Counties must under no circumstances be allowed to win these championships,' and when they asked how they should do it, he had replied that it would have to be done with the style mark. Lo and behold, in our next contest we had a style mark of two, and subsequently lost.

By this time, all our group knew what was happening, and as team captain I was ordered to go and protest to the officials. So off I went to challenge the National Coach, who was a Fifth Dan at the time.

Totally unabashed and looking down his nose at me, he said, 'I have no official position at these championships; I am only here as an observer.'

I replied, 'With all due respect, sir, you are the highest grade here and whatever you say will be taken notice of.'

One of Watanabe's courses. See how shiny with sweat we are! I'm in the back row, slightly left of centre.

Of course, all the officials denied the accusation, and I returned to my team. However, in the next contest our style marks were improved. In the event, London area won, and all credit to them – they were a good team, and had Margot Sathaye who was a class above everyone. Our team came second. The event finished a bit late for those of us who had to return to London, and I vividly remember running through the streets of Liverpool with my friends, all of us still wearing our judogi (judo clothes) and clutching our bags, desperate to catch the last train – which we did, by the skin of our teeth. We then had to take it in turns to use the loo on the train to get back into our civvies.

I became very disillusioned by what had happened. I remember thinking to myself on the long journey home, 'If that's the way they want to play, then I want no part in it.' I had no wish to compete or be involved in the way women's judo was going.

Practising Uchi Komi (Practise without throwing) on one of Watanabe's courses.

CHAPTER THREE
Emma Peel

Seven times thrown, eight times rise.
Jigoro Kano

I went to the Budokwai as often as I could, starting off with twice a week, then three times until eventually it was nearly every day. It was a bit of a torturous journey – and expensive. It involved a lot of travelling, always rushing to make sure I was on time and worrying that I would miss the last train. Once I was safely on the train I had to try to make sure that I didn't fall asleep and miss my stop. That never actually happened, thank goodness, but it was a constant nagging fear.

At that time I was training to be an industrial photographer, and studying for my qualifications on day release at Ealing College. One of our tutors, a man named Roy Gough, was a film stills man. He used to like to impress us students by bringing in examples of his work and showing us what films and TV shows he was working on. At this time most of the photographs were of Patrick McGoohan in Danger Man or Roger Moore in The Saint. We would all coo over them: 'Oh, Sir, did you really speak to Roger Moore...?' We were very impressed.

One day he showed us some photographs of men in army combat uniform. They were doing judo on a tatami (judo mat). 'Who are they?' I asked. The judo world at that time was quite small, and I wondered if I might know any of them.

'Oh, they're not actors,' he explained, 'they're stuntmen.'

I was stunned! 'Do you mean to say you can get paid for doing judo?' I asked. This was a light-bulb moment for me. People were actually getting paid for doing judo and there I was, as poor as a church mouse, permanently scratching around for the next penny in order to keep up my training. To get to the Budokwai cost me quite a bit in travelling expenses – buses, trains, tubes and more buses, and then back again later – to say nothing of having to pay for fees and judogi (judo clothes). In fact, on one occasion the Budokwai actually gave me a pair of trousers because the ones I was wearing were so patched.

I interrogated the poor man about this, but he wasn't very keen to help at first. He wanted me to continue with my studies. However, he did agree to pass my details on to one of the stuntmen he knew; and he eventually came back to me with the telephone number for a stuntman called Frank Maher, who had asked me to call him. I subsequently rang the number and had a chat with Frank. He wanted to know what I could do: could I swim? drive? ride? The list went on. He asked me to send him some photos and said he would get back to me.

After I had put the phone down, I thought to myself, 'What on earth do you think you're doing? What a cheek! Trying to muscle in on something you know nothing about! Do you really think he'll get back to you! Best forget about it...' – so I did.

About three months after the phone call, Watanabe was conducting a week-long course which I booked on and attended. Two hours in the morning and two hours in the afternoon, Monday to Friday. There was, for me, the usual marathon of travelling afterwards every day. I had one more day to go. On the Thursday evening I came through the front door, quite tired, and my mother greeted me all in a fluster:

'You're too late! You're too late! He said to call before eight o'clock!' It was now 8.10pm.

'Slow down Mum, what's this all about?' I managed to calm her down enough to understand that someone from *The Avengers* had called and wanted to speak to me. I rang anyway and spoke to Ray Austin, who was still available even though it was gone eight. Ray was the stunt arranger on *The Avengers* and he was looking for a stunt double for Diana Rigg who played Emma Peel. Frank Maher had passed my number on to him. They had been using a man (Billy Westley) but he had got injured. Diana is tall, and there were no tall stunt girls around; in fact there were only a handful of stunt girls and none of them were tall enough. Could I please come into the studio tomorrow to meet Ray and see if I would do? Could I? ... you bet! It meant missing the last day with Watanabe but I was keen to go.

I met Ray Austin, and he introduced me to Diana Rigg. I had to stand next to her while he and other important production people walked around us to see if I could be a suitable double. My impression was that it seemed to be a bit like buying a cow! 'You'll have to change your hair' (mine was long and dark, while Diana's was auburn and rested on her shoulders). 'You'll have to lose weight' (Diana was sensationally slim). But generally they seemed happy with me. 'Come and try out the car' – and the next thing I knew I was hurtling down the M1 in a pale silver-blue Lotus Elan with twenty-seven miles on the clock. Then it was a trip to London for a dress fitting, with arrangements made for a hair makeover.

After the fitting I called in to the Budokwai and was just in time to catch Watanabe as he was leaving at the end of the day, to make my apologies for missing the last day of his course. He was very kind about it.

This was another step forward for me. Even after I had passed my driving test, I had continued to travel into London on the train. London always seemed to be so frantically busy, and I was unsure about parking arrangements. I had driven to the studios and was sent into London from there, with just an A-Z map of the city to guide me (no satnav in those days). I had to make my way to the dressmakers and then on to the Budokwai, and by that time it was heading towards rush hour… Going around Hyde Park Corner for the first time – and in the rush hour – was quite an experience and rather scary.

I was sent to the Elizabeth Arden hairdressers in Bond Street to have my hair changed, and went on a desperate crash diet. I was young and very naive. Some bright spark told me about this infallible diet where you can lose weight quickly on nine hard-boiled eggs a day, water and nothing else… so that's what I did! Three eggs for breakfast, and the same for lunch and dinner. Being keen as I was, I did this for several weeks; and, I must say, it did work, until I reached a point where I would prefer to have nothing rather than another boiled egg! So I had to learn how to lose weight properly, starting by avoiding the tea lady who came round with a supply of the most gorgeous crusty cheese rolls on her trolley. During the time I was on *The Avengers*, I must have tried every kind of diet that had been thought of. It was a constant battle to stay slim, made all the more difficult because I was working so hard at judo.

One day on *The Avengers*, there was a group of us sitting waiting while the lighting was organised. Somehow it slipped out that I belonged to the Cookery Book Club. I confessed that although I wasn't allowed to eat the recipes, I did love to read them. At that moment Di Enright (Diana's stand-in) and everyone else started to laugh and admitted that they also belonged to the Cookery Book Club and felt the same way…

I went to the studios to rehearse with Ray and he said to me in a slightly accusing manner, 'I've been trying to register you with Equity' (the actors' union) 'and they say you are already registered!' My name at this time was Christine Child. It had not occurred to me that there could be anybody else with the same name, but apparently there was and she was registered with Equity.

'No,' I replied, 'that's not me.'

'Well,' Ray said, 'you'll have to change your name.'

I started to think, 'This is my chance to pick something unusual and exotic; something like – Natasha…? Olivia…? Roxanne…?' but Ray broke into my musings.

'You want to keep the same surname because it's easier with cheques, and keep the same initial for your first name… How about Cyd?' Ray had just returned to England after working on the film *Maroc 7* with Cyd Charisse.

'Well, what *about* Cyd,' I thought. 'Isn't there anything else?' At first I wasn't too sure about it, but Ray immediately began introducing me to people as Cyd Child. I found it hard to keep a straight face to begin with, but everyone else just accepted it and it began to feel normal, so I fairly quickly became used to it. My only problem was that, although I was still Chris to everyone at the Budokwai, if anyone called 'Syd' – the name of our Club Manager, Syd Hoare – I would react because I would think they had called me!

'Can you ride?' was the next question. 'Er, no,' was my reply. 'Well, you'd better go and learn then,' was the command. So every weekend that was free saw me off to riding lessons, on Saturday and Sunday mornings. My Dad, who had been in the Royal Horse Guards, made me a gift of a riding crop. He didn't say much but I think he was secretly pleased that I was now learning to ride.

The crop came in handy a few times. I was attending a riding school and the horses seemed to have their own characters. It took a while to find out what these were, and sometimes it could be a bit scary. One horse was known for playing his own little game. When you checked his girth before getting in the saddle, he would blow his stomach out so that everything felt tight. We had to walk a fair way before we came to Black Park where we could let go and have a canter; I had been warned to check him, so I kept checking as we walked along. It all seemed too good to be true and I couldn't believe it, but his girth still felt tight… 'Okay,' my teacher said, 'let's have a canter,' so off we went. We were going well – and then my horse sucked in his belly and everything became very loose. My saddle swiftly began to slide around, and I was in danger of falling off (you could almost hear the horse chuckling). I must have looked as if I was pretending to be an Apache rider in a western as the saddle was by now hanging on the side of the horse. I was wearing a new sweater and didn't want to spoil it by falling off, so I was hanging on to the horse's mane for dear life until I could stop him.

Then there was another horse who thought it was funny to terrify his rider by backing into traffic. This was really frightening. I was advised that if he did this, the remedy was to give him a flick with the riding crop and he would then behave himself. This worked, and I found that all I had to do was to make sure that he saw the crop when I mounted him. I would stick it in my boot and he knew it was there, and he would give no trouble and I wouldn't have to use it; but I did see other people sitting on him with ghastly white faces as he backed and turned into traffic with the car drivers hooting their horns!

There was another horse who would try to veer next to a tree so that it would hit you on the leg. All the horses seemed to be a bit bonkers. There was one who would try to roll on the ground, and another who would bolt given half a chance, taking you under low overhanging branches. My teacher had insisted that I buy a riding hat. I was an awkward size and the hat had to be ordered. When it eventually came, the first time I wore it the horse I was on bolted and whisked me under some low branches. My first day wearing it and I ended up with a dent in my new hat – but it could have been my head.

My thoughts on these experiences were that it was all good training. Bearing in mind that this was a school to learn to ride and we didn't have the experience to deal with these nutty horses, I'm surprised that we all survived. At that time in the film industry, merely sitting on a horse qualified as a stunt, as you don't know what they might do and there is no handbrake, and I wholeheartedly agreed with this.

My first day on set was on the *Avengers* episode 'The Fear Merchants' at Pinewood Studios. That was in September 1966. I was paid ten pounds per day. Ray made a point of telling me that from now on the rate would be fifteen pounds per day. As we worked on TV film contracts, I would also receive 'exploitation' which was the daily fee again if I worked, and royalties would be calculated on this as well.

Wardrobe dressed me head to toe in a dark green suede outfit with built-in boots and revealing holes around the body. At that time, this was considered rather daring, so I was given a blanket to wrap around me, and pointed in the right direction for the appropriate sound stage.

I entered the stage on my own. I had never been on one before and had no idea of what I should expect.

There was no sign of Ray Austin or Diana, and no one seemed interested in me; they were too busy shooting a scene. I found a quiet corner and sat down to wait.

I hadn't been there long when a tall man approached me with a call sheet and a pen in his hand. 'Would you mind giving me your autograph?' he said with a smile on his face.

'Me?' I replied, absolutely sure he couldn't possibly mean me – after all, I had only just been invented... 'Are

This photo is of Diana in the costume we had to wear for 'The Fear Merchants'.

My four wheeled Berkeley with chain drive motor bike engine.

The Austin Healey Sprite which was much more presentable..

This is my MGB GT which I loved!

you sure you want my autograph?'

'Yes,' he said, 'it'll be a bit of a laugh.'

Feeling well confused, I took the call sheet and wrote 'Cyd Child' on it. The man turned the sheet around, looked at the signature and glared at me. 'I suppose you think that's funny!' he roared and stamped away. I felt even more confused and sat there huddled in my blanket, wondering what else was going to happen.

A few minutes later Diana appeared on the set wearing the same costume as me. She walked confidently up to where the camera crew were working and they all greeted her in a friendly manner. A moment later the tall man sheepishly came back to me. 'I'm sorry,' he said, 'I thought you were Diana Rigg...'

Well, I thought, that bodes well for being a double. In fact, as time went on I would occasionally be mistaken for Diana. Messengers would come up to me and tell me I was wanted on the telephone. I learned to say to them, 'Is it Diana you want? Because I'm Cyd...'

I was quite shocked when, only a few weeks after joining this life, I was asked to give a donation to a fund for a stuntman (whom I didn't know) who had just been killed at work doing a fall. Before starting work on each new job we had to sign a 'blood chit', which was a disclaimer that the company thought would clear them if we hurt ourselves. There was no insurance for stunt people at this time, and all we could do was try to help each other. Over the following years, stunt people pushed for a register of members of the stunt profession, and we eventually managed to sort out a system of insurance with Equity. One of the problems we had was that it was quite common for extras to be offered a few extra quid to perform an easy stunt, with professional stunt people only called upon to do the scary stuff.

With a proper register with Equity, only stunt people would do anything that was called a stunt. It took a bit longer after that before we could get a rule that, wherever possible, women should double for women, as some men were quite happy to include doubling for women as part of what they did.

Life became like going to a special school. Each week, I would go to the studios and Ray would show me the script and say, 'This is the story, this is what Emma Peel has to do, and this is how you're going to do it,' and I would learn. It was hard work. I would get up at 5.30am in order to leave home at 6.30, arriving at the studio by 7.30 so that I was ready to go on set at 8.30. The day would often end at 5.45pm and, by the time I had changed back into my own clothes and driven home, it would be around 7.30-8pm. If we were on location the times might be extended, depending on how far away we were.

Working on location always seemed like a big adventure. We would be given 'location sheets' at the end of the day before. These would give us instructions on how to find the first location of the day plus any extra details which might be thought necessary. It was all rather secretive because sightseers were not wanted. Satnav had not been invented so we had to closely follow the directions, and we would be given extra help by mysterious little signs which had been left by someone helpful. These were small wooden arrows which had paper sheets attached with the Avengers logo of a silhouette of a small handgun with a rose in its barrel. When we had finished at the location we would all leave in convoy for the next one.

What was nice was that, if we were on location with Emma's Lotus Elan, I was often allowed to be the nominated driver. Then it was my responsibility to drive it to and from the location and keep it in my care. I loved days like these. When I first started doubling for Diana, my personal car was a four-wheeled Berkeley, which was unbelievably awful. It looked like a little red sports car, but in reality it was a fibreglass body with a motorbike engine. It looked okay, sounded dreadful and was not far off being a deathtrap! When I first bought it I took my mother out for a drive (fortunately around the countryside where we lived) and, with her weight extra in the car, it couldn't get up the hill near home and the car stopped. So I grabbed the handbrake – and it came off in my hand! At one time you could see the road under the footwell. I found this so disconcerting that I fibreglassed a piece of plastic over the hole. If you did a long journey in it and stopped, then it wouldn't start again unless you took the plugs out and gave them a bit of a scrape!

The first time I came back to the Berkeley after driving the Elan all day, I thought that something had happened to it. It didn't feel safe to drive, and I couldn't believe that I'd driven it to work that morning.

After a couple of miles I got used to it again, but I decided that when I had enough money I would get a better car that would not be so embarrassing. I subsequently bought a second-hand Austin Healey Sprite, which lasted for a while; and then eventually I bought a second-hand MGB GT, which I adored. I loved the sound of it and would drive with the window open so that I could listen to it.

I heard about one incident when a group of stuntmen (not on *The Avengers*) were returning to the studio in a car that had been used as a police car and was still bearing the police decals, which should have been removed. In a mad moment, the occupants (who were all wearing police uniforms) thought it would be hilarious to put the 'blues and twos' on and speed up the motorway. In the middle of all this fun the driver was suddenly brought to his senses by a tap on his side window, and when he looked there was a police motorcyclist riding alongside him! Suddenly wishing that he had never agreed to this, he wound his window down to see what the real policeman had to say, which was 'Can I help?'

Thinking quickly, the driver pointed up the motorway and shouted desperately, 'The black Mercedes!' to which the motorcyclist accelerated away. The group then swiftly left the motorway at the next exit, hurriedly removed all the police decals and as much of their uniforms as possible, then returned to the studio via the back roads!

Diana turned out to be a lovely person, great fun to work with and very professional. When we had a scene that involved me, I would be on set to see the end of any action that Diana was doing and try to copy Diana's movements as she finished the shot. She, in turn, would try to pick up from my last piece of action. One particular day made us laugh. Diana had a little white poodle called Poopey. He used to come on set and sit on her chair and wait for her while she was working. We were making the episode called 'Death's Door' and Diana and I were wearing identical costumes. We had chairs next to each other, and were having lots of fun taking turns on each bit of the fight. I would do my bit and come back to my chair, saying to Diana, 'Over to you!' and she would return saying, 'Your turn...' We did this a few times, and poor Poopey got quite confused. I sat down and Poopey jumped on my lap, looked me in the face and

Diana and Poopey.

This is the costume that Diana and I wore for the fight scene that confused poor Poopey so that he didn't know who was who.

'The Living Dead'

then looked so bewildered as he was expecting Diana, and instead it was me; she was standing behind him laughing!

The first time I used judo in stunt work, I was part of a group doing a fight scene. I was still very 'green' and naive and in awe of all the others. Ray was directing the fight, and maybe he wanted to impress me with his knowledge. He was saying things like, 'Joe will do this, Alf will do that, Fred will do this...' and then he said, '... and *you* will throw this guy with Tai-O-Toshi!' Well, when he said that it really woke me up, as the one thing out of all this that I really understood was, 'Throw him with Tai-O-Toshi,' so I thought I would give it my best shot. When the fight started and my turn came, I threw this chap with my best Tai-O-Toshi, as fast and as hard as I could. Big mistake! Immediately there was a lot of shouting:

'Stop! Stop! What do you think you're doing?!'

'You told me to throw him with Tai-O-Toshi,' I replied, feeling rather pained that my efforts were not being appreciated; I thought I'd managed a rather good throw.

Then I was told in no uncertain terms, 'You don't actually throw him. He'll do that himself!' Well, that put me in my place.

(For those who don't know, Tai-O-Toshi is also known as Valley Drop and is a throw where your opponent is pulled suddenly forward but you drop your body to one side and they fall over your outstretched leg.)

I was very rarely asked to do real throws, although there was one occasion on another *Avengers* episode, 'The Living Dead'. I had to double for Diana when Emma Peel was breaking out of a prison cell. The idea was that I would pick up the guard on my shoulders (Kata-Guruma which is known as shoulder wheel).

It was only a small cell and they wanted me to pick him up, spin him around and throw him down on the bed. The guard was played by another stuntman, Terry Plummer; he was very big, weighing perhaps around eighteen stone. There was no way to fake the throw; and I had to turn around in front of the camera, meaning that my face went past it – and I was doubling for Diana. In those days stunt people were not acknowledged. People must have suspected that stars had stunt doubles, but it was never admitted. As far as the general public knew, Diana did all her own stunts. The camera crew were worried that my face was going past the camera and they kept saying, 'Can you do it faster? It looks like Emma Peel is having trouble.'

With an eighteen-stone man across my shoulders I replied, 'Emma Peel *is* having trouble...'

Anyway, we did it, but there was a heck of a row about this scene. Jack Greenwood, the Production Controller, said: 'We're in trouble here. We've got the double's face going straight past the camera.'

That's why they wanted me to do it quicker,

because everyone got a good look at my face and they were afraid people would be writing in. However, on the day it was shown no one said a word, and there was nothing in the papers at all. The only mention was a letter to the *TV Times* remarking on the scene and asking how it was done...

As I have said, Diana's approach to work was very professional, and she expected to be treated professionally. One day I turned up for work and went into Wardrobe looking for my outfit. 'Oh, we haven't got a costume for you this time, you'll have to borrow Diana's.'

'Oh dear,' I thought, 'she's not going to like that...'

The unit was already working on the lot and I wasn't needed until later, so I wandered up in my own clothes and waited for the explosion. When Diana had finished the shot she was working on, she came up to me and said, 'Why aren't you changed?'

I reluctantly said, 'I can't get changed because you're wearing the clothes...'

Diana gave me a long hard stare. 'Come with me,' she said, grabbing my hand and dragging me off to the Studio Wardrobe without even telling the crew that she was leaving the set. No one was there. We used to have our own walk-in wardrobes for the costumes that were made for us specifically. We weren't the same shape: Diana had longer legs than me, and I had a longer body than her; and there were other differences as well, such as the fact that I took a bigger collar size. It was important that our costumes fitted closely as the catsuits were very clinging and didn't look good if they weren't figure-hugging.

Diana went into her wardrobe and I went into mine. I could hear her rattling through the coat hangers.

A hand came out with a catsuit hanging from it. 'Have you got one of these?'

I rattled through my hangers. 'No!'

'Okay, have you got one of these?'

'Yes!'

'Put it on!' So we both changed into the chosen outfit and went back up to the lot.

'Won't they have to reshoot what you've been doing?' I asked as we approached the film crew.

'That's their problem,' Diana said. 'If they want to play cheap, I'll give them a cheap performance;' and she made them reshoot all the takes she had already done that morning.

It was as well that we didn't try to share costumes, as I very often ruined them. There was one episode called 'You Have Just Been Murdered'. The producers felt that we really ought to have Emma in a leather catsuit as she hadn't been in one for a very long time and it was being remarked upon. A beautiful black and silver catsuit was made. It was lovely, made of soft glove leather, and had little chains across the front. It cost, I think, around £480, which in those days was a lot of money. Because of the cost, only one was made. Leather clothes are very difficult to wear if you are doing action. It doesn't stretch or give so it inhibits your movement.

I arrived on location and Ray was telling me what he wanted me to do: 'Okay, this baddie is blocking her way across the bridge and they fight; she slips and falls off the side of the bridge and manages to hold on...' We tried this and the underarms tore. 'She swings a leg up to zap him under the chin and get purchase to climb up... The crotch tore. We found we

Putting him in a spin

DIANA RIGG

IN "THE AVENGERS" the other Saturday, Diana Rigg apparently lifted up and gave an "airplane spin" to a man about three stone heavier than herself. Were there wires to help the lift? I thought I was fit and strong, but I cannot lift my husband, who is only two stone heavier than me.

(Mrs.) J. DIXON, Alexander Road, Liverpool.

● *ABC are keeping quiet on the tricks of the trade. Frankly I didn't believe it either, so don't go straining yourself Mrs. D.*

The Photographer, February 1967.

This photo was taken at the time while I was waiting for the correct costume.

'You Have Just Been Murdered'

A still from *The Man Who Had Power Over Women.*

were having to adapt all our moves to what we could do in the outfit. Just about everything seemed to produce tears and splits. Gladys, the Wardrobe lady, was following me about with a loaded sewing needle attempting to keep me stitched in! The beautiful catsuit was totally ruined, and we were never again asked to wear leather.

When Diana left and the Emma Peel episodes ended I was offered a chance to buy some of my costumes, but there were very few that were in a condition worth buying. I think catsuits and leather were preferred because there was this sort of sexy undercurrent to the whole thing.

'You Have Just Been Murdered' also featured a fight in the water with Les Crawford. Les was a seasoned stuntman who was playing the part of a baddie called Morgan. Ray Austin had said to us, 'I want lots of thrashing arms and legs and splashing so that you can't tell who's winning, but of course Emma wins in the end.' Les was intent on giving me a really good ducking; he thought it was hysterically funny to nearly drown me! As I got pushed underwater for the umpteenth time I thought to myself, 'She wins in the end – I know she does! It's in the script!'

As we wrapped for the day, I remember standing, swathed in towels, on the bank of the little lake we had been working in while the props man was rowing about picking me a huge bunch of water lilies! It was so surreal.

One day I was introduced to one of the writers, who told me how pleased he was that I was doubling for Diana. At that time there were not very many stunt girls and it was quite accepted for men to stand in for women. This practice had its limitations, though, as men are not convincing doubles for women. Their shape is all wrong and they move differently. Apparently, now that a woman was doubling for Diana, the writers could be more adventurous with their stories, knowing that it wouldn't be a problem.

Eventually we (the stunt girls) managed to get a ruling through Equity, the actors' union, that wherever possible, women should double for women. This was important because some men would quite cheerfully double for women, and no effort was made to find a female stunt double; this obviously limited the amount of work available for women.

For the episode 'Escape in Time', Emma had to be run down by a motorbike. We spent all day with me running about and a chap on a motorbike trying to run me over. They wanted me to dodge out of the way at the very last second. We kept doing it over and over again and the bike really felt close to me; I didn't feel I could make it any closer. The director, John Krish, was very appreciative; the next time I was called to the studio, he gave me a present of a very expensive Dior perfume – 'For all your hard work!' – which I thought was very kind. (Some months later, John Krish was directing the film *The Man Who Had Power Over Women* with Rod Taylor and, when he heard that stunt people were required for a particular scene, apparently said that he didn't care who was called so long as it included Cyd Child... I was rather stunned.

However, some weeks after 'Escape in Time' was filmed, I was called to the studio to reshoot the bit where the motorbike nearly hits me. This was to be done by a second unit with a different director. We went through the same rigamarole: 'It doesn't look close enough, Cyd; can you do it again, closer...' I was getting a bit fed up with this. I didn't see how I could get it any closer; I could already feel the rider brushing against me and the heat of the exhaust as he passed by.

So, when they said it again and we went for it again, I let the bike hit me – and then said, very sweetly, 'Was that close enough?'

The director looked a bit sheepish and said, 'Yes, I think we're okay now...'

One day we worked on an episode called 'The Bird Who Knew Too Much'; in this story, Emma has to do a magnificent dive from the high board of a swimming pool. Peter Elliott, who was a champion high diver, was hired to double Diana for the dive, and he did it superbly. However, there were a few things that gave away his masculinity... There was the run-up to the dive; and also, when he came back up to the surface, he tossed his hair back in the way only a man can. It didn't help that he was wearing a wig held on with string running from under his chin and over the top of his head.

'Cyd! Can you do the run-up and the surfacing please?'

I had a quick discussion with Peter on how best to smoothly blend this in. 'Have you done any trampolining?' he asked. I replied that I had. 'Okay, just run up and do a crash dive, that will blend in.'

Well, off I go, running along the top; leap off into a crash dive – and find that I am in mid-air from the top board and I'm not trained in high diving! So I curled up into a ball to hit the water, sank to the bottom of the pool, sat around for a moment or two – and came up to a lot of concerned faces looking at me. 'Thank goodness you're all right! We thought you'd killed yourself!'

They seemed satisfied with what they had and I wasn't asked to do it again. It was getting late, and cold, so we finished for the day. However, it's not easy to just go home when you are soaking wet and Wardrobe want the costume – right now! A hot bath had been laid on for Peter and me. However, there was only one bath, and Peter got in it first. I had to sit on the floor outside the bathroom, with a towel wrapped around me, waiting shivering for Peter to finish his ablutions... and he took his time!

'Murdersville' was another very involved episode. We started off with me in a red trouser suit running away from a helicopter, leaping over a fence and falling (all planned). However, the trousers split as soon as I landed – cue Wardrobe... They stitched me back in, but it happened again; so the decision was taken (as this was going to be a very active story) that we should reshoot it with Emma in a catsuit. After a telephone call to the studio, one was brought out to us by car.

There was a part of this tale where Emma is ducked, head first, on a witch's ducking stool. The director, Robert Asher, asked me how long I could stay underwater as he wanted all the ripples on the surface to go still. I said, 'I don't know. How about I stay down as long as I can and I'll wriggle my feet when I want to come up?'

'Okay, let's try that...' so we gave it a go. They tipped me back and down I went, backwards, head first into this mucky village pond, keeping my mouth tightly closed as it was very muddy and the water got dark as I went down. I was holding my breath and just letting an occasional bubble out when, all of a sudden, I was pulled up and out into the daylight. I was rather surprised as I hadn't wriggled my feet, and I questioned this with Bob Asher. He said, 'Yes, I know. I didn't like it. It made me feel sick!'

At the end of the story there is a fight (surprise, surprise) and Emma gets thrown against a table covered in custard pies.

'Escape in Time'

'The Bird Who Knew Too Much'

'Murdersville'
Emma is ducked in the village pond.

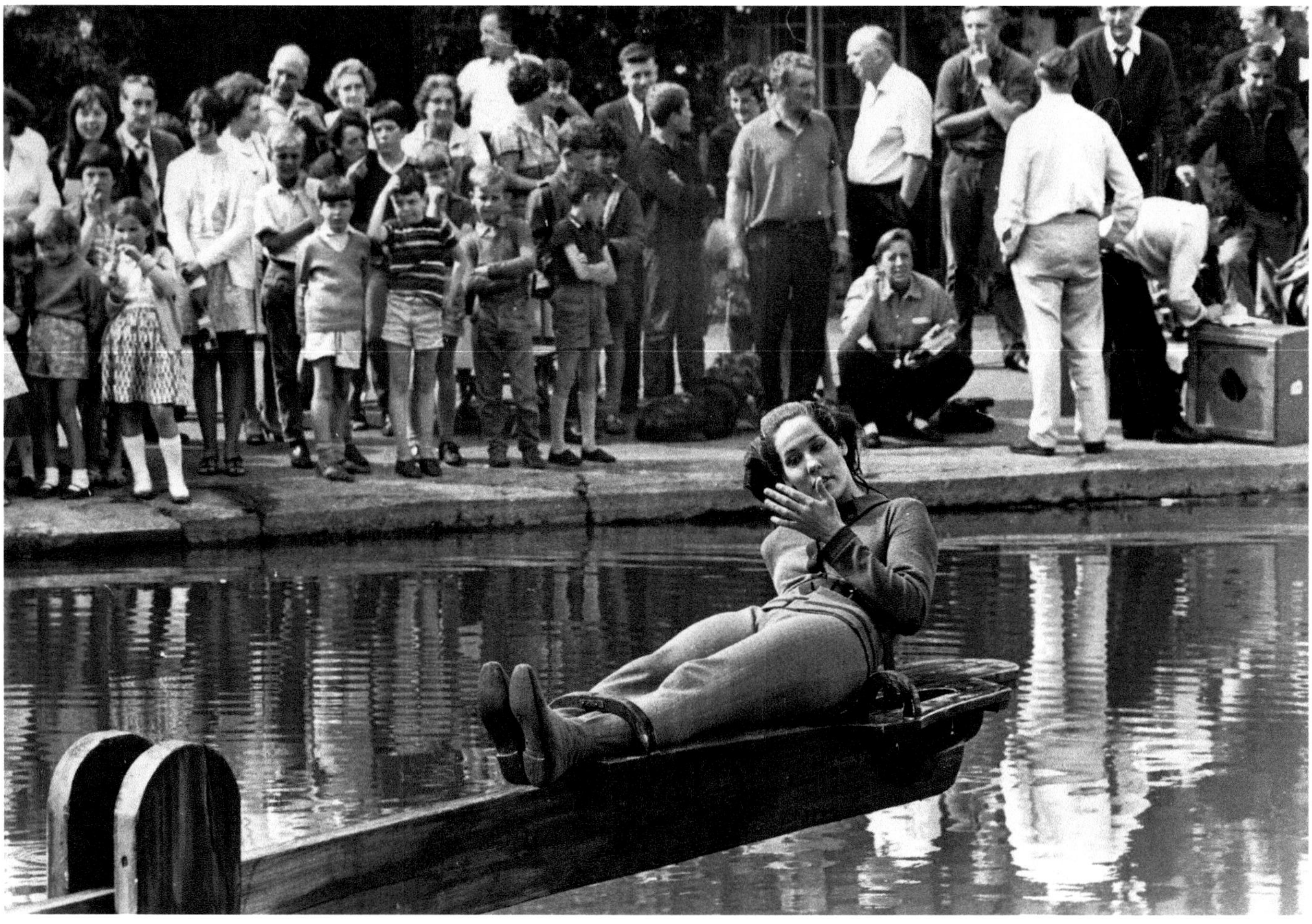

We did it and I landed square in them. As I heard the director say 'cut', I also heard a smothered hysterical snigger from above me, which turned out to be an electrician who couldn't help laughing... He'd enjoyed it anyway.

Another memorable episode was 'Return of the Cybernauts'. I had to be 'whacked' by a cybernaut and flung backwards over the settee in Steed's flat. Ray wanted it to be as dramatic as possible, so I went for it. In the end it worked better than I had hoped for and I went over the settee and hit the wall, smashing one of the picture frames in doing so.

In this episode we also did a car chase where Emma is supposed to be under the control of the maker of the cybernauts, Paul Beresford, played by Peter Cushing (who turned out to be a really nice man). In the story, Emma gets into her car and drives off at speed, nearly running over Steed (Paul Weston doubling for Patrick Macnee), and zooms around the corner and away. This was all shot in London. We arrived first thing in the morning, and Ray told me to go off for a little drive and 'get used to the car'. I thought I'd just drive around the block; however, London traffic being what it was (and is), that wasn't so easy. It was rush hour by this time. Feeling very conspicuous in an open-top Lotus Elan dressed as Emma Peel in an orange and pink suit with a miniskirt, I managed to find myself going the wrong way up a one-way street and not being able to do anything about it because of the crush of traffic. Luckily a very kind policeman helped me sort myself out (and didn't book me).

When it came to the filming, Ray said, 'Drive round the corner as fast as you can,' which I did. Unfortunately, the tyres screamed all the way round, and all the windows in the background were immediately filled with people looking to see what had happened. We couldn't use that shot so we had to do it again.

Later in the story, Emma is supposed to hurtle down the road with Steed chasing after her and then drive through a closed gate. I'd never done anything like that before. Once again, Ray instructed me: 'We've prepared the gate – just make sure that you're doing about forty-five when you hit it...' That was easier said than done. I had to try to look as if Steed is keeping up with me, when in fact the Elan could have left Steed's Bentley standing, so I was constantly looking in my mirror to keep the Bentley in sight and holding back. However, when the gate came into view I had to put my foot down and leave him behind in order to do the required forty-five mph, and I think it was probably more like sixty or seventy in the end. However, it all worked out according to plan. Interestingly the white paint from the wood of the gates made patterns all over the nose of the car – but didn't damage it.

'Dead Man's Treasure' was an episode that was particularly fun to do. We were having a beautiful summer, and we spent quite a few days driving about outside as the story is all about a car rally. The beginning of the episode also had a brilliant fight scene. Ray wanted me to dive over a desk to catch a baddie who is burgling an office. In order to make it work, Romo Gorrara (who was doubling for the baddie) and I had to time it so that I took off and he walked into the collision point, but it all went spectacularly well.

Rocky Taylor was the stunt double for Patrick Macnee when I first joined *The Avengers*. Steed's car was usually a vintage Bentley which was on loan from the secretary of the Bentley Club. On 'Dead Man's Treasure' there was an incident when Rocky reversed at speed and the engine decided to burst into flames. Great consternation but everything was okay in the end.

There was another occasion when Rocky was driving the Bentley and I was sitting next to him. We were filming a dream sequence and supposed to be careering down a narrow winding country lane. While we were rehearsing this, Rocky turned to me and said, 'Cyd, there's a strong possibility that the car could turn over here, so you will have to be ready to jump out... keep an eye out for a good spot...'

I looked out and all I could see was barbed wire and the ground sloping swiftly away covered in stinging nettles! So my reply was, 'No chance Rocky – I'm not going out there! If you lose it, I'm going in the footwell!' Fortunately that wasn't necessary...

Eventually, Rocky left us to work on *The Italian Job* and Paul Weston, who used to be Patrick's stand-in and double, took over the position of stunt double. He went on to become a highly regarded stuntman and stunt arranger, arranging stunts on big movies like the *James Bond* and *Superman* series.

'The Winged Avenger' was a story in which the villain can walk up walls and on the ceiling. To make this we had several different sets. There was a 'normal' set with the floor in the usual place, another with the walls at an angle and one more which was upside down. During the story, Emma has a fight with the baddie while they both have their feet attached to the ceiling. Some of the fight was done on the upside-down set, and some of it was done with me hanging upside down with my feet tied to a strap suspended from the ceiling of the studio stage. It was considered extremely funny to tie me in this position, upside down over the set, and then call a tea break! At the end of the fight Steed reaches up and holds Emma's hands and Emma (me) has to drop back down onto the normal floor; to do this we had another stuntman, Dinny Powell, who hung from a trapeze holding my feet so that he could let me go.

During the time I was doubling for Diana, my parents decided that they were going to move to Hand Cross in Sussex. My father actually thought that I would go with them. However, to do that would have meant that, instead of about an hour on average to get to the studio, it would take me about two and a half hours – and of course the same for the return journey. I really couldn't envisage doing this. I had to get up at

'From Venus With Love'

about 5.30am to get to work in time as it was. So I started hunting for a flat. I didn't have much time to find somewhere, and I didn't have much spare time in which to look either, so I couldn't be too choosy. However, I found quite a nice little pad which was the top floor of a house, living above the landlord, in Chalfont St Peter, Buckinghamshire.

There was an occasion while I was working on *The Avengers* when my car needed some work. I took it into a garage in Borehamwood, where the studios were. Unfortunately the garage told me that they wouldn't have it ready until the next day! I was stuck. I had been planning to go to the Budokwai after work, and I didn't know how I could go about getting back to my flat as it was out in the country.

Fortunately I ran into a stuntman I knew, the aforementioned Romo Gorrara, who lived in central London.

'Romo! I really need a lift tonight! Please, please, please can you give me a lift into London after work?'

'Yes, of course,' he laughed. Pleased to have sorted that journey out, thinking, 'I'll worry about the going home bit later,' I went back to work.

However, later in the day, Romo sought me out. He was working a short distance away on the film *The Dirty Dozen*. 'Cyd, I'm sorry, I can't give you a lift tonight. I've promised one of the actors I'll give him a lift and there's no spare room' (Romo drove an E-Type Jaguar).

I was horrified. I had no spare time to arrange anything else. 'But Romo, you promised,' I guilt-tripped him. 'Please, please, I'm stuck otherwise. Can't you take us both? I'll sit on his lap?!'

'I'll ask him,' was the reply.

So that, ladies and gentlemen, is how I had a lift into London in an E-Type, sitting on Donald Sutherland's lap!

In 'From Venus With Love', Emma Peel had to kick down a burning door to get out of a room. I had to borrow Diana's outfit for this. I thought it felt a bit uncomfortable at the time, but didn't realise until later that the reason for this was that I had it on back to front! No one seemed to notice.

The only time I was hurt during an episode of *The Avengers* was on an episode called 'Never, Never Say Die'. In the fight towards the end, Emma Peel had to be thrown into a wall; it went wrong and I badly bruised my back. I ended up having to lie down in my dressing room while the fight was changed so that Diana didn't need a stunt double.

The production schedule could be a bit hairy. We would start off trying to film a story every two weeks, working in sequence. However, if an episode wasn't finished in time, it could end up being filmed back to back with another one. We would start catching ourselves up because the series would be already showing on television. Sometimes we got to the stage of filming four episodes at once, and actually be only two weeks behind episodes that were showing in the USA.

Rehearsal for the Cybernaught to attack me.

'Dead Man's Treasure'

'Return of the Cybernaughts'

'From Venus With Love'

Funnily enough I didn't manage to see many of the *Avengers* episodes when they first came out. I was usually out training, and home video recorders had not been invented.

Gerry Crampton was a stuntman that I had worked with a few times on *The Avengers*, and he called me for a job on *The Mercenaries* which was a film he was working on at MGM Studios in Borehamwood (eventually the name was changed to *Dark of the Sun*). This was the first time that I had done any filming work other than *The Avengers* so it was quite exciting.

The story was about the unrest in the Congo; I had to play the part of a kidnapped nun. We were working on a set with a balcony, and the action featured civilians being assaulted and struggling. I had to be resisting a large man (Joe Powell) who is trying to rip my clothes off and we fall together from the balcony. Wardrobe dressed me in a pristine white nun's habit, complete with wimple and tie belt and a large cross. I thought I looked rather nice; but then I was told to go to be 'prepared'... I had to stand while a man slashed at my skirt and clothes with scissors. I stood very still – I was a bit worried about the sharpness of the scissors, and very aware how close they were to my legs! When he was happy with the result, my clothes (and I) were then sprayed with dirt. This was necessary as I had supposedly been 'dragged through the jungle'.

When it came to the take, I had to scream and struggle before we went over the rail. This was my first experience of acting, and it was a different experience to find the cameras actually wanting to see my face. It all went well and I was told, afterwards, that falling together is regarded as potentially dangerous because of the possibility of landing on each other.

Payment for films was made in a different way. You were paid for the day (possibly with adjustments), but there were no royalties. One thing I had to learn off by heart was my National Insurance number. The accountant would arrive at the end of the day and you were paid in cash, but you had to sign your daily contract with your NI number or you wouldn't be paid. I can still remember it even now!

Chitty Chitty Bang Bang was filmed at Pinewood Studios. There were a lot of stunt people involved in the factory scene. We were all dressed in Victorian clothes as workers in a sweet factory. Vats of 'sweet mixture' (which appeared to us to be coloured wallpaper paste) had to be tipped on the floor with us slipping, sliding and falling all over the place. I don't know what colouring they used in the mixture, but it made amazing, indelible stains on our skin! When I eventually got home I spent a great deal of time in the bath trying to get the red stain out of my hair, the green stain out of my legs... I actually had one leg red and the other green!

There was a very happy atmosphere among everybody, and one day when it came to lunchtime we all decided to go to a local pub for lunch. We didn't get changed as we only had an hour, so all these Victorian factory workers descended on this particular pub. We were all happy and laughing, and so were the other customers as we had our lunch. However, while we were there another bunch of film extras arrived with the same idea. They were all working on a war film being made at Pinewood and, like us, had stayed in costume due to time limitations. The problem was that they were all wearing Nazi uniform... We all knew that these were just British film extras having lunch; but it was amazing how the atmosphere changed, from happy to icy cold. It wasn't their fault, but we couldn't leave quickly enough.

A rare rest day, sunbathing in my Mum & Dad's garden.

On this film I also had to double Anna Quayle as the Child Catcher's wife when she slides down a giant slide into the Child Catcher's cage. I had to wear Anna's costume, and I was pleasantly surprised to find that she was exactly the same size as me.

I kept in touch with Diana for a while after she had moved on from *The Avengers*. When she was appearing in the play Abelard and Heloise at Wyndham's Theatre, we were both trying to help Alun Hughes, the dress designer. He had fallen on hard times, and Diana had got him a little job as her dresser on the production. I would pick him up at the end of the working week and take him back to my boat and feed him up, bringing him back to the theatre in time for the first performance of the week.

We gradually lost touch, but met up again at the *Avengers* video launch party. My son, Adam, asked me to ask Diana for her autograph. She very kindly wrote a few words on the back of my ticket, and Patrick Macnee signed it too.

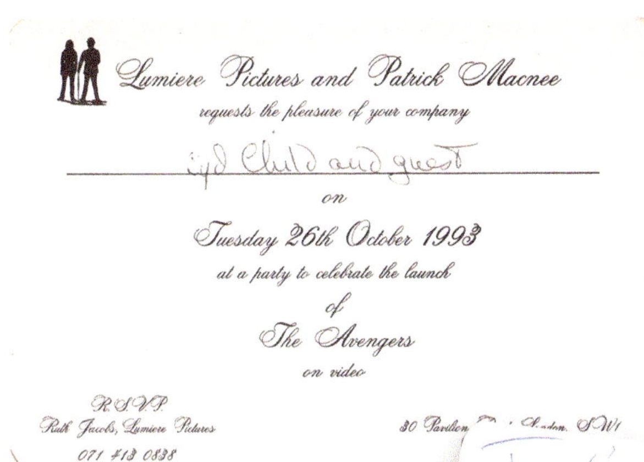

Lumiere Pictures and Patrick Macnee
requests the pleasure of your company
Cyd Child and guest
on
Tuesday 26th October 1993
at a party to celebrate the launch
of
The Avengers
on video
R.S.V.P.
Ruth Jacobs, Lumiere Pictures
071 413 0838

CHAPTER FOUR

Tara King

The greatest accomplishment is not in never falling, but in rising after you fall.
Vince Lombardi

When the last Emma Peel series of *The Avengers* finished, none of us knew what would happen. *The Avengers* was very big at the time, so obviously the producers would want to continue; but if they picked a new girl, would they want me? While I waited to find out, Gerry Crampton offered me work on the film *Hammerhead*, doubling for Diana Dors.

This was shot on location in Portugal, which was rather nice. The only fly in the ointment was that the locals did not take kindly to the fashion of the time. I had not been given much time to prepare before leaving England and had just brought with me clothes that I would normally wear at home. I found out that miniskirts and culottes were regarded with huge hostility by the locals. One evening, when I was out for dinner with some friends and wearing what I thought was a modest outfit (a loose catsuit with wide flared legs), a man tried to push me off the pavement. Another time, a young man on a bike rode directly at me one day as I walked along a pavement. I was rather concerned as I was carrying a bag filled with breakables that Gerry had asked me to bring to the location for him to give to people as presents. The man on the bike had ridden close by me a few times already and seemed to be getting ready to do something, so when he came back I was waiting for him and gave him a hearty push and shouted at him. He was rather taken aback by this and rode away.

Diana Dors turned out to be a cheerful, friendly person and I liked her very much. I was to double for her death fall from a cliff. She had my heartfelt sympathy for the way the press hounded her. They were relentless and would allow nothing to deter them. One day she and I were being taken to see the director to check on the outfit and whether I looked enough like her. We were ready and got into the car; however, the driver was briefly called away, and immediately photographers appeared from nowhere and stuck their heads in the car windows, ignoring our protests as they snapped away. Poor Diana could only try to smile, knowing that they would take pictures anyway and she wouldn't look good if she shouted at them. Fortunately, the driver returned and rescued us; I wondered later whether the paparazzi had paid him to vanish for a few minutes.

There was one funny incident at the hotel. Dave Prowse, the actor, was playing a bodyguard in the film. One day I was resting by the hotel pool and I saw him picking someone up above his head for a photograph. 'That's brilliant Dave,' I said, 'could you do that to me so that I can have a photo?'

'Of course,' was the reply, 'but I'll have to do it tomorrow 'cos I've got to rush now, and we need to try it out in the pool first in case I drop you!' So we arranged it for the next time that I had a day off.

I was quietly sunbathing by the pool waiting for him when a huge contingent of American 'gentlemen' suddenly arrived. They were apparently having some kind of convention at the hotel. I lay on my face on my towel, ignoring them, but I could hear every word they said – and I realised they were talking about me. 'Do you think she's lonely?' 'Shall we go over and keep her company?' plus other things! So I lay there plotting, working out how I could get as many of them as possible in the pool if they so much as touched me.

Just as they were building up confidence to come over, I heard a cheery 'Hi Cyd, sorry it's taken me so long!' and Dave had arrived. Now if you don't know what Dave Prowse looks like, he's a very tall, muscly bodybuilder; he was the actor under Darth Vader's helmet and cape in *Star Wars*, and he was also the Green Cross Code Man... My American 'friends' just melted away.

While I was in Portugal, I received word that the *Avengers* production team wanted to see me, so on my return to England I duly went to the studio. I was introduced to Linda Thorson, who had been chosen to play Tara King, the next *Avengers* girl. The general consensus was that I would be okay as a double – with the usual qualifiers such as 'need to lose weight' and

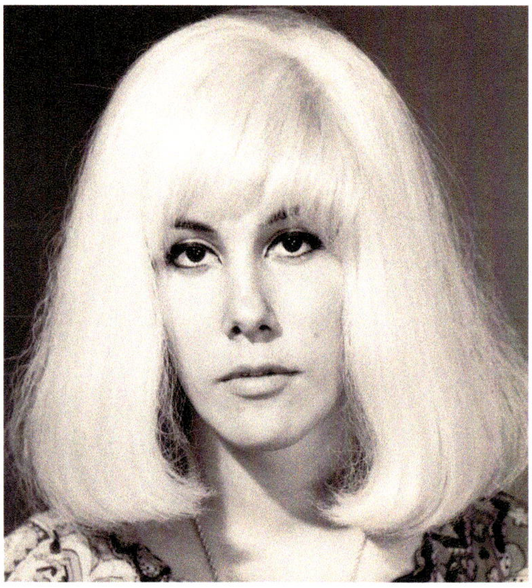

Doubling for Diana Dors.

Dave Prowse holding me over his head!

'change of hair style' and so on. Apparently, the idea was to make Tara a bit like Marilyn Monroe, and this would necessitate both of us having our hair bleached and styled. I pleaded to be allowed a wig but was dismissed with, 'It's a year's work and we don't want to use wigs.'

So off we both went to a well-known hairdresser's in the West End of London. My hair has a strong dark pigment and doesn't like to be lightened, so it resisted. I had to go back a few days later for my hair to be bleached again... and again... about nine times in three days! When it was finally done, I sat in the hairdresser's chair while his assistant took the hair clips out. She left the room and I waited for the main man to come and 'dress' my hair. I ran my hand over my head and it felt like it was covered in prawns.

The hair was dead, like straw, and so was Linda's! It was horrible. I felt rather sad. I had gone from having lovely long healthy hair to this. The hair was dressed and it didn't look too bad, so I resolved to make the best of it and booked to have my eyebrows bleached so that the effect was a little bit more natural.

The hair was difficult to live with. It had no body and couldn't hold a style. Colin Jameson, the studio hairdresser, would put my hair in rollers and leave them in. When the production assistant told us, 'We need Cyd in the next shot,' Colin would take the rollers out, dress the hair and I would do whatever needed to be done. When I had finished, Colin would put the rollers back in to wait for the next shot.

I became a bit of a hermit with my social life. Being naturally dark, my roots would start to show within a day or two and I couldn't make the hair do anything. I took to wearing a woolly hat after I saw people staring and sniggering at me. Poor Linda was also suffering; the hair on the back of her head was breaking off and disappearing. Colin was struggling to hide this by combing her curls over the space. Mine wasn't quite as bad as this, but it was like straw and would come out in chunks on the comb.

We both kept pleading for wigs, and one day when I was sitting in Hairdressing, preparing for work, Linda came rushing up to me in great excitement. 'Cyd, we're getting wigs!' she cried.

'That's wonderful,' was my reply as she rushed off again.

Colin, the hairdresser, looked at me solemnly. 'Don't get too excited,' he said. 'That's only for Linda.'

'But my hair is falling out too!' I cried in dismay. 'What about me?'

'You'll just have to put up with it,' was the answer. I was not happy. However, shortly afterwards I was allowed a wig.

The first few episodes of this new series had not felt good. Lots of the old familiar production faces had disappeared and we had a new one – John Bryce. He wanted to change everything, and it wasn't working. All the previous episodes I had worked on with Diana had had a completely different feel about them – you just knew that you were working on something successful; but now it all seemed amateurish.

The powers that be obviously felt the same. One day I came in and everything had changed. John Bryce had gone, and we now had Brian Clemens and Albert Fennell back and the atmosphere had brightened enormously. However, Ray Austin was no longer the stunt arranger as he had gone on to greater things and was now a film director. Our new stunt arranger was Joe Dunne, a very experienced stuntman whom I had worked with before.

Brian Clemens announced that he didn't like Tara blonde, and we were given dark wigs. The first two episodes that we had filmed

Me with my Dad.

were binned, although a few scenes were used in further stories – which meant that Linda had to talk about wearing wigs to cover the fact that these clips had a blonde Tara.

Linda and I were so pleased that we could at last do something about our hair. 'Dye it dark and cut it off,' we instructed Colin. When we were off set we both took to wearing loads of eye makeup, false eyelashes and huge earrings to divert attention from our hair.

One day Colin came in and announced that he would be leaving us as he had been contracted on a big film. Although we were pleased for him, we knew we would miss him as he was such a good hairdresser.

'Please can you cut my hair as short as you can before you go?' I asked, which he did. I ran my hand over it and, at the back, by my neck, my hand slipped. 'What have you done?' I asked.

'What d'you mean?' queried Colin.

'This bit at the bottom of my hair – it feels slippery...'

Colin began to laugh. 'That's your real hair,' he informed me, 'the new hair growing through.'

'Wow!' I said, 'cut some more off.' So Colin cut my hair as short as he could. He also cut Linda's, and we wore the dark wigs that we had been given for filming until our own hair was long enough to be used as 'Tara' on film. Colin had cut our real hair so well that it didn't need restyling until it was actually getting too long and needed a trim.

When we were filming an episode called 'False Witness' there was a fight in a vat of milk. Real milk! The props people said to me, 'It's a bit cold, we'll warm it up for you,' but it was a baking hot day so I begged them not to, just to leave it as it was. However, that was on the Friday and we didn't get to do the fight until the Monday... which was a very cold day! Props hadn't bothered to warm the milk, because I had told them on Friday not to bother. So we had very cold milk – which also smelt a bit off!

At the end of the fight I had to leap out of the vat on to the floor, and I was wearing leather boots which had become sodden with milk. There was splashed milk all over the floor. When my feet touched the ground, I slipped and skidded all over the place and went feet first, colliding with the studio lights which fell all around me. This was highly dangerous and one of the electricians rushed to 'save' me. However, he also found himself sliding about in the milk with me among the lights. Fortunately, we weren't electrocuted, but it was a bit scary!

In the same episode Tara has to chase a milk float and try to catch it; it speeds away and she falls over in the road. I tried to make this as dramatic as possible, going head over heels in the road. However, it was so effective that a little old lady who was passing by came over to me saying, 'Are you all right dear?'

What a sweetie!

Linda and I had suffered the hair saga together and had been on quite friendly terms. However, as time progressed things became a little bit more difficult. At this time Linda was twenty years old and this was her first big part. She wanted to do everything herself. It had even been a problem convincing her to use a lighting stand-in, which all the actors had; but now it became apparent that she wanted to do all the stunts herself as well. This caused problems for several reasons. Stunt doubles are used because the last thing you want is for your principal actor to be hurt; insurance won't allow the actors to do it as it costs a massive amount of money for a film crew to be kept waiting. Also, using a stunt double who knows what they are doing will make the actors look good. At that time everyone thought the actors did it anyway because the Production Office didn't admit that stunt doubles were used. For me, it meant that if I didn't work my salary was slashed. Linda would try to talk the directors into changing what was asked for in the script so she could do it herself. Previously, with Diana, we had tried to make everything we did as spectacular as possible, and now it was all being watered down. Linda would also try to wear a costume that didn't have a duplicate made for it, in the hope that she couldn't be doubled. If I was doubling for Tara, Linda would finish her part of the action and then walk off set. This didn't help with 'blending in' the use of doubles.

One day, we were working on location. It was a beautiful spot: a lovely meadow filled with buttercups and wild flowers. Even though the planned outfit had had a double made for it, Linda had picked another. I waited in a chair out of the way while she did her filming. Then one of the props guys came up to me and said, 'Do you know what she's saying about you? They said they wanted you in the next shot and she said, "But I'm wearing a miniskirt! Can you imagine Cyd in a miniskirt!" '

I was deeply hurt. It was true that we were both trying to lose weight and Linda was doing better than me, but I was still slim. We had both started off the same size, but I think that possibly Linda was using some kind of medical help – and the weight was falling off her. I was slowly following along behind on my diet. Linda had taken to telling all and sundry that my bum was bigger than hers...

Anyway, I was told that I was needed and that I would have to get changed into Linda's costume. By this time Linda was on her way back to the studio in her car; I had to hitch a ride in a breakdown wagon that happened to be going back there. When I walked into Wardrobe, the lady in charge was ironing the outfit that Linda's chauffeur had just walked in and thrown on the floor! So, I got changed and made my way back. I did the required shot, and then found a spare chair and sat down to wait to find out what was next.

It was a beautiful day, the meadow was full of flowers, the birds were singing, but I felt really miserable. Linda was making it plain that she didn't want me around; I was on reduced money because she didn't want me to double her; I couldn't lose weight fast enough. What should I do? I was actually thinking, 'Why am I doing this job? Why don't I find something else? What's the point of staying here?'

Patrick was sitting near me and had noticed how quiet I was. 'What's the matter Cyd?' he suddenly said. 'What's wrong?' Patrick was a lovely man, and he wheedled the whole story out of me and listened. Then he said, 'If I make an appointment for you with my doctor, will you go?'

'Well, yes,' I said.

'If you reach your target, I'll give you a bottle of champagne,' he said; then he was called away.

I thought about this and got rather worried. I didn't earn the same kind of money as Patrick and I wasn't sure that I could afford to pay a Harley Street doctor. I asked Jack Greenwood, one of the producers, if the company could pay for me but he said 'no'.

Patrick gave me the appointment and I went to see a very charming doctor, Dr Swan. He prescribed me some tablets, with guidelines on diet, and then amazed me by telling me that Patrick was paying! What a lovely man! Patrick was so kind.

I followed all instructions... and it worked. I lost weight fast. One day when we were on set, the Wardrobe lady came up to me and said, 'Are you wearing the right costume, because Linda thinks you're wearing hers?' Over her shoulder I could see Linda staring at me. So I went back into Wardrobe and swapped outfits: they were the same size! The Wardrobe lady told me Linda couldn't believe that I was now slimmer than she was – and she wasn't happy about it.

A few days later I was on set when Linda arrived. As she went to walk

Linda.

Me.

'All Done With Mirrors'

past me, she stopped, looked at me and said, 'I had a dream about you last night!'

'Did you?' I replied. 'What was it about?'

She gave me a long look and said, 'I dreamt I stabbed you to death with a hypodermic needle!' And then she walked away...

The actress Elizabeth Taylor had come to ABC Studios. There was great excitement on the first day that she arrived. The main stages were in a block of four with a road going around them where, if you were lucky/early, you might be able to park your car. Elizabeth Taylor was visiting to check on whether her dressing room was 'suitable'... We were all under instruction that there would be NO PARKING on the road outside the entrance she would be using. She arrived in a chauffeur-driven white Rolls Royce with red leather upholstery. All the corridors leading up to her dressing room, and just past it, had been freshly painted. Three of the normal dressing rooms had been knocked into one and had been fitted with a sunken bath. The next dressing room along had been fitted out for her personal hairdresser. Miss Taylor inspected all of this and announced that it was fine – except she didn't like the colour! So it was all repainted. When her filming was over, there was great interest in who might be the next recipient of this wonderful dressing room and the studio decided to give it to Patrick.

Patrick had told me that I could collect the promised bottle of champagne during the lunch hour when he was free, so I knocked on the door. He opened it with his charming smile and ushered me in. I was rather disconcerted to discover that he was totally naked! He graciously explained that he was a nudist (something I was completely unaware of) and liked to be naked when he was relaxing. 'You don't mind, do you?' he said disarmingly.

I thought to myself, 'How can I object to someone doing whatever they like in their own space?' However, I did feel somewhat uncomfortable; there was Patrick, completely buff naked, and I was fully dressed, and had no intention of removing my clothes... It felt a bit surreal. There was no threat in any way but I didn't feel I could stay. I thanked him for all his help and he congratulated me on reaching my target and I left. I didn't remind him about the champagne – it wasn't important. I couldn't help but think how ironic it was that Patrick was hailed as 'The Best Dressed Man on TV'.... and yet privately he preferred to wear no clothes at all!

Things with Linda gradually settled down as she began to realise that I was only trying to make her look good, and anyway no one knew that it was me. One thing that didn't change was that Linda was not allowed to do any driving on public roads as she hadn't passed her UK driving test and failed it at least five times.

When we were making *The Avengers* at Borehamwood, the stages we were using were back to back with those used by *The Saint*. Sometimes Roger Moore would pop in... and he was a great practical joker! In 'All Done With Mirrors' there was a scene where Tara was creeping stealthily up the staircase of a lighthouse, not sure if anyone is there. Linda was being filmed doing this and when she was almost at the top of the stairs, Roger came bounding down and frightened the life out of her! Totally unexpected and definitely not in the script. He thought this was hilarious... Mind you, once we'd all recovered from the shock, everyone else did too!

In the same episode I doubled for Linda in a fight scene with Bruno Elrington, who was a professional wrestler. Joe Dunne, the stunt arranger, came up to speak to me while we were working on the fight. I could see that he thought something was funny. He said, 'Bruno has just had a word with me; he said, " 'Ere, can you have a word with your girl

'Homicide & Old Lace'

'Noon Doomsday'

'All Done With Mirrors'

'All Done With Mirrors'

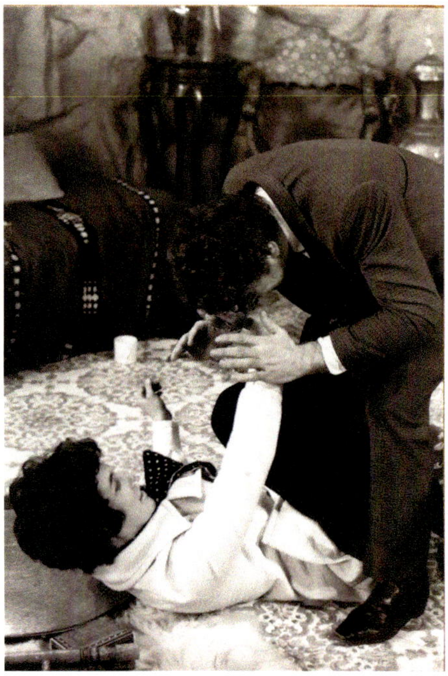

'Bizarre'

(me)? She really grabs hold of me." Apparently, professional wrestlers don't – and he wasn't happy with the way I did.

While working on *The Avengers*, I had always been on a daily contract, only paid for when I was needed. Now that I had been working in the industry for a while, I started to get work on other television shows and films; and one day *The Avengers* called and I was not available as I was committed elsewhere... Ray Austin actually knew about it as he had told me I should do this to make *The Avengers* realise that I should be under contract. Jack Greenwood contacted me and wanted me to sign a contract and I began to understand the problems that Diana had faced (although mine were small scale compared with hers). Before signing the offered contract, I calculated an average of how much I was earning per week on the current system; but the contract I was being offered was much less!

I refused to sign if it meant that I would be earning less money for the same work. Jack Greenwood must have spoken to Joe Dunne (the stunt arranger) who took me to one side to try to find out what the problem was and I showed him my calculations based on what I had previously earned. He was astounded! 'Bloody hell Cyd! You've been earning more than the artistes! You can't expect to get that!' However, I stuck with it and ended up having a difficult row with Jack Greenwood. He refused to budge – as did I... and I got as far as having my hand on the door handle of his office as I went to leave before he changed his mind. I hated being put in that situation. I don't like confrontations.

There was an embarrassing moment for me when Tara was required to do a cartwheel in the tag scene at the end of the episode 'The Curious Case of the Countless Clues'. Tara has played the whole episode with her leg in plaster. In the tag, Steed asks her how her leg is. Tara whips his hat off and, while holding it in her teeth, does a cartwheel across the floor, ending with her whipping around the fireman's pole (it's in her flat) and popping the hat on her own head as she smiles at him. True to form, Linda wanted to do this herself. The director wasn't so keen and wanted me to do it, and there was an argument. In the end the director insisted that we both do it so that he could choose the best one. The take he chose wasn't Linda's, and she wasn't happy. She shouldn't have felt bad. Everyone who watched it thought that she'd done it anyway.

The normal pattern for creating a fight was for the stunt/fight arranger to devise what he wanted based on what was in the script. He would then choreograph the fight with his chosen stunt people, and when he was satisfied with it the director and cameraman would be shown the result. Once everything was agreed we would rehearse it until we were confident with it. When filming began, we would start by doing a master shot with all the stunt people. This was the fight filmed in its entirety from beginning to end in one shot. Then the director would pick out parts of it where he could use the main artistes so that they could be filmed in close-up and you would get a good look at their faces. This would be cut together to look as if they had performed all the action. In the episode 'My Wildest Dream' Joe (Dunne) and I worked on a fight in an office of an optical company. We rehearsed it many times. I was doubling for Linda and was wearing a pair of short culottes which exposed most of my legs. This meant that I was unable to wear any padding to protect my legs or knees. We had rehearsed the fight so many times that it was quite slick and fast and became rather vicious. By the time we eventually filmed the scene my thighs were a mass of deep purple bruises and were painful to touch, but the resulting fight was very realistic.

When we were filming 'The Rotters', I had to wear a very short minidress. Whenever I had to do this, for decency's sake, I always wore two pairs of pants: one pair under my tights, and one pair on top which would also hold the tights up. Alf Joint was the baddie, chasing me around the woods with a large axe in his hand. At one point I slipped and fell, grazing my knee. First Aid arrived to clean it up, probably for continuity as Linda wasn't supposed to have blood all over her leg! I had to take off my tights so that they could get to the skin; knowing that I had another pair underneath, I removed the top pair of pants and the tights. There was a loud shriek from a small crowd of onlookers as a middle-aged lady clamped her hand over her husband's eyes! I did shout at her, 'It's okay, I'm wearing another pair,' but she didn't look convinced...

One December, just before Christmas, Joe Dunne said to me, 'I've got us some work, but keep it quiet because we'll be moonlighting.' I wasn't sure what he meant but I soon found out. We were working on a film called *Captain Nemo and the Underwater City* – at night! And *The Avengers* by day! So we did a day on *The Avengers* at the ABC studios and then drove up the road to the MGM Studios at the other end of Borehamwood.

There was a group of stunt people working on the film. We were supposed to be passengers on a ship that was sinking in a violent storm. We had a look around when we got there. There were hydraulic rams to make the ship (well, the part of a ship that we were working on) tip and sway violently, with wind machines making sixty mph winds. There were tip tanks that would chuck 'waves' made up of tons of water over the ship, and the local fire brigade were going to supply the 'rain' with hoses. We had a good look and digested what that was all going to mean, and then went to get changed.

Soon after, a crowd of extras arrived to be the rest of the passengers. They were laughing and joking and thinking what a great wheeze this was going to be. Then the director called over the tannoy: 'Before we go any further, can everyone please come and see the effects so that you know what to expect?' The extras came, smiling and giggling, to find out what was going to happen; you could see that they thought this was going to be such fun. We already knew! The effects started: the ship pitching crazily all over the place and huge heavy waves crashing over it, gale force winds and rain... You could see their faces drop. They suddenly realised why they were getting better money than usual, and wondered if they should have asked for more. There was no laughing now.

It was unbelievable. By night-time we were all set up on deck waiting to run for the lifeboats – in Victorian dress. The director said to me, 'When I call action, I want you to run towards the rail, and then everyone else follows.'

I said okay; then the props man came over to me and said, 'Can you hold this?' and gave me a birdcage with a cloth hanging over it!

'Great,' I thought, 'this gets easier by the moment!' Then we had to wait for the effects to reach full ferocity before the director could call action.

I don't know if you can picture this: it's night-time in December, so it's really cold, dark (with arc lights trained on us), the deck heaving, the waves crashing over us, the rain and the wind machines (which are actually old Spitfire engines mounted on a frame); you couldn't hear yourself think, let alone hear anyone calling 'action', so we just ran when we thought he might have

Fight rehearsal and final take for 'You'll Catch your Death'

'The Interrogators'

'The Rotters'

Continuity photo from 'Take Me to Your Leader'

'Whoever Shot Poor George Oblique Stroke XR40'

Rehearsal for 'Take me to your Leader'

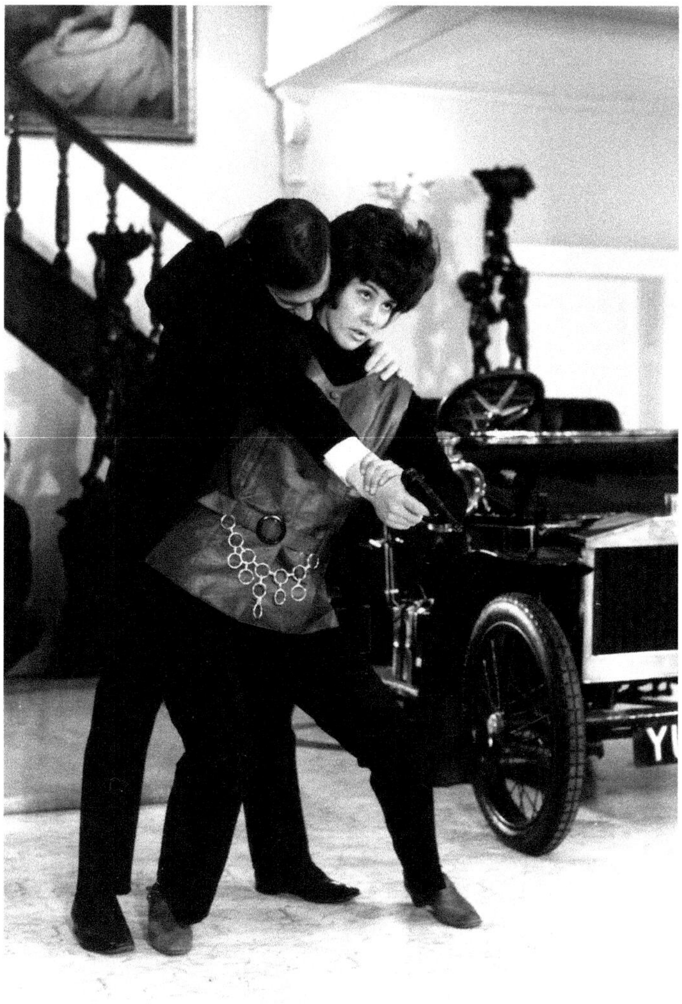

'Get - A - Way'

said it. Then we had to climb into 'Victorian' lifeboats which were lowered into the 'sea'. To create as much drama as possible, there had to be problems with the boats – colliding with each other, tipping over, dropping one end so that all the occupants were emptied into the water. Of course, all of us stunt people had to end up in the 'sea' one way or another – trying to swim in Victorian dress, which is not easy… It was a hell of a way to spend my birthday!

We didn't finish what was needed by the time dawn was breaking, so we had to come back the following night, which was Christmas Eve. Dawn breaking was about the time we were due back at the ABC Studios to work on *The Avengers* and we just about made it. I sat in the make-up chair and Peter, the make-up man, tilted it back so that he could work – and I promptly went off to sleep, only to be woken by Peter poking me in the cheek with his brush and laughing. Joe and I managed to get through what we were asked to do, but whenever we were given a break from action we kept nodding off. I found out later that the rest of the crew decided that Joe and I must be having an affair because we couldn't keep awake!

We went back to MGM that evening to finish the filming there. However, this night was a lot colder than the night before. There were now icicles hanging from the metal rails of our ship, and ice all over the deck, so it was very slippery. Someone lost their top hat in the water and by the time it was fished out it had so much ice on it, it looked like a piece of glacé fruit! Some kind soul had put a bottle of brandy in our caravan; but when we finally had a chance to drink some, we discovered that those people who had not been needed in our shot had sat in our caravan and had already started on it. We were a bit annoyed, as we stood there shivering and dripping wet; we felt we'd earned the reward.

When we finally finished in the early hours, I gratefully accepted an offer to sleep on the floor of a friend's house in Borehamwood. I was in no state to drive home to Old Windsor. We had been awake for forty-eight hours and been on the brandy… and it was now Christmas Day! After a few hours' sleep I pulled myself together and then drove down to Sussex to spend Christmas with my parents. When the film was released I watched it in great anticipation, looking to see how our work had appeared, and most of it seemed to have been cut out!

When it was finally announced that *The Avengers* was finishing, it was hard to believe. However, when we had the wrap party at the end, we had to face up to it. Normally, it's not the done thing to pester the artists that you are working with for autographs or photos; but I thought, 'This is my last chance,' so I said to Patrick Macnee, 'Patrick, could I possibly have a signed photo?'

'Yes of course,' he said, 'as long as you give me one of you in exchange.' He was such a lovely man.

I met up with Linda again at the *Avengers* video launch. The next time was *The Avengers* Fiftieth Anniversary event in 2011, which was admirably organised by the students at Chichester University. Ray Austin was there, John Hough (director), Brian Clemens (producer and writer), Bob Fuest (director), Honor Blackman (Cathy Gale), Linda Thorson (Tara King), me and lots of other people who had worked on the series. Unfortunately Diana couldn't come, but Patrick joined us on a video link. We were also joined by Paul O'Grady who is a huge fan of *The Avengers* (and I'm a fan of him). It was lovely to catch up with the old gang.

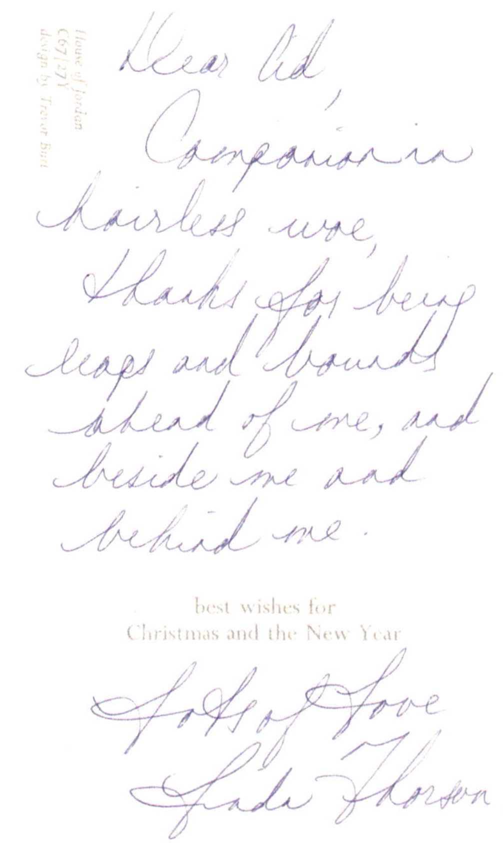

'The Curious Case of the Countless Clues'

CHAPTER FIVE

Cats, Rats and a Dog Called Emma

Dogs have owners; cats have staff.
Unknown

One day, when I was on the way to Borehamwood to meet a friend for lunch, my car was held up in a minor traffic jam. This was unusual because I was travelling down a small back lane that I regularly used as a shortcut as it didn't have much traffic. The cars in front would move forward by one car length, and then stop again. This happened several times until it was my turn. That was when I realised what the problem was. A small ginger mongrel dog was running about the road in a panic. She was terrified and in imminent danger of being run over.

I tried to call her to me but she wouldn't come. Every time I started to get close to her, she would run away. In the end I decided that it was no good, I couldn't help, and I was now very late for my lunch appointment, so I returned to my car. To my surprise, the dog followed me. I tried once more to call her to me but she ran around to the other side of the car and tried to squeeze under it. I gently pulled her out and gave her a cuddle. She was trembling and very frightened. I needed to get going so, deciding to sort out the problem after lunch, I put her in my car.

Later on, I took her to the police station closest to where I'd found her. I was informed that the nearest dog pound was at Rickmansworth! 'That's miles away,' I protested. 'Can I look after her and leave you my number in case anyone claims her?' To which the answer was 'yes'...

I called her Emma, as I was getting attached to the name, and we became firm friends. No one ever did claim her; when I took her to the vet, it was decided that she had been dumped. She was sadly neglected and only a few months old. She was very nervous of getting either into or out of any car. I found her very intelligent and willing to learn. Unfortunately my landlord didn't share my enthusiasm, and pets were not allowed in the flat I rented. So, rather than give Emma up, I had to look for somewhere else to live.

My boyfriend at the time was a rigger at the studio and ex-Royal Navy. I was introduced to the joy of boats, and ended up buying a Thames spritsail sailing barge to live on. I had no idea what I was taking on; it was a steep learning curve! The barge was called *Iota*. She had been built in 1886 and had belonged to one of two fleets owned by the Eastwood Brick Company. The boats in one fleet were named after English counties, while those in the fleet to which Iota belonged were all named after letters of the Greek alphabet. She had won a race in 1888, and there was a picture of the event on the wall.

Iota was moored on the river Thames at Old Windsor. There were no houses nearby and, when I first got her, I had to row across the river to get to her. It was very rural and quiet. I innocently moved all my possessions on board and prepared to set up home, accepting that life would be a little different now, with oil lamps and a chemical loo.

The first night was rather scary and a startling wake-up call. Emma and I huddled together as rats ran between the sides of the boat and the interior panelling. In the morning I discovered that the rats had climbed out of the bilges and run everywhere, in and out of the packets of washing powder and all over the place including the work surfaces in the galley, leaving a trail of muddy footprints. Emma and I had no time to waste. I was due at the studio for 7.30am. As I drove there I decided that I really must get a ship's cat as soon as possible! How, I wasn't sure...

I was in Wardrobe sorting out my costume for the day when my friend Alun Hughes came in. Alun was the hugely talented dress designer on *The Avengers* and a good friend of mine, with a wickedly sharp sense of humour which would have me in stitches. He was Welsh and spoke the language fluently; he could also bake a superb bara brith (a traditional Welsh tea bread).

'Cyd!' he exclaimed, 'would you like Victoria and Albert...?'

This took me by complete surprise! Victoria and Albert were Alun's much loved and very pampered

town cats. 'Yes, please!' I replied. I couldn't believe my luck. I'd only just decided I needed a cat, and here I was being offered two handsome felines. Alun looked most surprised. I don't think he was expecting such an immediate response. So it was agreed: I would collect them and take them home.

Alun lived in London, and I drove to his flat to pick the two of them up. They were both beautiful, large, long-haired cats. Victoria was jet black with gorgeous yellow eyes; Albert was larger, a tabby with a white bib and white boots and huge green eyes. My new friends were packed lovingly by Alun into a cardboard box.

I drove them home and everything seemed fine. By then it was night-time and, as I've already explained, to reach my boat I had to row across the river. The Thames is fairly wide and strong at Old Windsor, where Iota was moored. I placed the box on the rear bench seat next to Emma and commenced rowing.

Victoria and Albert were both quite big cats, and by this time they had had enough. As we reached the middle of the river they started to wriggle about and the box fell off the seat into the bottom of the boat and came open. Albert got out and was horrified to find that he had landed in water; only a little water, as you get in the bottom of a dinghy, but enough for him to decide that he wasn't staying there. He leapt over the side, where he had another shock when he found he was in even more water! He began to swim as fast as he could towards the nearest land, back the way we had come. Victoria was about to follow, so I grabbed her and stuffed her up my jumper. As I was now starting to drift downstream, I retrieved my oars and made for Iota. It's actually quite difficult to row with a reluctant cat inside your jumper! I let Emma inside the barge and shut Victoria in the main saloon, then promptly headed back after Albert.

I normally moored my dinghy by the garden of a lady called Chloe whom I was friendly with. I made for there, not sure whether Albert had managed to swim across the river. I was soon assured that he was okay: my torch showed a minor river of water running down the large willow tree on the bank, next to the river. I tried coaxing the sodden animal to climb down, but he would not relinquish his perch, so eventually I had no choice but to return to the boat empty-handed. The next day I informed Chloe of what had happened and asked her to let me know if Albert turned up.

After a week or more I began to despair that Albert would ever come back. I worried that Victoria would miss him and feel lonely; so when another friend of mine, the stunt girl Dorothy Ford, offered me a kitten, I said 'yes please'. I had a Rayburn stove in the galley which ran on solid fuel – anthracite, coal, driftwood, whatever was around at the time. The new kitten liked to sit in the ashes next to the Rayburn, so she became known as 'Cinders'.

A fortnight after Albert's disappearance, Chloe phoned to say that he had turned up! He was very beautiful and Chloe really wanted to keep him, but she very reluctantly handed him over.

The rat problem continued. The boat was kept off the bank by stand-off beams which floated on the water and pushed the boat away. The rats would run up the beams, get into the mechanism of the leeboards and into the barge – or run along the deck. They dug up the crocus bulbs that I had planted in pots and ate them. You knew where they had been because we had snow by then and you could see their footprints.

It took a while for the cats to work out a strategy for dealing with them. Albert decided he would sit in the middle of one of the beams and wait to catch the rats as they ran up it. Of course, they could see him a mile off and just used a different beam. He then changed tack and waited for them by sitting on top of the dustbin, which they sometimes raided. This didn't work either, as rats are not stupid and could see him.

The boat's interior was illuminated by oil lamps which I had to go round and individually light with a match when darkness fell. One night I got home late and started to light the lamps. As the light grew, I discovered the three cats lying on the chairs around the room. There was a distinct atmosphere; it was like they were waiting for me to notice something... then I did! There was a dead rat lying in the middle of the floor!

I must admit I squealed with delight, and my gang of three looked justifiably proud of themselves. I made a big fuss of them and gave them treats. After that they were on their way. There were no more problems with rats on the boat, and I think they cleared all the neighbouring land. They made a point of presenting me with presents of dead rats, which could be a trifle disconcerting – especially when they were dropped in from the skylight practically on top of you.

Victoria and Albert adjusted well to their new life. They became very used to living on a boat. They would jump down onto the stand-off beams and run along them to get to the bank from the boat. When the river flooded and the water went over the bank, I joined two beams together end to end; Victoria would trot along these as they floated and then quickly run through the shallow water to the land. All the cats learned very quickly to jump inside through the portholes onto a stool that I would leave for them. They became real ship's cats.

Emma came with me wherever I went. I would give her a run on the way to work, then hand her over to my friends the riggers, who would keep her in their hut. When it came to lunch I would give her a run again and take her back to the hut; she would get another run on the way home. Emma adapted very well to living on the boat. She had to jump up to the deck from the dinghy as the ladder was too thin for her to use. The main ladder down into the boat she could climb down and up, surprisingly, and looked very pleased with herself as she did it.

She was a good guard dog and would bark if anyone came near. She and the cats became friends and were quite happy together. Cinders would get into Emma's basket and curl up to sleep with her. At one time I had a problem with rainwater leaking in everywhere; as the water was dripping on my bed, I ended up sleeping on the floor in the main saloon and woke to find that the cats and Emma had joined me, having tucked themselves in with me wherever they could.

On board *Iota* with Emma.

When the river was in flood it would be necessary to put Emma in the dinghy and wade through the water to reach the land. I had a precious pair of waders which were very useful.

My parents lived in Sussex and I tried to spend every other weekend with them. I would stoke up the Rayburn on the Friday and it would still be just about alight when I returned on the Sunday evening, so the place didn't get cold. Albert took a dim view of this. He didn't like being left, and so one day when I returned he had gone. I searched everywhere for him but with no luck. I faced up to the fact that he was gone and then, a few weeks later, he came back. I made a big fuss of him and he seemed quite happy, and Victoria was glad to see him; but then the next time I went away, he left and didn't come back.

I was offered a little black half-Siamese kitten which I called 'Hawkins'. He was very talkative and would chat to me all the time. I had changed the parking arrangements for my car and now walked down the towpath to get home. Hawkins would wait for me on the way and call to me and escort me home. Now, when I went to visit my parents my menagerie came with me.

CHAPTER SIX
Iota

A small sailing craft is not only beautiful; it is seductive and full of strange promise and the hint of trouble.
Elwyn Brooks White

Iota, my floating home, was a 79-foot spritsail sailing barge and still had her masts. She had been converted to have an engine and living accommodation. The engine didn't work any more, but I wasn't worried as she was fine as a houseboat. She was moored at Old Windsor and I lived on her for seven years through rain and shine, fog and snow. She had no electricity and I had to use oil lamps for lighting, coal and wood for heating and propane gas for the cooker and fridge. This was before the age of mobile phones, so I had a telephone put in with lots of loose cable outside in case of floods (because the river would go up much higher).

There were three other boats moored nearby: *Romagini*, a large old motor torpedo boat which was rumoured to have been at Dunkirk; *Onda*, an 89-foot old sailing barge of a different design to *Iota*; and another houseboat which was a railway carriage jammed into an old dumb barge. We were not moored very close together, but we got to know one another and helped each other out when necessary.

When I first moved on there were no lamps at all and I had to go to a large ship chandler's to get some. I needed quite a few as Iota was a big boat, so I couldn't afford to buy them all in one go. I wanted to buy good ones in brass with a gimbal to keep them steady if the boat rocked, so I had to make occasional journeys to the chandler's to buy a few at a time (when I could afford it and when I had the time), plus all the other things that kept adding themselves to my list. I had a couple of free-standing oil lamps, but wall lamps were much more sensible. Paraffin could be bought at the garage when I filled up with petrol.

I also discovered that there was such a thing as a Primus iron, which ran on paraffin and was relatively simple to use when my clothes needed pressing.

The fires were built in so they weren't a problem. The difficulty that arose was that I couldn't have a coal delivery – there just wasn't anywhere for it to be delivered. My father had anthracite delivered to him in Sussex and I would shovel it into sacks and bring it home when I visited my parents. I decided on anthracite because it wouldn't produce sooty smoke. My MGB might have looked good at the time, but on occasions it had two hundredweight of coal in the back in four sacks of half a hundredweight each. I had worked out that I could just manage that. The tricky bit was lifting the sack off the dinghy and throwing it upwards onto the deck of the barge. It had to be done in one go or the dinghy would smartly drift away from the side and you were at risk of going head first (with coal) into the river. I never actually did this but it was a close-run thing.

Besides providing warmth, the Rayburn stove in the galley heated the water and could be used for cooking. There was also a cooker and fridge that ran on propane gas. This was supplied in tanks which had to be changed periodically when they were empty. The easiest way was to put the tanks in the dinghy and go to the nearest chandler's. Unfortunately the direction of the river's flow meant that I took the empty tanks downstream and when they were full (and heavy) I had to fight the current rowing back.

For water I had two huge tanks on board that I filled up when required via a pipe which came across a field – occasionally having to pump water from one tank to another to keep the weight balanced. The bilges had to have an eye kept on them and to be pumped out when necessary. There was a chemical loo which had to be transported across to the land when full, carried to the nearest field and emptied in a secret pit which served the houseboats. This was protected by a natural thick screen of stinging nettles...

I had a sort of garden... pots and window boxes on the deck where I could grow herbs and flowers. It was easy to water them – just drop a bucket on a line into the river and pour the water over...

Crossing the river in the dinghy could be dangerous and rather scary. I shall never forget coming home one day when it was foggy – and, of course, the fog is

worse on the river. At that time I was still parking my car across the river and using the dinghy to get home, although I had upgraded from oars to an outboard motor. I narrowly missed crashing into another boat in the fog as I crossed over, and then cautiously made my way upriver. Although I knew where my boat should be, I couldn't see a thing. At that time I hadn't been living there very long and didn't know what was further upriver past my boat, so I had no idea what perils I might be heading towards. I was sure I'd gone past her, but then luckily I spotted the wheelhouse because it was painted white, which was just as well as the main part of the barge was black.

The river was so powerful when it was in flood that it was terrifying and you didn't want to cross it if you could avoid it. Later, I made arrangements to park my car at the nearest house on my side of the river; from there I had to walk down the towpath and then release the dinghy, which was on a pulley attached to Iota. I kept the rope padlocked when I wasn't there. Once released, I could pull it over to me on the land, get in and then pull my way back to the boat. Walking down the towpath could be creepy (and muddy), and I preferred to do it without a torch on; I had the idea that if you shone your torch people could see where you were, so I only used it when absolutely necessary.

Some of the local people did not want us there, and I soon learned that it was prudent to have your mooring ropes tied to chains which were in turn attached to the mooring posts – otherwise the ropes might be cut! I also made sure that *Iota* was securely attached to an anchor which was sunk in a deep part of the river.

If the river became high due to excessive rain, it would be allowed to flood where our boats were moored, probably in an effort to try to keep it away from where the expensive houses were... This was always a worrying time. *Iota* had a flat bottom and the prevailing wind would come up the river and try to push her stern around. If the water was high, this would mean that she would float over the bank. I would need to push her off with a pole in case the water dropped and left her there. It also meant that I would have to use waders to walk through the water to get to dry land after I had tied up my dinghy.

On one occasion the water was so high that even this procedure was out of the question, so I took my dinghy to a different spot on the bank and tied it to a tree. When I came home later, in the dark, I untied the ropes (I had extended the pulley system as far as I could), got in with Emma, and made to go back home. The rope seemed extremely tight and difficult to use but we made it back and tied off the dinghy. I could hear a rushing noise and could see something alongside Iota and assumed it was a tree branch or similar that had been washed down by the floods. I got the boat hook and tried to push it away but it wouldn't go and steadfastly stayed alongside.

Now you don't want old trees to get caught underneath your boat because when the water goes down they will damage your underside; so I got my torch to find out what was going on. The thing looked familiar – and imagine my horror when I realised that this 'tree' was, in fact, my mooring post which had floated out of the bank!

My first thought was, 'What's holding us?' and I rushed to the bows to see if the anchor still held... and it did. I was rather worried as the anchor had only been expected to keep us in position, not to hold the entire weight of the boat!

With all the extra height of water I was worried that the anchor would be pulled out, so I let out some more anchor chain. There was a 'twang' from the mast as the telephone cable was pulled tight! Iota was now at a strange angle to the bank with her bows pointed out towards the middle of the river. There was so much water around me that it was more like being in the middle of a sea rather than next to a river bank. I was frightened that we were about to be swept downriver... so I 'abandoned ship'. The three cats were hastily put in a cat basket and I took them and Emma to my friend who lived nearby to be looked after while I sorted out what I could do. Fortunately this was all before I had my macaw living with me (see next chapter).

When I returned to *Iota*, she was still where I'd left her and didn't seem likely to go anywhere, so I started to calm down. After an unsettled night I woke in the morning to see if anything had changed. I was still in the middle of a huge stretch of water. I started to make breakfast and while I was doing this, I heard a boat making its way upriver. I rushed up on deck with Emma and discovered that it was a tug, who came over to us when I waved.

The skipper tied up alongside and came aboard with his crew to join in breakfast. In the course of conversation it turned out that he knew *Iota* from the days when she used to work! This was all a tremendous coincidence, especially the fact that they were coming upriver just when they were needed; normally you wouldn't see a tug on our part of the river. After breakfast, my new friends kept their tug alongside and pushed Iota back to where she should be and held her there while I took some nice long ropes and safely tied her up to a nearby telegraph pole. That time was the highest I had ever experienced the river.

Once, when I was working at the Omar Khayyam (more of that later), I came home in the early hours of the morning and discovered that my dinghy had sunk! I had to ask my friendly neighbour if I could borrow her swimming costume in order to retrieve it – there was no other way to get on board.

This all sounds very negative, but there were lots of positive sides to this kind of life. On days off, you were already at the river; just put your swimming things on when you get out of bed. No need to worry about traffic. Drinks could be put in a bucket and lowered over the side; they were beautifully cool when you wanted them. On one occasion I swam across the river (with Emma) to the small boat chandler's on the other side, to buy and eat an ice cream. Once on board, it was very private. Nobody on shore could reach you; if anyone tried to arrive by boat, you could hear them arriving. There were also, funnily enough, no draughts, so it was all very cosy.

Swans are magnificent birds and to see them take off to fly is quite breathtaking. They need quite a long 'runway' on the river, and when you watch you can hardly believe that they will actually manage to get in the air. As property of the Crown, they are listed by the 'swan-uppers' who periodically come down the river in boats making a note of where they are. Swans are very territorial and guard their patch of river

fiercely; they can also be incredibly cruel. I have seen them try to drown a dog that they didn't like swimming in their part of the river. Their technique is to put their feet on its head and beat down strongly with their huge powerful wings. They use this same technique on young swans that invade their territory looking for somewhere to live.

One day, I watched as a pair of swans bullied a young swan that wanted to be on their part of the river. He (or she?) was fully grown, but didn't fight back or seem to know what to do. He wandered off; however, later that day, when I returned home at night-time, he appeared, like a strange white ghost, floating next to *Iota* between the boat and the land. I had to take my dinghy alongside *Iota*, and he followed me. He came very close and seemed to want to be friendly. When I had finished mooring the dinghy, I fetched him a little bread, which he gobbled down. He looked very hungry, so I put a little bit of honey on some more bread. He stayed there. I think he felt safe because the other swans didn't like that area. I thought I would call him 'Cyril'.

The next day, I was on the bank talking to John, a neighbour from one of the other houseboats, when there was an almighty hubbub out on the river. Two adult swans were attacking my young swan friend; he didn't know what to do and came close to *Iota*, as he had the night before. I called him and he seemed to understand. He came quite close so I waded into the water and grasped him by the neck. The other swans were watching and slowly edging closer, so I scooped him up and tucked him under my arm. He didn't seem to mind and didn't struggle.

I asked John if he could help as we needed to contact the vet to ask what to do and I couldn't let go of my friend. I held on to Cyril while John went below to ring the vet. As I waited on the deck, Cyril reached down with his head to look inside and see what was going on.

The vet advised us to bring him in to the surgery as he may have swallowed a fishing hook. We had to cross the river to get to my car, so we climbed into the dinghy. John rowed while I still held on to Cyril, who was not at all perturbed, and all the way across the river we were followed by the other swans. It must have looked quite comical. John then drove my car, a little Wolseley Hornet, with me sitting in the back holding our friend, who was most interested as we drove down Windsor High Street; we did get some very astonished looks from the people in the street. We left him with the vet who treated him and he was then taken to a swan sanctuary.

There was another experience that I will never forget. I had come home in the afternoon. It was a glorious sunny day and I rowed across the river. As I slowly came round by the stern of *Iota*, I saw a family of kingfishers sitting alongside each other on one of the mooring ropes. There were two adults and two young ones. The approach of my dinghy had been silent and we took each other by surprise. One look at me and they were off in a bright turquoise flash of blue, but for one fleeting heartbeat I had a close-up view of one of my favourite birds.

I went through a phase of making home-made wine. I wanted to be self-sufficient and, wherever possible, made wine from fruits and flowers that grew around me such as elderflower, elderberry and honeysuckle. If fruit was cheap in

the shops I would make wine from it; I had a very successful batch of strawberry champagne which, when my friends discovered it, was completely consumed within a week!

I did once try making nettle beer; this looked a bit like Guinness, but it worried me so much when I realised how powerful it was that I only made one batch. It kicked the corks out with such violence that it looked like I had discovered oil – and the bottles were being stored in a cupboard next to the side of the barge... I was going to throw the rest of the batch away, but a neighbour liked the beer so much that he took it all. He invented a way to deal with it. He would stand the bottle in a large bowl and cover the top with another bowl; I had tied the corks down with string and he cut that with a knife! When the resulting black eruption exploded out of the bottle, the beer was contained back into the bowl and could then be poured in a controlled fashion into something to drink out of.

When Peter came into my life he used to bring his car battery down to the boat with him, so that we had the luxury of television at weekends on our little black-and-white portable TV.

In April 1974, the Royal Borough of Windsor and Maidenhead was formed; and in October that year, to mark the presentation of the Charter, the Queen toured the new borough by river steamer from Hurley to Windsor, visiting riverside parishes along the way. Peter and I, with friends and family, waved madly as she sailed by. It was all very exciting.

The queen travelling past.

Peter having just come aboard.

Life on the river was very enjoyable and interesting, and also helped me to keep fit for judo and stunt work. However, this idyllic carefree existence was about to change. The owner of our stretch of riverbank, a Mr Pollock, decided to sell to a new man – Mr Shanley. Mr Pollock never visited the riverbank and didn't care two hoots what went on there. Mr Shanley, however, was hostile and wanted us gone. He doubled the rent even though the lack of amenities stayed the same. At that time, and probably now, boat dwellers had no protection in law.

Onda, the 89 ft sailing barge which was my neighbour, had acquired a new owner, Basil, who was a retired Colonel of the Ghurkas. Basil was not inclined to put up with what we all agreed was an unfair situation. He arranged a meeting with Mr Shanley and I was asked to go along with him. As we walked up the driveway to the house, Basil said to me, 'Say nothing, regardless of what I say; then if it all goes wrong, you can deny that you were part of it.' I dutifully sat and listened to the pair of them threatening each other.

As we left, Basil, gentleman that he was, escorted me to my friend's house which was next door. I said to him, 'Basil, I really don't like the sound of what was said. I think you should go home and start digging the trenches and setting up the machine-gun nests! Something is going to happen!'

'Don't you worry my dear,' was the only reply. However... the following weekend *Onda* was gutted by fire. Basil survived but not all of his cats and dogs were so lucky. We contacted the police who agreed it was arson but said they had no way of tracing the culprit. My boyfriend, Peter, persuaded me that it was time for me to leave.

So... I sold *Iota*, we bought a house and I left my unconventional lifestyle behind.

CHAPTER SEVEN
A Macaw Called Chrome

She was not quite refined. She was not quite what you would call unrefined. She was the kind of person that keeps a parrot.
Mark Twain

I had gained a reputation at the studios as 'the mug that will take all the strays'. I was inundated with people telling me about this dog or that cat that desperately needed a home. I had to harden my heart and turn them away. To take on any more just wouldn't be fair on the ones I already had.

Then Diana Rigg asked me if I would like her blue and gold macaw.

'I'd love him Diana,' I said, 'but I've got cats and a dog, he wouldn't be safe...'

'Oh, that's not a problem Cyd,' was the reply, 'he can deal with them.'

'But I'm out all day and there are no windows for him to look out of...'

'Don't worry about that, he likes a chance to practise!' Diana had an answer for everything, and she was very persuasive.

As it happened, I was very friendly with an elderly lady with motor neurone disease. I had permission to park in the grounds of a large house owned by her daughter Hilly, who was a friend of mine; it was very convenient for my boat. I don't know what her real name was, but we all called her Ba. She occupied what used to be the music rooms, on the ground floor, with French windows leading onto the garden. I would sometimes get home very late and Ba, who was bedridden and often awake at night, would hear me walking past her window; frequently she would call out to me, and I would join her for a cup of tea and a natter.

On one of these occasions I told her of my quandary relating to Diana's parrot, who was called Chrome. 'Oh, my dear,' she said, 'I'd love to have him!'

'But, Ba,' I said, 'Diana says he swears...'

'That's not a problem,' Ba said, 'we'll put him up the corridor when the vicar comes.'

Ba was so keen and it was all agreed.

There was great excitement when Diana drove down with Chrome to deliver him to Ba. Diana got on with all the family like a house on fire. It was a lovely day, so she came on board my boat and we sat on the roof having drinks and watching the life of the river pass by. It was very amusing to see the faces of the people on the boats when they saw Diana Rigg sitting there; they couldn't believe their eyes.

Diana was in Abelard and Heloise at the time, and she told me all about the wicked jokes the actors would play on each other. For instance, as part of the play there were people in monks' dress standing in the shadows with their hands in prayer. One day, when one of the actors came on stage, they slipped an ice lolly into the praying hands. The monks couldn't do anything about it and had to stay there while the lolly melted and dripped down their arms. Another time, when the Bible was opened for the marriage scene, the actor involved discovered that there was a risqué photo in there to distract him... I gave Diana a bottle of my home-made potato wine to take back with her to the theatre. It's quite strong and I understand that the cast got rather merry on it... after the show, of course.

Chrome settled in with Ba very well. He seemed to understand how fragile she was. He had an enormous and very strong beak – he could crush a Brazil nut or walnut in one go – but he never hurt Ba. Chrome had a perch, he was never in a cage. Normally he was quite happy to stay on the perch, and if he fell off he would find the nearest convenient thing to climb up. There were occasions when Ba would wake to find him sitting on her chest when he had managed to get off his perch and had climbed up her bedding. He would look her right in the face and greet her with a loud 'Hello!' He would get hold of her fingers but never crush them, just chuckle away to himself.

Ba for her part was not frightened of him at all. Yet other people were. At that time Chrome was young and boisterous. He was very loud, and didn't seem to know his own strength. He thought it was funny to grab your finger and squeeze. He wanted to hear you say 'Ow!' Sometimes he would grab your finger and look you in the eye while you held your breath,

waiting for the pain... then he would say 'Ow!' and cackle with laughter.

He was a real character and great fun. He did originally, when I first met him, have an extensive vocabulary of swear words; but as he didn't hear them he gradually forgot them – apart from one beginning with 'f '... He realised that if he came out with that one then it caused a huge reaction. He saved it up and would surprise us when it was totally unexpected.

I remember one Sunday afternoon when I had gone to see Ba. She said to me, 'It's a lovely day Cyd, would you mind putting Chrome on the tree outside?' (there was one outside her French windows).

This I duly did. Chrome thought this was wonderful. He started climbing about, breaking bits off and dropping them down and chuckling to himself the whole time. Ba and I sat talking for quite a long time until eventually she said to me, 'Could you get Chrome in for me, dear? I think it's getting a bit colder now.'

So I went to the bottom of the tree and looked up. Chrome was just out of reach. 'Chrome, come on down,' I said to him nicely.

'No!' he shouted, and then commenced to climb further up the tree.

'Chrome, come on down,' I now shouted.

'F@#k off!' he shouted back as he now sat at the top of the tree. I looked around – fortunately there was no one else within earshot...

It took me quite a long time to persuade him to climb down, but that incident stayed in my mind and I always remembered what he was capable of. Ba thought it was very funny. She had a wonderful friendship with Chrome.

One day, Ba decided that Chrome's claws needed trimming and the vet was called. The vet had not had to do this before to a macaw. The claws were trimmed, but a little too much. There is a vein that runs down a bird's claws and you have to be careful not to cut too far up or you make them bleed.

Chrome's claws now bled. This is potentially dangerous as birds' blood is thinner than ours and there was a possibility that he could just bleed to death if the bleeding did not stop. The vet put little plasters on Chrome's claws and said he would return later to check on him. Chrome cut a slightly comic figure sitting on his perch with his toes covered in plasters, picking alternate feet up and peering at them and then saying 'Aaaaah' in a rather pathetic tone... The vet did return and Chrome was pronounced okay, but I promised myself (and Chrome) that this would never happen again.

Chrome stayed with Ba until, unfortunately, her health took a turn for the worse and she had to go into a hospice. Chrome stayed on his perch in her now empty room. He misbehaved and climbed up the curtains and ruined them. He was bored. I said to Hilly that if she didn't want to look after him, then I was quite happy to take him on now as I had realised that I could manage to look after him and he had got to know me. Hilly did try but she was slightly scared of Chrome (he was a big bird) and he started wrecking the place. So eventually I was given his care and he came to live with me on the boat.

He was a wonderful companion and we got to know each other very well. I handled him a lot and he became quite tame. When his claws needed cutting he would sit on my knee and I would clip the ends with my nail scissors, taking care not to cut too much off. Eventually, when it was too long and threatening his throat, he even let me cut the end off his beak – and I had to do that with a hacksaw!

He didn't have a cage; he sat on a large perch with a catch tray underneath. I would cover the tray with newspaper to catch all the rubbish that used to fall. When his new feathers were growing, he would rip the old ones out and drop them in the catch tray. I thought his feathers were beautiful. They were a fantastic iridescent blue on the outside and yellow underneath, which seemed amazing on a single feather. When he discarded his feathers, I would pick them up and save them, if they weren't too badly broken when he pulled them out. Chrome never missed a thing and he noticed this. I saw him watching me and he must have been thinking about it, because the next time he removed a feather, he was more careful and didn't break it, and he actually handed it over to me. I kept the best ones in a box, which I still have to this day – I had ideas about making a collage of him.

Eventually, his flight feathers started to grow and he began to experiment with trying to fly. I had read that these birds could fly thirty to forty miles without stopping and I was worried that he might get lost. So, Chrome and I paid a visit to the vet to see what we should do about this. The vet wasn't very keen to trim his feathers and said to me, 'Do you think he would come back to you if you allowed him to fly?' I had an immediate flashback to the time he was climbing up the tree and swearing at me; and I could visualise him flying around me, going from treetop to treetop telling me to f*** off. So I ended up trimming his feathers myself. It doesn't hurt, and I only trimmed off the end so that he couldn't fly and this was constantly replaced. He was quite happy.

Diana was right: he did like to practise, and he was quite mischievous. Rent was payable on my mooring and one day my rent collector came while I was out. He stood on the river bank, sinking into the mud, and called me. A voice from the boat said, 'Just a minute...' So he waited, but nobody came.

He called again, and the voice again said, 'Just a minute...' And so it went on until he left. He told me this story later because he thought it was me playing a mean joke on him; but you know who it was!

The Sandhurst military academy used to practise rowing their skiffs on our patch of river. They would do it during the week when the river was quiet. You would hear them from inside the boat: 'In... out... in... out... row!' And, of course, the inevitable happened. One day, there was a little echo: 'In (in)... out (out)... in (in)... out (out)... row (row)...' He did it while I was there; I looked out of a porthole – the oars were all over the place and they were all looking in different directions to see who the prankster was. I didn't dare say.

We used to get large 'shuffle boats' full of tourists on the river. One beautiful day I had allowed Chrome to come up on deck. I had put a chair on the deck and he was sitting on the back of it. There was a lock just around the corner of the river and we knew there was a shuffle boat in there as you could hear the engines throbbing and the murmur of voices. Eventually, the lock was opened and the boat came out and started downriver. Iota was moored on a bend, which actually showed her off rather well. I could hear the voices on the boat: 'Oh look at that boat – isn't it lovely... Oooh look, there's a parrot on the boat... Oooh look at that parrot...' Click, click, click went the cameras. By this time nearly everyone on the boat was leaning over the starboard side. Chrome resolutely stared straight ahead and ignored them. Then, as the shuffle boat was just alongside, he suddenly turned to face his admirers and, at the top of his voice, shouted his ultimate putdown: 'F#@k off!' There was a deafening silence as the boat chugged on its way; no one said a word and you could just hear the throbbing of the engines as it carried on downstream...

Now please don't get the impression that this was all Chrome could say. He had a wide vocabulary of other words and phrases, and he knew what they meant. He knew that you said 'Hello' when someone arrived and 'Bye' when they left; 'Want some water' if he was thirsty, and if he wanted to scrounge some food off you he would say 'Nice?' as you were putting the food into your mouth... and he would keep repeating it until you gave him some. If you cheated and gave him something that he wasn't impressed with he would say it again with a very sarcastic twist. He knew my dog's name and would shout 'Emma!' at the top of his voice when he saw her trying to sneak away. And he loved to sing. Opera was his favourite, but he also liked Barbra Streisand and hymns. He would join in at the top of his voice.

When he first came to me he had a wooden perch which was very worn. He had whittled it away and it was going thin at one end. My boyfriend Peter (Gallie) said, 'I'll change it for you,' and put in a new one. Chrome ripped that up in about a week. 'All right! We'll go for a teak one then, we can soon sort that out.' However, Chrome ripped the teak one up in just a few days. We didn't like the idea of metal because we thought it would give him cold feet, but he had to have that in the end. The food pots on the end of the perch were loose, so Peter tightened them up with a spanner. Chrome watched him do it – and then he undid the nuts again. He thought it was the most wonderful game.

Chrome had already had a taste of the film and

television world when he worked with Diana on 'The Bird Who Knew Too Much', an episode of *The Avengers*. He also appeared in various other screen roles. A film crew came to Iota to do some location work for the TV series *Special Branch* one day, and Chrome very quickly learned 'action' and 'cut'. This caused a bit of a problem. I had been sitting with him to make sure he behaved himself. I was beginning to feel that I needed the loo; I heard the call 'cut' and the director saying they were going to move the camera. This sounded like a good time to seize the opportunity to take a break, so I left Chrome and nipped into the bathroom. As I locked the door I heard 'action' from the director. It was too late – I couldn't get back in time, and there was an immediate loud cry of 'cut!' from Chrome.

I was given some work on *The Return of the Pink Panther*, doubling for Catherine Schell. I was the burglar in the museum, dodging the laser traps, stealing the diamond and escaping from the security men. For several days it was just me, Joe Dunne the stunt arranger, and the film crew. Blake Edwards, the director, was very interested in martial arts and used to know Bruce Lee. In between takes we would sit and chat. He was lovely to talk to and at some point I told him about Chrome. He became quite animated and insisted that I bring him in so that he could meet him. Blake loved him and wanted to use him. I subsequently realised that Blake seemed to have a soft spot for parrots and often had a little cameo role for a parrot in his films.

Chrome and I were subsequently called in on *The Pink Panther Strikes Again*. We went on to the set to find Blake and walked in on a rehearsal. Michael Robbins was rehearsing his part. He played a butler who moonlighted as a drag artist singing in a gay club. The soundtrack was playing and Michael was practising miming to it. Of course, it just happened to be Chrome's style of music and he immediately joined in, at great volume, which caused huge laughter all round.

I had to play the part of a bouncer called Bruno, with Chrome on my shoulder. Chrome was supposed to mess on Peter Sellers' (Clouseau's) shoulder, but they had to fake it because Chrome would never do such a thing. There was subsequently a big fight and Chrome, for safety, was put on a large bowl of fruit. You can imagine his delight with that; what a perk of the job! He got so sticky as he gorged himself that I had to give his feet and beak a good wash that evening when we got home!

It was also good to have a chance to chat with Peter Sellers. He used to do judo at the London Judo Society and had given them a cup to award each year. He was pleased to hear that the cup was still being competed for.

I worked on the James Bond film *For Your Eyes Only*. We spent about a month in Corfu filming, and while we were there I got talking to Barbara Broccoli and Michael Wilson. I had found out that in the story there was a parrot. I asked if they had cast the parrot yet and was told that they would be auditioning when we returned to England. So I managed to get Chrome included in the auditions. I was told that what they were looking for was for him to look as if he was talking; then they could dub speech on. So, armed with a pot of peanut butter, I would wipe a little inside his beak and he would try to lick it off. It worked perfectly, and he was hired.

I was told he had got the job but that they would also have a 'standby parrot' for when he got tired. I said, 'You must be joking – he won't get tired. This is right up his street. He's going to love this!'

Despite my reassurances, the standby parrot was hired; but he stayed outside the set for a couple of days until it was realised that Chrome was fine on his own. He enjoyed himself immensely. I polished his beak for him with coconut oil and he looked wonderful.

The props department had contacted me asking about 'his cage'. I explained that he didn't have a cage so they insisted that I lent them his perch so that they could make it look good. So Chrome ended up with a wonderful brass custom-made perch designed just for him! Which we still have.

He became friends with all the crew, and those who were nervous of him he worked on until they also loved him. There was a lady working with the Wardrobe team who was extremely wary of him. She would walk away whenever he was near. Chrome noticed this and decided he wanted to be friends...

He was allowed a lot of freedom on the set and, provided he didn't cause trouble, he could roam around. When this lady moved away he would follow and sidle up to her, trying to be his most charming, cocking his head on one side and saying 'hello', until eventually she gave in and they made friends to the point where one day she came up to me with Chrome on her shoulder and asked me if it was 'okay to take him for a walk'... Chrome liked to walk along the top of the sets; if he came across Roger Moore and Cubby Broccoli playing backgammon, he would stay there, watching, looking from side to side observing their moves.

John Glen, the director, asked me if Chrome could 'do something' with a watch; so my husband Peter sat with him all evening playing with Chrome with his own watch. The next day, Chrome did his bit with the cameras and everyone was satisfied. We didn't know how exactly the shot was going to be used until we saw the film... and Chrome was talking to 'Maggie Thatcher' through Bond's watch.

I did have one worrying experience when I was taking him to the studio. We were filming at Pinewood and I had to transport Chrome there. As he didn't have a cage, our usual mode of travel was for him to sit on my shoulder while I drove. It really wasn't dangerous. He was quite happy to sit there quietly; he never caused trouble, but sometimes he attracted attention from other people so I liked to take the back roads. Everything went fine until I pulled out of the lane onto the bigger road next to Pinewood. As I joined the road a police car drove up behind me. I had a sinking feeling

On the Set of
For Your Eyes Only.

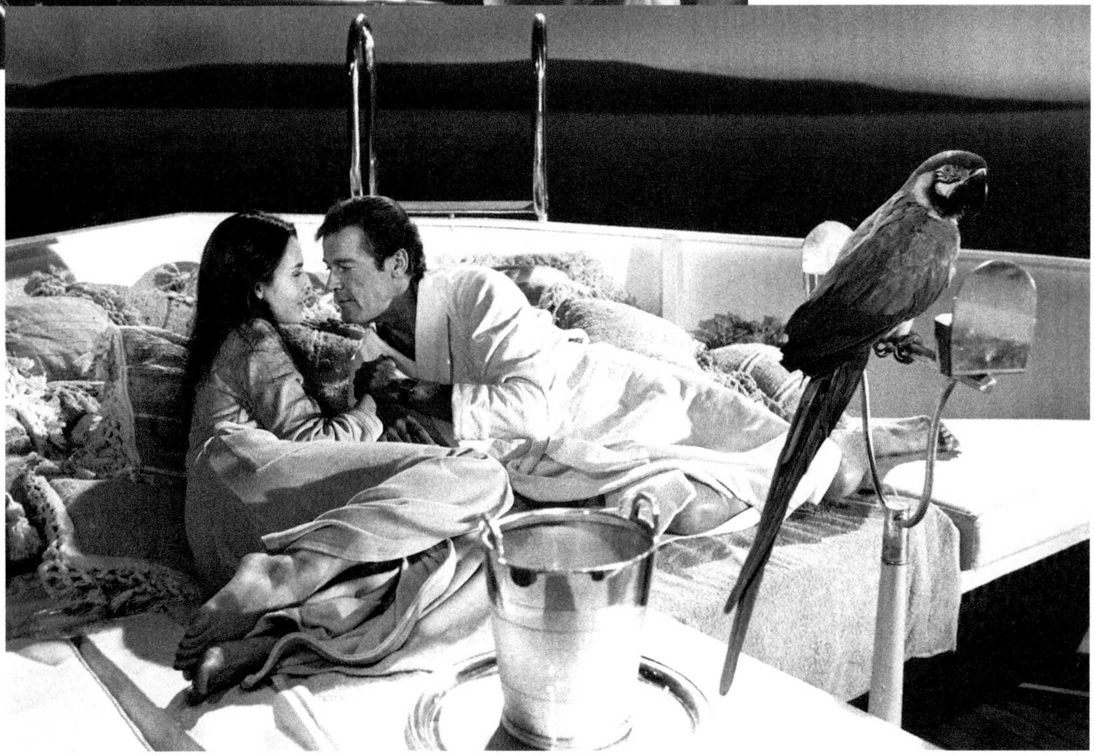

With John Glen, director of *For Your Eyes Only*.

With Cubby Broccoli.

With Lewis Collins.

when I saw them. I was almost at the entrance to the studios, thinking 'If I could just get to the gates…' The police car followed me and flashed his blue lights, so I had to stop.

The policeman walked up to my window. 'Good morning madam; are you in the habit of driving around with a wild animal in your car?'

'He's very tame and I'm just taking him to work…'

'To work?' he exclaimed rather sarcastically, quite unimpressed. He was not happy and proceeded to lecture me.

Chrome, in the meantime, wanted to know what was going on. He walked from my left shoulder to my right and peered out of the window at the police officer, who glanced at him and tried to ignore him. Not to be deterred, Chrome walked a little bit further down my arm to get nearer to him. 'Hello,' said Chrome. The officer tried to pretend he wasn't there. 'Hello,' said Chrome again, even louder. 'Hello!' He wasn't going to let it go.

The officer wasn't sure what to do with him, and hurriedly told me not to do it again and let us go. Rather relieved, we made it through the gate.

One day, while Chrome was working on this film, I took some friends to lunch. Chrome couldn't come with me so I left him in my car, sitting on the back of the driver's seat with Barbra Streisand playing on the tape player – he loved Barbra Streisand. A little while later the continuity lady came up to me, with a smile, and said, 'I've just walked past your car and your parrot is singing away!'

He made such an impact that he was asked for again and returned in the Bond film *The Living Daylights*.

I eventually moved off the boat and settled into a house with my husband, and when our children came along we got involved with the local 'under fives' group. Chrome was very obliging at having his photograph taken with various punters to raise money. Here he is with Lewis Collins who had come to open the show.

Chrome liked to play about in our garden. He liked to strip the bark off the trees so we gave him his own 'tree' which was a dead elderberry tree that we 'planted' in the garden especially for him, to prevent him from ruining our apple tree. He had a wonderful time stripping his tree, and we would then tie little 'puzzles' around the tree to entertain him. These were usually walnuts or Brazils which were tied to pieces of string for him to hoist up and deal with. Cracking a walnut or Brazil was child's play to him with that great big beak. In fact, sometimes he helped us out with dealing with the Christmas nuts; he thought this was wonderful.

Chrome loved playing with water and his greatest treat was to have a chance of a bath, so we would take him out into the garden, pour water over him and give him a chance to splash about. However, giving him such freedom came with a cost and he contracted an illness from the wild birds in the garden. We had to take him for treatment to Regent's Park Animal Hospital, where they took great care of him and restored him to health. We were told that, as he was now on their records, he could be treated as an outpatient should he have any problems in the future. Pete went to collect him when he was ready to go as I had just given birth.

'Do you have his cage?' he was asked.

'Er, no, but I do have his coat.' We had a child's jacket which we used to wrap around him to keep him warm on the way to the car. Chrome never had a cage. Pete said the man's face was a picture.

When we had our third child we decided that we needed a bigger house, so we moved down to Devon.

Of course Chrome came with us. He settled down very well. He was now our only pet. However, a few years later he became ill with what would eventually turn out to be diabetes. He was the first parrot to be so diagnosed with diabetes in this country. It took a lot of tests to discover what his problem was and, once again, the Regent's Park Animal Hospital gave advice. Chrome stayed with us this time as we lived in Devon and it is a long way from London. His blood tests were sent to the hospital. He became very ill, but once it was decided to put him on insulin injections he recovered. So every morning I had to give him an insulin injection into his tummy. He was so good about it. He would let me tip him onto his back on my lap and put up with the injection. It was wonderful to see him return to his old self.

However, sometime later he picked up an airborne infection and went quickly downhill and died. We were devastated. I don't know how he managed to get diabetes. We only ever gave him natural foods – nuts, fruit, vegetables and seeds. It wasn't that he was being given sweet things. His treat used to be to be given the inside of peppers: red, green or yellow, he loved them all. He would hold the stem with his foot and delicately pick off the seeds. I still think of him every time I cut one.

CHAPTER EIGHT
Throws and Throwing

Anyone can throw a ball, but try throwing something that is trying to throw you.
Neil Adams MBE, Ninth Dan

I was beginning to feel a little bit 'lost' with my judo. I enjoyed it but I was going nowhere. I had reached Second Dan in 1964 and yet, five years on, there was no chance in sight of ever being able to move up.

After my experience at the first women's team championships I had no wish to be involved with women's competition, but I wanted something to motivate me.

Apparently, there was a lack of British women for the Olympic throwing events, and so a televised appeal went out for girls to train for the team. They particularly wanted tall female athletes with 'kinetic' ability: that is, to be able to control your movement and direct your muscles with your mind. One of the preferred groups was 'judo girls', as well as gymnasts. I thought I would give it a go. Out of eight hundred and thirty-two applicants, I was one of those accepted; I joined 'Maria Hartman's Throwers' and worked on discus, javelin and shot.

It was interesting, and the training was hard work. However, the people already involved in these activities did not welcome us and were rather hostile. They thought that, because we had been recruited through a television appeal, we would get preferential treatment. So we kept to our little group, training together and encouraging each other.

We usually trained at the Crystal Palace, in all weathers. This was a new experience for me: running around the track on a little path that had been made through the snow, starting off with many layers and gradually shedding them as we warmed up; having a bucket of hot water to drop the shot in so that it didn't get too cold; throwing a discus which would then slice under the snow making it difficult to find (it was best to practise with a handful so that you could throw them first and then search for all of them at the same time). It was very different to the dojo (training room) that I was used to.

Our coach, Joe, had various ideas to improve our strength and fitness. One of his favourites was to make us wear a vest filled with lead and run up the steps of the Crystal Palace Stadium. He wanted to improve our 'explosive' strength. The vest had sixteen pounds of lead in it, and we took it in turns. We used the highest set of steps and the idea was to sprint up to the top, two steps at a time, and walk down; hop up on the right leg, walk down; sprint to the top again, walk down; hop up on the left leg, walk down; and lastly sprint to the top once more, walk down and give the vest to the next person. It was hard... The worst bit was the walking down, when your legs had turned to jelly. I remember once standing at the top; I had finally finished my turn but didn't trust my legs to carry me down. My group were waiting at the bottom shouting, 'Bring it down!' (the vest) and I was shouting, 'If you want it, come and fetch it!'

It was quite embarrassing when an athletic event was held at the Crystal Palace and the public would come to watch and fill all the seats in the stadium. We would have no idea until we walked in and found all the seats full of people. We then had to puff and pant up and down the steps in the lead vest as usual, with everyone watching, because we were not allowed to skip our training. We took it in turns to look after this infamous vest until the next week's session. On one occasion one of my friends had the vest in her training bag and a very kind gentleman tried to help carry her bag. His face was a picture when he went to pick it up.

The Crystal Palace was on the far side of London from Old Windsor in Berkshire, where my barge was moored, and travelling to and from training was a bit of a convoluted journey. I never knew which was the best way to go and was always trying different routes. One day I was passing comparatively near to the Budokwai, and it 'called' to me... I went in and was welcomed by all my old friends.

'How lovely to see you! Haven't seen you for ages, are you going to practise?'

'I haven't got a kit with me...'

'Don't worry, we'll lend you one!' Well, I joined in

STUNT GIRL CYD REALLY THROWS THEM NOW

CYD CHILD is the beauty who took brawn into a man's world—and found success.

As a judo fanatic she rough and tumbled her way to a black belt. As a stunt girl she took the bruises that earned Diana Rigg TV fame in the Avengers series.

☆

And now comes a chance to win world acclaim herself. As a result of an appeal from the Women's Amateur Athletic Associatiton she is one of the girls being taught the javelin and discus in preparation for the 1972 Olympic Games in Munich.

'I am not kidding myself I am going to become an Olympic star,' said 24-year-old Cyd, after her second coaching session at Crystal Palace yesterday. 'I've never done athletics throwing in my life, but I'll have a darned good try to become a success at it.'

Judo has been Cyd's sport for the past ten years. 'Now that I am a 2nd Dan I am finding it a bit difficult to go any higher, so it will be good for me to have a new sporting target.'

Marea Hartman, secretary of the Women's AAA, who made the TV appeal for Olympic field event talent to boost Britain's strength, has had 832 applications for the coaching tests.

'It's been a wonderful response,' she says. 'I know we possess the talent to knock the hides off the Russians and anybody else in these events, if only we can find it and give it the chance to flourish.'

ROY MOOR

Daily Mail, November 1969

and, being well out of practise, I was wiped all over the mat; but I thoroughly enjoyed myself. I never went back to the throwing events. The decision was a bit awkward, as I had the infamous lead jacket in the boot of my car and had to make arrangements to get it picked up. I decided that I would return to judo, but only to practise at the Budokwai and not to take part in any competitions.

Charlie Palmer started a kata class on Saturday afternoons. Kata is a formal presentation of judo. You work together with a partner to demonstrate the kata that you have chosen. At that time there were three popular ones that you were frequently asked for when taking part in a Dan grading. These were nage-no-kata, or kata of throws; katame-no-kata, kata of groundwork; and ju-no-kata, or kata of 'suppleness' – although 'ju' doesn't have a simple translation into English. Besides suppleness, it also means gentleness or softness, but it is more than that. Quoting from T. P. Leggett's book on ju-no-kata:

'The word Ju, literally softness, has a technical meaning in Judo. The classical example is a willow which gives before the fury of the tempest, so that at the end its flexible branches remain unbroken, whereas the rigid oak is uprooted. Sometimes the principle is misunderstood as complete non-resistance. But it should be noted that the willow does use some strength, in that it keeps its root firm; it is only that it does not directly resist the force of the wind. Similarly, in Judo, force is not directly resisted: but there is indirect resistance. The indirect resistance is based on balance, skill and strategy.'

I enjoyed these classes and attended regularly. We worked on the three main katas, but we were also introduced to others, such as Gonosen-no-kata (kata of counters), Kime-no-kata (kata of self defence), Itsutsu-no-kata (kata of the five principles) and Koshiki-no-kata (ancient kata). Kata needs a great deal of practice and discipline. Every move has to be correct and as it has always been done, and also you need to convey the meaning of what you are doing. It is challenging but that's what grips you.

Charlie was a perfectionist and would not allow any sloppy work. In katame-no-kata there is a certain amount of walking backwards and forwards on your knees, back upright. Charlie would get us to practise this while he walked among us with a shinai in his hand, resting on his shoulder. A shinai is a bamboo practice sword which is used in kendo (the Japanese sport of sword fighting). If you bobbed up and down while you were walking on your knees you could expect Charlie to give you a brisk tap on the head to remind you to stay level as required.

Eventually Charlie relinquished his role as ladies' instructor and kata instructor at the Budokwai. He just couldn't manage the time with his work commitments. I was tremendously honoured to be asked to take over these classes, and was ladies' instructor at the Budokwai for about fifteen years. I also became a registered instructor with the Inner London Education Authority and taught at several schools in London, including the London Oratory and the Queensgate School in Kensington. Various clubs around the country would sometimes ask me to give courses, and I also trained some police cadets. Being a fan of of the TV police drama Z Cars, I have kept a letter that I had from a Chief Superintendent Barlow. He is obviously not the character from the show, but it appealed to my sense of humour.

The Saturday kata class was taken over by John Cornish when he returned to England from Japan. The first European to perform kata at the All Japan Championships in front of the Emperor, kata was John's speciality and he was keen to promote it in this country. His knowledge was extensive, and he introduced me to go-shin-jutsu (judo self-defence kata) which seemed to be his favourite. In return I helped him refresh his ju-no-kata which he had not had cause to practise for a while. Having reached the grade of Fourth Dan at judo during his time in Japan, John continued to progress and eventually became a Seventh Dan. He was also a high grade at aikido, and encouraged me to learn and practise this with a Japanese lady who was staying in London for a while and who wanted to keep up her practice.

John was an amazing man. He was very quietly spoken, and a kind and considerate sensei; married to a Japanese lady, he was also interested in ikebana (flower arrangement).

At one time the ladies' changing room at the Budokwai was used as the male high grades' changing room, except on occasions when there were ladies' lessons; apparently it was a priority for the male Dan grades that went back to the origins of time. Unfortunately, we ladies were not aware of this. I blithely used the changing room as I always did, and quite often I was there at other times than during the ladies' lessons as I also gave private tuition and joined in kendo and aikido classes. All the male Dan grades had realised this and had graciously given up their 'rights' as they knew the changing room was being used – all except for Charles Mack (known as Charlie) who was not going to be moved. Charlie Mack was one of the higher Dan grades who, as well as being a Fifth Dan at judo, was also very proficient in karate and aikido. He took part in classes that I was not involved in, so I knew him vaguely by sight but did not really know him. He had trained in Japan, was a traditionalist and wanted things to stay as they always had been. I don't think he was particularly interested at that time in the fact that ladies wanted to learn judo. I was completely unaware of all this and, one day, I was in the changing room, had a shower and was halfway dressed when he walked in... We had a bit of an argument and I managed to get the rest of my clothes on and leave. He managed to claim the room for that day, but from then on the changing room was designated 'Ladies Only'.

My friend Christine Wildman and I would often pair up to work together in the Saturday kata class. In 1970 Chris persuaded me to be her partner and enter the National Kata Championships, held with the National Team Championships which was still a no-go area for the public! We worked very hard to perfect our kata. Tony Reay and other high-grade teachers at the Budokwai would give us critical advice.

As I am slightly taller than Chris, we had decided that it would look better if Chris was Tori (the one who is attacked but overwhelms their opponent with superior skill) and I would be Uke (who attacks but is overwhelmed). You cooperate to make the kata work, so there is no snobbery involved.

We entered in nage-no-kata (kata of the throws) and ju-no-kata (kata of suppleness). There are five sections to the nage-no-kata, with three throws in each, and they have to be performed on both right and left. This meant that in a single performance of the whole kata, I had to be thrown thirty times – and we practised over and over again! By the time the championship was almost upon us, my feet were so sore with all the break-falls that it hurt to walk, and we had to adapt our practising. We eased back a bit, and I recovered enough that we managed to perform the katas at the Championship. The whole kata had to be shown, from beginning to end.

We won gold in both. It was a sensational feeling. I felt as if we had painted an incredible picture in the air which had then melted away. All the hard work was worth it.

The Budokwai is not just a judo club; the word budo covers many martial arts and several others were practised there, including karate, aikido and kendo. Kendo is a martial art derived from kenjutsu which is the ancient form of Japanese swordsmanship as used by the Samurai class. When practising kendo the participant wears a jacket similar to (but not the same as) a judo jacket; big, wide floor-length trousers known as hakama; and Japanese armour that covers the head and shoulders, chest and hands/arms. The practice sword called a 'shinai', mentioned above, is generally used; this is made up of bamboo strips bound together. The 'proper' sword called a 'katana' is only used for display purposes.

I had watched some of the kendo classes and wanted to have a go, so I enrolled and joined in. This was a totally different discipline with a fascinating history and I enjoyed the classes immensely. One of the things that I liked was that there was no differentiation between male and female – you were just participants. In fact, in Japanese history, there were women who fought as Samurai. These were known as onna-bugeisha, which translates as 'warrior women'. They used all the weapons that the male Samurai had, such as the swords, horses and archery, but also favoured one which was specifically designed for them – the naginata. This is like a sword on a long stick and gave them better balance considering their smaller stature. Their story is fascinating and well worth a read, if you want to look them up.

There was one occasion that I thought was very funny. Our club took part in a team competition. Normally, the teams would do a formal kneeling bow to each other before beginning and each participant would have their armour next to them. You would be able to get a good look at the person you were up against. Due to time limitations, the first two contestants in each team were asked to make the formal team bow with their armour already on, ready to begin. As the lowest grade in the team, I was first on and made my bow, armour on, ready to start. My opponent was wearing a black jacket signifying that he was a Dan (master) grade. This was equivalent to a black belt grade in judo. I was a mere low-ranking kyu (student) grade and as such my jacket was white with criss-cross black stitching on it, signifying that I had not yet reached Dan grade. My thoughts were, 'I haven't got a hope, but I'll try to give him a run for his money...'

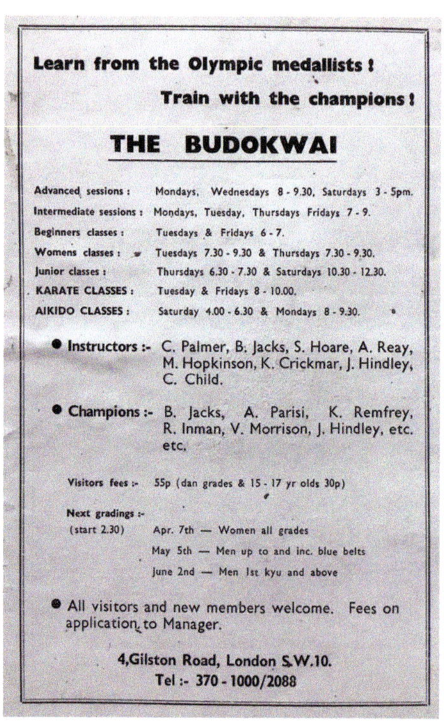

When we began he went for me hammer and tongs, but I fought back as hard as I could and it took him a little while before he inevitably won. Now, I'm tall for a girl and with all the armour on, he couldn't tell and probably thought I was a young lad (girls being in the minority). At the end of the match, the formal bow to end is made with the armour removed... When we all did this, he was furious and threw a bit of a tantrum. He was obviously very unhappy that he hadn't achieved a quicker victory since his opponent had been a mere female!

Compared with kendo it was more difficult to achieve 'equality' for women in judo. Some men (more usually the older ones) didn't approve of women getting involved in judo. To begin with, women had tried to replicate the same judo that they saw the men performing which did not necessarily suit a woman's build. It has taken a while for women to develop their own kind of style which involves much more reliance on suppleness and speed.

However, respect is earned, not given, and it depends much more on what your performance is like when you are on the mat rather than how much you can talk about it when you are not practising. The younger men seemed to accept us more, but only if they could see that you were serious about your judo.

CHAPTER NINE

No Blade of Grass

The brave do not live forever, but the cautious do not live at all.
Japanese saying

The stunt business in TV and films operated like a community of close families, which is understandable if you think that you might have to rely for your life on the person you are working with. Consequently, there were various top stunt arrangers who each had a circle of people that they preferred to use – their own 'family'. Obviously, if a particular double was needed, either for their skills or their looks, then they would be requested. Gradually, over the years that I had been working on The Avengers, I had got to know more and more stunt people. Once they had got used to me and trusted me, I started to get called on for other productions.

One of these was *No Blade of Grass* which was filmed on location in the Lake District. I was one of a marauding gang of bikers who were preying on vulnerable people in a world where there is a severe global famine; a bit like the Indians attacking a wagon train in the old cowboy films. It was quite hard going. The weather was unusually hot and we were wearing leather biker gear, and the director (Cornel Wilde) would keep us standing by and in position ready to go for long periods. This meant that we seemed to be constantly desperate for water. I lost seven pounds that week even though we had a huge full English breakfast every morning! I didn't realise this had happened until I put my own clothes on to drive home and found that they nearly dropped off me.

We had to ride around our victims in a gun battle. I had to be shot and fall off the motorbike on which I was riding pillion. The director asked if I could be dragged along. We initially told him that it would be difficult to organise, but we had to do it twice and on the second take my foot got caught and I was dragged along, so he did get what he wanted in the end.

The driver of my bike was Jack Silk who was a very experienced motorbike rider. There were a number of serious concerns in planning the stunt. There was a danger that I would unbalance Jack as I left the bike, and if that happened we didn't know what the result would be. It was also possible that a riderless bike might hit me. The most worrying problem, though, was with some of the other riders. Only a few of our group were professional stunt people; the rest were mostly amateurs who, although they were keen bikers, had no idea of the discipline required in organising the kind of shots that we were working on. There was one guy who 'thought it would look good' to do his own thing when I did the fall from the bike – and nearly ran over me! The boys took him behind a bush and 'had a word'...

Working on a 'daily' basis on a variety of different productions meant that quite often you had no idea what the story was about, and you just did what was required that day. For instance: 'Can you put these clothes on and fall down these stairs? ... Action... Cut... Thank you very much – goodbye!'

Consequently, sometimes I know that I worked on a particular production but can't remember what I did. For instance, I know that I worked on *Space 1999* several times, as a stunt double for various actors; but the only time I remember what I did was when I played the part of a guard on the episode 'Devil's Moon'. This was because I was playing a part and could recognise myself when it was shown.

The same goes for *UFO*, which I worked on a few times but I can only remember doubling for Wanda Ventham diving through a car window. I didn't have a chance of getting to know Wanda but she seemed to be a very calm and friendly person. Another time involved doing some car driving. I also remember being in a harness, hanging close to the ceiling of the stage (quite high), and we were 'working in space'.

Sometimes, when I am watching repeats on TV, a situation happens in the story that seems familiar and I think, 'I did something here, I remember the costume...' Sometimes it will all come back to me but often only after the action has happened.

There was also *Blake's 7* for the BBC, which I worked on several times. All I remember of that is

No Blade of Grass

having to wear a very expensive make-up which gave you a pale, unearthly reflective look – and working in Wookey Hole caves, which was rather creepy. The lights made weird shadows everywhere so there were always dark areas. I did quite a bit of work as a kind of alien guard; and at one time I had to balance on top of some very slippery damp rocks, which was slightly worrying.

Once I worked on an Italian TV series that I never knew the name of, or indeed the story. I had to be a body drifting down the Thames. As I float rather too easily, I had to tie weights around my ankles, wrists and body before getting in the water. I shall never forget the horrified expressions on the faces of some onlookers who had come to see what we were filming. I think they thought I was a suicide as I disappeared under the water and drifted through the weir!

It was also difficult to keep track of what the film companies were doing with the material they had shot. We were supposedly entitled to royalties on our work, depending on the contract (was it TV, TV film, film...?). I once worked on a film where Terry Walsh and myself had to ride a tandem in our underwear and end up in the village pond (don't ask, I don't know what the story was about – the film was called *I'm Not Feeling Myself Tonight*). I don't think the film made it to the cinema; but one Christmas, while watching the TV, I saw an advert for the forthcoming Boxing Day sales and among other clips was the one of me and Terry going into the pond! Theoretically, Terry and I should have had royalties on that but it was too difficult to track down.

I also did quite a few odd days working on safety films for the Central Office of Information: going through a windscreen, as a passenger and then another time as the driver (the moral being, wear your seatbelt); getting knocked over by a car overtaking on a zebra crossing (don't overtake at crossings); hitting my face on a glass door (beware glass doors)... stuff like that. There are so many entries on my records which just give the name of the film and how many days, and I don't know what I did.

On one occasion a group of us had to do a commercial for car tyres. We worked on a new section of the M40 motorway which had not yet been opened. The story was that the car in which I was a passenger was driving along in the outside lane when the windscreen gets shattered by a stone; the driver loses control and swerves across the central reservation into the oncoming traffic on the other side. In order to make the windscreen shatter on cue, I had to jab a sharp instrument into the corner – it was quite exciting...

Then there was a COI film that I worked on where the message was, don't overtake at pedestrian crossings. I arrived in the morning at the designated pedestrian crossing and I was a bit early so I had to hang around. There was a policeman there so eventually we got chatting. He told me that he was there for safety as 'some stunt girl is going to be hit by a car'.

'That's me!' I cried.

'Really?' He was quite astonished. I think he didn't expect a stunt girl to look like a normal human being...

Everyone arrived and we worked out what we were going to do and how we were going to do it, including what shopping I should carry for dramatic effect – things that would roll all over the place or smash such as eggs and fruit. We did the shot several times, and when we had finished a man rushed over and gave me a huge bouquet of flowers. He owned the florist's just across the road and had been watching us all day. What a kind thought! There are some lovely people in the world.

I worked for the BBC on *The Goodies* quite a few times. There wasn't much difference between working for the BBC or ITV, except the BBC were meaner with their money. *The Goodies* were a lovely bunch and great fun to work with; and the stories were always quite bizarre. I remember I had to impersonate Barbara Cartland on one episode – even though I was a completely different height and shape! I think it was a wrestling scene with another stunt girl. Another time I had to be a nurse holding Bill Oddie all wrapped up in a blanket to make him look like a newborn baby.

For the episode 'Scoutrageous' we were supposed to be 'the Salvation Army in training' with machine guns and so on, which we filmed in Brecon in Wales where they train the real army. I had to learn how to use a Vickers machine gun. You couldn't just pull the trigger, because the blanks had wax in them which would jam the gun, so you had to learn the procedure to unjam it; fun, but absolutely deafening! The difficult bit was that the director wanted me to smile angelically as I fired the gun. Pretty tricky while you are holding the gun with both hands, it's vibrating like crazy and the noise is unbelievable! I'd always wanted a chance to fire a machine gun; usually, if one was involved in any action I did, then the gun had to be fired by the artist as it was a close-up.

We did another episode where I had to be an American tourist wearing a witch's hat who catches fire and has to jump into the moat of an old castle (it was always a bit daft); that was freezing! The moat was fed by an underground spring. I had a car waiting for me when I finished so that I could be wrapped in towels and driven to a nearby pub for a prearranged hot bath. I got in the car with my teeth chattering and, as he set off, the driver said, 'There's a bottle of brandy under the seat!' I found it and gratefully had a few swigs. By the time I got in the bath I was numb. I sat in the hot water and watched my skin turn from blue, through various shades of pink – and still couldn't feel a thing. Possibly the brandy was involved a bit...

Tim Brook-Taylor and Graeme Garden posing helpfully for me, and Billy Oddie relaxing between takes.

On the left, my 'Valkyrie ' outfit.

Another time I had to swim underwater in a swimming pool, and then come up and burst out of the water trying to sing in an operatic style, like 'The Ride of the Valkyries'!

There was a film called *All Coppers Are...* for which we had to film a riot with a police line trying to hold it. It was filmed outside on the lot at Pinewood and involved lots of pushing and shoving and angry words. We were given 'bricks' made of foam rubber to throw at the 'police'. However, this was not enough for some people. There were some in the crowd who seemed unable to accept that this was not for real and that the 'police' were not real policemen... I would call them professional rioters!

These people started soaking the foam bricks in water to make them heavy, so that when they were thrown, it hurt... Then they started searching around for real bricks to throw... At that time (1971) we still had the old currency and had not yet gone decimal. The old pennies were large and heavy. The troublemakers started throwing these pennies at the 'police' which was quite dangerous as they could cut faces. The situation became rather unpleasant. Unfortunately, in a crowd of people it is difficult to identify who is doing this, but a warning went out and the scene was eventually completed. It made me realise how difficult it must be for our police force to deal with situations like this.

CHAPTER TEN

Out From Behind Closed Doors

You win or you learn.

In the year 1971, things started to happen. On 7 March I managed to become a Third Dan. It was rather unexpected. A lady I know called Anne Swinton asked me to take part in a grading for her to get her Third Dan. It was always difficult to get enough ladies together for a Dan grading as you needed a minimum of six people for the examination to work. I agreed, but at the back of my mind I was thinking, 'Yes, I'll take part, but it's not a done deal that you'll win; I'm not giving it away...' On the day, Anne didn't turn up; but we had our six ladies, which made it enough to run the grading anyway, and I managed to succeed.

The Budokwai did a show in the Earls Court Exhibition Centre. This was a tricky one for me. I had been asked to do a self-defence display (wearing a dress); but the kendo class wanted me to join in their routine (in the big wide Japanese trousers known as hakama, as well as armour), and also Jane Peach and I were to perform nage-no-kata (in judogi). It turned out the changing rooms were on the top floor of this vast building – and our display was on the ground floor!

'I've got a problem!' I said to the organisers, in panic. 'I'll never be able to get changed in between displays! I can't run up and down in time!'

'We'll see what we can do,' was the reply.

I ended up with a little room just outside the main arena where the horses and so on would come in when they were needed. There was a small group of soldiers who were part of the event. They were relaxing, having a fag near the entrance, and this dishevelled woman kept running in and out of the door, changing her clothes each time. I must say, I got some strange looks from them.

I discovered that the CKI system was no longer being used and women now had the same scoring method as the men; so I was persuaded to be a part of the London Area team for the National Team Championships, and we won gold.

Later in the year, on 6 October 1971, the very first Women's Individual Open Championships were held at Bracknell Sports Centre, and this was an exciting new step for women. Lots of my friends had put their names down to enter and I thought I would give it a go. In order to enter, all participants had to produce a medical certificate to prove that they were fit to compete. Accordingly, I went to see my doctor for the desired paperwork and while I was there I asked him about the swelling that had appeared on the right side of my neck. He told me that he would do some tests as he wasn't sure... and he would have the results in two weeks but he thought that it was probably either glandular fever or leukaemia...! I was shocked! For the next two weeks I was mentally sorting out my will.

My weight category was heavyweight (above seventy kilos). I was very nervous, and this was not helped when I discovered that there were newspaper and television reporters there – and someone warned me that they were looking for 'the *Avengers* girl'. I really didn't want to be interviewed before competing; I just wanted to be left alone. So I hid in plain sight in large groups of competitors who were warming up.

The event itself was well organised. There were one hundred and nine entries, including eleven from West Germany. There were also three Dutch observers and a promise of a team from the USA the following year. I achieved bronze in the open (Chris Wildman won gold!) and I won my weight category.

Nerves and emotions then overcame me and I embarrassed myself by bursting into tears.

I had food for thought after my last contest with Elke Mogebier, the German lady I met in the final. It was the first time I had encountered a female opponent who looked me right in the eye. I realised that all the women I practised with were smaller than me. I thought to myself that, if I was to repeat this experience and compete at an international level, then I must find taller people with whom to practise.

Once the championships were finished with, my

This is the Nage No Kata that Peaches and I performed at the Earl's Court show. I was Uki to Peaches' Tori.

The Victorious London Area Team - 1971, with our Team Manager, Syd Hoare.

Brian Jacks.

neck went back to its normal size. The results from the doctor were negative and he decided that it was all due to stress... phew!

Thinking about the height issue, I decided that perhaps I could join in the men's Olympic training class at the Budokwai, run by Brian Jacks. This was a men-only class aimed at the elite grades. Brian was a top competitor. In 1964, at the age of sixteen, he was the youngest person to be selected for the European Championships, and won a gold medal in the junior middleweight section. In the same year he was selected for the Olympic Games in Tokyo. He went on to win bronze in the Munich Olympics in 1972 and was also selected for the team in 1976. In 1967 he won a bronze medal in the World Championships.

Brian won the British Open six times and the European Championships five times (twice as a junior and three times as a senior). Bear in mind that his category, middleweight, always has a huge number of competitors. Eventually, Brian became famous for taking part in the TV programme Superstars and beat the cream of British and European sportsmen to win two years in succession. He was a tremendous ambassador for judo and, whenever he was interviewed by the press, he always made sure he was wearing his Budokwai sweatshirt!

I asked Brian if I could join in his class, and he said, 'You'll have to ask the manager.' I asked the manager (Syd Hoare) and he said, 'You'll have to ask Brian...' and so it went on. Nobody wanted to make a decision. After a lot of arguing and discussion by the Budokwai committee, it was eventually agreed that I could join in with the proviso that if any other woman wanted to join in, then I would have to leave the class. I learned later that the problem was that the powers that be were worried that allowing women into the class might lower the standard. My argument was that the class was so hard that it was unlikely that any other woman would want to join in; and also the class was so big, usually around seventy people, that allowing one woman in (me) wouldn't make any difference, especially as I wanted to work and I didn't want to be treated differently.

These classes were enormously hard work but they did help me a great deal and I did enjoy them. I tried to make a point of only training with light, light-middleweight and middleweight men who were closer to my own weight, but sometimes I could not avoid training with heavier people. Keith Remfry and Tony Sweeney were both heavyweights but had a wonderful fluid style which was beneficial to me. There was also Angelo Parisi who was light-heavyweight, fast and supple and attacking on both sides.

Brian treated me the same as everyone else and I suffered the same. The warm-up always started off with lots of sprints up and down the dojo, and whoever was last each time had to do ten press-ups. Initially that was often me, and he would shout 'go' to start the next run before I had finished the press-ups, so I would be eternally last (and doing more press-ups). Also, if Brian thought that not enough enthusiasm was going into the press-ups, he would take off his belt, double it and use it as a whip – to encourage you... I quickly learned to make sure that I wasn't last.

The 'British Bulldog' game at the end of the class was positively terrifying, and I would often hide in the doorway if it was a big class, which it usually was, as I was in danger of being smashed into the walls!

However, most people in the class just accepted me as another body and made no allowances. This was great and just what I needed.

I think I should also point out that in those days, in any of the classes, both men's and women's, we trained for two hours non-stop and there were no water breaks – the opinion being that to drink water would mean it 'slopping about' inside you as we worked. Today, everyone seems to have a water bottle handy and is constantly drinking from it. We also had to ask permission if we needed to leave the class. You couldn't just walk out; that would be insulting to the sensei.

I trained regularly in the elite class with the men, and joined in with the courses and displays that Brian would run. Angelo Parisi was a young member of the class and Brian had taken him under his wing as it was obvious that Angelo had potential, so we would often be on the same courses. Angelo has an amazing ability to absorb new moves just by seeing them done, and he didn't always know how to explain the mechanics of the movement, so Angelo would show the technique and Brian would explain how he did it. When we were doing the courses, Brian would say things like, 'Show 'em your dustbin throw Ange,' and Angelo would oblige and Brian would explain how it was done. Brian also liked to challenge members of the audience at displays – usually large heavy non-judo men – to try to get out of my kesa-gatame, my favourite hold-down. This used to worry me a bit as some of them were very strong and I was worried that they might escape and then I would have let Brian down. He was well known for his superb uchi-mata (inner thigh reaping throw) and he helped me to make it my favourite technique; and with this intensive training I managed to win the British Open, in my weight category, for five consecutive years from 1971 to 1975 and also in the Open category as well in 1973.

Two young brothers had come to the Budokwai to learn judo; their names were Quentin and Steven Kingsbury. Their father would come to watch from the doorway. People were very friendly and, in the course of conversation, we found out that he was a doctor. At that time judo players, and for that matter all sportspeople, did not have any specialist medical care. If you had a problem you had to go and see your GP – who would usually consider that you had brought this on yourself, and you would simply be told 'to rest'. It gradually became the norm that people would ask Dr Ken Kingsbury about their injuries: 'Oh Ken, can I just ask your advice about my shoulder/knee/back etc...' and he didn't mind helping. He was very knowledgeable, and had many contacts in the medical profession. Over time, Ken became a sort of health guru for us all, sorting out our problems. If you had an injury, your first port of call was Ken. He would arrange for you to see an expert to get you sorted out. The deal was that you had to ring Ken as soon as you left the hospital and tell him what the verdict was. If he was not happy with the result, he would send you to another expert, until you were sorted out.

Angelo Parisi and Keith Remfry.

He began to travel with the British judo team; I think they may have been the first sports team to travel with their own doctor. When he was at the Olympics he had the same sort of experience that he had previously had with us – people coming up and asking about their injuries – only now they were from other sports. He was an amazing man and helped everyone he could.

Ken also gave us advice about training. Not just the ladies: mainly the Olympic men. He pointed out that when we make an attack we stop breathing, so we should try to do some training with restricted breathing. His idea was that if we carried weights in our hands whilst running, this would do the trick.

The weights had to be light enough that you could keep your arms bent and your hands close to your chest and possibly swing them, but heavy enough to make you work. He developed a method of calculating the optimum weight for each person, and he would use old pill tins filled with lead shot. The tins were a good shape to hold in your hand, but the noise of the rattling lead was a bit unnerving. I used to go out for a run after practice, with the key for the door in my pocket because everyone would have gone home by the time I got back. Just a few miles holding Ken's lead-shot pill tins... It was surreal, padding around South Kensington and Earl's Court, late in the evening, in the dark, with these pill tins sounding like I was shaking maracas! People leapt out of my way; I think they thought I was some kind of maniac. You didn't have to go far before you could taste blood in your mouth, and by the time I got back I could

This is Ken supervising treatment on my right ankle which was always giving trouble.

hardly stand and had the greatest difficulty in getting the key in the lock as my hands were shaking so much!

However, I considered this preferable to some of Ken's other ideas. For a while Keith Remfry turned up for practice with small sandbags strapped to his wrists and ankles. This looked very uncomfortable.

Keith Remfry was our genial giant. He won bronze twice in the world championships, and silver in the Open class in the 1976 Olympics. Although he was a big man, he was supple and had a fluid, mobile style, which made him one of the few heavyweights that I enjoyed practising with. Surprisingly to me, he had no objection to practising with me and would even ask me for randori.

Ken was always coming up with new ideas. Another one he had involved beating your own result. The idea was that you had a group of exercises to do; I think it was ten different ones and they were best done with a partner. You had to work ferociously for one minute and then rest for one minute until you had completed all of them, writing down your scores as you went. We always started with the sprint. You sprinted ten yards as many times as you could in one minute, then you had your minute's rest (in that time you wrote down your score while your partner was doing their sprints). Then you continued with the next exercise. They were things like press-ups, sit-ups, skipping, burpees, kickbacks with alternate legs, and squats with your partner on your shoulders – stuff like that – with only one minute's rest in between and notes taken of your results. Next time you tried to better your previous score. It's amazing how hard it gets. There were three or four of us among the Budokwai ladies that were in the International Squad and we decided that we would do this twice a week before our class. What was interesting was that we had no strength left after doing this and yet our judo improved!

Funnily enough, there were quite a few ladies who arrived for the class and found us all collapsed around the walls, who then decided that they would do it too... No amount of 'you don't have to do this' would dissuade them and we ended up with quite a gang joining in.

I became great friends with Ken and his wife; and, when Peter managed to get me away from my boat and into a house, we lived not very far from them. Ken enlisted me to help him in a research project he had started with the Sports Council, studying the treatment of sports injuries, which lasted for a year or more. Along with Ken's assistant, a lady called Jean, I had to travel to various hospitals around the country giving the Sports Injury Clinics computer-printed forms and taking back the completed ones.

Sometimes Ken would get annoyed when the forms were too vague, and I would have to take them back and ask for more information – which could be quite daunting when you were dealing with a senior doctor.

Ken also did various studies on us. I remember one day he turned up to Brian's class with clipboards and wanted to check our heart rates and recovery times. The chosen method was to pick a body, check the heart rate and then make that person work flat out for a short time, just a few minutes. That doesn't sound too bad – but flat out is flat out. It was continuous attacking, no rests at all, with Brian and his belt and everyone shouting to keep that person going. When the time was up the body collapsed on the floor and the heart rate was taken again, and a second time after thirty seconds, then again and again as the person recovered. Ken was noting all this down. He did this test on all the members of the Olympic squad that were present. This was Brian's Olympic training class so all these people were men (except me). I noticed that Ken was avoiding me and I didn't understand why. Then everyone decided that I should be included, so it was my turn... and it was a nightmare! At the end I dropped to the floor and Ken couldn't feel a pulse! He looked concerned and asked if I was okay. I managed to gasp out 'yes' and he kept checking me until he did get a pulse. I eventually learned that women's pulse rates are faster than men's; and I'll swear that I had no pulse because all the valves were completely open and all the blood was just one continuous flow! Well, that's what it felt like! Ken looked a bit bemused at all his results and said that we were all off the scale of what he had expected, based on results he had obtained from athletes, and that he would have to go away and recalculate.

Ken also decided that we needed a proper system of rehydrating as we all sweated so much, and he began work with a manufacturer (Beechams?) to produce a sports rehydrating drink called 'Dynamo'. Sometimes he would bring samples in so that we could give our opinions and ideas on the flavours. Ken also organised special enhanced vitamin tablets for the elite competitors as he felt that we were burning up and washing out our nutrients with the amount of training we were doing.

I had begun working in the BJA head office on a 'when I was free' basis. The BJA was always short of money. On one occasion, Tony Reay, the General Secretary, asked me to order the medals for the upcoming Men's British Open Championships. He told me that we couldn't afford to have trophies this time, only medals; then he said that we couldn't afford to have the ribbons on the medals! 'You can't do that!' I said in horror. 'You can't just stick a medal in someone's hand! Can we afford the ribbon if I buy it from a haberdashery shop and I'll stitch it on?' – and this was agreed. So that year I took all the medals home and stitched the necessary ribbons on. Another year we couldn't afford trophies for the Women's British Open and I got Tony to agree to pottery commemorative plates instead and a potter friend of mine made them.

As well as Brian's Olympic training class, I still continued to join in all the ladies' classes so I was at the Budokwai most days. One of the ladies in these classes was Gill Kenneally who was a friend of mine. Sometimes I slept on the wooden floor of the flat she shared with a group of other girls rather than rush for the last train. When you have a young body you can put up with a lot...

One thing we ladies bitterly resented was that when we entered a major championship, we were required to produce a medical certificate to prove that we were female, that we were not pregnant and that we were fit and able to take part in a judo competition. If you were an athlete taking part in equestrian events or you were a high diver, this was not considered necessary; but if you were going to 'fight', then you were regarded with suspicion. It was annoying, time-wasting and expensive. I'm sure our GPs were not impressed either.

In 1972, things really started to happen. Great Britain was invited to take part in an international competition for women, held in Yugoslavia. It was decided to form a women's squad to give us a pool of players to enter major championships. The eliminations were held at the Crystal Palace in one of the gyms. Four players were selected for each weight category to create the squad. In order to give everyone a fair chance, those of us in the squad had to travel all over the country to train in different dojos. The idea was that, as we all had to pay our own expenses, then this was a fairer system as everyone at some time would have a training session near them. We usually had to sleep on the mat, and I vividly remember a time when we had to sleep in the Sheffield Police dojo. In the morning, we tried to have a shower and the showers were extremely cold – with green mould on the tiles and freezing water!

Another time, Heather Ford and I, with a few others, were travelling to a training session in a car... and the car broke down. We arrived very late, in the dark, and everyone else had gone to sleep, so we had to creep in to find a corner of the mat to sleep on – not easy in the dark.

I managed to win my weight category in the squad selections and had hoped that, with that success and my win at the previous British Open, I might be put in the team for Yugoslavia, but I was not selected.

However, our team did well in an event with nine countries competing. They brought back one gold and two bronzes.

Building on the success of the Yugoslavian trip, the GB Women's Judo team set off again in May to Gelsenkirchen in West Germany for another international tournament, once again paying all expenses ourselves. There were sixteen of us. Brian Jacks, Angelo Parisi and Dave Lawrence came to see us off at Heathrow Airport. Brian pinched my 'fur' coat and pretended to be a bear chasing the girls around – which drew a little bit of attention our way.

There were four countries taking part: West Germany, Austria, Holland and Great Britain. As we

The team for the Italian Championships in 1972.

My contest against De Cal.

entered the stadium for the championship, everything seemed very 'alien' and I could feel my nerves increasing. All around me were foreign voices and I felt very far from home. The loudspeaker was playing the latest pop music, and suddenly we heard a track which was doing very well in the charts at the time: 'Amazing Grace' played by the band of the Royal Scots Dragoon Guards. I'm not Scottish, but Scotland is part of Great Britain, and it was wonderful to hear the bagpipes: very comforting, like a little bit of home. I loved it.

A hard and exciting day's judo gave Great Britain a total of eight medals from twelve players. My friend Chris Wildman and I both won gold, and the team also won one silver and five bronzes. Our medals were presented and we were given flowers by handsome young German men, which was rather unexpected.

In July, we were off again, this time to St Vincent in Italy for the Italian Women's Championships. We were a team of five with six supporters; Ken and Sylvia Kingsbury and a group of friends from the Budokwai came to see us off at Heathrow. Once again we were financing ourselves, so we all had slightly different travel arrangements. Pat Cottis, one of our supporters, had travelled via Gatwick and we met up with her at the Milan Central Station after transferring there from the airport. Our train left at 2.35am and stopped at every station with two changes en route. It also had wooden seats! We finally arrived in St Vincent at 8.30am on Friday 28 July and at our hotel shortly after.

Six countries were taking part: Italy, West Germany, Yugoslavia, Finland, Turkey and Great Britain.

Lebanon were expected but did not arrive. Mrs Jean Gilmour, Second Dan and referee, had travelled with us and was expecting to referee. She had a problem with the officials, who didn't like the idea of a woman refereeing and said she could judge instead. Jean told them in no uncertain terms that she had not travelled all this way just to judge. So the officials relented and said that she could referee the first match of the day! Her refereeing was of the highest standard and she came in for a great deal of praise from all, particularly the other referees who were all men.

I discovered the drawback of competing in the heavyweight category. The lower limit was sixty-five kilos but there was no upper limit. I didn't allow myself to get too heavy as I needed to be able to double for smaller people in my stunt work, so I was usually no heavier than about seventy-three kilos. Margherita De Cal, the Italian girl that I had to fight, was around ninety kilos!

I had attacked her with uchi-mata (inner thigh throw). This was my favourite technique and I was strong at it. Unfortunately, De Cal was so heavy and strong that it didn't work. However, her resistance made her balance change backwards, so I changed my uchi-mata into ko-uchi-gari (small inside reap) and took her backwards.

De Cal landed flat on her back (with impetus) which should have given me an ippon, but the Italian referee gave me wazari. It didn't matter; I won anyway.

We brought home three bronzes with one gold – that was me.

Some people went home immediately after the event, some went on to other places and I stayed in St Vincent for a few extra days as my ticket had, for some unknown reason, been cheaper if I stayed longer. So I had a couple of days on my own, which was slightly difficult as I don't speak Italian while the locals in St Vincent speak Italian with French as their second language. My French was the basic French that I had learned in school.

The day of my return started out okay. I had managed to ask the hotel staff (in French) to wake me up in time to get to the station for the train to Milan, and that part of the plan went well. However, when I arrived at the station, there was no train. I waited and waited; still no train. I tried to ask the station staff what was going on, but they could only speak Italian.

With a rising sense of panic I discovered that the only people in the town who spoke English worked in the Tourist Information Centre. I made my way there – walking, with my bags – to discover that although they said they spoke English, it was not easy to understand. However, after a difficult conversation I managed to get the message that the reason the train had not come was that there was a rail strike! So I had to get a bus from St Vincent to Milan, constantly worrying that I might not make my flight. In the event, however, I arrived in good time, and even managed to buy the Italian watermelon that Angelo had requested – although it was a heavy liability to carry back!

4 November 1972 was the second Women's British Open, and this time we had teams from the USA, West Germany, Holland and Switzerland taking part as well. My weight category was still classed as heavyweight but was changed to sixty-eight kilos and above, and I managed to hold on to my title from the previous year.

The Japanese coach for Poland, Tomita San, had called in at the Budokwai on his way home to Japan as he had finished his stint in Poland. He was very interested in what was going on with the women and decided that he would like to see the British Open Championships for Women. As he didn't have much English, I acted as liaison for him as much as I could.

The medal presentation was a little confusing. We were directed to a podium which was rather high, and I stood on the number one area, and I'm tall anyway... Charlie Palmer walked up to present the medals – and his face was just above my knees. We looked at each other and grinned. There was no chance that Charlie would be able to reach up and get a medal around my neck, so I crouched down to get level with him. He was in a jovial mood. He was my teacher and my friend and in a moment of exuberance he kissed me. There was no harm in it. It was just a moment of fun. No offence meant or taken.

I was also furiously stitching in between bouts, to finish a dress that I wanted to wear that evening. Apart from being the ladies' British Open, it was also the day of the wedding of Brian Jacks and his long-standing girlfriend Julie. I had

Receiving the gold medal at the Italian Championships .

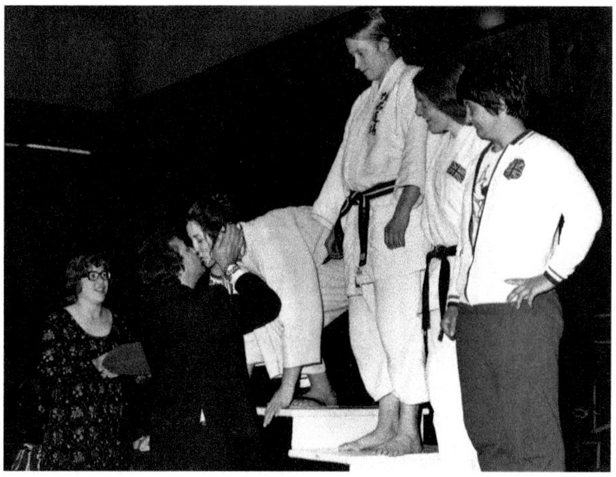

Medal Presentation 1972.

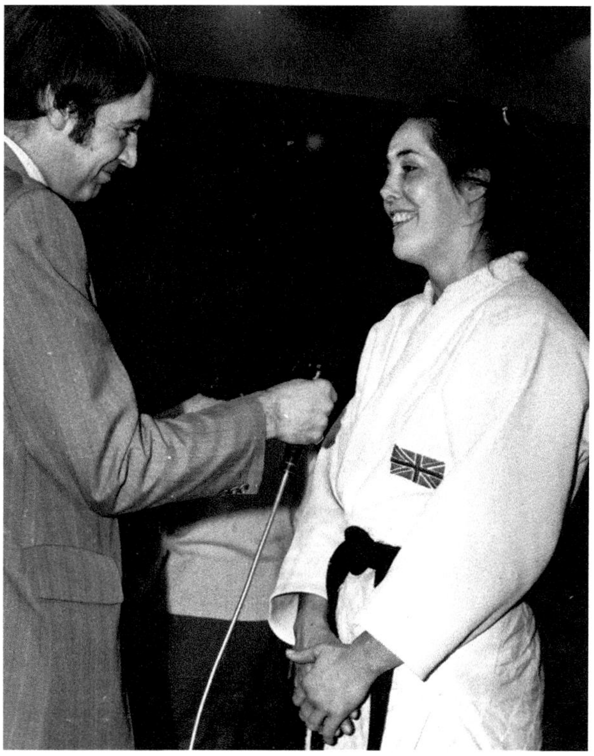

Being Interviewed by the BBC.

Publicity photo featuring (from Left to Right) Brian Jacks, Chris Wildman, Dave Lawrence, Me, and Dave Starbrook.

Left: Final of the British Open 1972 Against Maureen Braziel of U.S.A.

Below: Eliminations for the British Open 1972. Holding Maggie Burgess.

been unable to go to the wedding because of the championships but fully intended to get to the reception that evening. It was being held at the Budokwai, and everyone I knew was going.

I did manage to complete my dress and enjoyed the party... and also got to know the man who was eventually to become my husband – Peter Gallie. We had seen each other at the club but had never before had an opportunity to chat to each other. He was tall, dark and blue-eyed and had a wonderful smile. I can't remember what we talked about, but we discovered that we shared the same sense of humour and got on like a house on fire. We have now been together for forty-eight years!

CHAPTER ELEVEN

Our Miss Fred

The brave do not live forever, but the cautious do not live at all.

There was a film called *Our Miss Fred* which starred Danny La Rue. I was called to the production office regarding work on this film, which I knew nothing at all about. The lady interviewing me suddenly gave me a costume to put on and said that if it looked okay in it, then I was hired. I put it on and my heart sank. I was often called to double for people who were smaller than me, and very often I would struggle to wear their costume. This was worse. I could hardly do it up, and it felt very tight and revealing. I couldn't escape; I had to return to the lady and show her, thinking, 'This is really embarrassing...'

However, she said, 'That's fine, you're supposed to be a French tart.' Oh, okay then...

On the day, a group of us rendezvoused at an airfield. The plot was that Danny La Rue, dressed as a French tart and accompanied by a party of similarly attired ladies, was trying to escape Nazi-occupied France in an old car which would be attached to a barrage balloon. A very sensible RAF type approached and asked us all to follow him to a room in a large hangar. He then told us that we ought to know that if the cable holding the barrage balloon to the ground should break, the balloon would continue to rise and it would be impossible to bring it back; so we may need to parachute out of the car 'if things go wrong'. That sounded a trifle worrying... 'Do any of you know how to use a parachute?' His face dropped a bit when all but one of us confessed that no, we didn't. The only person who did was Del Baker, and he had brought his own with him!

We were given a hasty lesson whereby our friendly RAF man endeavoured to explain what we would need to do in the event of an emergency descent. The parachutes would stay on the floor of the car and would only be put on if we needed them; we were cautioned that we should under no circumstances jump out unless we were more than five hundred feet off the ground. This was when it dawned on us that we were not getting enough money for this job! Usually, you had a daily rate and then there might be an 'adjustment' of extra money if what you were being asked to do was above and beyond. The adjustment would be payable each time you had to do the shot, unless the reshoot was your fault – then you did it again for free. At that time twenty-five pounds was about what you would expect for a daily rate, and then there should have been an agreed adjustment for each time we went up under the balloon.

We were being offered twenty-five pounds for the day with no adjustments. In those days twenty-five pounds was worth a lot more than it is today, but still not enough for what we were being asked to do.

However, it was better than nothing, and we were there already; and the woman in charge said if we wouldn't do it she would ask the local parachute club to do it.

We had to be in a kind of basket which was made to look like a car hanging underneath the balloon, pretending to fire guns over the side. We had a bit of a problem because when the wind turned the car around, you could see that it wasn't real. We did it once, and then someone had this brilliant idea that we should let off smoke flares when we were in the air, so we had to go up a second time – and then there was a panic to get us down again as someone else had realised that the balloon was filled with hydrogen and we shouldn't be setting off flares...

All in all we went up under the balloon five times, which by my reckoning was five pounds a time, going up several hundred feet each time. On the last occasion the woman who had caused us so much angst decided that, as we had a spare parachute and she thought it was such an easy job, she would come up with us. So up we went again. By this time the wind was picking up and, when we got up to full height, the car started to spin around a bit. There was a rather loud banging noise and the car shuddered. The woman screamed and threw herself to the floor shouting, 'The cable has broken!'

This is me with my friend, fellow stunt woman, Dorothy Ford.

'Oh, sod it,' I thought. 'This job gets better and better... where's my parachute?!' With a mental picture of me, dressed as a French tart, wearing a German helmet, parachuting down to earth showing the world my knickers and suspenders! But it turned out that the cable wasn't broken; it was just the car twisting and turning and buffeting against the cable. We all had a secret smile to ourselves and each other at her distress as she sat on the floor trembling and hugging her knees while we were winched back down. She looked rather shamefaced as she got out.

Karma does happen!

Life had changed after *The Avengers* finished. I no longer had a regular job, and this felt strange. I did get occasional jobs doing stunt work but you didn't always get much prior notice; so, to be sure of having enough money to pay the rent and live, I took on other work. At first I thought that, as I had qualifications in photography, I would try and find something in the photographic world. I hadn't realised until I tried that there were far more photographers than there were positions available. After a lot of hunting, I eventually managed to get a job in a restaurant called the Omar Khayyam; it was an Arabic restaurant with belly dancers. The dancers would do their dance and then move among the tables posing for photographs with the customers. I had to take these photographs and then try to get the customers to buy them. When they agreed, I had to gallop up the back stairs to the cash desk to get this put on their bill. The photographs then had to be processed and printed as quickly as possible so that they could be delivered to the customer at their hotel (they were always visitors). The wife of the owner had offered to deliver these for me, and for a while this worked quite well.

I didn't start work until about 10.00pm and I would then finish in the early hours. This left me time to take on film work when it came, and also I could continue with my judo training. However, I had been given this job because the previous girl needed to take time off; one day, she returned and obviously wanted her job back. The owner's wife, who turned out to be a friend of this lady, now announced that she wouldn't be able to deliver the photos any more. I realised what was happening and thought, 'Okay, I'll deliver them myself.' So after I finished work at some ridiculous time in the morning, I would then trawl around all the big posh London hotels delivering photographs.

My car at this time was a clapped-out little Wolseley Hornet which was always grubby. Emma, my dog, always accompanied me; she stayed in the car while I was working. I was expected to wear semi-evening dress for my job. One day, I drew up at the front entrance of this very smart London hotel (I can't remember the name) and the doorman, in full regalia and wearing impeccable white gloves, walked up to my car. I was sure he was going to tell me to go away and stop disgracing his smart frontage. I prepared myself to tell him that I would only be a sec', but I just needed to drop off this package at reception. However, without batting an eyelid, he opened the driver's door for me in a very grand manner. I said 'Thank you' as grandly as I could, and took my envelope in. He was waiting when I came out and opened the door for me again with a twinkle in his eye. I swooshed into the driver's seat with my long skirt and thanked him again. It was pure pantomime. I hope he didn't get his smart gloves dirty touching my car...

There was a singer who worked at the Omar Khayyam; she sang with the English group who did a stint between the Arabic sessions. Her name was Norma Stoneman and she came from Australia. She was tiny but had a fantastic voice and an amazing smile which lit up her whole face. One evening, she had finished her session and I bumped into her as she was preparing to leave. She looked entirely different. When Norma was singing she looked very glamorous with a long sparkly evening dress; now, she had removed her make-up and was wearing jeans and a leather jacket.

'Where are you off to?' I said, rather startled.

'Oh, I'm catching the night bus and I don't want to attract attention...'

I had a moment's thought of what travelling on the night bus must be like. 'Where do you have to go to?' I asked.

'Earl's Court,' was the reply.

'Can you wait?' I said. 'I'm just finishing up, then I'll be leaving and I have to go past Earl's Court.' That was the start of a fantastic friendship which has lasted even after Norma went back to Australia.

Every night I would give Norma a lift home and one night, as usual, we came out of the restaurant to find my car. It was still just about going; on this occasion, the starter motor was beginning to die and I had parked the car on a hill so that I could bump-start it if necessary. As we walked towards the car we ran into a group of policemen. The Omar Khayyam was in the City of London and there were often lots of police around. They chatted to us and asked what we were doing, and we told them. We must have looked an incongruous pair. Norma, petite and dainty with short blonde hair, jeans, trainers and a leather jacket. Me, tall and towering over her, with long dark hair, long skirt and high heels. They walked with us to the car and I began to feel a bit nervous. What if the car wouldn't start? How would they feel about me bump-starting it? I shouldn't have worried. Norma and I elegantly swished into the car, joining my dog who was waiting for me; and it didn't start. I rather self-consciously began to get out to push – and once they realised what was happening the policemen

This is the kind of photo I was doing. I didn't take this one, but it was taken when I went to the Omar Khayyam for my birthday and my friend Soraya danced on our table.

laughingly pushed us down the road!

One evening, I was startled to receive a phone call while I was at work; it was Gerry Crampton! 'I'm in Munich, I need you here; I'm working on a film called *Assignment Munich*... Can you come out tomorrow? Get your ticket, I'll meet you from the airport and refund your money.' That was a bit of a panic. Things were not so nice at the restaurant any more and I knew that they wanted any excuse to get rid of me, so I wasn't really bothered; I knew I would probably lose the job, but I didn't care. I had to make an excuse to leave work as soon as I could to get home and pack, and make arrangements for my cats and Emma the dog. I managed to get one hour's sleep. My clothes were packed without being pressed; my father picked me up in the morning to get me to the airport and take possession of my dog.

I arrived in Munich and looked for Gerry at the airport, but there was no sign. I don't speak German.

I began to panic a bit, not helped by the lack of sleep. I went to the customer service desk, where a very haughty lady said in heavily accented English that she had a message for me that had been telephoned in; she then handed over a scrap of paper with an address written on it and a name. Apparently, I was to make my own way to this address and would then be reimbursed with my expenses. I had come in such a rush that I had no money with me, and in common with most people at that time I did not have a credit card. As soon as the paper was in my hand, this lady lost interest in me and turned to someone else. This was in the days before modern technology and such things as mobile phones, so I had no way to contact Gerry.

I made my way out to the taxi rank, thinking to myself, 'I need to find someone who speaks English so that I can explain.' I walked down the line of taxis asking the drivers if they spoke English, and eventually found a really kind and helpful man who listened carefully to my dilemma and then told me that, although he did understand and would like to help, I would have to go to the front of the queue and take the first taxi there; he would explain my situation to the driver for me.

The man who was designated as my driver did not look overjoyed to see me. My new German friend assured me that the man understood that I would pay him when I got to my destination; however, he had the look of an extremely pissed-off German paratrooper from WW2. He put my luggage in the boot of his car and off we went. I had no idea where we were going – the paper only had an address.

We went into the centre of Munich and eventually ended up outside a very large building which looked like a bank. My driver (Hermann, as I was beginning to think of him) gestured that this was the place.

It didn't look like it to me. I thought I was probably being sent to an office or a hotel. It turned out that this was a bank! I went in; they were just closing and didn't really want to listen to me. I had to find someone who spoke English and ask to see the person whose name was on the paper. Heads were slowly shaken; nobody knew anyone of that name. Heart now thumping, I was directed to the next floor. No, no one knew anyone by that name. I had no idea what to do next; and then I thought of grumpy Hermann, leaning against his car with his arms folded, and my luggage in his boot... and I couldn't help it – I started to cry.

A very kind German man rushed to help me and, wonder of wonders, he spoke English. He took me to his office, sat me in a chair and listened to the whole story. Together, we tried to do a bit of detective work. Once I had calmed down I mentally went over every word that Gerry had said to me when we had our telephone conversation – was it only last night? – and I remembered him saying that he was staying at the Holiday Inn. I asked this lovely man if he would mind calling the hotel and asking if there was a room booked for Cyd Child – and there was! This Good Samaritan then paid off Hermann, recovered my luggage and drove me to the hotel. What a star! I got his name and took him money a few days later, although he kept telling me that it wasn't necessary.

When I arrived at the hotel, no one from the film company was around, so I checked in, got the key for my room and arranged for the clothes in my luggage to be pressed so that they were more presentable. I was told what time everyone was expected back, so I waited in reception for Gerry. I found out later that the address given to the lady at the airport customer service desk, which should have been for the Munich film studios, had been taken down incorrectly – it was the German equivalent of someone writing '16' instead of '60'.

Apart from my journey, everything else about this job was fine. Everyone was very friendly and helpful.

I made friends with the actor Pernell Roberts, who was in the film, and his (then) wife, Kara. We are still friends and keep in touch with each other even though Kara lives in California. We were working at night in a railway station and were kept supplied with the most gorgeous goulash soup. Funnily enough, Gerry pointed out one of the crew who really had been a paratrooper in the last war: tall, blond (going slightly grey), blue-eyed – and he was a pussycat, with a smile that lit up his face.

When I returned to England, I found out that I had indeed lost my job at the restaurant; and I worked for a while selling ice cream on the Strand for the Parisi family – Angelo's Dad. At that time Angelo was just another fellow judoka. Little did any of us realise that he would go on to become one of the world's most outstanding judo players.

On one occasion I worked on a film called *Pope Joan*, which was being filmed at Bray Studios, just up the road from where I lived – quite convenient really. It was night shooting. The action that we were doing involved a horde of marauding Saxons who sack and burn a nunnery; I don't know any more about the story. I was dressed as a medieval nun, in a long homespun dress with a roughly woven veil.

We were told that for a particular shot we were to be background action. The nunnery was going to be on fire and we were to be running about in the flames. Olivia De Havilland was going to be tied to a cross which would be dragged away by a horse. Rocky Taylor and Joe Dunne (both of whom I knew from my time on *The Avengers*) were dressed as Saxons and had to be chasing me. We went to have a good look at what we were dealing with. The set was built like an authentic medieval nunnery. It had three storeys, all made of wood, with walkways outside doorways, with steps up to each level; the steps were made from split tree trunks. It looked very good. We were to start at the top at the furthest end; it was a big set.

We worked out our action. We were going to start on a kind of wooden landing with Rocky and another Saxon climbing over the rail. I was to struggle with Joe, break away and run along the walkway, negotiating the steps along the way; they were going to catch me at one point. We would struggle again and I'd get away, and we would keep repeating this while the shot was going on. Each window had a fishtail burner for propane gas to make the fire, and we asked special effects to show us how far the flames would come out of the window so that we knew how much room we would have on the walkway.

So far, so good.

On the day, there we were. I was standing in the middle of the landing with Joe close enough to grab me, and Rocky and another Saxon poised ready to climb over the rail. 'Stand by' was called; 'light the flames'; 'turn up the flames'. The flames were *much* bigger than we had expected! It started to get rather hot; you could hear the wood crackling as it started to catch fire, and smoke was beginning to drift around us – and *still* no one had called 'action', so we had to stay where we were. The director was having a word with Olivia De Havilland who was tied to her cross. It was now getting *very* hot. Rocky was not happy as he was close to a fire, and he started shouting at the camera crew. I was holding my skirt away from my legs as the cloth felt like it would burn me. After what seemed like an eternity, 'action' was finally called and we were off like greyhounds out of the trap!

By this time you couldn't see where you were going, with black smoke everywhere. I couldn't see the steps, my veil dropped over my face and I fell down the stairs. When I got up I trod on the inside of my skirt and fell again. In fact, I think I fell down every set of stairs. I could hear Joe's voice calling behind me, 'Don't stop Cyd! Keep going! Keep going! Forget the action...' Never mind the action; the guys overtook me (I practically had footprints on my back) and beat me to the exit! And then they were gone... 'to have a word...'

None of what we had done was usable as the whole of the background was wreathed in thick black smoke; so we had to do it all again, with the crew understanding that the flames would not be quite so high this time, and that 'action' would be called as soon as the flames were ready.

CHAPTER TWELVE

International Competition

Sweat more in training; bleed less in battle.

There is a particular kind of training called Kangeiko, also known as Winter Practice. The idea is that you train every day very early in the morning for ten days during the winter when it is cold and miserable. Overcoming the unpleasantness of rising early and training in freezing conditions instils a mental toughness and a never-give-up attitude. There is a similar practice which takes place in dedicated clubs, in the hottest part of the summer, during the hottest part of the day with the windows closed. This is known as Shochu Geiko. You need to be very serious about your training to take part in either of these events!

Brian Jacks was invited to take part in the Kangeiko/Winter Practice at the Judo Clube de Portugal in January 1973. Unfortunately, Brian was already committed elsewhere so he asked Angelo Parisi, me and Dave Lawrence to go instead. We flew out from Heathrow on 3 January which was also Angelo's birthday! Our plane fare, hotel accommodation and food were all taken care of. All we had to do was practise judo with the club members for two hours every morning and another two hours in the evening.

By now Angelo was beginning to make a name for himself. He had won a gold medal in the British Open and the Europeans, and also a bronze medal in the Olympics in Munich the previous year. He would go on to win the British Open that year and also in 1975, before marrying a French lady and departing to France, for whom he was to win four gold medals in the French championships, three gold medals in the Europeans and two gold Olympic medals!

At the hotel we had a suite to ourselves; I think the staff were very confused because whenever they wanted to clean the rooms we always seemed to be asleep. We would rise very early, be picked up and driven to the club, practise (hard), come back to the hotel and have breakfast, then go back to bed for a while – leaving our sweaty judogi draped over the radiators... We would be collected and taken for lunch (prepared by a lovely Portuguese lady who spoke no English), and then various volunteers from the club would take us sightseeing around Lisbon before the evening practice. It was difficult to get our jackets dry as we were constantly training, and working hard in a wet sweaty jacket tends to make your skin sore.

We were taken under the wing of Kobayashi Sensei. Some months later when I met him at the European Championships, he told me that he had arranged with Okano San in Japan for me to go out there to train. I felt extremely honoured but I had to say that I couldn't go. I was by then in a relationship with the man who eventually became my husband and I didn't want to disappear off to Japan for what could be years...

Trials to establish who was in the Women's Judo Squad were now held every year, and in February 1973 we actually also had five female referees! Go girls! I managed to retain my place.

A team was selected to enter the Swiss Open Championships on 6 May in Balerna. There were teams from Switzerland (obviously), Canada, France, Belgium, Germany, Holland, Italy and Great Britain. We sent a large team, entering as many people as the Swiss would allow. We won two gold, one silver, five bronzes and a trophy for the best team of the championships. Chris Wildman and I were the two golds.

As usual we had to pay all fares and expenses ourselves.

Summer 1973 saw us off again, this time to St Lorenzen in Italy for the Italian Grand Prix on 4/5 August. Again we had to make our own travel arrangements and cover all costs. Of course we went the cheapest way, with the last leg being by train (with wooden seats) overnight. It was such a long journey and we were so tired when we arrived. I was sharing a room with Maggie Burgess and we just crashed out – I went into such a deep sleep.

Against Ellen Cobb in the 1973 Selection Trails.

Against Pat Johnock in the 1973 Selection Trails.

Some bright spark had decided that we would have a training session that day. I remember something waking me – I didn't know what it was... It was like I was lying under a deep, dark layer of something. I had to struggle through all these layers to get the top, like I was at the bottom of the sea. When I reached the top I opened my eyes, wondering what had called me. Maggie was also opening her eyes; we looked at each other and said, 'What was that?' Maggie said, 'Perhaps someone's waking us for the training session?' I opened the door but there was no one there – the hotel was silent.

Maggie and I got dressed and went to look for the others, but they had all gone. We had slept through the wake-up call, and the last knock had been because they were going; so not only did we miss the training session but we didn't finish our sleep either. Needless to say, Ellen Cobb, our team captain, gave us a lot of stick about missing the training – she thought we had done it on purpose!

There were six nations taking part: Czechoslovakia, Great Britain, Italy, Switzerland, Turkey and Yugoslavia. We took two gold and three bronze; Chris Wildman and I were the two gold.

We had a day to relax before we returned home, and the weather was beautiful. We were miles from anywhere and we thought that, after all our hard work, we would just have a lazy day sitting out in the sun – there was no one around. We had the place to ourselves. Eventually two old ladies also came outside and sat a little way away from us. We were just enjoying the sun, lying in our bikinis.

After we had been there for quite a while, a young Italian soldier walked past the hotel. He was in uniform so I suppose he was going to work. He paused when he saw this group of girls and then came over to talk to us, saying he wanted to practise his English. I could foresee trouble, so I turned onto my front and thought I would ignore him and take no part in the conversation. It was a mistake to talk to him, and after a while the others realised this, but there was no getting rid of him. His chat gradually became more and more suggestive so that he was becoming a pest.

He was annoyed that I stayed with my back to him and kept trying to persuade me to turn over. I said to my friend nearby, 'Has he got one of those hats with a feather on it?' I had to ask as I couldn't see.

'Yes,' she said.

'Can you pass it over?' She did; so I got hold of the feather, bent it in two and passed it back. Thinking about it, I suppose it was a bit mean, but he was becoming really annoying and we wanted him to go – and he had no intention of leaving.

Our hotel was out in the countryside, part way up a mountain (probably the cheapest around since we were paying), and it had one of those swimming pools that sit on top of the ground and you have to climb in. We started to talk to each other in English slang that he didn't understand. Marie Fourt said, 'I think "mushti" wants a dip,' and we all agreed. We were a team! We all rose as one and grabbed hold of him by the arms and legs. He started to struggle, and then you could see on his face that he thought this was some kind of game and he relaxed. We ran over to the pool with him. As we were about to throw him in, my bikini top pinged undone on the back. Liz put her hands over his eyes as someone did it up for me, and we threw him into the middle of the pool. No judo, just teamwork! The two old Italian ladies were laughing so much that they nearly fell off their chairs.

We grabbed our things and ran for the hotel, picking up his hat on the way. We vanished into our rooms. A bit later Marie came to the room Maggie and I shared. 'Have you got his hat?' she said. 'Let me have it,' so I did. 'He's not getting that back!' she said as she left. A bit later he came back to the hotel looking for it, wearing a dry uniform with a very wet area where his pants were. I don't know if he did ever get his hat back; I rather doubt it.

We ladies tried to enter all the foreign open championships that we could. This was pretty hard because of having to finance everything ourselves. Some of the 'old guard' of judo men were very much against what we were trying to do. One day, I was having an argument with Tony Reay about whether or not we could have Great Britain blazer badges, and I said to him, 'Why are you being so difficult and obstructive to us?' and he said, 'Well, we had to struggle, so you should too...' Things improved gradually. The younger ones, such as Brian Jacks, Roy Inman and Keith Remfry, were very encouraging and helpful. Brian even came to one of the Women's British Open Championships and brought a group from his class to cheer us on.

The third British Open Championships were held on 24 November 1973, and this time my weight category was sixty-eight kilos and above. It was at the Crystal Palace as we had outgrown Bracknell Sports Centre. Entries were from Germany, Holland, Sweden, Switzerland, Eire and Great Britain. There were one hundred and fifty-five entries which included sixty-five for the Open. I had a really good day, winning both my own category and the Open; as a result, I was presented by Anne Swinton with her trophy for the best player, which is a bonsai tree. I was also given the Pam Hogg trophy for the Personality of the Year.

Team for the Italian Grand Prix 1973.

Top Team Swiss Championships. This is our victorious team with our medals and trophies - best team of the competition.

This photo shows Liz Viney MBE in the middle with the trophy for best team with Chris Wildman (on the Right) and me on the Left with our trophies and gold medals.

Eliminations during the British Open 1973.

Presentation for gold medal for the heavyweight category British Open 1973.

Presentation for winning the Open Category of the British Open 1973.

The Anne Swindon trophy for the most outstanding competitor of the British Open.

Relaxing between bouts during the day.

These were all the trophies that
I had won that year - 1973.

All my medals so far.

The trophy for the most
successful competitor in the British Open
Championships 1973.

Brian did a series on 'Judo for Beginners' in the Observer magazine
and asked me to help out with some pictures.

CHAPTER THIRTEEN

European Championships

Judo is the only Olympic sport that permits torture.
Vladimir Putin

The year 1974 started well. I secured my place in the Women's Squad at the National Trials and achieved my Fourth Dan on 7 March.

The Dutch International Championships were held at the Rodalhal in Kerkrade on 7 April. It was for men and women. We stayed at the Rolduc Monastery which took us a bit by surprise. The nuns were like ghosts; food was laid out for breakfast but there was no sign of anybody – a bit like *Beauty and the Beast*... It was also a bit of an eye-opener for those of us who had never encountered a continental breakfast of cold meats, cheeses and bread.

The doors were not locked, and a group of young Dutchmen decided to disrupt our sleep the night before the championship and came running into our rooms after we had gone to sleep, switching the lights on and banging doors and then running off. Our dedicated judo mother, Liz Viney, decided she would put a stop to that and moved her bed out into the corridor, just the other side of the swing doors that they had been crashing through. Liz spent the night there and there were no further disturbances.

Once again there was a problem regarding the referee that we had brought with us, Jean Gilmour. She was female! That was unheard of and wouldn't do at all! All the officials were male. They tried to tell Jean that she couldn't be used, but she rounded on them so fiercely that they backed down on the spot and she proved herself one of the best referees there.

There were seven countries taking part: Holland, Great Britain, France, West Germany, Ireland, Switzerland and Belgium. We took four gold (Lynn Tilley, Pam Scullard, Cydatty Bogie and me), one silver and six bronzes. My only disappointment was that no medals were given, only trophies. I have always preferred medals.

I had been working in the head office of the BJA for some time. It was an ad hoc arrangement which worked quite well. I was paid only for the hours I worked, so I could still do stunt work, and there was no problem in taking time off for judo events and to sort out judo-related injuries. I was now made Assistant General Secretary. This was also the year when London hosted the Twenty-third European Championships for men, on 2-5 May. This was really hard work. Ena Anderson and I were the main dogsbodies and we were busy from 7.30am to gone 10.00pm. We had thought that being on the BJA staff would enable us to have a ringside seat, but it didn't really work out like that.

We were given overnight accommodation at the Crystal Palace ('basic' is the only word that describes that), and we called in at the local Chinese restaurant each evening, as they were closing, to buy whatever they had left over and then ate it in our room (cell). We were so tired. Each morning there was a wake-up call at the crack of dawn, or what felt like it, from a loudspeaker set in the wall of the room, and one morning I found myself trying to rip it out of the wall before I totally woke up!

However, the event went well. The culmination was a team event of Great Britain versus Russia. In the intermission before the match took place, the Band of the Coldstream Guards had been playing; Dave Starbrook had a word with them and they played all patriotic tunes such as 'Land of Hope and Glory' and 'Rule Britannia' so the crowd was whipped up to a frenzy. The atmosphere was incredible. First one side would score, then the other. It was beginning to look as if Russia would win. Keith Remfry, our heavyweight, was the last person to fight and he had a hard match which went to time. The signal came for the end of time; Keith's opponent relaxed because he thought it was the end of the bout... however, the referee had not yet called 'sore made' (which ends the match). Keith immediately seized the opportunity and threw his opponent for ippon! The place erupted! It was so exciting! Everyone leapt to their feet cheering. When the scores were added up, the result was a draw. All the officials got together and

This photograph was taken by Terence Donovan, the well known photographer, who became an enthusiastic member of the Budokwai. This photo is currently displayed in the foyer of the Budokwai

announced that three random members of the teams would need to fight again to decide the result. Unfortunately for us, Russia won in the end, but it was an amazing experience.

I thought I would have a go at organising some ladies-only gradings at the Budokwai. This was in the hope that we could make some progress at improving the state of ladies' Dan gradings, which were particularly difficult to arrange at the time because there weren't very many of us and Second Dan was about as far as most people could get. The BJA head office in London had lists of all the clubs within reasonable travelling distance of the Budokwai: the London Area, Northern Home Counties and the South. I notified all those that had ladies listed as members, along with any other clubs that I thought might have ladies who would be interested. The system worked quite well; we started to get a lot of ladies attending, and we managed to include ladies' Dan gradings as well. Brian Jacks agreed to be one of the examiners, and the eminent referee Gordon Mortimer agreed to referee and that made sure that there were no arguments. We had a very successful system.

The Fourth Women's British Open was held at the beginning of November 1974. This time I was competing in the new heavyweight category of seventy-two kilos and above. Competitors came in large groups from many other countries – the USA, Canada, Sweden, France, Germany, Yugoslavia, Holland and Switzerland – as well as, of course, Great Britain. Afterwards we had many letters from both competitors and officials from overseas, saying that the Women's British Open Championships was now the best women's event in the world. To quote one, 'The atmosphere is the friendliest I have yet encountered and yet the competition standard is the highest.' I held on to my title and was also given the Dame Enid Russell-Smith trophy as the person who had done the most to promote women's judo, which was a lovely surprise. Trevor Williams, who had donated the Trevor Williams Geemat trophy given to the heavyweight winner, decided to let me keep it as I had won it for the last four consecutive years.

At last the European Judo Union decided to hold the first European Judo Tournament for Women. This was known as the Coppa Europa and was held in Genoa on 30 November/1 December 1974. The idea was to experiment with the idea of a European Championships for Women. Liz decided that it was time for her to step down as Women's British Team Coach/Manager and Roy Inman took over. I knew Roy well from the Budokwai: he had been a successful international competitor for the past twelve years and this looked like a good move.

On the journey, Chris Wildman and I were sitting behind the team managers and I could hear them talking. They were discussing how many medals they expected to take home! I found this quite shocking and said so to Chris. In my mind I felt that I would do my best to succeed; but we had no idea what opposition we were going to meet, and who knew what the outcome would be. It is a wonderful thing to be an unknown trying to win – there is no pressure. However, when you are an established champion the stress is quite different; everyone is watching you. The competition is trying to bring you down, analysing your every move, and your own side confidently expect you to win, while you yourself are not sure what awaits you.

We got the distinct impression that this championship wasn't expected to be a success. The venue was a large hall that was normally used for car shows; consequently it had a concrete floor! This made any falls on the mat rather hard.

Eleven countries took part, and other countries sent observers. Each British girl was allowed to enter one category only, in order that the greatest possible number of Senior Women's Squad members

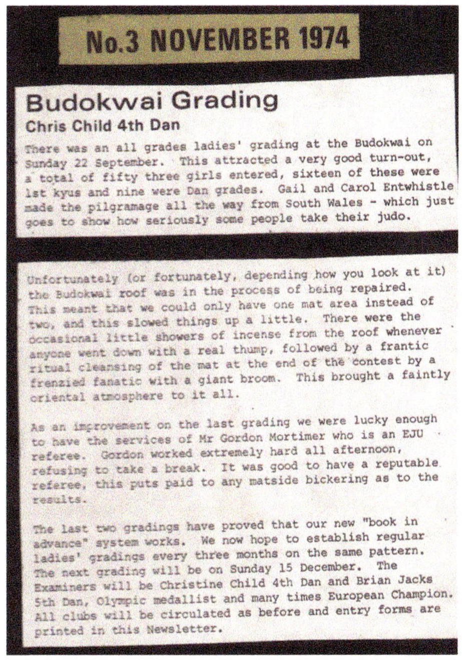

No.3 NOVEMBER 1974

Budokwai Grading

Chris Child 4th Dan

There was an all grades ladies' grading at the Budokwai on Sunday 22 September. This attracted a very good turn-out, a total of fifty three girls entered, sixteen of these were 1st kyus and nine were Dan grades. Gail and Carol Entwhistle made the pilgramage all the way from South Wales - which just goes to show how seriously some people take their judo.

Unfortunately (or fortunately, depending how you look at it) the Budokwai roof was in the process of being repaired. This meant that we could only have one mat area instead of two, and this slowed things up a little. There were the occasional little showers of incense from the roof whenever anyone went down with a real thump, followed by a frantic ritual cleansing of the mat at the end of the contest by a frenzied fanatic with a giant broom. This brought a faintly oriental atmosphere to it all.

As an improvement on the last grading we were lucky enough to have the services of Mr Gordon Mortimer who is an EJU referee. Gordon worked extremely hard all afternoon, refusing to take a break. It was good to have a reputable referee, this puts paid to any matside bickering as to the results.

The last two gradings have proved that our new "book in advance" system works. We now hope to establish regular ladies' gradings every three months on the same pattern. The next grading will be on Sunday 15 December. The Examiners will be Christine Child 4th Dan and Brian Jacks 5th Dan, Olympic medallist and many times European Champion. All clubs will be circulated as before and entry forms are printed in this Newsletter.

Roy Inman.

Receiving the trophy and standing for our National Anthem.

Lyn Tilley and I celebrating our golds after the Coppa Europa (It's beer, we couldn't afford Champagne...)

Chris Wildman and I do our dance during the Japanese party...I'm nearest the camera.

could experience high-level competition. Roy Inman travelled with us as the official coach for the team, and Captain Ray Mitchell was selected by the EJU as the British referee. Great Britain achieved two golds (Lynn Tilley and me), two silvers and three bronze. Once again I had to fight De Cal, and this time she was weighing in at around one hundred and eight kilos! My teammate Maggie McKenna was my opponent in the final, so Great Britain took gold and silver.

The event was judged to be a complete success by all concerned. We celebrated by dunking Roy in a large fountain. To do this we had to enlist the help of my opponent Margherita De Cal because she understood English. Genoa had a one-way traffic system and we needed our coach driver (who didn't speak English) to take a different route back to our hotel in order to take us to the fountain. We took Roy by surprise. He thought he was posing for a photo with the team around him, sitting on the edge of the fountain. He told us afterwards that, as he came back to the surface, all he could see was a sea of red, white and blue running away. We then discovered that he didn't have a change of clothes so he had to travel home in Chris Wildman's jeans!

Roy told us that before returning home he thought we should celebrate with a Japanese party.

'What's that?' I asked.

'Oh, everyone has to sing a song,' says Roy.

I was sharing a room with Chris Wildman and she gave me a long look.

I said, 'I'm not very good at singing.'

'Neither am I,' said Chris. 'I've got an idea: let's do a dance instead...' So we did a spoof cancan, hiding behind a Union Jack with knee and elbow supports and various daft bits of clothing – we had borrowed some big knickers and vests. Roy told us later that he didn't see much of it because he was laughing so much that he couldn't keep his eyes open.

Of course, competing and training at this level meant that I incurred many injuries, over and above the usual bruises, haematomas, mat burns and bits of skin missing. Here are some of the more 'interesting' ones...

Iris Dehnel was a master of ashi-waza (ankle/leg techniques) and I dearly wanted to learn from her, so every practice I would ask her for randori (free practice) and try to absorb some of her ability. We would usually end up moving very fast around the dojo, which was the small dojo allocated for the ladies' classes, downstairs at the Budokwai. One day we crashed into the wall and I twisted my right ankle. I had torn a ligament. I was told not to practise while it healed, but inevitably I returned too early. This has resulted in a weak right ankle that will give way far too easily and has necessitated frequent physiotherapy at St Mary's Hospital, Paddington.

Syd Hoare accidentally kicked me very hard in my right ear which has now gone partly deaf.

I have dislocated my right index finger so many times that I learned to restore it myself and it has now settled in a slightly weird position which, although it doesn't hurt, looks deformed.

During squad training I sheared through an upper molar which then had to be removed and replaced with a (very expensive) bridge.

While training in Brian's Olympic training class, I developed a backache which got progressively worse. As I had a big competition coming up in two weeks, I needed to know: should I train or should I rest? Ken Kingsbury sent me to St Mary's Hospital, where I was told to rest. Ken wasn't satisfied with this and sent me to the New Charing Cross Hospital, where the consultant told me I had stress fractures in the small bones in my back, and if I continued training then these would pass into the big bones and I would be in serious trouble. This time when I called Ken from outside the hospital I was in tears. Ken was reassuring: 'Don't worry about what he said; did he do X-rays?'

'Yes,' I replied.

'Okay then, I want you to go back in and see this other consultant...'

He gave me a name. The new doctor told me a different story. 'There are no stress fractures, but the bones are slightly subluxated (out of place). It's fine to keep training but I want you to come here for physiotherapy every day.' I was also told to put my mattress on the floor to sleep on and support my back as much as possible. All this I did. I managed to defend my title and win at the championships (German Open), but the back problem wasn't solved.

A couple of weeks afterwards I said to Ken, 'It's still there, the back pain.'

'Okay,' he said, 'I don't know why everyone bypasses him, I want you to go to the Head of the Physiotherapy Department.' This I did. I was weighed and measured and asked to touch my toes (something I have always been able to do and can still do now).

The consultant looked at me doing this and told me that there was nothing wrong with my back and that I was 'being too sensitive after the championships and should snap out of it and forget about it'.

I told Ken. 'I've had enough of this,' he said. 'Do you mind if we see someone else and I stay in the room with you for the diagnosis?' I was beginning to feel a little reluctant to see anyone else, thinking perhaps it was just me and I should try to snap out of it. However, Ken persuaded me to go with him to see another consultant in Harley Street who was an osteopath. This man said I had a bone in the middle of my back that had turned around the wrong way, and the muscles in my left leg were trying to compensate and had lifted and shortened by an inch (two and a half centimetres). He did some work there and then, which was amazingly gentle and managed to lower the leg by half an inch. I had to return the following week and he finished restoring the bone back to where it should have been and there were no further problems. An amazing man!

Vacinuff Morrison used to fight as a light-middleweight and I liked to practise with him. He was fast and supple and was a good partner to work with. One evening we crashed to the floor together and I landed very heavily on my right shoulder. It felt as if the inside of my right shoulder had 'kissed' the inside of my left shoulder; it was very painful and lost all its strength. Ken Kingsbury discovered that about five of the bones in my shoulder were slightly out of place. With great effort Ken managed to put all but one back in position. I vividly remember lying on the floor of his son's bedroom and being instructed to pull on a pole which ran from floor to ceiling while Ken knelt over me trying to push the bones back in. Goodness knows what it would have looked like to anyone walking in!

He sent me to see various experts to try to fix the last bone, the top rib; however, I was told that the only solution was that they could make a hole in me and insert a tool a bit like a tyre lever and crowbar it back into place – but it might slip out again. Eventually I had to accept that it was going to stay out of place and reeducate the muscles.

This happened at a time when Brian Jacks and I had decided to enter the National Kata Championships with nage-no-kata (kata of the throws) and were frequently practising it – and I was Uke, the one who attacks and is repulsed, so I was being thrown a lot. It was weird because I would feel okay until I was thrown, and then as I went through the air it was absolute agony – but as soon as I landed the pain would be gone. However, we persevered and things were going well until Brian dislocated his back in an international competition and we had to pull out.

My shoulder injury occurred just before the 1975 Dutch Championships, and for the first time I had to pull out of a competition because of injury and was unable to go to defend my title. One small consolation was that my name was mentioned in the Guinness Book of Records as the holder of the most British titles in the women's judo events. This remained unchallenged until 1991.

I didn't enter any tournaments that year until the British Open, which was held at the Crystal Palace on 8 November 1975. Eleven countries took part, the oversea participants outnumbering the home contingent. The countries taking part were: Austria, Belgium, Canada, France, Holland, Sweden, Switzerland, West Germany, United States, New Zealand and Great Britain. There were also delegates from the European and Oceania Judo Unions who were making notes with a view to a future world event for women.

During one of the eliminations I tore a ligament in my left knee. This meant that I had to withdraw from the Open and had to fight the final of the over seventy-two kilos category with a knee full of novocaine.

I did manage to hold on to my title, and in time the knee healed; however, I have learned that when doctors say, 'You may get arthritis in that when you're

JUDO

Origins Judo is a modern combat sport which developed out of an amalgam of several old Japanese fighting arts, the most popular of which was ju-jitsu (jiu-jitsu), which is thought to be of pre-Christian Chinese origin. Judo has greatly developed since 1882, when it was first devised by Dr. Jigoro Kano.

World and Olympic titles World championships were inaugurated in Tōkyō on 5 May 1956. The only man to have won 4 world titles is Wilhem Ruska (Netherlands), who won the 1967 Heavyweight, the 1971 Heavyweight and the 1972 Olympic Heavyweight and Open titles. In the European championships (instituted in 1951) only Great Britain (1957–58–59) and the U.S.S.R. (1972–73–74) have won 3 consecutive titles.

British titles The greatest number of titles (inst. 1966) won is nine by David Starbrook (b. 9 Aug. 1945) (5th dan) who won the middleweight title 1969–70, the light-heavyweight 1971–75 and the open division 1970–71. The women's championships were instituted in 1971. Christine Child (4th dan) has won most titles with five wins: the heavyweight in 1971–74 and the open division in 1973.

Highest grade The efficiency grades in Judo are divided into pupil (*kyu*) and master (*dan*) grades. The highest awarded is the extremely rare red belt *Judan* (*10th dan*), given only to seven men so far. The Judo protocol provides for an *11th dan* (*Juichidan*) who also would wear a red belt and even a *12th dan* who would wear a white belt twice as wide as an ordinary belt, but these have never been bestowed. The highest British native Judo grade is *7th dan* by Trevor P. Leggett (b. 22 Aug. 1914,) Charles S. Palmer and Geoff Gleeson.

Marathon The longest recorded Judo marathon with continuous play by two of 6 Judoka in 5 min stints is 50 hr from the Dufftown and District Judo Club, Keith, Grampian, on 13–15 Sept. 1974.

My entry in the Guinness Book of Records.

Trevor Williams presenting me with his new Williams Geemat trophy. He gave me the previous one to keep as I had won it four years in succession.

Team for the first official European Championships for Women.

older,' what they actually mean is, 'You *will* get arthritis in it when you're older.' Ask any veteran judoka and I bet they tell you all about the old injuries.

It had been announced that the first official European Championships for Women would be held in Munich on 12/13 December 1975. I told everyone that if I could win my category in that, then I would retire from competition. I was finding it harder and harder to juggle training with work and a home life. In those days there was no sponsorship of any kind.

This time I had been entered in my weight category, seventy-two kilos and over, and also in the Open, which would be run on consecutive days. Most of the other teams were housed in the Holiday Inn, but due to lack of money the British team was housed outside Munich in a youth hostel. It was clean and pleasant, but we had a problem on the first day of competition: the bus sent to collect us broke down en route and we were extremely late arriving. The competitions had started by the time we arrived, the fights being run out of sequence in order to avoid the ones that had British girls in them. Poor Jackie Redmond was the first one of us to compete; she had to change on the bus and more or less run straight on to the mat. Dazed and upset by the scramble to get there in time, she had no opportunity to prepare herself and consequently lost her match.

We all had a hard day and my final was, once again, against De Cal, which I was relieved to win. De Cal managed to get a koka (three point score) at the beginning and then was penalised for passivity. I then scored a wazari (seven point) from a throw and then held her down to finish with ippon (full point).

Charlie Palmer was sitting at the officials' table trying to look impassive. He told me afterwards how difficult it had been for him.

They put all the medal winners on the rostrum and gave us medals, trophies, flowers, certificates and special judogi as presents; and then, as we turned to go, a couple of officials came up to me while I was still on the rostrum and demanded that I go with them for drug testing. I was completely unprepared for this. With arms full of stuff I was trying to catch one of my team to take it all for me and look after it, while these people were insisting that I went with them now!

They took me to a room with a loo in the corner with the door removed. Liz was not allowed in with me: she was shut outside. I was handed a glass jug and told to take it into the loo and pee in it – while they watched me! Well, that's not something I'd ever done before; and what with running to the loo all day and not eating or drinking much (nerves), I was rather dehydrated and couldn't give them what they wanted. We tried turning the taps on – no joy... but after about an hour I managed to squeeze out just enough and they let me go.

I opened the door of the room to find Liz waiting for me... and Charlie Palmer! He was waiting to give us a lift back to our hotel. I thought that was a very kind thought. Unfortunately it was now so late that I couldn't get any food anywhere – and I was starving. It must have been around eleven o'clock and I really needed to get to bed as I was competing again the next day. Apparently you can get colds from stress; I had found over the last few trips abroad that I would leave England in good health and would step off the plane with a full head cold. This trip was no exception and I had a stinker. Liz and Gill Shelton went through the list of remedies and forbidden drugs and decided that all I could have was Friar's Balsam, which didn't help much. It took me quite a while to wind down from the day and go to sleep.

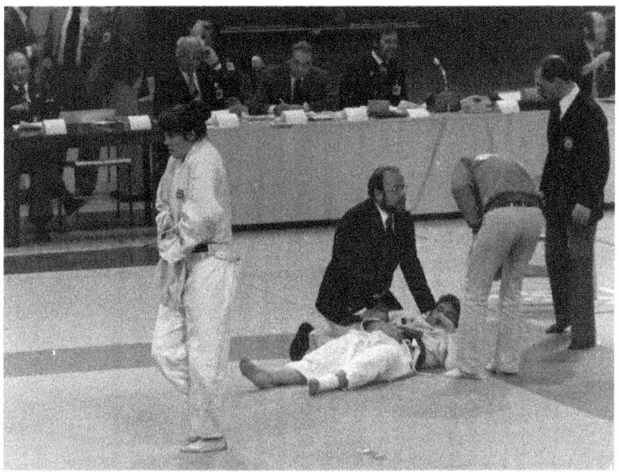

The end of my match against Liotard of Holland. She had succumbed to a strangle.

This is just to show that Liotard was not hurt and there were no hard feelings.We had met in contest several times before.

This is the beginning of my bout against De Cal.

Me with the Gold medal for the first Women's European Judo Championships.

However, the next day I was competing in the Open. I managed to win my first three contests but then lost by five points to Pierre of France who went on to win. I was, actually, completely drained by then. Nowadays, there is a break between the Open and the other categories so that competitors can have a rest day.

Charles Palmer, thoughtfully, also treated the whole British team and supporters to a guided coach tour of Munich on the Sunday morning.

The judogi that the champions received was a very special present. It had machine embroidery on the bottom of the left front which said (in German), 'The 1st Women's Europeans', with the German shield. I liked it very much, until I discovered that it was a size 150! I thought to myself, 'This was obviously organised by a man. Who else would consider that a woman who won the heavyweight category would be the same size as one who won the lightweight category?' However, once the error was realised, the organisers whisked it away. I thought, 'Just my luck, that's the last I'll see of that and I rather liked it too...' To my surprise and pleasure, eventually I received an identical one in the correct size – 180.

I always preferred medals to trophies. I have kept the medals, and the trophies have been passed on. Two of them are with our local judo club, Drake Judo Club, to be given annually to the most improved youngsters: one for the girls and one for the boys.

We always meet up with old friends at the various Budokwai anniversary dinners. The photo below is a vain attempt to take a picture of all the Budokwai members who had been in the national team. It became pandemonium as practically everyone in the room tried to be in it!

With Charles Palmer.

Here is my collection. It covers most of the championships that I entered, except for the Dutch Open because the year I won it they weren't giving medals, only trophies...

All in all I won eighteen gold medals – fourteen in international competition.

1. Kata Championships (with Chris Wildman) – Nage-No-Kata
2. Kata Championships (with Chris Wildman) – Ju-No-Kata
3. Team Championships (London Area) 1971
4. British Open +70kg 1971
5. British Open Open Category (Bronze) 1971
6. German Whitsun Tournament 1972
7. Italian Open 1972
8. British Open +68kg 1972
9. Swiss Open 1973
10. German Open 1973
11. Italian Grand Prix 1973
12. British Open +68kg 1973
13. British Open 1973 Open Category
14. Team Championships (London Area) 1974
15. British Open +72kg 1974
16. Coppa Europa 1974
17. British Open +72kg 1975
18. First Official European Championships 1975

CHAPTER FOURTEEN
The Pink Panther

You have to live before you die, or you'll die before you live.
Peter Sellers

Joe Dunne was working on *The Return of the Pink Panther* and called me to double for Catherine Schell. In the story, she is a burglar breaking into a museum to steal the Pink Panther diamond. Joe had already doubled for Catherine on location in Morocco; now he wanted me to do the stuff inside the museum, which was a set at Shepperton Studios. This turned out to be rather fun. It was just me, the film crew and Blake Edwards, the director.

In the scene, the burglar creeps through a museum, locates the laser-beam sensors with a hairspray, and slides under them in various ways. She then produces a contraption from her pocket to hold the burglar alarm down while she steals the diamond. Joe sent me off to practise using this, so I spent some time crawling around my dressing-room floor getting used to playing with this gadget. It was time well spent. When it came to filming, I managed to use it as if I knew how to.

At the end of this particular part of the story, I had to be lying in a large shadow when one of the security guards accidentally sets off the alarm, causing a door to drop which 'Catherine' has to dive under. Even though this was a set, the door was an extremely heavy one, so I didn't want it to land on me. The first take Joe wasn't happy with. 'Can you do it like that but make it a little closer?' So I held back a fraction and then dived under the door again. 'Hold back a bit more...' So I went a little bit later again. Joe was by now cueing me, giving me the signal when to go. The trouble was, I was leaving later, and later... but going faster, and faster... However, we did manage to get good timing in the end!

Later in the film there is a fight in a Japanese restaurant so I am dressed as a Japanese waitress. Unfortunately, I am about a foot taller than all the other Japanese ladies... However, with all the action, I don't think it shows.

We were called again when *The Pink Panther Strikes Again* was in production. In this story, I had to play a butch bouncer in a gay club. I had a short wig to hide my long hair and Chrome sat on my shoulder. The actress Dyan Cannon was also working on this film, and when she heard Chrome singing away in my dressing room she came in to see him. She was quite taken with him. Blake Edwards also loved Chrome, but my voice had to be dubbed as it was deemed not to be masculine enough!

I had the same problem when I worked on the TV series *Minder* in the episode 'A Nice Little Wine'. I had to play the part of the lesbian girlfriend of a girl in the story called Jo, and once again my voice was dubbed... In the scene I was involved in, we were on location in a ground-floor flat in London. The director had set up in a room with the camera facing a door in one wall. He wanted Arthur Daley (George Cole) to come in through the door, dragging with him the villainess. Shortly after, I had to come through the same door, followed a moment later by Terry McCann (Dennis Waterman). This sounds okay, except that the door actually led into a very small downstairs bathroom, in which we all had to wait until we were called. The only way we could do it was if Dennis and I stood in the bath, and then there was room for George Cole and the actress to squeeze in and close the door. We duly squashed in – very close together... I said to Dennis, 'I can now say that I've been in the bath with Dennis Waterman,' which gave us all a giggle.

The next Pink Panther film was *The Revenge of the Pink Panther* and once again a large contingent of stunt people were working on it. Peter Sellers was in good form. He was a great giggler. This meant that sometimes he would start to dissolve into giggles during a take and all around him would start to laugh as well. When Peter started to crack up, we would all give Blake Edwards a quick look; and if he was laughing, we knew it was okay to join in... and Blake would let Peter get away with it – for a while... However, eventually, he would decide that time was

being wasted and he wouldn't laugh. When that happened, we wouldn't laugh either. When Peter realised that his audience were no longer laughing, he would switch off and get back to work.

It was a funny scene. Peter and Burt Kwouk had entered a bar in disguise. They were both wearing black make-up with huge Afro wigs, loud satin outfits and massive platform shoes. It was so overdone that it was hilarious just to look at them. We spent days working on this, but in the end the scene was cut from the film.

On another occasion I was one of a group of stunt people who were asked to make a safety film to be shown to commercial aircrew, to demonstrate the procedure if their plane had to ditch into the ocean. We all had to travel to the seaside, complete with our wetsuits, and were taken out to sea the next day. The idea was that the ditched airplane would be simulated by the boat we were all on and the real aircrew would release and inflate the life rafts; we, as passengers, would obey instructions and leap off the ship (plane), swim to the life rafts and climb in. The life rafts being used were real, and it was a bit thought-provoking to find that they actually didn't want to inflate! The first one was thrown into the sea and the aircrew tugged the cord that ought to inflate it – as per procedure – but nothing happened! The same thing happened to the next one... and these had been taken off working airliners! However, eventually we managed to get one inflated and we got on with it.

The Pink Panther Strikes Again with Chrome.

In January 1973 the stunting fraternity managed to secure a Stunt Register with Equity (the actors' union). This enabled us to protect our work so that only registered stunt people could work on films and television, but more importantly it enabled us to have insurance at last. The fees were quite high, but fair; and we would have cover if we were hurt or killed.

Modesty Blaise is a character created by Peter O'Donnell. He wrote many books about Modesty and her sidekick Willie Garvin. Stories about Modesty and Willie were also printed as comic strips in the *Evening Standard* and other newspapers. I have loved reading these books, and wrote to Peter to tell him how much I admired his writing. We became firm friends. I used to meet him sometimes for lunch in his office. I called it his 'eyrie' because it was at the top of an old building in Fleet Street and you had to climb up loads of rickety wooden stairs to get there. We would sit and chinwag, talking about all sorts of things. Sometimes he would come to watch our judo competitions.

Peter told me one day that he had a new artist doing the illustrations for the comic strips and that he was having trouble making the illustrator understand the moves he was describing in the fights. Peter said he had an idea that might help. He wanted to make up a book of photos of the various moves, which he would number, and then he could quote the numbers to the artist. He asked if Brian and I could do the moves in front of a photographer.

So one afternoon, Brian and I spent a few hours at the Budokwai with Peter and a photographer. Bearing in mind what these photos were needed for, I started off wearing trousers and a jumper; however, after just a few moves I split the trousers and had to resort to wearing my Budokwai tracksuit trousers.

Peter told me later that his idea had worked and helped him a lot. There was a film called *Modesty Blaise* which was supposed to be based on Peter's books; and before you ask, no, I did not work on it. In fact Peter hated it. He said there was only one line that he wrote in the entire film. He eventually bought the rights for the film so that it could never be shown again.

Brian demonstrating his amazing drop kick!

This is Peter O'Donnell with my two boys on one of our visits for lunch.

Stunts Incorporated

AT a closed meeting in London last week, the nation's stuntmen got together and opened a register, the chief aim of which is to secure insurance cover. It's a strange way to make a living, we thought, and went along to the Prince of Wales Feathers in Warren Street where, we'd discovered, some of the stuntmen occasionally gather and drink their fresh orange juice.

We found Gerry Crampton, very much the king of the trade, his droll old pal Joe Dunne, who's a great deal funnier than the many stars he doubles for, and Cyd Child, a judo champion and the muscle behind television's Mrs Emma Peel. They're a handsome trio, which is what we said to them, and Gerry Crampton said: "What did you expect—cauliflower ears and squashed noses?"

Insurance is clearly prudent for anybody going in for scraps with Sean Connery and John Wayne and jumping through fifth-floor windows, but as Gerry Crampton said, at the top end of the trade where some make £10,000 a year, they have their own insurance and don't need the union's.

"And in any case, you might be taking risks, but they're calculated. Nobody respects you for a stunt that's very likely to kill yourself. People like Burt Lancaster and Kirk Douglas know a real stuntman when they see one, and they don't want to work with amateurs who can't calculate a risk.

"It's a matter of being a technician—knowing just what can be done and what can't."

Our trio in the picture often work together—"Well," says Cyd Child, "would you stand in the middle of the road and let somebody you don't know drive a car at you?" and when you ask them if they ever get hurt they say no, but that's not counting leopard claws in your back and trivialities like smashed ribs.

But their pal Jack Cooper, who has dived 78 feet into water and 78 feet on to cardboard boxes and prefers the boxes ("Boy, that water's hard") tells us he did once get "a nasty whack." He had to do a 45-foot fall and some mattresses had been prepared. Nightfall interrupted shooting and they resumed first thing the following morning. Unhappily, the mattresses were of straw, had got wet and froze overnight. Which was how he got his nasty whack.

If it's action you want: Joe Dunne, Cyd Child, Gerry Crampton

THE SUNDAY TIMES, JANUARY 28 1973

Brian & me demonstrating more moves for *Modesty Blaise*.

Self Defence World Magazine
Jan 1975

CHAPTER FIFTEEN
Purdey

Respect is earnt not given.

The European Championships were over and I was trying to get used to the idea that I was no longer going to compete. Various people, including my fiancé, didn't believe me; and I thought, 'They will all understand when I don't enter the selections for the Women's Squad.' Then the phone rang...

It was Ray Austin. Seven years after *The Avengers* had finished, there was going to be a resurrection! *The New Avengers* was on its way. Ray asked me to come to Pinewood to see him and we had a chat. He wanted me to be the fight arranger! The new series would have Patrick Macnee returning as Steed, and he would have two assistants, not one: Joanna Lumley (Purdey) and Gareth Hunt (Gambit). Ray asked me to get Joanna and Gareth as fit as possible before we started shooting – in three weeks! Joanna's character, Purdey, was supposed to be extremely fit and supple, an ex-ballet dancer who was also brave and capable of fighting baddies.

Joanna is a wonderful, lovely person with a refreshing sense of fun. We took over the old band room at Pinewood which we made into a kind of gym. I introduced Joanna and Gareth to the joys of shuttle runs, circuits and suchlike followed by lots of stretching. They worked very hard for an hour in the morning every day, and afterwards Joanna even had an hour's ballet tuition after our session while Gareth worked on weights the other side of the room.

I had said to Ray, 'How far do you want us to go? Because what I've been doing for myself may be too extreme for Jo and Gareth.'

His face remained impassive as he thought for a while; then he said, 'Go all the way! I want them really fit!' So we did.

Amazingly, neither Joanna nor Gareth raised any objections, and they both worked very hard. Poor Gareth suffered a bit with the stretches but endured it all with good humour. They really did do some hard training, sometimes very hard. I told them, 'You're going to hate me. You're really going to hate me!'

However, Jo was pleased with the end results despite the fact that she'd cried, 'Enough! I hate it, I hate it!' towards the end. She told me later, after she had done some filming, that the cameramen couldn't keep up with her when she was running and had to ask her to slow down. Jo always put her heart and soul into any action. Ray doesn't say a lot but he seemed pleased.

When shooting began we had a bit of a problem with the costumes. For a while they were designed by Catherine Buckley who would just send highly expensive clothes to the studio. Well, I remember going into Wardrobe one morning and the lady in charge was looking very worried. She said, 'Look at this! What am I supposed to do with these things? We've got this scene with Purdey scrambling through the woods, mud and whatnot, and look what she's sent me,' and she showed me the costume with a label on it that said, 'Not to be washed. Not to be dry cleaned'! And there was no double outfit for it either. It was absolutely ridiculous! Another outfit was an olive-green body-stocking fighting suit, which Joanna didn't seem to like very much. I heard her say, 'Here comes Purdey, dressed in green slime!'

On one of the first episodes that we made, Purdey was shown practising in a dojo. They had dressed her in a very stylish gi similar in style to the traditional judogi and made of soft silky velvet. It looked very glamorous, but there was a problem that we judo ladies know all too well – what do you wear underneath? No one had considered this, so Jo came and found me to ask what I would recommend. At that time, contest ladies wore leotards, and that's what I suggested. Wardrobe didn't have anything like that but I happened to have mine in my bag... So, if you ever see that episode, Purdey is wearing my leotard!

In the episode, the man Purdey is practising with was doubled by a stuntman named Val Musetti who at that time was a Second Dan at judo. This was good for

Joanna Lumley at the Press Launch.

The New Avengers Team.

what we wanted and we rehearsed a very mobile randori (which unfortunately was only used in part).

There was another episode called 'Gnaws' where I used something that Brian Jacks and I had been messing about with, for fun. Brian had this idea that you could get thrown with seoi nage (shoulder throw) and land in position to then throw your attacker with the same throw. It looked quite spectacular, so I included it in the fight scene.

Joanna was keen for me to double for her, but Ray was unsure about it; so Joanna did as much as possible herself, and we used various different stunt doubles when we had to. One day, Jo had an idea. She arranged for me to visit her hairdresser and have a wig cut on my head to double her hair. She then asked me to come to the studio and hide in her dressing room. Jo managed to borrow an outfit from Wardrobe that had a duplicate, and we dressed ourselves in these outfits and I put the wig on. We then went down onto the set and Joanna insisted that we had a screen test to see if I could double for her. This was done, and all agreed that it worked! I was now Jo's stunt double as well as the fight arranger!

Gareth had a very droll sense of humour. On one occasion it was necessary for Gambit to break into a room and I needed Gareth to jump down from the window ledge to the floor. Gareth couldn't understand my directions so he asked me to show him, which I did. There was a little pause and then he said, 'Can you do it again, in a suit?'

There was an episode called 'Sleeper' where a large part of London has been put to sleep, except they missed Purdey and the baddies are chasing her around trying to catch and kill her. At one point Purdey is driving a Mini and gets shot at with a machine gun which shatters the front windscreen; she has to knock the broken windscreen out of the way with her arm in order to keep driving. Unfortunately for me, Purdey is wearing silk pyjamas and I ended up with a host of glass splinters sticking out of my arm and no standby First Aid. I ended up in an old public toilet trying to wash the glass out under a tap. The next day we had a standby ambulance and the medic belatedly cleaned and bandaged my arm for me. Some years later I had an itchy spot on the back of my hand; I teased it, and a long thin splinter of glass came wriggling out!

The New Avengers did not operate in the same way as the original *Avengers*. There was a lot of penny-pinching. I was the stunt arranger for the first thirteen episodes but they would only call me when there were stunts, and I was only paid for the days I was there. They wouldn't let me work on other days to sort stuff out or prepare. Stunt people were only called on the days when we had to work. The way things operated on *The New Avengers*, which I could never fathom, was that the second assistant did a lot of the calling of stunt doubles, without consulting the stunt arranger, whereas usually that was the province of the stunt/fight arranger.

In the episode 'Gnaws' we had a fight scene in a sewer. The filming of the fight had been almost completed but we needed one more day. We had two male actors with stunt doubles and I was told that the company couldn't afford to have me as well (as fight arranger). I had just fought to keep the doubles and yet I was now being told that I wasn't wanted. This would never have happened on the original *Avengers*; you wouldn't shoot a fight scene without the fight arranger present.

Of course, Ray Austin was often the director and it was probably thought that, if they had him, they didn't need anyone else as he was once the stunt arranger on *The Avengers*. Patrick would try very hard to help me out. He'd say, 'I think Cyd should be here whenever we're doing anything that involves action,' but they didn't always listen.

On one episode, 'Dirtier by the Dozen', Purdey is supposed to be stuck in a minefield and Gambit rescues her by hanging from a rope ladder suspended from a helicopter. Marc Boyle (who was going to double Gambit) and I prepared for it, bought the necessary harnesses and visited the helicopter pilot to talk it through; but we were never called. The producers had talked Jo and Gareth into doing it themselves. This saved the stunt fee. Some years later, when I was working for the BBC in Wales, I heard an actress talking to the make-up girl about that sequence. I was incensed to hear her say that the stunt people had 'chickened out' and the actors had had to do it themselves!

The penny-pinching got worse; and, when the second series of *The New Avengers* was planned, they dispensed with my services totally.

Getting the kick into the action. Austin directs a close-up shot of the Lumley leg for an *Avenger* episode.

This is an old newspaper cutting and you can see Ray looking through the camera and me next to Jo.

CHAPTER SIXTEEN
Life After Competition

Perfection is not obtainable but if we chase perfection we can catch excellence.
Vince Lombardi

It felt rather strange not to be involved with the Squad Trials in 1976 as I had retired from competition. However, Roy Inman had taken over as squad manager and coach, and he asked me to be involved in the training of the squad. Over the following years he also asked me to travel abroad with the team as their manager. There also came a vacancy on the promotions panel and I was asked to join. This was the panel that checked the veracity of all the Dan grade promotions to make sure that they had been conducted properly. At that time it was Dr Phyllis Elliott, Roy Inman and me. Years earlier, I had waited in fear and trembling, to find out if my grading had been validated... and now I was one of the group that was doing the checking! How times had changed! Later in the year, at the British Open, I was given life membership of the BJA and the Vic Terry Trophy for Personality of the Year.

In 1977 Peter and I were married in the little church at Old Windsor. We kept it as a small, relaxed, traditional wedding. I made my dress and our cake, and our very good friends Wendy and David very kindly gave us the use of their house for the reception, which was convenient as it was right next to the church. We gave all the guests free film for their cameras and told them to take whatever photos they liked, on the condition that they let us have the negatives afterwards; remember, this was before the digital age! This had some amusing repercussions, as when we walked out of the church we found ourselves surrounded with everyone's debris – jackets, bags and so on – and a wall of friends and relatives facing us, cameras at the ready.

My friend Margot Sathaye was steeped in judo and spent a large part of her life in Japan where, on 16 February 1978, she received her Fifth Dan. This made her the first British woman to achieve that grade. I became the second on 25 May the same year, when I became the first woman to reach Fifth Dan in the UK.

Margot was an amazing person. Her standard of judo was exceptional and way ahead of the rest of us. She was quiet and reserved and at her happiest when she was doing judo. Margot never said a lot and I was astonished to receive a present from her, from Japan, which was a 5th Dan Obi (belt) from the Kodokan, with my name embroidered on it in Japanese. I treasure it.

Being a team manager is almost as stressful as being a competitor – perhaps more so. On one trip I had a large team of girls who were all young teenagers going for a competition in West Germany. We had set off from Heathrow okay, but then we needed to change planes at Frankfurt, which was when we discovered that there were not enough seats in the next plane to accommodate the entire team. The BJA had not booked the seats so we were taking pot luck. Two people had to wait at Frankfurt to catch the following plane, so I left the assistant manager (Marion Woodard) and one of the lightweight competitors.

During the flight I realised that one of the girls kept asking her friend if she was all right. I sensed alarm bells ringing and asked the young lady if there was a problem. She told me that the friend suffered from severe claustrophobia and, as this was a small plane, she was worried about her. After hearing that, so was I! With visions of one of my team trying to hurl herself out of the door, I also kept a close eye on her...

We arrived safely at our destination to discover that we had lost some of our luggage, and also there was a problem with our directions. The BJA had blithely told me that the airport was only about fifty metres from our hotel, but as we were surrounded by fields this was patently not so. To make matters worse, no one seemed to speak English and we had no German.

I tried to swallow a rising panic and decided to ask for help at the Lufthansa desk; surely they would have someone who spoke English? They did! This wonderfully helpful man spoke excellent English. He helped me fill in the forms for the missing luggage and then to work out what had gone wrong regarding our

Dr. Ken Kingsbury presents me with the Vic Terry Trophy.

Peter and I were married at Old Windsor.

The British Team: Left to right. Maureen Bennett, Heather Ford, Me, Jane Bridge, Avril Malley, Connie Armstrong, Ann Hughes and Julie Cross.

destination. The place we needed to get to turned out to be thirty miles away, not fifty metres; and as I worried about how I was going to transport all these girls there... he offered to take us in an airline crew bus! A real angel!

We had to leave word for Marion to travel by taxi and to look out for the missing luggage, and our guardian angel told us that we would be picked up for the return journey on the Sunday morning. So, Sunday morning at 5.30am found me and my group in our GB uniform, standing on a corner in a tiny little German town, hoping and praying that Lufthansa would not let us down. I had no idea what I would do if they did; the BJA do not provide you with spare cash. But there was no need to worry: the Lufthansa bus arrived as promised.

In March 1978 Great Britain sent a Senior Women's team to join in a tri-nation tournament in Paris. The countries taking part were Great Britain, Belgium and France (who fielded two teams). We did well, coming second place. However, the next day when we had to travel home, it snowed! The lady who had been looking after us while we were in France escorted us to the airport – and then disappeared. We were left to deal with what turned out to be sheer chaos, all by ourselves.

We checked in as normal; however, the airfield was covered in a thick layer of snow. Shortly after we checked in, our flight was cancelled. By this time we had gone through to Departures. I had to leave the girls with a severe warning to 'Stay there – I'll be back,' find my way back to the desk and recover our bags. We were then stuck for the rest of the day, waiting to see what flight we would be on.

Despite the rules about supplying delayed passengers with food, we didn't receive any until 4.30pm, by which time we were absolutely famished. Through the windows we could see planes being de-iced in preparation for take-off; but precious few were actually leaving, and some were being de-iced for a second time. We were just kept waiting – and waiting...

Eventually, after about ten hours, we were allowed on a plane; apparently it would be the last plane of the day! We were de-iced; I kept thinking of the Munich air disaster and praying that it would not be this team... how long did the de-icing last? There was a bunch of cheerfully drunk Irishmen on board (the free drinks had kicked in) and one was escorted firmly off after his language got too colourful and loud. So we were rather a rowdy flight.

What started to bother me was what was going to happen when we arrived back in England. These girls were supposed to be in my care. It was obvious that we were going to arrive very late at Heathrow, in the middle of the night; and some of the team had a long journey afterwards, travelling by train up north. I asked them what they were planning to do; they might get to London, but the trains going north would be finished for the day.

'Oh, don't worry Chris – we'll sleep at the station.'

That made the hairs on the back of my neck stand on end! 'Surely that's not safe!'

'Chris, really, don't worry, we've done it before!'

We were greeted at Heathrow by Roy Inman (our coach) and my husband, Peter. I was so relieved to see them that when Roy said 'How did it go?' I gabbled my reply so fast that no one could understand what I said. 'Slow down, slow down!' Roy laughingly replied. He was just happy that we had all come safely home.

There was a team visit to Austria. Again, we were dealing with large amounts of snow. One of our team was injured and an ambulance was called. However, unlike Britain where we have the National Health Service, the ambulance would not take our competitor without prior payment. Next problem: we had no money (surprise, surprise). I was desperate. The President of the Austrian Judo Federation was sitting with the VIPs; I vaguely knew him from my days as a competitor, and he was also a friend of Charles Palmer, so I went up to him and told him my problem. He was such a kind man. He magnanimously said, 'Don't worry, the Austrian Judo Federation will pay.' Without his help, I have no idea what I would have done.

In 1980 we again sent a team to the Austrian Open in Kufstein. We were treated with so much friendliness and, at the championships, one man made a point of talking to us and said that he ran a toboggan business up the mountain; if we wanted to visit him, we could have a free go. Well, the entire team wanted to take him up on his offer, so the next day saw us going up on the ski lift (which was free) to visit him. We were not equipped for such an adventure: all we had to wear was our team tracksuits and trainers, but it was a beautiful sunny day so we thought we would be okay. He greeted us with a huge smile and, true to his word, sent us off on his toboggans.

Of course, it hadn't occurred to us that we had no idea of how to control one, so we all had a rather hair-raising (and exciting) trip down the mountain. Most of us made it down okay; however, poor Heather Ford had a nasty accident which was an argument between a large log pile, the toboggan and Heather – and the toboggan won! This resulted in her needing special care with her seating arrangements for the journey home. I had to do a tour of the local town looking for a circular cushion: no luck; so I ended up buying two heart-shaped cushions which, when put together, sort of made the right shape. Heather informs me that she still has them.

I was also involved with the training of the squad. I'm not sure how impressed Roy was when the physiotherapist and I took the girls to a private room and recommended that, if they were serious about winning important championships, then they should consider going on 'the pill' in order to control their periods. When young women are put under stress it is highly likely that they will start their period. So, the day of a championship – and, for the inexperienced, squad training sessions – would bring a period on. On this particular day, Charlotte (the physiotherapist) and I had both been inundated with young women asking if we had 'anything to help out' because their period had started unexpectedly.

Charlotte and I had a brief chat and decided that we really needed to speak to the girls en masse and explain a few home truths to them, so that they all knew. Obviously, Roy was excluded from this talk...

This photo is of Margot with Noritomi Masako who was her sensei and one of the first women ever to attain 6th Dan.

Rusty Kanokogi.

We women were now well on our way. Now that we had European championships, we could push for world championships and after that the Olympics. Rusty Kanokogi in America was a titan in women's judo. In 1959 Rusty famously entered a YMCA judo championship in Utica disguised as a man (because women were not allowed to compete). She taped down her breasts and won the contest, but when it was discovered that she was a woman she was stripped of her medal. Rusty organised the first women's world championships in New York in 1980 and was instrumental in bringing women's judo to the 1988 Summer Olympics. In 2008, the government of Japan awarded Rusty the Order of the Rising Sun Gold Rays Rosette, one of Japan's highest civilian honours bestowed on a foreigner who has made a positive influence on Japanese society. She died in 2009, but before she died she was re-awarded the YMCA medal that had been taken from her. Her ashes are interred in the Kanokogi samurai gravesite in Kumamoto, Japan and the stone is etched in gold with the words 'Rusty Kanokogi, American Samurai'.

Squad training - Brian Jacks as coach.

CHAPTER SEVENTEEN
Superman

There is a superhero in all of us.
Superman

The film *The Stick Up* (originally titled *Mud*) was filmed entirely on location in Devon, with David Soul in the leading role. I was called to play the part of the Amazon Lady who is a fairground mud-wrestler in 1935 England. In the story, David Soul's girlfriend takes on the challenge of trying to win a mud-wrestling bout against the Amazon Lady to try to win some money. It doesn't go well and David Soul joins in. We all ended up well and truly covered in mud.

The awkward thing for me was that – despite my way of life – I have a sensitive side, and react badly to some substances. For instance, caffeine upsets my stomach, and I'm allergic to swimming-pool water and penicillin. The mud that was inside the wrestling ring was made with potting compost, and it had lime in it. I came out in a rash all over, and discovered that I'm allergic to lime. So whenever we were getting ready to shoot, the actors (who didn't have a problem) had to wait while the stunt girl was covered in Vaseline before we could start.

The cast and crew were billeted in various bed and breakfast establishments around the local countryside and we would get together in the evenings. On one occasion we all met for the evening at the hotel which was our main headquarters. We had a very sociable time culminating in David Soul entertaining us by singing and playing his guitar. We all felt a little uncomfortable when he asked us to teach him some English folk songs - and nobody knew any! He was very friendly. At the time we all knew him from *Starsky and Hutch*, we hadn't realised that he could sing as well.

Hanover Street was a film set in World War Two, including the London Blitz. Obviously, filming a scene of the Blitz involved a stunt crew. We began with a typical 1940s street in London at the end of the day: people coming home from work, walking along the pavement, getting off a double-decker bus and crossing the road. Then it all began: explosions, fires and people running about and shouting. We worked through the night. The fires were very realistic, and there was a weird unearthly screaming which was caused by the amount of propane gas being pumped from a gas tanker hidden behind the set. Apparently, in order to get enough gas for all the fires that were going on, someone had to stand on the safety valve and that was what was causing the noise!

I wasn't born when the Blitz was going on, but some of my friends were Londoners from the East End and had lived through it. Working on this story, and the accuracy of the set, brought back many memories for them and I heard many touching stories of their experiences.

The first and second *Superman* movies were filmed together and involved a number of different crowd scenes. At one time we were shooting night scenes at Pinewood on a set which was supposed to be summertime in New York; however, it was actually wintertime in England. We started off wearing thermal underwear beneath our summer clothes, but the next night when we turned up for work Wardrobe said to us, 'I'm terribly sorry, ladies, but there's a risk that your underwear may show, so I'm afraid you can't wear the thermal stuff; I've bought a selection of Marks & Spencer undies and you can make your own choice...' It was very cold so we all stayed well wrapped up until the first assistant warned us that it was almost time; then we would have to take off the ski boots and thick coats and pretend it was summer. (Pete had bought me the ski boots after the first night, because he wasn't happy with me getting into bed in the early hours of the morning 'like a block of ice' as he put it...)

What was delightful was seeing the faces of the small children who had been allowed on the set to see Superman. Their eyes were huge and round as they were introduced to Christopher Reeve but they couldn't take their eyes off his feet. Superman had to have clean soles to his boots when he was 'flying' and

Christopher Reeves as Superman.

In the story, the supervillains were causing trouble and taunting Superman. We started off with explosions on cars and lorries, then chunks of rubble falling all around us and the ground shaking, after which we were blown down the street by giant wind machines. The trick was to be able to reinvent yourself after the take and make yourself look like a new person, to make sure that you continued to work on the film. The policy seemed to be that if the camera paid any attention to you, such as if you had a line, then afterwards you were sent home. I had a large bag of wigs and managed to survive being seven different people before I was given a line – 'Superman help us!' – while 'rubble' rained down on me. After that I had to leave.

On another occasion, we arrived at Pinewood ready to work but were promptly taken to caravans and told to stay there. This was slightly strange, as usually at Pinewood we would have dressing rooms; but, heigh-ho, we went along with it. Our stay in the caravans seemed to last a long time and we started to question each other: 'Does anyone know why we have to stay in here?' with all sorts of answers being suggested. Obviously no one did know.

After a while we discovered that the scene we would be filming was of an earthquake. The set was a street; each 'house' was held up by a crane with cables, and the cranes had to swing about and make

Terry Walsh and I beginning to be blown down the street!

the houses shake. The action was being practised with all the people out of the way. What was rather unsettling was that apparently some of the 'houses' had fallen flat on their faces.

When we were finally allowed on set we worked rather hard on making the scene look authentic. It was impossible to completely rehearse the action; you could only have a sketchy outline of what you wanted to do. We did nine takes. I had to climb up a ladder inside a 'house' to emerge at a window and then, when the 'house' began to shake, make my way out onto the porch and climb down the outside whatever way I could. It's not easy trying to keep your balance with everything going backwards, forwards, sideways, up and down, with nothing to hold onto – while trying to keep your skirt down at the same time!

In the first take my 'husband', without looking back over his shoulder at me, shot out of the window and vanished. I was left sitting on top of the porch of 'my house' contemplating the best way down and trying to realistically scream...

We all thought that the end result ought to be pretty good. However, a few weeks later we were called back to do it again and we had a different director who, apparently, was very experienced with earthquakes. We were given lessons on how difficult it was to walk during an earthquake as he was not happy with our previous efforts... We did all the action again and he appeared satisfied, but our work was not included in the final film.

At least that is what I thought until recently! While chatting to a very knowledgeable fan, Philip Hawkins, he told me that in the extended version of the film, the earthquake scene was included and to my delight I was finally able to see it.

I was called to double an actress on *The London Affair*. I had no idea what the story was about, but it was necessary for me to jump into the water of the docks in London. That was the nasty bit; the water in the docks was very dirty, unhygienic – and cold. Ships were known to discharge their bilge water and toilets into the river. However, I was covered by my tetanus shots, and had managed to find a wetsuit that just covered my body (no arms and legs).

The next problem was that the actress was tiny! I worried that I would be sent home but was assured that for this shot, height wouldn't matter.

CHAPTER EIGHTEEN
Bollywood

You have to dream before your dreams can come true.
Dr A. P. J. Abdul Kalam

The phone rang; it was Gerry Crampton, calling from India: would I be able to come out to Bombay? He needed me... so there I was, on my way!

I'd visited various countries before, but I'd never made a long-haul flight and certainly not on my own. After the last fiasco when I'd gone to work for Gerry in Germany, I was a bit worried that he would not be there when I arrived, but he promised he wouldn't let me down.

The flight stopped to refuel at Dubai, but I stayed on the plane as I felt sure that if I got off then something would happen and I would miss the flight. We arrived at Bombay and I collected my luggage and went through all the airport checks; no sign of Gerry... I made my way through the airport – no sign of Gerry... I was beginning to panic a bit but forced myself to be calm. What was I going to do this time if he didn't show up? I stepped out of the airport into dazzling sunshine – no Gerry; then I heard a shout from a cafe across the road, and there he was. I was so relieved.

I found that we were staying at the Holiday Inn at Juhu Beach with the other westerners working on the film. There were also the flight crews from various commercial airlines, and some Canadian helicopter pilots who flew to the offshore oil rigs. We were right next to the beach, but I was warned not to go there on my own; and we had a security guard by the gate.

The film was called *Shaan* and the stars were Amitabh Bachchan and Shashi Kapoor. The production team and crew were Indian, and there were a few English people as well: James Allen (camera operator), John Grant (special effects), Gerry Crampton (stunts) and now me. We were later joined by David Campling who was the sound editor. I was to double the two leading ladies. One was called Parveen Babi and she was very beautiful. I was sent for a dress fitting as I needed two outfits, both the same style but one a dark pink and the other one yellow. The tailor making these outfits had a kiosk on the pavement and I was measured, over my clothes, in full view of the passing public!

We worked hard, with long days and no Sundays off. Shashi and Amitabh were very friendly and spoke perfect English so we all got on like a house on fire, although it was rather amazing to see the reverence that their public held them in. They were treated like gods! Amitabh gave me a souvenir photo; some years later I was surprised to see the same picture being used in *Slumdog Millionaire*.

We were given expenses but I found I wasn't using them. They were given in cash - rupees. These had to be spent as I couldn't take them back to England. There were no shops nearby although you could barter with people who hung about near the hotel. If you sat on the wall between the hotel and the beach this signalled that you were interested and various people would gravitate to you. Did you want to buy peacock feathers or have your photograph taken with a monkey? I bought some rocks from a 'rock wallah'. These were quite interesting. They were rocks which had been tapped with a hammer so that they were in two pieces showing the crystals inside them. I didn't buy anything else as I am not very good at bartering, so friends had advised me to go to a 'government shop' where they fix a fair price.

Pete had waved me off from England with a request to 'bring me back an elephant!' So, when I finally got a day off, I borrowed Gerry's car and driver and went into Bombay to shop. My driver took me to a government shop and I was amazed at the display of handmade elephants. They were made of various different woods and patterns ranging from tiny to massive! It took me some time to make a selection! This shop impressed me so much that I returned there several times while I was in India. It fascinated me.

Shashi Kapoor was married to Jennifer Kendal, sister to Felicity Kendal who starred in *The Good Life*. Jennifer was very kind and invited us to their home to have a traditional Sunday roast, which she cooked for us – in case we were getting homesick!

Relaxing in the grounds of our hotel in my effort to get a bit of a tan before returning home.

This is me with Shashi Kapoor.

The stunt crew with Gerry in the middle and me next to him.

I was subsequently given an additional role as a bodyguard in the film, and here I am playing with a fake rock!

Amitabh Bachchan

When it was time for me to go home to England, I was very kindly given a farewell gift of the costume I had worn to double Parveen Babi.

After this expedition, I decided that it was too difficult to try to continue to be involved with the Women's Judo Squad and I spoke to Roy Inman, the coach, and withdrew. It was impossible for the squad to rely on me as stunt work was too random and took up most of my time.

lan Hume

CHAPTER NINETEEN
For Your Eyes Only

Anything is possible if you've got enough nerve.
J.K.Rowling

Another phone call: this time I was asked to go to Pinewood Studios to see if I would be a suitable double for Carole Bouquet on the new James Bond film, *For Your Eyes Only*. This was agreed and I was then told to prepare to be working in Corfu and Greece. Work permits were arranged through the company.

The stunt team knew that we would be doing a certain amount of sub-aqua work, so we had a few sessions in Dorothy Ford's private pool to make sure that we were all happy and that we had all the equipment that we wanted. Dorothy was a regular member of the James Bond stunt team and was also a friend of mine.

I was having difficulty staying underwater to practise mask clearing and vividly remember Greg Powell saying to me, 'Don't worry Cyd, I'll sort that out' – and a giant hand landed on my head and pushed me down and held me there.

Then came the day of travel to Corfu. It was refreshingly different to what I was used to. There was no restriction on the weight of luggage, which was fortunate bearing in mind all the stuff I had to bring with me. A large shiny black chauffeur-driven limousine arrived at my house to pick me up, and the driver didn't complain that he had to wait because I wasn't ready.

We all met at Luton airport and we had our own plane with Monarch Airlines – flight number M007. They settled us down in seats towards the back of the aircraft and we were offered Buck's Fizz all round.

When it came time for me to find the loo I was directed to a door at the side of a partition separating us from the front. I went through, and discovered that the whole of the inside of the rest of the plane had been stripped out. There were no seats, and the plane was full of the equipment that we were going to need: cameras, lighting and everything else. All strapped down and covered in nets. We were obviously a very professional unit. When we arrived we were all then transported by bus to our hotel by the beach.

There were lots of beach activities that we could take part in, for a fee, if we wished to. Martin Grace, Roger Moore's stunt double, decided he would go waterskiing whenever he could, which was usually quite late in the day. He could be seen waterskiing around the bay in the sunset!

I thought I'd have a go at the paragliding. For this they strap a parachute to you with a long line leading down to a speedboat; as it takes off you get lifted into the air on the parachute, and the boat then tows you round the bay. It's great fun and, when they think you've had enough, they cut the boat's engines and drop you in the sea.

The occupants of the hotel were largely made up of people working on the film. We worked long hours, trying to make as much use of the light as we could. Dawn to dusk sounds about right; so in the morning, at the crack of dawn, when it was time to wake up you could hear alarms going off all over the hotel. I thought this rather amusing...

We started filming around a swimming pool. There was a bit of a shortage of girls to decorate the pool so Dorothy and I got roped in as well. The hairdresser pinned bougainvillea in my hair and I felt very glamorous. However, when we were rehearsing the fight, the man playing one of the baddies kept dropping his gun into the pool – in the deep end, which was about eighteen feet deep. No one seemed very keen to go in and fetch it. Bob Simmons, the stunt arranger, went around asking various people who all turned out to have a good excuse not to go in, so eventually he asked me to swim down and pick it up. I wasn't very keen as I knew it would ruin my lovely new hairdo; but no one else wanted to do it, and Bob was in charge, so I ended up having to swim down and pick it up. It was then dropped in again... and again... and the pool was filled with seawater which made me so buoyant that it was difficult to get down. My bougainvillea was totally flattened.

Preparing to go paragliding.

Waiting for the speed boat to pull me up.

I had to double Carole Bouquet arriving in a seaplane. Sounds simple; however, she had a beautiful white couture outfit with trousers and I had to take them off to paddle through the sea to get on the plane. Which meant that I had to try to get the trousers back on while we were flying, and it was only a little plane...

Also, it had been decided that while we were up in the air, they would film the plane swooping down to shoot at the ship. Again, that sounds simple, but in the shot Carole Bouquet is not in the plane. This meant that I had to try to hide in the back of this very small plane, so that I could not be seen. With the pilot going through attacking manoeuvres, for a time I experienced negative G and was weightless floating about in the back of the plane – along with all the bits and pieces that had been stored there – but trying to keep out of sight.

On the occasions when we weren't actually filming we were practising being dragged around the bay behind a speedboat. That is, Roger and Carole were supposed to be tied together and then dragged through the water. We were trying to get used to this and working out safety procedures and how long you could hold your breath while having rushing water gushing over your face. It's amazing how much salt you can collect in your hair when you do this for hours on end!

Cassandra Harris had to be mown down by a dune buggy, and I was her double. For this piece of action, the Remy Julienne team was in charge of the driving. They were a family of stunt drivers, and the youngest brother was going to do the action with me. We practised what we planned to do, starting off slowly and then increasing the speed until we were satisfied with the result. When it came time to shoot the scene I was sent to the Wardrobe caravan to get my costume. I had no idea what it looked like and didn't know where to look. The Wardrobe mistress handed me a small brown paper bag.

'What's that?' I said, thinking she was offering me a sweet.

'That's your costume...'

Mystified, I looked in the bag. Inside it was the smallest bikini I had ever seen.

'Is this it? I exclaimed, thinking, 'It's going to be difficult to wear any pads with this...'

'Oh, and there's this as well,' she said, handing me a see-through chiffon top, which didn't help the problem of the pads at all.

The stand-in for the camera set-up, who was a local Greek girl, thought the top was so risqué that she refused to wear it even with her own clothes underneath!

My day turned even more sour when I discovered that the elder brother in the Remy Julienne team had told his younger brother that he was going to do the shot in his place; and, of course, I had not rehearsed with him. When we did it, he was going much faster than I had practised with his brother. With this kind of action, you don't feel inclined to mess around and I just wanted to do the shot and get it over with, so I didn't make a fuss. However, he was going much too fast, and if you look in the sequence of photos you can see that I took a headlamp off with my legs and smashed the windscreen with my face!

I then had to wait an hour for a local doctor to arrive and put stitches in my lip – and he didn't believe in local anaesthetic either...

Fortunately, we only had to do it once. As you can see, there was no way you could wear any pads for protection.

Cassandra Harris and Roger Moore at the start of the action.

The beginning of the action for me.

My leg takes the headlamp
off and my face breaks
the windscreen.

There's a part of the story where a large powerboat has to run down Bond and Melina in the sea. This piece of action was allotted to Graeme Crowther and me. It was actually quite scary. As you duck-dived and tried to swim down you had no idea how far down you had made it. The sea was very clear but very deep at the point where we were working; all you could see was blue. Also the water was very buoyant and I found it difficult to get down. However, we dived and swam like fury. Just for once, I think I might have been ahead of Graeme; and all the time you could hear the engines of the boat getting louder and louder – and then as it went overhead you sensed something that felt like a fingernail stroke across your back. It gave me the creeps. I know it wasn't, but part of me kept thinking it was the propeller, and every time it happened I would freeze. We had to do it several times; but in the film, for all our effort, we look like footballs floating in the sea.

One day, the second assistant came to find me and said that I was needed for a shot later in the day (Magic Hour they call it, when the light starts to change at the end of the day). 'What do I have to do?' I asked. He rushed off shouting scene numbers over his shoulder – which didn't help as I didn't have a copy of the script. I began a hunt for a script to find out what the action was. When I finally tracked one down, I discovered that we would be shooting a scene at the end of the film. Carole Bouquet and Roger Moore were supposed to dive naked off the ship! The other members of the stunt team thought that this was hilariously funny as they climbed into Roger's powerboat to leave us and go back to the hotel.

The make-up lady wanted to sort me out to remove all my white lines from sunbathing; and Wardrobe offered me these special 'invisible' pants that were made of a very thin stretchy material, a bit like tights, which had very soft edges so that they didn't dig in and show a line. I gratefully accepted her offer.

Martin Grace, Roger's stunt double, had previously said that he wasn't bothered about going naked, but when he found out about my 'special' pants, he changed his mind and said he would wear a pair too. So the pair of us stood on the bows of the ship, with make-up doing their best to give us a convincing all-over tan; and all the time there was a procession of men climbing out of hatches and doors in that area of the ship with duties that 'just had to be done', but were quite obviously just wanting to have a look.

I had never dived from such a height before, but Martin said, 'Just follow me!' So off we went.

'What the hell was that!' was the cry from the camera crew, who were in a small boat filming from sea level. My dive had been very close to a belly flop! 'Let's go again; quickly, the light's going.'

So we had to do it again, but it was okay the next time. I think the Greek fishermen who had to haul us out of the water were a little bit bemused by our appearance, and I couldn't help laughing. However, when the film was cut together, the scene was removed and I was upstaged by my own parrot!

The film *The Sender* was a bit scary. The scene we were working on was when the 'sender' is having an operation and bursts into flames. I don't know the rest of the story. When the stunt crew arrived and went on set, which was designed to represent an operating theatre, we found that there were little tiny gutters running everywhere. I asked what these were for – and found it a bit chilling when I was told that they were for the propane gas to run along for the fire... I'm not very keen on working with fire. I'll do it if asked, but I have a healthy respect for fire. When it came to the scene we had to run away from various fireballs, and some of our team ended up with singed eyebrows and hair!

In *Space Riders* I had to be part of a cabaret composed of two women wrestling in whitewash! I was dressed in a leopard-skin bikini and had to come down a 'death slide' to arrive in the wrestling ring...

Roberta Gibbs and I were asked to work on the long-running soap opera *Coronation Street*, to check on the safety of a shot they were planning. The plan was for a car to roll down a slope with two of the barmaids in it and land up in a lake. No one was sure how far the car would roll or how deep the water would get. We all trundled out onto the moor. Roberta and I had brought our wetsuits, but we hadn't been given a caravan and there was a freezing cold wind. We decided to put off getting changed until the last minute; and we had another problem in that we had nowhere to leave our handbags. When we did it, the car just rolled and rolled! What we didn't know was that although it was supposed to be secret, someone had been sneakily taking photos, and the next day – there we were in the newspaper.

NOT-SO-DRY RUN: Stunt girls Roberta Gills and Cyd Child scramble from the runaway car.

IN THE DRINK

By KEN TOSSELL

A drop too much for Street's Fred

BRITAIN'S most famous barmaids landed in the drink yesterday.

Bet Lynch and Betty

CHAPTER TWENTY
A Change of Direction

The laughter of a child is the light of the home.

In 1981 Peter and I were blessed with a son. It took us some time to decide on a name as there were so many suggestions coming at us from all directions; however, we eventually settled on Robin.

Robin's arrival changed a great many aspects of our lives. It was no longer a simple thing to just jump in the car and go off to judo. Film work had to be carefully managed to make sure that I had someone who could look after him. I could no longer give an immediate answer if there was a telephone call saying 'Can you work for me tomorrow?' Peter and I had decided that we wanted to look after our children ourselves. We could not see the point in going to work to earn money to give to someone else to look after them. Consequently, if I had a call, I needed to check to see if Pete or my Mum could be free before I could answer yes or no.

There was one day when I was doing a film shoot for Pioneer, the audio equipment manufacturer. The idea was that I had to represent the Statue of Liberty looking fed up. Robin and I had previously gone up to London for the day for me to try out the costume. A very nice friendly young man fitted me for the head; I had to point out that I was human and did actually need to breathe, as it completely covered my head and had no air holes whatsoever. He had completely missed this necessity, and rushed to rectify the problem. I was given one tiny hole where the mouth was; the only way I could survive was by keeping extremely calm, concentrating on my breathing and trying not to panic.

On the actual day, my aunt and uncle were looking after Robin, and I rang them at lunchtime to make sure that everything was okay. It turned out that Robin had fallen and cut his face. They assured me that everything was all right, but I just wanted to get home as soon as possible to check on him. This was not so easy. We had almost finished but had to wait for the final photos to be processed to be sure that they were okay. I was dressed in long, thick drapes; any exposed skin was painted with green make-up, and then, of course, there was the head. When they finished, I was keen to just go; I had to make a tube journey, then pick up my car to drive home... Oh no. They refused to let me go until I had washed off all the green make-up, using a tiny inefficient shower which was not up to the job. I had to be really insistent before they would let me go.

'But Cyd, you've still got green make-up behind your ears... and in your ears!'

'But I don't care. What does it matter? The people I meet won't see me again...'

My approach to stunt work had changed. When I first started it was a bit of a challenge – could I do it? Could I do something that other people couldn't? It was a bit daredevil. It never occurred to me that I could be seriously hurt. My mind only thought: live or die. If I was called on a job, I wanted it to last as long as possible. Extended days and overtime were fine; if one day became two or three days or a week into longer – great. Now I had a small child dependent on me, and my attitude was different. Previously, when I was asked if I could work, I only wanted to know where and when. Now my questions were different. I had one telephone call saying, was I free, and I found myself asking, 'What do you want me to do?' and when the answer was 'Hang on to the outside of a train...' my reply was 'Why?'

Hearing myself asking this was rather shocking to me. I had realised that the job was no longer live or die; I had to face the fact that I could end up with serious injuries which might mean that I would not be able to look after my son. I thought to myself, 'If anything happens to me, who would look after Robin?' The answer was plainly Pete, but he wouldn't be able to do it on his own. He needed to work to pay the bills, so he would need help. My mind ticked off a list of possible helpers: his Mum, my Mum... and I thought, 'I don't want Robin to be brought up by anyone else, I want him to be brought up by me!'

Robin. 9 months. July 1982.

Me as the statue of liberty, I was more than fed up that day.

So the glamour of the job began to fade. I hated it if I was too late home to see Robin before he went to bed. I would go into his room and get his things ready for the next day, making no effort to be quiet, hoping that he might wake up; but he slept too deeply. Of course, I would have to leave very early and he would still be asleep when I left. One week I was working every day and didn't see Robin awake for a whole week; and in that week his top teeth started to drop down. So the last time I had seen him, he had no teeth; and the next time he had a whole mass of them and his face looked different – and I'd missed it! I no longer actively looked for work, just accepting those jobs that I could manage.

On 25 May 1983 I received my Sixth Dan, the first woman in the UK to be given this grade. I found it hard to get my head around this. In my earlier days at the Budokwai, the only Sixth Dan I knew was T. P. Leggett, and he was the only one in this country and treated almost like a god. I never thought it possible that I might one day get to be the same grade. The only grade I really aimed for was Fourth Dan because, at that time, that was Margot Sathaye's grade. When you have a Sixth Dan belt, or higher, you can wear a red-and-white blocked belt instead of a black one. This denotes you as a high-grade teacher. If you wish to just teach, or you are getting a bit frail and don't want to be roughed up, you wear the red-and-white belt. If you want to join in and be treated the same as everyone else, or maybe compete, then you wear your black belt. It's your choice.

Three years later Robin had a brother, Adam. I accepted less and less stunt work and started to earn pin money by stitching appliqué pictures on sweatshirts and towels. I have always enjoyed handicrafts, and I could do this at home.

Four years later the boys had a sister, Zara. We now began to feel that our house wasn't big enough. We considered what we could do to enlarge it, but we'd already extended it as much as we could; it had started off as a little two-up two-down semi-detached cottage and there is a limit to what you can do.

We discovered that, if we sold our house and moved to Devon, we could afford a four-bedroom detached house with a large double garage, and clear our mortgage!

So we moved to West Devon, into an old stone-walled barn which had been converted. The living area was a huge room upstairs where the hay had been, and the bedrooms were downstairs where the cattle had been kept. The house was surrounded by a good-sized garden with a stream running down the side.

Pete was especially pleased to have a very large double garage with a workshop. It was so peaceful and beautiful there. The locals were very friendly, and we slowly put down our roots and settled in. The children loved it even though the difference was amazing. We were well out into the country with two buses a week – one on a Tuesday and one on a Friday. Robin started at the local school, which had a total of twenty-seven people, staff and students – quite a change from his previous school where there were thirty-two in his class alone. He blossomed.

In fact we all blossomed. The children did well in their school. As it was a small country school, the pupils benefited from lots of individual attention from the teachers; and living deep in the countryside is very soothing for the soul. We made lots of friends among the people who lived nearby.

After Zara was born, I felt that I needed to get involved with exercise in order to try to get fit again, so I joined the aerobics class at the local leisure centre. I say local but, in the countryside, local usually means a bit of a drive; in our case it meant a drive to Launceston in Cornwall. Robin and Adam joined the swimming classes, as did Zara when she was old enough. Pete went in the 'studio' to use the rowing machines and I joined in aerobics classes. I have always enjoyed dancing and exercising to music so this was fun.

We noticed that there was a poster on the wall for the local judo club; Robin was interested, so we enrolled him. We thought we would leave the judo teachers to get on with their work and not interfere; we nearly got away with it...

Adam and me.

However, one evening, while I was taking part in the usual aerobics class, I noticed a face peering through the little glass panel of the gym door. I didn't take much notice; but when the class finished and I came out, I discovered that the face belonged to a lady called Beth Altabas who coincidentally had been in my judo class at the Budokwai. She had recognised me and told the manager of the leisure centre, who then mentioned it to the people who were running the judo club. We were trapped! So we were now involved in the local judo club. We didn't really mind; it was just that we hadn't want to interfere with the way they did things.

In due course, Adam also joined in judo, and eventually Zara as well. All the children enjoyed it for a while but they were never 'bitten by the bug'. First Robin, then Adam and then Zara dropped out of judo and put all their concentration into swimming, in which they all had a natural ability and they excelled. We didn't mind. They had a curiosity about judo and wanted to try it out, but swimming was much more their thing. All three became extremely competent swimmers and very good lifeguards, and Robin even went on to become a lifeguard trainer. Everyone has to go with their own passion. Although judo has been a big part of mine and Peter's lives, we wouldn't want to force it on our children if they didn't really want to do it.

Pete with the boys.

The Western Area put me forward for my Seventh Dan which I received in January 1998. This was something I never, ever believed I would obtain. Earning my First Dan (black belt) had been a special milestone for me; however, the grade that meant the most was when I received my Fifth Dan (fifth grade of black belt), as that was the grade that Watanabe had when he was at the Budokwai. I admired him enormously and never dreamt it would be possible for me to achieve that level. At the time it was the highest competitive grade; all grades after Fifth Dan were for services to judo.

I continued with the aerobics classes and also joined in 'step' which I really enjoyed. Pete made friends with other people who used the rowing machines and became more and more involved with the rowing. He bought a Concept 2 machine and started on a 'Row a Million Metres' challenge. I had a bit of a go but didn't take it too seriously.

One day, Sue Buckley, our step/aerobics instructor, said to me, 'There's a course on soon to qualify as an instructor – you should enter.'

This came out of the blue and took me by surprise. 'No, it's okay Sue,' I said, 'I'm quite happy to keep coming to your classes.'

Zara, aged 3 years.

AA BREAKDOWN SERVICE

PATROLMAN

'Oh, that's a shame,' she said. 'I want some time off next year and I was hoping you'd cover me...'

Well, that set off alarm bells. I really enjoyed Sue's classes; but there had been, on occasion, classes that were covered by other people, and these had been a bit of a disaster. So I began to think seriously about doing the course, and eventually bit the bullet and put my name down. It was hard work and very involved but I succeeded.

In order to get as much experience as possible I started a regular class in our village. This was fun and rather necessary. I hadn't considered all the extra expenses of buying equipment, professional memberships and insurance. I was offered classes at Launceston Leisure Centre and covered classes for people who needed time off. When you do these classes you don't just walk in and take the class, although that's what it looks like. You actually spend quite a bit of time preparing, and this means doing the exercise on your own before you arrive for the class. I found I was steadily losing half a pound in weight every week, whatever I ate, which was a terrific side-effect!

Sue and I stayed great friends and I still went to her classes. The line-dancing craze arrived and we went off together to get qualified to teach that as well. It was all a little bit crazy. While we were on the course, the leisure centre manager had advertised line-dancing classes, without consulting us, and told everyone that the first class would be a free taster! We arrived to do this with hardly any time to prepare and discovered the centre absolutely packed with people. You couldn't move. We had to try and get all these people into the one gym; they were all crushed up against the door and we couldn't get past to get in and take the class. In the end we had to go through the offices at the back. We had no microphones at this point and our CD player struggled to be heard with so many people squashed into the room.

However, enough people enjoyed the evening for the manager to decide that we would put on regular classes, and we discovered that we were much in demand at other sites as well; for several years we did a Saturday evening session at Liskeard Leisure Centre. We gave ourselves a name, 'Moonshine', and put out flyers. Phil, the leisure centre manager for Launceston, also started to hire us out to schools.

In 1997 Pete entered the British Indoor Rowing Championships and persuaded me to enter as well. Fortunately for me this was divided into age categories, and I managed to scrape through to a gold medal. The following year, we went back again and this time it was a silver medal.

Sue introduced me to fitness weekends, which were available to fitness addicts and instructors. The ones we most liked to go to were run by a group called M-Brace Fitness. They used to take over holiday camps in their off season, for the weekend. Sue and I would rent a caravan along with other friends that wanted to come. Everything would kick off on the Friday evening with each of the presenters giving a fifteen-minute 'sample' of their class; that was exhausting on its own. The next day would start around 7.00am with a run (to be avoided if you could, but you wouldn't be allowed to because they would take the run through your caravan); then a short break for breakfast, followed by activities every hour for the rest of the day, finishing at around 5.00 or 5.30.

Montreal Olympic rowing medallist, Hugh Matheson presenting me with my silver medal.

Our shop.

Swim School Principal Chris.

Swimming Teacher Chris.

You were given a spreadsheet of activities with a choice of four or five different classes each hour. For instance, step might be in the area next to the pool, tai chi or yoga might be in the nightclub, and so on, with the instructors changing every hour. Aerobics and dance-related classes might be in one of the large halls, aqua aerobics and aqua tai chi would be in the pool; there were also other classes such as power stretching, circuits and nutrition. You needed to study the chart the night before and work out which classes you wanted to go to, and then it was a matter of running from class to class, trying to write notes when you could.

Sue and I always wanted to do the step classes run by Fitz (Fitzroy Gaynes) who had his own version of step called Step-a-Jam. These classes were so much fun that I would go to all of them: beginner, advanced, whatever, I didn't care. We also did the ones run by Delvin Clarke; and we discovered that with both of these instructors it was not enough just to turn up in time for the class – you needed to do the class that was on previously, because people who had been in those would stay on their steps and you wouldn't be able to find an available step to join in. Sometimes, if the instructor was very popular, then you might have to do the two previous classes...

Once the Saturday classes finished you had a shower, something to eat and then a rest; because then, in the evening, there was a party, often fancy dress and always involving a lot of dancing, which finished late, and then there might be an after party... and, of course, it was all repeated the next day (without the evening activities because you probably had to travel home). The whole thing was tremendous fun and hard work – my calves used to be like concrete by the time we had finished. There were often massage teams and you could book a session with them. I think I booked a massage every day!

Peter was an extremely able microscope salesman. He had even sold microscopes to NASA. However, this work involved a massive amount of driving, especially since we were now living in the depths of Devon. So, some years later when the village shop came up for sale, we decided to buy it; we thought that this could be a good change of direction and we fancied the challenge. The shop was sadly neglected, and we worked hard and turned it into a thriving little business, trying for an image of 'The Olde Curiosity Shoppe' and selling predominantly local and West Country produce. During our last few years there we made a speciality of bespoke hampers, and at Christmas we would average around seventy-five of them. On Christmas Eve we would give free sherry and mince pies to our customers and the shop would be heaving, with a party atmosphere.

During the time we were in the shop, Peter decided that he would like to get a World War Two Willys jeep. He found one he wanted – in Watford. One of the local farmers allowed him to borrow his trailer and the pair of them drove off to collect it. This became Pete's new hobby. It is a 1943 Willys jeep, which would have had an expected life in WW2 of six weeks. He stripped it down, serviced and painted it.

After about five years, we decided that it was time to sell the shop and take on other jobs. Our son Robin was working as a duty manager at the local swimming pool, Meadowlands in Tavistock, and he managed to get me a part-time job there. Of course, the manager had my CV, so I hadn't been there long before he asked if I would like to teach the aquafit class. Aquafit is like aerobics in the water, but there is more to it than that. I said that I would like to but I would need to do the proper training first, and this was arranged. Shortly afterwards I was asked if I would like to train as a swimming teacher... This was the beginning.

In the next town, Okehampton, the pool was being replaced by a new leisure centre called Parklands, and our manager was also the manager for this as well. He asked if I would like to be the studio coordinator for this site and organise the classes. This appealed to me. There are lots of opportunities in the leisure industry if you are prepared to train; at one time I was studio coordinator and studio instructor at Parklands and also swim school principal at both Meadowlands and Parklands. I was very busy, looking after both swim schools, teaching swimming, aquafit, aerobics, step and body balance on a regular basis and various private lessons and specialised classes. Eventually, this all became a bit too much and I was allowed to choose which site I wanted to stay with, but I had to give one up.

CHAPTER TWENTY-ONE

Back to the 1940s

Life's too short to drive a boring vehicle...

One day when Pete and I were in Tavistock, we saw a small convoy of World War Two military vehicles. The drivers were obviously friends; we got talking to them and discovered that they were a club – which, of course, Pete ended up joining. He would disappear to club meetings and take his jeep to events, eventually persuading me to get involved as well.

It's fun driving the jeep but you need to concentrate. The brakes are nothing like modern brakes and you need to leave a much longer stopping distance. The steering will wander given half a chance. The mirrors vibrate all the time, and there's no heating; if you put the canvas doors on then everything steams up; the rain comes down the inside of the windscreen as well as the outside; and the windscreen wipers are hand-driven. No mod cons at all – and you're sitting on the petrol tank!

One of the most scary things was when we crossed over to Cornwall on the Saltash ferry and we were last on, so we were on the sloping ramp with the motorbikes immediately behind us. I was holding on to the handbrake and praying that the brakes would hold until the bikes drove off. Thank goodness they did...

To begin with, the jeep was all that seemed necessary, but after a while we found that we felt out of place driving it around in ordinary clothes; so after that we wore green military gear. We gradually started wearing more and more uniform as we got involved with big events where it was really requested.

After a few years, Pete decided that he also wanted to get a 1943 Dodge Command Car. This was great fun. It was like a very big jeep, and a bit of a challenge to drive as it had crash gears. Having a trusting, liberated husband, I was allowed to drive it – a bit of an honour given that the previous owner hadn't allowed his wife behind the wheel. It was hard work; two and a half tons of armoured metal which could reach speeds of sixty miles an hour with 1940s brakes, no seat belts and wartime lights. The engine had a fabulous sound. However, there was one small improvement on the jeep: vacuum windscreen wipers – although they did have the disadvantage of slowing down when you went uphill. It wasn't quite the same as driving a Lotus Elan, but definitely needed driving skills. It did mean that I would have a vehicle to drive whenever we went to an event, as we would often take both and part of the fun of having these vehicles is the driving of them. Pete didn't mind me driving his babies, although he did buy me an off-road driving course as a birthday present...

At the military vehicle events everyone tries to educate the public on the history of their vehicle, and we also learned a lot from veterans who would visit. Pete would put out information regarding the Command Car; in his research he discovered that the vehicle was built for the use of commanding officers, but they quickly decided that they preferred a jeep as the Dodge would be a target for enemy snipers. The only commander who liked the vehicle was General George Patton – and he had a fleet of them. So Pete made a mannequin of General Patton who could sit in the back of the vehicle, or even stand up if you tied his hands to the rail. This was great except his head frequently fell off when we were driving around, and our friends would laughingly pick it up and return it to us.

We found that if we put the model in a chair next to the Dodge when we were in camp, he created a lot of interest with visitors, and people would want their photo taken with him; so Pete decided that he would acquire the correct uniform and become 'General Patton'. I would have to drive, as generals have a driver; fortunately, General Patton's driver was a lady.

We have been involved with the Military Vehicle Trust for many years now, and have taken part in big events such as the War and Peace Show and also the Normandy D-Day Commemorations. One year we went to Normandy and also on to Falaise; in total we drove twelve hundred miles on that trip. There is a

Riding the steam train at the Buckfastleigh show. You get a free ride if you are in uniform.

The Veterans Parade at Weymouth during 'Armour & Embarkation' 2012. 'George Patton' with his lady driver and three re-enactors making us look good.

Visiting the beach at Arromanches on 5th June 2009 as everyone is preparing for the 65th anniversary of D-Day (the following day).

114 UXB

POLICE

Anytime Now!

Anytime Now!
TFF 369

recognised medical condition, known about since World War Two: 'jeep bum' – ouch! – and we know all about it.

As we have got older we decided that it would be sensible to sell the Command Car; it was beginning to be a bit of a struggle to maintain because it was so big. We still have the jeep, although we are not as keen on camping as we used to be.

I loved teaching swimming and specialised in teaching disabled adults and children, and nervous adults. However, one day, while staying with friends, I suffered a heart attack. I took this as a warning and gradually gave up regular work and retired from my job at the pool. It is so easy to carry on with your life as if nothing will ever change; but it does, and all the time your body gets older. There comes a time when you realise that life is limited and now is the time to enjoy every moment. I needed to concentrate on my own health.

The heart doctor had advised regular exercise, and I managed to convince him that my chosen exercise was going to be swimming. My knees are now too dodgy, and my back complains if it has to stay upright for any length of time, so regular walks are best avoided. So I make myself have three swimming sessions a week and swim a mile each time; so far, so good.

We have recently moved to a bungalow on the edge of Tavistock. Life is different now. There is a bus service every hour, instead of twice a week which is what it was in the village where we used to live! If we wanted to we could have takeaway food delivered to our door, although I must admit we haven't tried that yet. My time now is spent doing my regular swimming, working on the garden when the weather allows me, a variety of sewing and knitting projects and sometimes, when asked, getting involved in various judo-related events.

CHAPTER TWENTY-TWO
The Last Word

Sore made* *('That is all').
Judo refereeing term

Looking back, a lot has changed for women during my life. When I was a child, women were not considered equal to men. Women have had to push and push to be allowed the same opportunities. Even when I was an adult it was extremely difficult to be accepted for a mortgage. In the judo world, women started off with no competition at all; then the first women's championship was held without the public because it was considered indecent; and then, when we had the first international championships for women, we had to have a doctor's note to say that we were female, not pregnant, and fit to do judo. We also had our championships on different days to the men. *Now* the championships for men and women are held on the same day at the same place – and a mixed team, of men and women, is suggested for the next Olympics. With stunt work, too, there was a lot of resistance to women doing stunts to begin with but now it is quite acceptable. We *are* progressing. To be absolutely honest, I wonder if the fact that women had to fight so hard to be recognised might have helped me, because it gave me a fierce desire to prove that we ladies are just as able as the men.

My personal battle was in the field of competition judo. I wanted to be given the opportunity to compete on the same level as the men. We ladies fought to be allowed to fight. Very gradually the barriers came down.

Other women were fighting for equality in other aspects of judo, for instance, refereeing. To begin with, most of the judo hierarchy considered women referees to be inferior and a bit of a joke. These ladies had their own battle trying to get recognised as worthwhile referees.

One lady, Belinda Petty, was a regular in my ladies class at the Budokwai. She reached the grade of Second Dan and developed an interest in refereeing. She became very competent and wanted to get involved in refereeing the big events. She found that she was limited to ladies' events; and that, although men could referee ladies' events, the reverse was not true – ladies were not allowed to referee men's events. So, even though Belinda had all the necessary qualifications, she was only allowed to referee women's national championships. Eventually, this was extended to all male events at area and club level. She was not allowed to referee at national events such as the All England men's competition. The feeble excuse for this was that she might not be strong enough to interfere at times of danger. This was the start of a three-year battle for Belinda which culminated in an industrial tribunal, by a unanimous vote, finding the British Judo Association guilty of sex discrimination. Belinda now has the right to referee at top men's events. The court decision has also affected the way women are treated in other sports besides judo.

Rusty Kanokogi in the USA battled for equality and justice for women in judo in her own way using the law courts. It was due to Rusty that the first Women's World Championships were held in 1988.

The Avengers has developed a momentum of its own. It has become cult viewing and is now being shown all over the world at any time of the day. There is a massive fan base of people who love the show. It has withstood the test of time, probably because it is quality-made. It always used the latest technology, well-known actors wanted to work on it, and we had the finest directors, designers and writers. It is quite something to think that a programme that we worked on so long ago has been constantly watched and enjoyed all these years, collecting new fans all the time. *The Avengers* has been a very important part of my life and I have enjoyed every minute.

What I have always loved about film work is that every day is different. You can never be sure about

* Pronounced So-re ma-de

Left: Belinda Petty refereeing at a competition.

Right: Rusty Kanokogi known as the 'Mother of Women's Judo'.

what will be involved, so each day is fresh. Apart from all the stunt doubling, I have also been asked to play small parts and I have been: a nun, a Hell's Angel, a witch, a tart, a hag, a nurse, a crinolined lady, a corpse, a bodyguard, a New York cop, a bouncer, an alien, an Indian dancer, a mud wrestler and numerous everyday people. I can also say that Roger Moore has 'caught' me in his arms (*Crossplot*), I have fought with Paul Newman (*The Mackintosh Man*), carried Peter Sellers on my shoulders (*The Pink Panther Strikes Again*), shared a bath with Dennis Waterman (*Minder*) and have been mud wrestling with David Soul (*The Stick Up*)... It has all been fun.

APPENDIX ONE
Film and Television work

This list is not totally complete. Some of my records have been lost (for example, I worked on *The Goodies* many times but don't have a list of all the episode titles) so I have had to rely on my memory... and I know I've missed a few. There were also various safety films, TV commercials and TV interviews which I have not recorded.

1966-67 ***The Avengers*** (TV series) Regular stunt double on colour series for Diana Rigg and other people as necessary

1966 ***The Baron*** (TV series) Stunt performer

1967 ***Hammerhead*** (film) Stunt double for Diana Dors

1967 ***The Mercenaries*** (film, a.k.a. Dark of the Sun) Stunt nun

1967 ***The Prisoner*** (TV series, ep. 'Hammer Into Anvil') Stunt performer

1967-69 ***The Avengers*** (TV series) Regular stunt double for Linda Thorson for entire series and other people as necessary

1969 ***Arthur, Arthur*** (film) Stunt double for Margaret Courtenay

1969 ***Captain Nemo and the Underwater City*** (film) Stunt artiste

1969 ***Chitty Chitty Bang Bang*** (film) Stunt performer and stunt double for Anna Quayle

1969 ***Crossplot*** (film)Stunt double

1969 ***Randall & Hopkirk*** (deceased) (TV series) Stunt performer

1969 ***The Saint*** (TV series) Stunt performer

1970 ***No Blade of Grass*** (film) Stunt Hell's Angel

1970? ***Barclays Bank*** film 'Watch It' Stunt performer

1970 ***The Man Who Had Power Over Women*** (film) Stunt artiste

1970-71 ***UFO*** (TV series):

1970 – ep. 'The Psychobombs' Stunt double for Deborah Grant

1971 – ep. 'The Dalotek Affair' a.k.a. 'Crater 236'

1971 – ep. 'Timelash' Stunt double for Wanda Ventham

1971 ***The Persuaders*** (TV series, ep. 'To The Death, Baby') Stunt double for Jennie Linden

1972 ***Virgin Witch*** (film) Stunt double

1972 ***Assignment: Munich*** (film) Stunt double

1972 ***Our Miss Fred*** (film) Stunt performer

1972 ***Pope Joan*** (film) Stunt nun

1972 ***Spyder's Web*** (TV series) Stunt double

1972 ***The Protectors*** (TV series) Stunt artiste

1972 ***All Coppers Are*** (film) Stunt performer

1973 ***The Goodies*** (TV series, ep. 'Camelot') Stunt artiste

1973 ***The Mackintosh Man*** (film) Stunt double

1974 ***Alfie Darling*** (film) Stunt driver

1974 ***Brannigan*** (film) Stunt pub customer

1975 ***I'm Not Feeling Myself Tonight*** (film) Stunt artiste

1975 ***Return of the Pink Panther*** (film) Stunt performer and stunt double for Catherine Schell

1975 ***Royal Flash*** (film)Stunt Victorian tart

1975 ***Side by Side*** (film) Stunt performer

1975 ***The Romantic Rebellion*** (film) Stunt citizen

1976 C***entral Office of Information:*** 'Flashing Mirror' Stunt performer

1976 ***Pardon My Genie*** (TV series, ep. 'Travel by Sleeper') Stunt artiste

1976 ***Boeing 747 life raft safety film*** Stunt aircraft passenger

1976 ***Space 1999*** (TV series):

1976 – ep. 'Space Warp' Stunt double for Barbara Bain

1976 – ep. 'Devil's Moon' Guard and stunt double

1976 – ep. 'Bringers of Wonder' Stunt double for Catherine Schell

1976 ***The Pink Panther Strikes Again*** (film) Stunt bouncer and stunt geisha

1976 ***Thriller*** (TV series, ep. 'Ladykiller')

1976-77 ***The New Avengers*** (TV series) Stunt arranger for the series
– ep. 'The Midas Touch' Stunt double for Joanna Lumley
– ep. 'The House of Cards' Stunt double for Joanna Lumley
– ep. 'Gnaws' Stunt double for Joanna Lumley
– ep. 'The Last of the Cybernauts...?'
– ep. 'Sleeper' Stunt double for Joanna Lumley
– ep. 'Obsession'
– ep. 'Trap'
– ep. 'Hostage'
– ep. 'Angels of Death'
– ep. 'Dirtier by the Dozen'
– ep. 'To Catch a Rat'
– ep. 'Cat Amongst the Pigeons'
– ep. 'Faces'
– ep. 'Tale of the Big Why'
1977 ***Eustace & Hilda*** (TV series) Stunt artiste
1977 ***Gangsters*** (TV)
1977 ***ICI safety film***: 'Have a Nice Day Dear' Stunt artiste
1977 ***Revenge of the Pink Panther*** (film) Stunt performer
1977 ***The Stick Up*** (film, a.k.a. Mud) The Amazon Lady
1977-79 ***The Goodies*** (TV series):
– ep. 'Scoutrageous' Stunt performer
– ep. 'War Babies' Stunt performer
– ep. 'Kitten Kong' Stunt performer
1978 ***Sherlock Holmes*** (TV series) Stunt performer
1978 ***Blake's 7*** (TV series, ep. 'Project Avalon') Stunt alien
1978 ***Hanover Street*** (film) Stunt passer-by
1978 ***Superman*** (film) Stunt passer-by
1978 ***The London Affair*** (film) Stunt double
1978 ***The Revenge of the Pink Panther*** (film) Stunt performer
1979 ***Grange Hill*** (TV series) Stunt arranger
1979 ***Murder by Decree*** (film) Stunt artiste
1979 ***Superman II*** (film) Stunt passer-by
1980 ***Caleb Williams*** (TV series) Stunt performer
1980 ***Dragonslayer*** (film) Stunt villager
1980 ***For Your Eyes Only*** (film) Stunt artiste & stunt double for Cassandra Harris & Carole Bouquet
1980 ***Hammer House of Horror*** (TV series, ep. 'Rude Awakening') Stunt performer
1980 ***Minder*** (TV series, ep. 'A Nice Little Wine') 'Jo' (named role)
1980 ***Pobol y Cwm*** (TV series) Stunt driver
1980 ***Servowarm Central Heating Commercial***: 'Deferred Credit' Stunt performer
1980 ***Shaan*** (film) Stunt artiste and stunt double
1980 ***A Tale of Two Cities*** (film) Stunt performer
1980 ***The Enigma Files*** (TV series, ep. 'The Fit Up') Stunt performer
1981 ***Venom*** (film) Stunt artiste
1982 ***Coronation Street*** (TV series) Stunt artiste
1982 ***Curse of the Pink Panther*** (film) Stunt artiste
1982 ***The Sender*** (film) Stunt nurse
1982 ***Trail of the Pink Panther*** (film) Stunt artiste
1982 ***Servowarm Central Heating Commercial***: 'Question Time' Stunt performer
1983 ***Driving Ambition*** (TV series) Stunt driving double for Anne Carroll
1983 ***Robin of Sherwood*** (TV series) Stunt villager
1983 ***Space Riders*** (film) Stunt performer
1983 ***Supergirl*** (film) Stunt performer
1984 ***Pioneer Stereo*** (TV commercial)
1986 ***Three Kinds of Heat*** (film) 'Buyer' and stunt double for Victoria Barrett & Shakti Chen
1992 ***Without Walls*** (TV series, ep. 'The Avengers') Archive footage from *The Avengers*
1998 **The Avengers - The Journey Back** self
1999 ***Funny Turns*** (TV series, ep. 'Penelope Keith') Archive footage from *The Avengers*
2000 ***Avenging the Avengers*** self

APPENDIX TWO
Judo Achievements

18.8.63	First Kyu. Graded by Ken Maynard at local club
	Joined the Budokwai
8.9.64	First Dan. Graded by C. Palmer (Fifth Dan) & A. Sweeney (Fourth Dan), at the Budokwai
7.9.65	Second Dan. Graded by C. Palmer (Fifth Dan) & K. Watanabe (Fifth Dan), at the Budokwai
1966	First Team Championships – Silver in Northern Home Counties Team
1968-76	Budokwai Ladies' Instructor
1970	Kata Championships with Chris Wildman (two gold medals: for Nage-no-Kata and Ju-no-Kata)
7.3.71	Third Dan. Promoted by the Promotion Sub-Committee
1971	Team Championships – Gold in London Area Team
	First British Open Championships: Heavy weight +70kg – Gold, Open – Bronze
1972	German Whitsun Tournament – Gold
	Italian Open (St Vincent) – Gold
	British Open +68kg – Gold
	Became a Senior Examiner
1973	Swiss Open – Gold
	German Open – Gold
	Italian Grand Prix – Gold
	British Open in two categories: Heavy weight +68kg – Gold, Open – Gold
	Anne Swinton trophy for Best Player of the British Open
	Pam Hogg trophy – Personality of the Year
7.3.74	Fourth Dan. Promoted by the Promotion Sub-Committee
1974	Team Championships – Gold in London Area Team
	Dutch Open – Gold
	British Open: Heavyweight +72kg – Gold
	Coppa Europa (European Tournament) – Gold
	Dame Enid Russell-Smith Trophy for services to women's judo
	Became Assistant General Secretary of the BJA; joined Women's Sub-Committee
1975	British Open: Heavyweight +72kg – Gold
	First Official European Championships – Gold
	Mentioned in the Guinness Book of Records as most women's British titles. This stood until 1991.
1976	Retired from competition
	Became Assistant Team Manager & Coach to the British Women's Squad
	Vic Terry Trophy for Personality of the Year
1977	Joined Promotions Panel
	Given Life Membership of BJA
	Given Honorary Membership of the Budokwai
25.5.78	Fifth Dan. Promoted by the Promotion Sub-Committee
25.5.83	Sixth Dan. Promoted by the Promotion Sub-Committee
	Mentioned in the Guinness Book of Records as highest women's grade
29.1.98	Seventh Dan. Promoted by the Promotion Sub-Committee

Acknowledgements

I wish to thank my husband, Peter, for all his encouragement, support and help in writing this book.

I also owe a huge debt to the Budokwai: to all those people who taught and advised me, and the members who practised with me.

I would like to thank the following people for allowing me to use their photos:
- The family of Terence Donovan – archive@terencedonovan.co.uk
- The family of Peter O'Donnell
- Marion Woodard for allowing me to use her husband Graham's photographs
- Dave Finch © Copyright photos by Dave Finch

Many thanks also to Joanna Lumley, Brian Jacks and Liz Viney MBE for giving some of their precious time to write words to introduce this book.

Thanks go to my friend, Dave Rogers, the author of many Avengers books who inspired and encouraged me.

I would also like to thank the following people for their help and support:
- Paul Ajala
- Bruce Blakesee
- Chris Bentley
- Dick Fiddy (British Film Institute)
- John Pinnell
- Dino Armagan (AVA Sports)
- Massimo Moretti and Studio Canal
- Mark Witherspoon for all his hard work in creating the cover for this book

... and all those friends and family who have been interested and encouraged me.

The Big Class Racing Yachts

John Leather

STANFORD MARITIME
LONDON

Stanford Maritime Limited
Member Company of the George Philip Group
12–14 Long Acre London WC2E 9LP
Editor Phoebe Mason

First published in Great Britain 1982

Set in Monophoto Ehrhardt 453 10/11 by
Tameside Filmsetting Limited, Ashton-u-Lyne, Lancashire
Printed in Great Britain by
Butler & Tanner Limited, Frome and London

British Library Cataloguing in Publication Data
Leather, John
The big class racing yachts.
1. Yacht racing – History
I. Title
797.1′4 GV826.5

ISBN 0-540-07417-9

Jacket painting by N. Sotheby Pitcher
'His Majesty's Yacht *Britannia* Training at Cowes, 1913'
Watercolour, sold at Bonhams in 1982
Reproduced by kind permission of Bonhams, Montpelier Galleries,
Montpelier Street, Knightsbridge, London SW7 1HH

Other books by John Leather

Gaff Rig
The Northseamen
Clinker Boatbuilding
Panorama of Gaff Rig (with Roger Smith)
World Warships in Review 1860–1906
Modern Developments in Yacht Design (with David Cannell)
Spritsails and Lugsails
The Sailor's Coast
The Salty Shore
Sail and Oar
Colin Archer and the Seaworthy Double-ender

Introduction to the Big Class

Extraordinary size and exceptional speed are a fascinating combination and, more than forty years after the big-class yachts last raced, people are still intrigued by their complexity and majesty.

Big-yacht racing existed in Britain from the end of the eighteenth century until 1937, in America from the 1880s until 1937, and in Germany from 1891 to 1914. These three were the only nations to sail racers of the largest size. In Britain large yachts first raced at regattas, and occasionally in match races, during the summer – principally on the east and south coasts and sometimes on the Welsh coast. The tradition of medium and large sized racing yachts competing in a round of fixtures has its origins in the late 1840s, and by the 1870s it was a firmly established custom. Commencing with the Thames matches in May, the racing fleet worked its way through a full season's programme of regattas organized by yacht clubs, which provided the prize money. From the Thames it was 'down Swin' to Harwich regatta, 'up Swin' to the Thames mouth, and then the Nore to Dover, Dover to Ostend, perhaps Dover to Calais, then round to the Solent for racing inside, and sometimes outside, the Isle of Wight. After that they would go west down the Channel, round Land's End, and up the Irish Sea to Liverpool, to Barrow, on to the Clyde perhaps for a fortnight's racing, and back towards the south coast. They also visited regattas at Belfast Lough, Kingstown, Queenstown (Cork) and perhaps at Penzance and Falmouth. Then came the Solent and Cowes Week and after that, in later years, regattas at Bournemouth, Weymouth, Torbay and Dartmouth; the latter were held towards the end of the season early in September, after which the racers were laid up at their various home ports, usually where their skippers lived.

As their passage making was usually under trysail and headsails, and in all conditions, and the yachts covered several thousand miles each summer, they were often hard pushed to arrive on time at some fixtures. Occasionally a racer in a hurry set her mainsail, perhaps an old one, and achieved a fast passage. On August 29, 1898 *Yachting World* reported:

> The *Satanita*, with Sir Maurice Fitzgerald on board, made a record passage from Land's End to Valencia [in southern Ireland] last week doing the distance, about 250 miles, in twenty hours. The storm on Wednesday night was terrific but the big yawl carried her mainsail all through the night, and logged an average of over 12 knots.

From the mid-1890s to the early 1900s a few British large-class racers sailed out for a series of winter regattas on the Riviera, leaving in February and returning in late April to refit for the British season. Heavy weather was often encountered in the Bay of Biscay and the Gulf of Lyon. The racing at Nice, Cannes and other resorts was keen and welcomed by owners and crews as an extension of the racing year. The regattas coincided with the fashionable Riviera winter season, and racing was organized by French clubs such as the Société Nautique de Cannes and Nice Club Nautique, which provided generous prizes and also offered racing for smaller yachts. This pleasant interlude died out around 1903. Typically, the season commenced with races at Nice at the end of February, then moved to regattas at Menton and San Remo in early March, Monaco in mid-March, and concluded with the Cannes regattas in late March and early April, after which the yachts sailed for England.

By the 1930s the British big class was largely restricted to the east and south coast regattas but short forays were made across the English Channel to race at Le Havre, Deauville and Trouville in mid-season; the 12 Metre class also participated at these fixtures.

In America large-yacht racing took place in the East Coast states of New York, Connecticut, Rhode Island, Massachusetts, New Jersey and occasionally Maine – all within reach of the metropolitan centres where many of their owners had business interests. The American season tended to be shorter than in Britain, but the racing was no less keen. The round of regattas attracting large racers was less formal, and the ebb and flow of interest in this class was substantially influenced by the defence of the America's Cup. Won in 1851 by the schooner *America* on a course round the Isle of Wight against British yachts and subsequently instituted as a challenge cup, it has been successfully defended twenty-three times by the New York Yacht Club: the Cup is still yachting's most prestigious trophy. During the period covered by this book the large American sloops, equivalent to the British cutters, were built principally to contend for the Cup defence. Most other large American racers were rigged as schooners, and many of them were particularly beautiful.

Major regattas were held at Larchmont, New York in June and July, when Larchment Week attracted a large entry in all classes. But perhaps the principal event of the American yacht-racing season was the annual August 'cruise' of the New York Yacht Club, eastwards from the home waters near New York; this commemorated the first cruise, held in 1844. This week or ten-day event involved passage races from port to port as well as major regattas at Newport, Rhode Island and also often at Marblehead. By order of the Commodore, yachts of club members gathered at a port in Long Island Sound and for up to ten days competed in passage races; the fleet of sailing, cruising, steam and later motor yachts accompanied them in the journey to various ports along the coast. Sometimes the fleet went eastward round Cape Cod to visit Provincetown and Marblehead. Invariably they arrived at Newport for a major regatta where the prizes were valuable challenge cups.

Typically, the fleet assembled at New London; then there was a passage race and cruise in company to Newport where the Astor and the King's Cup were sailed for, and on the next leg they went to Vineyard Haven, off the southern Massachusetts coast. They then sailed for Provincetown on the tip of Cape Cod, every passage being raced by large and medium sized yachts, and from there to Marblehead, home of the influential Eastern Yacht Club, for a combined regatta. Sometimes the cruise ended there and the yachts dispersed, some returning westwards towards Long Island Sound, others cruising eastwards to the coasts of New Hampshire and Maine before returning for laying up.

Germany had no tradition of racing large yachts and little of other pleasure sailing until the early 1890s, when the Emperor Wilhelm II bought the ex-British racing cutter *Thistle*, built in 1887 as an America's Cup challenger under Scottish skipper John Barr, and renamed her *Meteor*. He encouraged German noblemen and business magnates to own large yachts and did everything possible to help Germans to take up sailing in craft of all sizes. This was principally to engender interest in maritime affairs and stimulate interest and approval for his ideas of naval expansion, but it was perhaps also an attempt to transform the series of regattas known as Kiel Week into a spectacle which might rival Cowes Week. Kiel Week embraced a programme of regattas and passage racing stretching from the river Elbe, on the North Sea coast, to Swinemunde on the Baltic coast of Germany. The series of events was organized by the Norddeutscher Regatta Verein of Hamburg, the Imperial Yacht Club of Kiel and the Lübecker Yacht Club of Lübeck. This season of midsummer racing, which was intended to attract British first-class and other racers as well as some American yachts, usually commenced in mid-June with a regatta on the Elbe at Cuxhaven. It was followed by the racing fleet's passage through the Kiel Canal to a series of regattas at Kiel, an ocean match from Kiel to Eckernförde in Schleswig-Holstein, and a handicap race back to Kiel. An ocean match from Kiel to Travemunde was followed by a regatta, then a race to Warnemunde and another from Travemunde to Swinemunde, where the 'week' ended early in July. There was also racing for smaller rating class yachts and for cruisers of all sizes.

Everything possible was done to induce foreign yachts to compete. To attract British participation, the German Emperor instituted the Heligoland Gold Cup Race from Dover to the island of Heligoland, off the German North Sea coast. The event succeeded in attracting many yachts, at first a mixed bag of large cruisers and a few fast cruising yachts. Later some large racing schooners and yawls participated, including *Susanne*, *Meteor*, *Germania*, *Cicely*, *Navahoe*, *Valdora* and *Hamburg*.

Inevitably the large German racers became dependent on the British racing programme, and the first three *Meteor*s were skippered and manned by English crews, and the first two were designed and built in Britain. The American designed and built *Meteor III* of 1902 was the last foreign-built large German racer, and after 1907 the German designer Max Oertz developed several large schooners for notable owners, including the Kaiser, and these gradually came to be skippered and manned by Germans.

The term 'rating rules' refers to the various rules governing measurement of yachts to ensure that they conformed to class requirements. A rating might be expressed in feet or metres and was obtained from measurements of the yacht made by the official measurer or declared by her designer. They included the waterline length and the sail area of specified sails and usually many other factors such as displacement, half-girth of the hull at various positions, maximum and minimum breadths, depths, draft, length of overhangs; there were also restrictive measurements to check undesirable trends in hull or rig design and sometimes specified minimum weight of masts, minimum accommodation requirements and so on. Various bodies established, administered and frequently reviewed the rules, in Britain the Yacht Racing Association which after 1906 acted in conjunction with the International Yacht Racing Union for those racing in classes which had an 'international rating'. In America the situation was different, with many of the larger yacht clubs rating yachts under their own, sometimes conflicting, rules. The subject is covered in more detail below.

The speeds attained by the large racers are frequently speculated upon, and an average for the 90 ft waterline cutters of the 1890s, such as *Britannia*, *Meteor* and *Shamrock (I)*, was 14 to 14½ knots, reaching in a fresh breeze. The schooner *Rainbow* was credited with 16 knots on a reach in the Channel in 1898. The large racing yachts built in Britain and America after 1929 under the American J Class rules had a much smaller sail area than the old cutters and schooners and generally only attained about 11½ to 12 knots.

This survey of large racing yachts starts in 1893 because for several years before that very few were built, and British and American yachtsmen were apprehensive about the effect that the existing rating rules would have on the sport. Suddenly, late in 1892, two large cutters were ordered in Britain and an equally large sloop in America; the intentions of the owners in both countries were to cross the Atlantic to challenge for various cups. Their unusual hull forms were very exciting: a long, overhanging bow and stern, a deep fin keel and concentrated ballast, a healthy beam and a powerful three-headsail cutter rig (called a sloop in America). Enthusiasm mounted and within a few months nine first-class racing yachts were ordered in the two countries. All these proved to be graceful and advanced in design, surpassing their predecessors whose clipper or plumb bows and longer keel profiles had developed under the influence of earlier rating rules. The hull form of these great yachts closely resembled that of the many recently evolved small rating classes. They promised speed and ability but were regarded by many as 'machines', while others condemned their graceful overhangs as 'ugly' – such is fashion.

In Britain the building boom commenced when the Earl of Dunraven commissioned George Watson to design a new cutter which would be named *Valkyrie II* and was to challenge for the America's Cup in 1893. On hearing of this, the Prince of Wales, later King Edward VII, commissioned another first-class cutter from Watson, and further down the Clyde William Fife (III) received an order for the big cutter *Calluna*; while at Southampton Joseph Soper was instructed to design the mighty *Satanita*. In America, the steel-hulled *Jubilee* was designed by John B. Paine, son of the owner General Paine, and built by George Lawley & Son at Boston. She was the largest fin-keel yacht then built and had two centreboards, a small board being fitted in the bow. However, she was unsuccessful. Stewart & Binney, who had taken over the yacht-design business of Edward Burgess after his death in 1891, received an order to design the *Pilgrim* and Nathanael G. Herreshoff was to produce two large sloops, *Navahoe* and *Colonia*. All these great yachts came out for the season of 1893, which must stand as the most exicting in the sport's history; the excitement was enhanced when Herreshoff received a further order for the big sloop *Vigilant* early in 1893. Of these designers, Herreshoff, Soper, Paine and Stewart & Binney had not previously designed a large racing yacht, though most had experienced success in smaller classes.

From that season of 1893 until 1937 the big-class cutters, sloops and a few yawls and schooners dominated the headlines in yachting and the activities and achievements of their owners, designers, builders, captains and crews became public knowledge, particularly during the contests for the America's Cup – all of which involved a British challenger sailing across the Atlantic to meet an American defender. But most of the intervening summers, except when Britain, Germany and America were at war, saw a fleet of big-class racers active in the regular round of the yachting year in Britain and America, and in the German Baltic regattas from the mid-1890s until 1914. The first-class racing cutters and sloops of this period were of similar dimensions throughout though sail areas and rigs varied considerably. Some notable larger schooners of different dizes were also built.

The evolution of the large racing yacht extended over 150 years, from the 1780s until its abrupt end in 1937. It included yachts of many types, hull forms and rigs, designed and built to various rating rules, and would need a complicated and fascinating study of many volumes to describe fully. This book is restricted to a pictorial glance at some aspects of the large racers of Britain, America and Germany between 1893 and 1937 – the period of the flowering of the greatest racers. Contemporary photography enables us to comprehend them accurately.

Whatever may be thought of the social conditions which produced the concentrated wealth encouraging their conception, the way problems concerning the frequent extremes of their design, construction and maintenance were overcome remains a striking and intriguing aspect of yachting. It required considerable technical ability and superb helmsmanship and seamanship if success was to be achieved. As a spectacle, these yachts remain unsurpassed and the impression of their speed, size and majesty lives on for generations who never saw them. My excuse for writing this book is that these yachts have fascinated me since, as a youngster in the little Essex maritime village of Rowhedge during the 1930s and 1940s, I knew some of their skippers and hands. Indeed, many of them were relatives of mine, and I heard much of the craft and experiences of the professionals who manned these yachts. This now-vanished breed of seafarers were specialists with a fund of sailing knowledge.

Rating Measurement Rules

The Yacht Racing Association was formed in Britain in 1875 with individual yachtsmen and twenty yacht clubs as members, but the prestigious Royal Yacht Squadron, Royal Thames Yacht Club and New Thames Yacht Club remained aloof for some years, being content to continue with their own system of time scales for rating allowances. The Y.R.A. adopted the existing Thames Tonnage rule of: Length on deck from fore side of stem to after side of sternpost × Breadth over plank amidships (or greatest breadth) × $\frac{1}{2}$ Breadth, all divided by 94 = Tonnage. Classes of 5, 10, 15, 20, 40, 80 and over 80 tons were formed for racing and flourished for a time. In 1878 this rule was amended to measure length on the waterline instead of length on deck. Under earlier rules this factor of the formula had restricted British racing yachts to a plumb stem but after 1881 designers were free to indulge in other forms of bow and in 1880 the fast 10-tonner *Buttercup* came out with a clipper stem, the appearance of which caused as much consternation as the rounded stems of the large yachts of 1893 were to do. Before this, yachts had been designed for racing within the constraints of a rule which forced them to have a plumb stem to obtain the longest waterline length. The breadth on deck could be little more than the breadth at the waterline so as to obtain the maximum stability from form of hull in which beam carried a heavy penalty and the need to place the ballast keel as low as possible resulted in a long, straight and almost level keel.

In 1881 the rule was amended to: Add the breadth to the length and multiply the sum thus obtained by itself and by the breadth, then divide the product by 1730 and the quotient should be the Tonnage in tons and hundreds of a ton. This rule caused the building of even longer and narrower racing yachts in Britain and it soon began to become unpopular.

In 1886 a new formula was adopted, at first rather hesitently as it appeared dangerously simple and it included sail area. It was

$$L \times SA \div 6000 = \text{Rating (as a number)}.$$

Large British racers (and all small ones) of the period up to a change of rating rule in 1896 were designed and built to this simple formula which became known as the Length and Sail Area Rule. It was explored rather timidly at first, but when the plate and bulb keel small 'Raters' appeared in the early 1890s in America and in Britain their snub overhanging bows, counter sterns and rather dish-like sections were to influence the minds of designers of larger racers and one of the early results was an increase in beam in larger racers, allowing masts to be stayed without having to use channels to gain increased spread and also affording generous deck space, which improved sail handling and sheeting arrangements.

Despite the new rule large-yacht racing in Britain was listless for another seven years and consisted of a 'menagerie' class of craft racing on time allowance, which has never been satisfactory to owners, skippers, crews or designers. In 1886 the season was supported by the same larger racers which had battled against each other in the summer round of the British coastal regattas. Principal among them were the cutters *Irex* 85 tons and *Marjorie* 68 tons and the yawl *Wendur* 128 tons. The cutter *Genesta* 80 tons and the similar sized *Lorna*, *Erycina*, *Marguerite* and *Vanduara* also raced at times while the new steel cutter *Galatea*, designed and built in 1886 to race for the America's Cup, was a failure.

The new rule took effect in the Cup challenger *Thistle*, designed by G. L. Watson for a Scottish syndicate headed by James Bell. She was built of steel by the shipbuilding yard of D. & W. Henderson of Glasgow, who were to build many large racing and other yachts designed by Watson. This graceful clipper bowed cutter was 108.05 ft overall length, 86.46 ft waterline length, 20.03 ft beam and 13.8 ft draft. Displacement was 138 tons of which ballast weight was 62 tons in her lead keel and a small amount of internal trimming. She beat *Irex* and *Genesta* but not too convincingly, and failed to beat the American sloop *Volunteer*. Extraordinary secrecy was preserved during her building, launching and completion but she was not particularly radical other than being well rounded in underwater profile and of course shaped to minimize wetted surface, consistent with adequate lateral plane. She rated at 120. *Thistle* raced with the British large class in 1890 and had the best record for the season against the new *Iverna* which was designed by Alexander Richardson of Liverpool, then a noted designer of racers and other larger yachts, to replace another of his designs, the cutter *Irex*, both owned by John Jameson who was the most knowledgeable owner of a large racer of that time. Her other competitors in the continuing mixed size big class included the successful *Yarana* (62 rating) owned by Paul Ralli and the first *Valkyrie*, owned by the Earl of Dunraven.

In 1891 and 1892 *Iverna* was the best yacht in the class, which in 1892 consisted of only her and *Thistle*, which had been bought by the German Emperor and renamed *Meteor*. During these doldrum years the best sport was in the yachts of moderate and small size, particularly in the 20- and 40-raters. In these craft the hull form was advancing rapidly under the new rule, in which the removal of restriction of beam resulted in the hull sections gradually becoming of the 'wineglass' shape now regarded as 'classic' but which was then advanced. By the early 1890s this had extended to the fairly large racing yachts of the 40-rating class; about 75 ft long overall and in some of which the long and graceful counter was balanced by the rounded outreaching stem and well cut away forefoot. These features were to be further developed in the surprising number of large racers ordered in winter of 1892–3 in which the designers incorporated the lessons learned from smaller yachts in their various interpretations both in Britain and America to produce some of the most attractive racing yachts ever built.

New racers for the big class continued to be built with enthusiasm until the rating rule was changed in 1896. *Ailsa* came out in 1895 as did the semi-racer *Hester*, a smaller yacht than the first-class racers which was allowed to race with them on time allowance. By then the Length and Sail Area Rule had developed faults, particularly in that the yachts were being designed with too little displacement and, in the smaller classes, little space below. It was encouraging light displacement craft with deep fin keels and fairly hard bilges and a tendency to fuller bows. Accordingly, in 1895 the Length and Sail Area Rule was superseded by the Linear Rating Rule, principally devised by the British hydrodynamicist William Froude, who took much interest in racing yacht form besides his memorable work on larger ships. The formula was $\frac{1}{2}$ (L + B + 0.75 G + 0.5 SA) = Linear Rating. Factor G was the girth of the hull including all keel, from waterline to waterline at a position 0.6 of the waterline length from the stem. This was measured by a tape in contact with the outside planking of the yacht. The new classes were 18, 24, 30, 36, 42, 52, 65 and over 65 Linear Rating; this approximated to their waterline length in feet. Several large British yachts were designed and built to this rule but by the turn of the century British large-class racing was again at a low ebb and included yachts much smaller than *Britannia*, *Satanita*, *Ailsa* and their contemporaries, and the sport declined for some years.

In 1901 the girth measurement in the Linear Rating Rule was altered, the upper point of measurement to be taken at 0.55 of the waterline length abaft the stem and taken to the sheer and an additional girth measurement, the chain girth, was taken by a tape stretched tightly around the hull and under the keel. This was subtracted from the skin girth and the girth difference (d) was multiplied by 4 and added to 0.75 G. This became effective in 1902, when the divisor was altered to 2.1. Moveable keels were also measured as if fixed, when lowered. This was of interest to designers of large-class yachts in Britain as several had been built with centreboards working through the ballast keel, though they were usually regarded as experimental and soon removed or altered.

In 1905 there was a movement towards completely reviewing the rules for rating racing yachts in Britain and Europe in order to produce yachts of all sizes which were of wholesome form and construction and in an attempt to build craft which would be more durable than existing racers and might be converted to useful cruisers when their racing days were over. This latter applied particularly to the larger classes. At an international conference in London in 1906 attended by sixteen nations, the delegates amended the Y.R.A. Rule. Waterline length was increased by the addition of penalties to discourage the flat beamy bows and sterns of the scow-type yachts which had developed during the previous ten years, the girth multiplier was reduced to 0.50 and the multiplier of the factor d was reduced to 3. The sail factor was amended to $\frac{1}{3}$. The position of the girth station was changed and the freeboard was measured at each end of the waterline and at the amidships girth station. This was added to the end of the formula as a minus factor. The rule was:

$$L+B+\tfrac{1}{2}G+3d+\tfrac{1}{3}\sqrt{SA}-F=\text{Rating in Metres.}$$

This rule came into force in 1908 and was intended to remain until 1917. Classes of 5, 6, 7, 8, 9, 10, 12, 14, 15, 20 and over 20 metres rating were built or envisaged. At the upper end of the rating the 19 and 23 Metre classes emerged as practical sized yachts. There were also larger schooners which were rated in this way, usually referred to as the A Class in many regattas.

There was a further international conference of British and European nations in 1920 and the formula was amended to:

$$(L+\tfrac{1}{4}G+2d\sqrt{SA}-F)\div 2.5.$$

Centreboards were then prohibited.

In 1933 the rule was further amended, but as from 1930 all British and American large-class yachts were being rated by the American J Class rule, it is unnecessary to discuss the International Rule further here.

In all this the Americans remained aloof, using rules of their own devising until in 1929 it was decided that Britain would adopt the American J Class rule for yachts of about 23 Metre (rating) size and the Americans would adopt the International Rule for yachts of 12 metres and under. This brought to an end the difficulties of negotiation that had been needed before each challenge for the America's Cup, to agree the rating formula under which the yachts would be designed – usually an American formula of which the British had little or no experience.

In the United States yachts of all sizes were raced under many differing rules of rating until well into the twentieth century. Various yacht clubs had their own rating rule and a yacht's rating might alter from regatta to regatta. The North American Yachting Union was formed in 1897 in an attempt to co-ordinate and rationalize this situation, but had limited success with a rule they adopted from the British rule of 1896 and by 1900 it was abandoned. In 1903 the New York Yacht Club, regarded as pre-eminent in American yachting, adopted the Universal Rule which had been formulated by Nathanael Herreshoff over many years. It was a comprehensive rating rule which the club commended to others. They acted through the Atlantic Coast Conference to promote it, however it was not until 1925 that the North American Yacht Racing Union was formed to govern North American yacht racing nationally. America remained aloof from the international conference held in London in 1906 when sixteen nations agreed on a rating rule which would serve Britain, Europe and Scandinavia and, they hoped, America also.

Around 1900 some American racing classes were designated by a letter, M, P, Q and R being the most numerous. Unfortunately the letters stood for differing classes of yacht in some clubs, which was confusing. In the New York Yacht Club the class J was to be of 68 rating, approximating to a 75 ft waterline length, and was the basis of a challenge on behalf of Sir Thomas Lipton in 1907 which was not accepted by the club on the basis of the deed of gift of the America's Cup; the proposed yachts were considered too small for the trophy's prestige and 90-footers were thought appropriate!

Until the N.A.Y.R.U. was formed in 1925 racing in North America was not organized under a national body, as it had been in Britain and many European countries for many years. In 1927 the Union adopted the 6, 8, 10 and 12 Metre International Yacht Racing Union classes to enhance opportunity for competition, while retaining the existing American Universal Rule of Measurement for classes such as M, P, Q and R. In 1929 revived interest in the America's Cup with a challenge for 1930 resulted in new large yachts being built to defend it against the British challenger, designed to the J Class of the New York Yacht Club rating rule on a waterline length not less than 76 ft. Only six American and four British Js were to be built before the class became obsolete in 1937.

The Owners

The necessary conditions for the construction of these majestic craft were peace, monetary stability, and sailing men of considerable wealth and leisure who were willing to bear the high cost of building and owning a large racer. In Britain these were principally noblemen or owners of large businesses. In America they were usually wealthy businessmen and millionaires, when that now-devalued word meant people of extreme wealth. In Germany, before 1914 Kaiser Wilhelm II induced many rich industrialists to invest in large racing yachts to further Germany's efforts to rival Britain, and thus to gain his favour. An owner required considerable means to stand the heavy cost of maintaining a first-class racing yacht, whose large sail area frequently meant broken spars and damaged sails and gear in hard weather. Also, each winter, many racers were altered extensively. Sometimes whole sail plans were scrapped or redesigned or hull forms partly amended after a few seasons' use to obtain some desired improvement or rule advantage. All this could be afforded in the days of low labour costs and highly skilled, hard-working craftsmen, but a similar financial commitment today would be immense. Even then comparatively few could afford it.

Yachting is now mainly an amateur sport, but the owners were then invariably 'gentlemen', and it is hard to appreciate its social structure before 1939. 'Fancy paying men to enjoy your sailing for you!' mused a retired professional who had spent a lifetime racing other people's yachts. Certainly it seems that the captains and crews got most of the fun as well as their living until the 1930s. The owner's function was to provide money for building, equipping, manning and maintaining the yacht in the best manner. His enjoyment was usually pride of ownership of a large yacht and seeing her carry his colours at the masthead. Also, of course, he hoped to see her win, and perhaps be on board, occasionally even holding the helm under the skipper's guidance. Some – a very few – understood the details of the yacht's construction, handling and performance, but most owners regarded racing yachts as rich men today regard racehorses – as an exciting pastime which offers the chance of considerable sporting success, provided there is the right combination of design, construction, captain and crew. A few, who had usually graduated from the smaller classes and from a business background, thoroughly understood yachts themselves and in some cases handled her in all racing conditions. Owners such as Sir William Burton and Thomas Sopwith could match their skill as helmsmen against the best professional skippers of their day, but it was a skill hard won.

The Designers

Those who designed the large racers were men distinguished in an eclectic field. No one personality was dominant, and several were of considerable standing. William Fife (III) was a designer and builder of yachts at the village of Fairlie, on the Ayrshire shore of the lower Clyde. He was born in 1857 into the third generation of a noted family of yachtbuilders, entered the business under his father and spent his whole life designing and building yachts, a long career spanning the prime and decline of large-class racing. He was an intuitive designer with purpose and integrity, and his yachts were characterized by sweetness of line and distinctive profiles. It was said that he placed beauty of form above success in competition.

Fife produced many fine racers in the smaller classes and his larger yachts included the unsuccessful *Calluna* (1893); the successful *Ailsa* (1895); *Shamrock* (1899) and *Shamrock III* (1903), the latter both America's Cup challengers; *Shamrock* (1908) and *White Heather II* (1907), both 23 Metres; *Susanne* (1904); *Waterwitch* (1911); and *Cambria* (1928), which was the first large-class racer designed with bermudian rig. From the successful 20-tonner *Clara* (1884) to the fine offshore racer *Evenlode* (1937) the names of his yachts are like a roll of honour: the 40-tonners *Annasona* and *Bloodhound*; the 40-rater *Isolde*; *Julnar*; *Valdora*; *Moonbeam*; *Sumurun*; *Rendezvous* and many others, besides many 6, 8, 12 and 15 Metre and smaller cruising yachts.

Fife's early work influenced American yacht design. *Clara*, 20 tons, wonderfully successful in her first season, was afterwards sold to America and raced there under Scottish skipper John Barr. For two years she was almost unbeatable in the American 55 ft class. In 1888 Fife designed and his yard built the cutter *Minerva* for an American and she was sailed across to America by John's younger half-brother Charles Barr, who there laid the foundation of his racing career in her two successful seasons with the 40 ft class.

The various international conferences to formulate rating rules for racing yachts did not take full advantage of Fife's knowledge and experience. If they had, a more wholesome type of big racer might have emerged, perhaps one like the fine yawl *Valdora* of 1903, a 106 ton racing cruiser which combined speed, seaworthiness and beauty.

In his late years Fife designed the beautiful offshore racing yachts *Latifa* and *Evenlode*. He died in 1944 and his long career stretched from the lean, over-sparred cutters of the 1880s to the fine sea-going offshore yachts of the 1930s, making him the unquestioned patriach of yacht design and construction; no one else worked as long and with such integrity as Fife, and the yachts built at Fairlie were among the finest in the world.

One of his rivals was George Watson, a Glasgow designer who had served his time in shipbuilding and was educated as a naval architect. He ran a taut design team which produced many of the most graceful and famous racing yachts in history. Watson's dry and canny business ways and shrewdness, which were typical of his background, brought him fame, and his office's prodigious output throughout the 1890s, when his draughtsmen were designing craft from small raters to huge steam yachts, besides Royal National Life-boat Institution lifeboats and some small commercial craft, was unparalleled and probably contributed to his early death aged fifty-three in 1904. His best-remembered racer is the *Britannia*, but there were many other famous designs among his office's total output of over four hundred.

Joseph Soper of Southampton designed a few large racers as well as many other yachts of most types, and was succeeded by his son. His most successful creation was the great *Satanita*, which thirty-four year old Soper was commissioned to design on Christmas morning 1892 – 'the best Christmas present I ever had' – and he worked almost non-stop until her lines, sail plan, weights and centres were determined, so that the loftsman could start laying her lines down immediately after the short holiday. Her beautiful, wineglass-like sections were typical of Soper's individual style and were reminiscent of many yachts designed in Southampton by the Paynes and earlier by Shergold, draughtsman at Hatcher's yard. Less well known was Soper's large cutter *Aurora*, launched by J. & G. Fay in 1897 for C. D. Rose. Her construction was delayed by a shipwrights' strike: she was not launched until 1 July and did not start racing until Cowes Week, so Captain 'Cook' Diaper of Itchen, near Southampton, and his crew had little time to tune her up. Like the *Satanita*, she showed great speed on a reach against *Britannia*, *Meteor* and the smaller *Bona*. A faulty rudder put her out of several races, but in twelve starts she won three first prizes and one second so did not do badly. She raced again in 1898 with little success and was laid up in 1899.

Soper designed the 93 ft waterline schooner *Clara*, which was built in 1900 by J. & G. Fay for Max Guilleaume, a German yachtsman. She was successful in large-class racing, sailed at first by Captain Hoskins and then by Captain Edward Gould of Brightlingsea.

Charles Nicholson became one of the most renowned British yacht designers. In 1886 he started at the family firm of Camper & Nicholson, the Gosport yachtbuilders, then under the direction of his father Ben Nicholson. The yard was founded in 1782 by Francis Amos. Afterwards, Ben Nicholson worked there and eventually bought out William Camper, who had gone into partnership with Amos.

Charles Nicholson was allowed to experiment with design at an early age and during the 1890s began to produce designs for fast craft in the small-rating classes. However, the yard obtained most of its income from building and repairing cruising yachts, and in the early years of the twentieth century began to build in steel; at first they built steam yachts and then early motor yachts and a few large racers and cruisers. Like his contemporaries Nicholson is credited with a large output; he achieved this, like many yacht designers, by laying out the general concept, leaving the detailed draughting and calculations to the chief draughtsman and the drawing office staff at the yard. The 73 ft waterline cutter *Nyria* was designed and built in 1906 as a moderate sized racer for competition with the varied collection of yachts then racing in Britain under the handicap system during a temporary collapse of true big-class racing. She was not a spectacular success, but the 23 Metre *Brynhild II* of 1907 eventually became famous as a fast yacht, despite the ill-luck which culminated in her sinking while racing in 1910. The 19 Metre *Norada* was successful in a magnificent class of four yachts which might have supplanted the mixed big class because they were cheaper and provided better sport. In 1913 Nicholson produced the splendid large racing schooner *Margherita* which sailed to the top of the A Class schooners despite a strong challenge from the Kaiser's *Meteor* and other fine racing schooners.

Shamrock IV was designed and built at Gosport in 1914 to race for the America's Cup, but the outbreak of war caused her to be laid up in America until 1920, when she came close to winning it. In 1921 Charles Nicholson superintended the design of a bermudian rig for the old *Nyria*, which was the first large-class racer to carry it – and it brought her success. Other big bermudian racers followed: *Astra* (1928), *Candida* (1929), *Shamrock V* (1930), *Velsheda* (1933), *Endeavour* (1934), and *Endeavour II* (1936) – Nicholson's last large racer and the last British first-class racing yacht. Charles Nicholson continued to superintend the design of racing yachts in the family yard until the early 1950s, and died in 1954.

Herbert W. White was a partner in White Bros. (Southampton), yachtbuilders on the River Itchen, Hampshire. He did most of the designing for the yard, principally of keelboats and cruising yachts, and occasionally of small-class racers. His most notable yacht was the big cutter *Terpsichore*, launched in 1920 and later renamed *Lulworth*; this was a 186 ton cutter which raced in the large class until the 1930s and always seemed more of a ship than her contemporaries with less freeboard. She was a powerful yacht which could win convincingly in some conditions but was heavy work for her crew.

Nathanael G. Herreshoff is regarded as the greatest American yacht designer. He was born in 1848 and died in 1938; during his long life he devoted himself to designing and supervising the construction of steam engines and steam and sailing yachts, including many racers. Most of the large number of craft he designed were built at Bristol, Rhode Island, first at the yard of his brother J. B. Herreshoff and later by the Herreshoff Manufacturing Co., established there when the brothers went into partnership. By training and inclination Nathanael Herreshoff was a mechanical engineer rather than a naval architect and shipbuilder. He came into yacht design and construction almost by accident, although he had designed, built and sailed small sailing and steam craft from the late 1860s. He was principally an innovator but he also willingly adapted the ideas of others. His design and construction were often ingeniously successful, sometimes not. His method of creating a hull form was to carve a half-model in wood: the lines were lifted from this and transferred to paper, an intuitive method not used by his contemporaries and probably reflecting his lack of training in naval architecture and ship construction. His approach to hull weights also appears to have been unorthodox and George Owen, who for a few years worked as a draughtsman at the Herreshoff yard, recalled a notable difference between his own carefully calculated weights for a large racer and those of N. G. H., who quickly modified his own assessment. Like Nicholson, Fife and Watson, Herreshoff was a prolific designer who directed the efforts of a team of draughtsman and oversaw the construction of yachts built under the daily supervision of foremen in the various departments of the company. Until 1915 his brother John managed the firm's financial affairs, leaving Nathanael free to concentrate on design and production.

Strong-willed, enthusiastic and almost totally dedicated to his work, the man had genius but he could be a trial to everyone around him at times. Most of his yachts were fast and successful but some had failings. *Vigilant* (1893) lacked draft and stability, and lost efficiency from her excessive angles of heel. The mixture of bronze and aluminimum plating in the hull of *Defender*, the 1895 Cup winner, led to inevitable interaction in salt water and led to the early scrapping of a fine racer. *Resolute* (1914) was a poor performer reaching or running, and her slack bilges, a characteristic of Herreshoff design, caused her to roll heavily off the wind, while her hull construction was so light that she frequently had to return to the yard for strengthening; the mast and rig went overboard in trials, which made her crew jumpy for the 1920 series.

Nevertheless, Nathanael Herreshoff designed all six America's Cup defenders between 1893 and 1920, competing successfully against the best British designers and builders of the time. He was unquestionably among the greatest of racing-yacht designers, but he was not infallible and would probably be surprised at the aura which surrounds his memory.

William Gardner was another distinguished American yacht designer for thirty years after he began business in 1888. He completed a thorough training in naval architecture and shipbuilding in America and Britain. Typical of the times, his first commissions were for two 46 ft waterline sloops, and the next was for a 90-footer! A large number of racers and cruisers of all sizes were produced by his office, including the noted three-masted schooner *Atlantic*, which won the Transatlantic Race in 1905. In 1914 Gardner was commissioned by Alexander S. Cochran to design the sloop *Vanitie* as a contender for the America's Cup defence against *Shamrock IV*. She showed speed equal to the Herreshoff-designed *Resolute*, and sometimes outsailed her, but was not a consistent performer in lighter winds. However, she continued racing under various rigs until 1930. Gardner retired in 1925 because of failing health. He had also designed many steam yachts and some commercial vessels.

Several fine shooners which were successful as racers or cruisers were designed by Archibald Cary Smith of New York, who was born in 1837. Unlike most of his contemporaries, Smith had worked at the practical laying-off and construction of small wooden yachts during an apprenticeship with Bob Fish, a noted designer, builder and sailor of yachts large and small, at Pamrapo, New Jersey. He also received instruction in draughting from shipbuilder W. W. Bates. However, Smith then decided to take up marine art for a living but continued occasionally to design yachts by draughting rather than by first carving half-models, at the time a method commonly used by American designers of yachts and small craft. Some of these yachts were large, such as the 100 ft waterline schooner *Intrepid* of 1878. Smith's 67 ft 5 in sloop *Mischief* (1879) was selected to defend the America's Cup against the Canadian challenger *Atalanta* in 1881: thereafter, yacht design became his professional career. The 110 ft waterline schooner *Yampa*, designed as a cruiser, proved successful in racing and was later sold to the German Emperor, to be renamed *Iduna*; this led to an order in 1902 for the fine racing/cruising schooner *Meteor III*. The influence of her original owner, for whom Smith designed several yachts, brought an unusual commission to design the 300 ft sound steamers *Richard Peck*, *City of Lowell* and *C. W. Chapin*, each capable of over 20 knots. Smith preferred to design craft for steel construction and produced sailing, steam and auxiliary yachts and many cruising craft. As the practice expanded Smith took into partnership Harry C. Barbey and engaged a staff of draughtsmen; the firm was called Cary Smith & Barbey.

The hull design of the racing schooners *Elmina*, *Amorita*, *Muriel* and *Meteor III*, built between 1901 and 1903, was in contrast to the fashionable shallow hull form which had a small area of midship section, a hard bilge and a slim, deep fin keel of small lateral area. Smith produced a hull with deep-V sections, generally slack in the bilge and with full lower sections and generous lateral plane below water – yet these were conspicuously fast yachts. The success of this type was repeated in 1905, when the firm, by then Cary Smith & Ferris, designed the 87 ft waterline racing schooner *Elmina* for F. F. Brewster, and again with the magnificent 100 ft waterline racing schooner *Enchantress* in 1911, for William C. Iselin.

The life of this talented, cultured and unassuming man ended soon afterwards. He was one of the greatest designers of large yachts, but is now little known. His work appears to have influenced Edward Burgess (1848–91), another noted American designer of the period 1883 to 1891.

B. B. Crowninshield of Boston designed many fast commercial sailing craft and yachts. He had a thorough technical training and, after a few years in general commerce in the western states, joined John R. Purdon, a Boston yacht designer and broker. A year later, in 1897, Crowninshield set up a business in Boston as a yacht designer. His first commission was for the 21 ft knockabout sloop *Mongoose*, which beat three Herreshoff boats in the class that season. He made a reputation for knockabout yachts in New England and was soon designing larger racers and cruising craft. (Knockabout sloops were a type of small keel yacht that originated in America circa 1898. A single headsail tacked to the stemhead, in contrast to the majority of small keel racers that had short bowsprits.) In 1901 Crowninshield was commissioned to design the giant 140 ft sloop *Independence* for Thomas W. Lawson, a Boston stockbroker who wished to contend for the defence of the America's Cup against *Shamrock II*. This was a challenge not only for selection as defender but to the New York Yacht Club, who by then regarded themselves as guardians of the trophy. It was also a challenge to the recent monopoly of design of the large yachts for Cup defence by Nathanael Herreshoff and his staff. Unfortunately Crowninshield's imaginative racer was unsuccessful, and as Boston did not make further challenges he was not again asked to produce a first-class boat, though he continued to design yachts of all sizes as well as fishing and cargo vessels for many years.

Another American designer, who produced one large racer, was George Owen. Trained as a mechanical engineer, he worked as Herreshoff's yard as a draughtsman between 1898 and 1901. Subsequently he reverted to mechanical engineering for a period but designed yachts in his spare time, gaining a reputation for smaller racers. After four years' work as a draughtsman at the Fore River Shipbuilding Co. he established himself as a yacht designer in 1908, continuing to produce small and medium sized racers and a few commercial vessels.

George Owen's big chance came in 1914 when he was commissioned by a syndicate of yacht owners from New York, Philadelphia and Boston to design the sloop *Defiance* as a contender for the trials for the America's Cup defence against *Shamrock IV*. *Defiance* was a beautifully built yacht with a double-skin mahogany hull and a deck full of winches, but unfortunately she was disappointing in performance. Owen continued to design yachts and in 1915 was appointed to the naval architecture faculty of the Massachusetts Institute of Technology, later becoming a professor of naval architecture. He also continued to design racing and cruising yachts. He sailed until 1957 and died in 1959, the last designer of the great racers in the old tradition, and perhaps the best liked.

W. Starling Burgess became a noted designer of American yachts and was responsible for the America's Cup defenders *Enterprise* (1930), *Rainbow* (1934), and probably also for *Ranger* (1937), on which the young Olin J. Stephens collaborated. Although this was to be his only work on a large-class racing yacht, Olin Stephens subsequently became the dean of international yacht designers, with half a century of successful designs of all types behind him. Both men reputedly draughted two sets of lines for this project. These were tank-tested and the most efficient model was selected. The designers resolved not to disclose whose hull form was chosen and this secrecy is said to have been maintained.

The father of W. Starling Burgess was Edward Burgess, a contemporary of Nathanael G. Herreshoff, who took up yacht design in 1884 after an early career in natural history. He designed many notable American yachts, among them the Cup defenders *Puritan*, *Mayflower* and *Volunteer*, and some fast fishing schooners. After his death in 1891 his young sons were educated as engineers. W. Starling Burgess turned to yacht design and produced attractive craft of many types, including some successful racers and fine cruisers. During the First World War he designed a few aircraft. His brother C. P. Burgess, a naval engineer, was also involved in the design of aluminium structures and designed the Duralumin mast for *Enterprise* in 1930; this was a 162 ft spar which weighed only 4000 pounds without fittings – about a quarter less than a wooden equivalent. Starling Burgess described the design of *Enterprise* as 'a fair and normal model, freakish in no way', but she was fitted with many rig innovations including a trangular section boom with a flat top about 4 ft wide, with cross-tracks allowing the mainsail foot to form whatever curve was desired: this was afterwards called the 'Park Avenue boom'. Burgess's innovative flair and experience was allied to that of Olin Stephens in the *Ranger* project in 1936–7. Their combined ability was enhanced by the availability of the new towing tank of the Stevens Institute of Technology, where Professor Kenneth S. Davidson had evolved an ingenious method of testing sailing models in which the driving force of the wind, its heeling force and its component of leeway were closely registered by the mechanical resistance of springs and balance weights. In testing a model's speed to windward the designers were able to plot speed made good to windward directly against wind speed.

As Charles Nicholson had given the lines of the *Endeavour* of 1934 to Burgess, who had responded with the lines of the *Rainbow*, the American team were able to evaluate her performance, and also that of models of the *Rainbow* and *Weetamoe*, and proceed from there with the design of the *Ranger*, confident that their model testing was providing results in agreement with the full-sized yachts. *Ranger* was the last large racing yacht built. She easily defeated the challenging *Endeavour II*, designed in the usual way, without tank testing. Starling Burgess designed yachts until 1941 and died about 1948.

Clinton Crane also designed one large racing sloop: the 1930 Cup-defence contender *Weetamoe*. Crane was of a wealthy industrial family and commenced a training in naval architecture and shipbuilding, but was attracted to yacht design. After studies, he entered the profession in 1899, becoming involved in the design of many sizes and types of yacht. In 1912 he left yacht design to manage the family mining firm for the next thirty-five years, but he continued to design yachts as an amateur.

Weetamoe (1930) was his most outstanding racer but he also designed several 6, 8 and 12 Metre yachts. During his career he was responsible for a wide range of craft, from small, one-design classes to large cruisers such as the 277 ft steam yacht *Vanadis*, the 218 ft steel barque *Aloha* and other comparable craft. Clinton Crane died in 1958 aged eighty-five.

L. Francis Herreshoff was a younger son of Nathanael G. Herreshoff. After training at the family yard in Bristol, Rhode Island he became a talented draughtsman and a designer of sail and power yachts until his death in 1972. He produced many racers, one of which was the large-class *Whirlwind* (1930), for the Cup defence trials against *Shamrock V*. She was the only first-class racer to be designed with a canoe stern and had many unusual features, but she was poorly balanced and no match for *Enterprise*. L. Francis Herreshoff worked from his homes at Manchester and later Marblehead, Massachusetts and was a splendidly eccentric and outspoken personality, an able yacht sailor and a writer with the rare gift of inspiring others.

The J Class *Yankee* (1930) was the sole large racing yacht designed by the firm of Paine, Belknap & Skene. Frank C. Paine was the younger son of General Paine who owned the America's Cup defenders *Volunteer*, *Mayflower* and *Puritan*, and was the brother of John Paine who designed *Jubilee* in 1893. Frank Paine had a substantial interest in the yacht yard of George Lawley & Son at south Boston, was an able racing helmsman and a man of means. It is probable that much of the actual design for *Yankee* was done by Norman Skene.

Max Oertz of Hamburg was Germany's only designer of large racing yachts, producing the fine large schooners *Germania* (1908), 366 tons; *Meteor IV* (1909), 400 tons; and *Meteor V* (1914), 355 tons. Born in 1871, Oertz was educated at the naval academy in Berlin, where he also enjoyed sailing the small centreboard craft on the local lakes. He studied shipbuilding in a yard on the River Weser and on leaving the academy joined a noted yacht designer at Helsingfors (then Russian) to gain experience. He became manager of Esch's yacht yard at St Petersburg in Russia and afterwards returned to Germany, opening a yacht design office in Berlin. Soon afterwards he went into partnership with Hans Harder, who had also studied at the academy, and in 1897 they established a yacht yard at Neuhof am Reihstieg, near Hamburg, starting with the design and construction of the 20-rater *Elly*; they also built four other yachts in their first year, besides small craft.

The yard flourished and later became the Max Oertz Yachtwerft, concentrating principally on smaller yachts of 25 to 40 ft in length, with a few larger cruisers and an occasional moderate sized racer. Oertz produced the designs, but many of the yachts were not built at the yard, including the large racing schooners. He also designed and built small motor craft and fishing vessels. His knowledge of construction techniques was wide and complemented his considerable ability as a naval architect. He remained in business during the 1920s.

The Builders

The builders of the large racers deserved a recognition they rarely received. They often built these yachts at a loss – sometimes to keep men employed so teams would not be broken up until other, more profitable, work appeared; occasionally, perhaps, for prestige and advertising. In Britain, the large racers were built in two main areas during the period this survey covers: on the Clyde and at Southampton, Itchen and Gosport. The highest skills of draughtsmen, loftsmen, shipwrights, platers, joiners, riggers, painters and engineers were needed in the construction of these finely finished craft.

During the 1890s and early 1900s several Clyde builders of steel steamships also built some fine racing yachts. Notable were D. & W. Henderson & Co. of Meadowside, Glasgow who built many large racing yachts on berths alongside the cargo ships which were their principal concern. These yachts included *Britannia* (1893), *Valkyrie II* (1893), *Valkyrie III* (1895), *Meteor II* (1896), *Rainbow* (1898), *Gleniffer* (1899) and *Distant Shore*, later renamed *Kariad* (1900). All these were designed by George Watson and Co.

A. & J. Inglis of Glasgow were contemporaries of Henderson and built the large racers *Calluna* (1893), *Ailsa* (1895) and *Waterwitch* (1911), all designed by William Fife of Fairlie. At Dumbarton, W. Denney & Bros. built *Shamrock II* in 1901 to Watson's design and *Shamrock III* (1903) to Fife's design. Their principal work was on destroyers, cargo and cross-Channel ships and special service craft. The yard of W. Fife & Son built the 23 Metre rating *Shamrock* in 1908 and *Cambria* (1928), besides many other yachts, large and small. On the Thames, Denny's rivals John I. Thornycroft & Co., who were leading builders of torpedo boats and destroyers, built the first *Shamrock* (1899) in their yards at Chiswick and Millwall, after the design of William Fife.

On the south coast, J. & G. Fay & Co. of Northam, Southampton built *Satanita* (1893), *Aurora* (1897), the fine schooner *Clara* (1900), and *Cicely* (1902). The first three were designed by Joseph Soper and the last by Fife. At Itchen, White Bros. built *Terpsichore*, later to be renamed *Lulworth* (1920). At Gosport, Camper & Nicholson built: *Nyria* (1906), *Brynhild II* (1907), *Margherita* (1913), *Shamrock IV* (1914), *Astra* (1928), *Candida* (1929), *Shamrock V* (1930), *Velsheda* (1933), *Endeavour* (1934) and *Endeavour II* (1936).

American builders were concentrated in the states of New York, Rhode Island, Massachusetts and Maine. These included George Lawley & Son of South Boston, Massachusetts who launched *Jubilee* (1893), *Independence* (1901), *Elmina* (1905), *Enchantress* (1911), *Vanitie* (1914), *Yankee* (1930) and *Whirlwind* (1930).

The Herreshoff Manufacturing Co. built *Navahoe* (1893), *Vigilant* (1893), *Colonia* (1893), *Defender* (1895), *Columbia* (1899), *Constitution* (1901), *Reliance* (1903), *Resolute* (1914), *Weetamoe* (1930), *Enterprise* (1930) and *Rainbow* (1934) – all defenders or potential defenders of the America's Cup. They also built the large racing schooners *Ingomar* (1903), *Queen* (1906), *Irolita II* (1906), *Westward* (1910), *Elena* (1911), *Vagrant* (1913) and *Katoura* (1914).

The Townsend-Downie Shipbuilding Co. of New York built the schooner *Meteor III* in 1902, and the Bath Ironworks in Maine, a shipbuilding company, launched *Ranger* in 1937.

Steel shipbuilers Pusey & Jones built *Pilgrim* (1893) at Wilmington, Delaware.

In Germany, Krupps Germania Werft at Kiel built the great racing schooners *Germania* (1908), *Meteor IV* (1909) and *Meteor V* (1914).

The Sailmakers

Of the various craftsmen who contribute to the success or failure of a racing yacht, the sailmakers are often overlooked. Designing and making sails of the sizes used by large racing or cruising yachts required considerable artistic and scientific skill, particularly in the cutting and making up; the complete mainsail for a first-class cutter or a large schooner or yawl could not be spread out at once on the sail-loft floor, and its shape could not be seen as a whole or its cut corrected until it was bent and hoisted for the first time on the yacht.

During the mid- and late nineteenth century the firm of Lapthorn of Gosport in Hampshire were prominent makers of sails for racing yachts of all sizes, as well as for cruisers. At Cowes, the loft of Ratsey flourished and made sails for many large racers. Eventually these businesses combined to become Ratsey & Lapthorn. During the period covered by this book the Ratsey loft was directed by Thomas Ratsey, a most experienced and inventive sailmaker and yacht sailor and a man of stout principles who, when approached in 1894 to make new sails for the visiting American racer *Vigilant* – whose Herreshoff sails were badly out of shape – politely refused, maintaining that there should be competition between different sailmakers as well as between different designers, builders and crews. There may have been more than national pride in this: probably Thomas Ratsey felt that the attention paid to designers, builders, skippers and crews blinded many to the efforts and advances made by sailmakers in the cut and strength of sails, particularly in England – yet the sailmakers' work contributed so much to the success or failure of a racer. Many of Thomas Ratsey's innovations were first tried out in sails for his own favourite cutter *Dolly Varden*, which was raced and cruised in the Solent area for decades. He made sails for royalty, nobles and commoners with the same care and attention, and the Earl of Dunraven, owner of the *Valkyrie*s, considered him as 'one of England's foremost gentlemen'.

American makers of sails for large racing yachts included Wilson & Griffin and Robert E. Morton, both of New York City, and Wilson & Silsby of Boston and Cousens & Pratt of Marblehead. The Wilson family were excellent sailmakers and one of them was responsible for making the sails of the schooner *America* in 1851 for her visit to race in England. Early in the 1890s the Herreshoff Manufacturing Co. decided to establish their own loft at the yard in Bristol, Rhode Island for sail repairs and in 1894 this was enlarged to make sails for yachts of all sizes. Unfortunately, at first the cut and finish of the sails was not good though it was later improved. Whatever the maker, up to 1920 the sails of every America's Cup defender and of most other large American racers were made from Lowell canvas.

Competition crept in around the turn of the century when Ratsey & Lapthorn, the English sailmakers, opened a loft at City Island, New York in 1902, which continues to flourish.

The Skippers

The large racing yachts were commanded by professional captains and were manned by professional yacht sailors, all thoroughly experienced in racing. Skill in yacht racing became the particular pride of many seafarers from certain communities. In winter most of them manned smacks or other small fishing vessels in the North Sea, the Solent, the English Channel, the Scottish west coast, or along Long Island Sound, the southern New England coastal waters and the coast of Maine. This wonderful school of seamanship was responsible for their smartness under canvas, and even the greatest of the many racing skippers from the Essex coast, the Solent or Long Island knew the feel of the dredge or trawl warp before they held the tiller lines of the world's fastest yachts. The crews were intelligent seamen whose anticipation of the mates' and skippers' orders ensured smart handling – essential when, after hours of racing, competitors were often only separated by seconds.

The skill, judgement and determination of the professional captains and crews of the racers often made the reputations of yacht designers. Racing captains rose solely by merit in a hard school and were in complete charge of these huge racers, which might have crews of up to thirty-five and, in some extreme American examples, fifty or more. Although the crews were ill paid by present standards, substantial prize money could be won by yachts which finished first, second and third, and a proportion of this money was divided among the winning crews. At the season's end, British skippers whose command showed a long string of prize flags – miniatures of their yacht's racing flag – were well rewarded and many built smacks and houses with their prize money, usually naming them for the yacht whose skilful handling had made their construction possible.

Many leading English captains and crews came from the little Essex maritime village of Rowhedge, on the River Colne. When *Valkyrie II*, *Britannia*, *Satanita* and *Calluna* were being built in the winter of 1892–3 the command of all these big-class racers was offered to racing skippers from Rowhedge, such was its fame. William Cranfield commanded the *Valkyrie II*, Thomas Jay the *Satanita* and John Carter was offered command of both the *Britannia* and *Calluna* but chose the royal cutter.

William Cranfield skippered many large racers, including *Yarana*, *Valkyrie*, *Valkyrie II* and *Valkyrie III*. Tom Jay skippered the large racers *Satanita*, *Ailsa* and *Rainbow*. John Carter commanded the *Britannia* until his death in 1910, though she was laid up for a period and he was released until again required. He was succeeded by his son Jack R. Carter, who sailed her until 1913. All these men commanded smaller racers and other yachts of various types at other stages of their careers, and their fellow villagers skippered and manned many other racing and cruising yachts until 1939, earning their living in winter in the fleet of cutter and ketch rigged smacks owned at Rowhedge where almost every male in the population of eleven hundred was either a sailor or a ship and boat builder. Wivenhoe, a similar village on the opposite bank of the Colne, produced a notable racing skipper in Albert Turner, who sailed *Shamrock IV* in 1914 and 1920 and was for many years afterwards captain of the *Britannia*.

The town of Brightlingsea at the mouth of the River Colne, was the home of many racing captains and crews. Robert Wringe sailed *Ailsa*, *Shamrock*, *Susanne* and others. Edward Gould raced the German schooner *Clara*. Edward Sycamore skippered many memorable racers including *Bona*, *Distant Shore*, *Shamrock*, *Shamrock* (23 Metre), the German-owned *Navahoe*, and for a time the schooner *Westward*. Thomas Skeats sailed the 'small' big-class racer *Bona* and later the somewhat similar *Moonbeam* (1920). Captain Loveless sailed the *Meteor IV* in 1912.

From Tollesbury, a small village on the nearby River Blackwater, Stephen Barbrook commanded *Brynhild II* and Charles Leavett was captain of *Britannia* during 1920–1. Edward Heard skippered *Astra*, *Shamrock V*, and *Endeavour* as a trial yacht during the Cup challenge of 1937. From the Solent area came Ben Parker of Itchen who sailed the German Emperor's *Meteor II* and *Meteor III*; Captain 'Cook' Diaper sailed *Aurora* and Alfred Diaper *Westward* when she was owned by T. B. F. Davis. On the Hamble River Charles Bevis of Bursledon sailed *Ailsa, Satanita, Sybarita, White Heather II* and *Lulworth*, and George Williams from Hamble village skippered both *Endeavour* and *Endeavour II*.

Gosport, on Portsmouth Harbour, produced several racing skippers. Robert Gomes raced the German Emperor's first *Meteor* (originally the British *Thistle*) and for a time *Meteor II*, and went to America with *Sybarita*. Charles Mountifield sailed the mighty *Sybarita* with Captain Bevis, and later commanded *White Heather* and *Velsheda* in the 1930s. Captain Pound skippered *Astra* early in her career. Alfred Embling sailed the schooners *Waterwitch* and *Margherita*, and Stephen Ray the *Nyria*. Joseph Gilbey from the village of Bosham on Chichester Harbour skippered *Candida*.

There was one Irish racing skipper of large yachts. William O'Neill of Kingstown, who sailed the *Ivernia* against the newer big-class yachts in 1893–4 and earlier the big cutter *Irex*. On the Clyde, Archie Hogarth from Portincross, Ayrshire commanded *Calluna* and *Bona*, was joint skipper of the first *Shamrock* with Captain Wringe, and later captained *Lulworth*.

These great racing skippers were above all fine helmsmen, particularly to windward, and they had wonderful judgement. They also had the ability to consider the hull and rig as a whole and tune the yachts to perfection, besides coordinating the work of a crew of perhaps thirty-five hands. To keep their place in the prize lists they had to anticipate the tactics of their equally experienced rivals, know the racing rules thoroughly, and have such calm nerves that they could be stretched to the utmost without flinching: an error at the helm of one of these giants could not only shatter their reputation but might also cost the lives of several men. Captains in the 1890s earned from £3 10s. to £4 per week and were all found when in commission; an owner would put his captain on a winter retainer to ensure he was available at all times for consultation on alterations to the yacht or to advise on a new design and, most important of all, so that he was again at the helm of the owner's yacht next season. Besides this, captains had a reasonable share of the prize money, and a successful racing skipper could live comfortably by the standards of the times, often putting money into local property.

Many British owners were unable to be on board during every race and some had no wish to be so. Thus they would sometimes have an owner's representative on board, usually a wealthy friend with sailing pretensions who maintained the owner's social contacts in his absence and corresponded with him by phone and telegram.

The captain had sole charge of the yacht and her crew and was responsible for the yacht's condition and business. The captain's opinion was respected by the owner and, when racing, the tactics and handling were left up to him. An excellent relationship usually existed between the owner and his skipper and in some cases they became friends in the formal manner then dictated by their differing social backgrounds. When racing in other than familiar waters, captains often took a 'racing pilot', usually a reliable local fisherman who specialized in this work and drew on his comprehensive knowledge of depths, tides, shoals and local wind and weather patterns, since the big class might only come once a year to his home ground. Skippers tried to use the same pilot each year.

Sir William P. Burton was the first British amateur to take charge of a large yacht while racing. In 1914 and 1920 he shared the helm of

Shamrock IV with Captain Albert Turner, who had been his racing skipper in various large yachts. T. B. F. Davis, Herman Andreae, H. F. Paul, Thomas Sopwith and Fred Sigrist sailed their own large-class yachts and were thoroughly knowledgeable about rules and tactics, but were helped by their skippers on tides, courses, winds and sail shifts and were backed by well chosen and trained racing crews. This movement to amateur helmsmen in large racers commenced in the 1920s and increased during the 1930s, though all the yachts carried a professional skipper who could relieve the owner at the wheel at any time. Apart from racing organization and advice, the skipper was also responsible for taking the yacht safely around the coast or across the Channel to various fixtures. Some owners, such as Sir William Berry, King George V and R. H. Lee, occasionally took the helm when racing; however, though they knew the rules and formulated tactics they had little opportunity to perfect their knowledge, so their yachts were usually raced by their captains or by other amateur helmsmen. Sir Philip Hunloke sailed *Britannia* with Captain Turner between 1921 and 1935 and the combination was successful. Designers such as Charles E. Nicholson and William Fife (III) occasionally took the helm of their creations, usually during trials or after alterations, sometimes on a rare day out.

In America the professional racing captains were principally from the oystering villages on the shores of Long Island, particularly Islip and Greenport. They included Captain Henry C. Haff of the *Mayflower, Volunteer, Colonia, Vigilant, Defender* and *Independence*; and Clayton Haff and Harry P. Haff of the *Resolute* and *Vanitie*, all from Islip. William H. Dennis of Greenport, on the northeastern shore, sailed the schooners *Elmina* and *Elena* and the sloop *Vanite*. Uriah Rhodes was a noted skipper of large racers, including *Defender* in 1899 and *Constitution* in 1901. Some others came from Massachusetts, including Aubrey Crocker, who sailed *Navahoe* and earlier *Puritan*, and Edward Sherlock of South Boston who raced the unsuccessful *Pilgrim* in 1893 and later the fine schooners *Yampa* and *Amorita*. Martin Stone of Swampscott and Hezikiah Newcombe of Wellfleet on Cape Cod raced *Jubilee* against *Defender* in the 1895 trials for the America's Cup defender.

Some English and Scottish skippers were invited over by American owners to race their yachts. Robert Wringe of Brightlingsea sailed the Herreshoff-built *Mineola* in 1900 with an Essex crew; this was a 106 ft sloop, one of four built as a class in an attempt to revive American interest in sizeable racing yachts for other purposes than for America's Cup defence. The owners of these yachts were all millionaires.

Cornelius Vanderbilt's *Rainbow* had an English crew under Captain George Parker of Itchen, in a closely matched class. When the big racer *Ailsa* was sold to an American she was taken over and subsequently raced by William Maskell of Brightlingsea, and Robert Gomes went out with the *Sybarita*. Charles Barr from Gourock in Scotland became a well-known skipper of large American racers, sailing *Navahoe*, *Vigilant*, *Columbia*, *Reliance*, *Ingomar* and *Westward*.

During trials and her defence of the America's Cup in 1893, *Vigilant* was under Captain William Hansen, a naturalized Norwegian; his handling of her in the first trial race led to the owners' requesting that Nathanael Herreshoff, her designer, steer her when racing, with the captain standing by and in charge of her racing crew of seventy. When *Vigilant* visited Britain in 1894 to race against the large class she made the transatlantic voyage under Captain Leander A. Jeffries, an eminent skipper of schooner yachts and an able navigator. Captain Henry Haff took charge for racing.

Amateur helmsmen appeared in the large class much earlier in America than in Britain. Charles Smithers was a distinguished amateur helmsman before 1915, sailing with success against excellent professional captains. However, there was another side to this trend. American owners and several of their friends were usually on board their yachts when racing, and this group of perhaps four or five amateurs frequently voiced opinions on tactics and handling to the skipper which conflicted with his professional judgement. This could interrupt the captain's concentration on the yacht's handling, which should have had his undivided attention, and these groups – politely termed the 'afterguard' by American yachting writers – were undoubtedly a great annoyance to many skippers. A 1901 observer was scathing about the behaviour of the large parties of amateurs usually carried by the American Cup defence candidates:

> The curse of these boats and the prolific cause of errors in handling is the presence on their decks

of a number of men who are not paid to be there. A man may be a great amateur sailor and an excellent helmsman in a small way, but he has his place, and it is not yet yoked up with a professional in the divided management of a big racing machine. If you hire a man to sail and have charge of one of these boats, let him have the command untrammeled by the presence of any persons except those he can command to obey or dismiss as he sees fit. This putting a man into the position of skipper of a racing boat and then surrounding him with a lot of men whose opinions he is obliged to listen to and whose presence he cannot rid himself of is not fair to the man nor beneficial to the boat. All the skippers complain of the presence of these amateurs and would gladly rid themselves of their presence, but they do not dare to. If these men were hired like themselves they could bounce them, but as it is they have to put up with their company, no matter how much they may be in the way.

After 1918 the American big class was sailed by amateur helmsmen including Charles F. Adams, Harold S. Vanderbilt, Gerard B. Lambert, Clinton Crane, Sherman S. Hoyt and George Nichols; they were backed by professional skippers such as Captains George Monsell, John Christiansen and Gust Olsen, with full professional crews, which by then were often Scandinavians.

There were few German racing skippers in large yachts and the first three of the Kaiser's *Meteor*s were raced successively by the English skippers Robert Gomes, Ben Parker and Robert Wringe. Robert Duncan from the Clyde was also 'lent' by his owner James Coats to the Kaiser for a short period. Captain Peters was the most accomplished German racing skipper and was generally referred to as coming 'from Hamburg', though he is believed to have originated from one of the Elbe fishing villages. Captain Peters first came to Britain in charge of the 65 ft Linear Rater cutter *Kommodore*, which he sailed with considerable skill. He afterwards skippered the large schooner *Hamburg* (originally the British *Rainbow*) and was well liked and respected as a racing captain. In 1907 he took charge of the Emperor's *Meteor III*, succeeding Robert Wringe, who had sailed her after Ben Parker was taken fatally ill in 1905. A German skipper appears to have been in command thereafter, though as late as 1912 Englishman Captain Loveless was sailing on board *Meteor IV*, presumably as joint skipper or adviser. The crews of the *Meteor*s and other large German yachts continued to include a proportion of English hands for several years, and smaller German racers, particularly the 15 Metre class, were largely skippered and manned by Englishmen until 1914.

The Crews

The professional hands of the British racing yachts were, like their skippers, almost invariably from small fishing communities. Many were from the Rivers Colne and Blackwater in northeast Essex: Rowhedge, Wivenhoe, Brightlingsea, and after the 1890s also from Tollesbury and a little later West Mersea. Others came from the Solent area – Itchen, Southampton, Hythe, Hamble, Bursledon, Gosport, Cowes, St Helens, Emsworth and Bosham on Chichester Harbour and from Poole in Dorset. Scotland provided men from Gourock, Largs, Fairlie, Dunoon, Port Bannatyne, Saltcoats, Blairmore, Sandbank, the Isle of Skye and Tarbert. Smaller numbers came from little ports and villages in Cornwall and Devon: Port Isaac, Penzance, Newlyn, Gorran Haven, Mevagissy, Looe, Brixham, Dartmouth, Plymouth and Exmouth, but these were more in evidence during the period 1919 to 1939, and for a time during the tremendous expansion of large racing yachts in the 1890s. Occasionally, hands came from small places which had no established connection with the sport: Whitstable in Kent; Pin Mill, Aldeburgh and Loewstoft in Suffolk. All were good seamen – sailors of the sail. This book is as much a tribute to their skill, and that of the captains and mates, as it is to their designers and owners, whose doings have already been extensively documented and who have been associated with most of the glory of these imposing yachts, while the captains and crews whose skill at the helm, on deck and aloft made them go are hardly recorded.

In America the racing yacht crews were from small oystering and fishing towns and villages on the shores of Long Island, New York, Connecticut, Rhode Island, New Jersey, Massachusetts and Maine. Many were from Long Island ports including Port Jefferson, Greenport, Islip, Oyster Bay, Northport, Huntingdon, Sayville and New Rochelle, with some from New York City and City Island. Connecticut yachtsmen hailed from Stamford, Southport, New London, Bridgeport, Stratford, New Haven, South Norwalk, Greenwich, Rowayton and Fair Haven. Rhode Island men were from Newport, Bristol, Providence and Warren. The Massachusetts yacht hands and skippers came from Provincetown, Wellfleet, Marblehead, Lynn, Cohasset, Hull, Hingham, Martha's Vineyard, Plymouth, Duxbury, Kingston, Chatham, Swampscott, Manchester, Boston and Gloucester. New Jersey men from Keyport served in some racers and most of the Maine hands came from the Penobscot Bay area. Perhaps the most interesting of these communities, which were so similar to the homes of their British counterparts, was Deer Isle, Maine where the communities of Stonington and Green's Landing provided men for American racing yachts and cruising craft at the turn of the century; they became known as the 'Deer Isle boys'. Many British yacht skippers and hands also sailed American owned yachts at various times, and after 1900 an increasing number of Scandinavian sailors appeared in the crews of American racers and they, particularly the clannish Norwegians, gradually began to outnumber native Americans, some becoming mates and a few captains under amateur helmsmen of the period. English hands sailed in many German yachts until 1914.

The German professional crews were principally from fishing communities on the River Elbe, the German Baltic coast particularly around Kiel, and Schleswig-Holstein. Some German naval personnel were also seconded to the yachts owned by the Kaiser.

Apart from the captains, first and second mates, stewards and cooks, the racing hands were usually young men between twenty and thirty years old, usually with the traditional background of winter fishing under sail and summer yachting; they often rose quickly from smaller yachts to be selected for the crew of a big racer. They were superb fore-and-aft seamen, able to work as a team with perfect drill, yet also able to think and act independently; from their knowledge of racing tactics they could anticipate orders, which were executed with lightning speed. They were also skilled in rope, wire and canvas work, and could maintain a good varnish and paint finish after the yacht left her fitting-out yard. This finish was lovingly cared for by the mate, who was responsible to the captain for the yacht's smartness in every way. When the crew set a spinnaker it was with the exact coordination of an experienced team. When the skipper ordered 'All hands on the mainsheet!' thirty powerful men were hauling in unison within seconds, with the refined expertise that amateurs would never be able to attain on a canted and heaving deck. When it was in – and those 4000 sq ft mainsails took some sheeting in a breeze – the mainsheet man instantly cast his rope stopper around it at the traditional order of 'Belay! Try that!' and all hands melted away to lie around the weather deck, crouched intelligently into positions of the least windage, with their noses over the weather footrail, carefully noting the tactics of the most dangerous rivals. In the silence, the slightest quiver of an opponent's sail, the least check on a sheet or some half-concealed movement, and so many inquiring eyes were on their own boat's helmsman: 'Did you see that, skipper?' If he had, they knew, although not a word was exchanged; if he had not, he understood the message on every face and at once traced the cause. Instinctively these men were ready at the 'Lee-ho!' or 'Look alive boys!' The sails were all silently adjusted, tackles and leads cleared for every point of sailing – and often without a single order until the crucial one, which the yacht herself seemed to obey. Keen on their work and good at it as they were, the crews were poorly paid. They were, generally speaking, a fine type of man, physically and mentally alert and taking as great a pride in their yacht as if she belonged to them. If they saw her before she was planked up, they would criticize her expertly and, after a short trial spin, would offer as sound an opinion as could be given.

From their weekly wage (£1 6*s*. in the 1890s; £3 in the mid-1930s) the crew 'found themselves' in food. At the start of the season one of them was appointed fo'c'sle cook and caterer, the others paying him a small amount each week for their food (5*s*. in the 1890s), and at the end of the season they expected to receive a few shillings back. The cook's was a difficult job, as all hands had good appetites and expected plenty of food. Each morning in port or at an anchorage the caterer went ashore with his basket for fresh provisions. Usually the fo'c'sle cook came to an arrangement with the steward and made stews with what was left over from serving the saloon table, supplemented by plum duff and spotted dick, which were cheap and filling. Surprisingly, coffee made into a thick syrup with condensed milk and sugar was often preferred to tea in the fo'c'sle of a British racer.

Naturally the smartest hands were picked for the most exacting jobs such as mastheadsman or bowsprit-endsman, which might carry increases in pay and prospects of advancement towards a mate's berth. In the days when bowsprits protruded 30 ft or more outboard and huge jibs were set and handled from them, the bowsprit-endsman's position was a wet and uncomfortable one, but of all the jobs on board a racer the mastheadsman's was the most dangerous. Large racers had one, and sometimes two, mastheadsmen, whose duties included being aloft anywhere to the topmast head – 160 ft above the waterline – before and during racing, to clear sails and topsail yards when these were hoisted or lowered and to check gear and rigging. They also laced the topsail luff to the topmast – no mean task when head-to-wind in a breeze with a 2000 sq ft topsail attempting to shake the men off the gantline. At all times they were checking gear for chafe and inefficiency. A mastheadsman combined the ability of a racing seaman with the head of a steeplejack. Quick wits and a sharp knife were his best friends when he was working aloft from his perch on the spreaders, maybe 100 ft above the yacht's foaming wake. For this work he received extra pay of a few shillings each week and he certainly earned it. Many paid the price of their daring and fell to their deaths; others went on to become successful racing mates.

The principal problem of the racing hands was how to dry their canvas racing suits and other clothing properly; these were frequently soaked from the previous day's racing. In wet weather there was little chance of a dry outfit. Constant hauling on hemp ropes resulted in split fingers and, after a few days' hard weather, many fingers were bound with brown tarred hemp for protection and to aid healing.

The introduction of bermudian rig into the large-class racing yachts during the 1920s led to a reduction in the crew needed to handle them – from the thirty-five to thirty-seven carried in the big British cutters and schooners of the 1890s and the early years of the twentieth century to the twenty-two needed for the smaller 23 Metre yachts of 1907–14. There was a further reduction of hands to a total of nineteen professionals in the J Class yachts such as *Endeavour*, which had a sail area, excluding spinnaker, of 7520 sq ft compared with the 13,028 sq ft set by *Valkyrie III* in 1895 and the 16,159 sq ft on the American *Reliance* of 1903, which needed over fifty men to sail her and up to seventy when racing.

During the 1920s and 1930s, crews' wages averaged £3 per week with 5*s*. of this deducted each week as 'good conduct money', payable as a lump sum at the end of the season as an added incentive for hands to remain with the yacht throughout, which they almost invariably did. Prize money was then paid at the rate of £1 per man for a first prize, 15*s*. for a second prize and 10*s*. for crossing the line with no prize. This was also paid as a lump sum at the end of the season.

At that time the racing crews were drawn from a wider selection of communities than before, but they were all from a winter background of fishing under sail in small craft.

A Day's Racing

A typical day's racing on board a British first-class racer commenced at 6.30 a.m. with cups of tea for all hands. Then the crew went barefoot on deck to scrub down, the buckets of sea water being drawn by the first and second mates. Scrubbing completed, chamois cloths were used to dry the deck down as well as possible and to clean and polish all brass and bronze fittings. The sail coat came off the mainsail and the foresail if she was a schooner, or the mizzen if a yawl. Some of the headsails would be put in stops, many hands kneeling at intervals along the deck at the leech or luff of the sail while it was bunched carefully towards the luff and the resulting long, thin sausage was lightly stopped with weak ropeyarn, which would part instantly when the sheet was pulled hard to break the sail out. This saved much time at starts and was often used at other times, particularly for spinnakers and jib topsails. Breakfast was at 8.00 a.m. and all hands made the most of it as there would not be another sit-down meal until the race was over, the yacht anchored and everything again stowed and shipshape – probably four or five o'clock in the afternoon.

Captain and mates would be about the deck discussing gear and leads, mastheadsmen might be aloft for the same purpose, hands would be busy stowing moveables below, steward and cook carefully packing crockery into cupboards against heeling. The caterer and a hand would probably go quickly ashore to obtain some fresh provisions; the steward might accompany them, particularly if there was to be a large party of owner's guests on board for the day's racing. Perhaps two or three hands would be told off to wash around the waterline and the sides in the dinghy and others would be preparing spinnakers and large headsails in the fo'c'sle, carrying the heavy sail bags from stowages in the counter or elsewhere.

Meanwhile, the owner and his family and guests would probably be staying at the yacht club, or on board the owner's steam or motor yacht, on a similar chartered yacht or on one owned by a friend. A few owners did live on board a large racer for short periods, but the bustle of life, the exigencies of preparation for race days and the frequent passagemaking meant that it was not a restful atmosphere, and few of the owner's party would have enjoyed it for long.

Usually, therefore, the owner and his family and friends came on in a launch an hour or so before the start, which might be at 10.00 a.m., but for about one and a half hours previously the racers were got under weigh and stood softly out of the anchorage, gradually setting mainsails and jibs, topsails and staysails and, depending on rig, foresails and mizzens. The crew tuned sails and rigging as they went, so that, by the time the class was near the starting line, shortly before the ten-minute gun, everything was in the best possible condition and all hands were at their racing stations. The skipper was at the tiller or wheel unless, as in the 1920s and 1930s, the yacht was to be steered by an amateur, when the skipper stood by to provide assistance and advice and give the orders to the crew. The first mate was in charge forward and the second mate aft; the latter oversaw all the handling of the running and shifting (preventer) backstay purchases, the mainsheet, and the handling of the sheets for jib, staysail, jib topsail and spinnaker sheets and guys. The first mate was responsible for supervising the anchor work, the set and trim of headsails and spinnakers, the lookout when racing, and keeping an eye on the tactics of rivals ahead or approaching who might not be able to be seen by the skipper or helmsman. He might also signal to the skipper how close the headsails would stand to windward, and perhaps his most difficult task was to establish the correct set of a jib topsail when going to windward. His was one of the most exacting jobs on board.

The hands were positioned about the deck in stations which, in the judgement of the skipper and mates, would result in the most efficient handling at the greatest speed for various sailing situations. They moved quickly and quietly to their posts and when not needed lay on deck to reduce windage.

To the crew of a large racer, a day's racing, usually over a course of 40 miles or so, was wearing work. The course was often a run from the start to the lee mark, then a beat back, twice around. Other courses were triangular and could involve rounding several marks varying from navigation buoys to light vessels or mark boats, which might be steam yachts, chartered passenger steamers crowded with members of the club organizing the regatta, or chartered fishing vessels with large ensigns at the masthead for ease of visibility.

Beating to windward in racing often meant tacking every few minutes, and the considerable sheeting, trimming, handling and setting of sails, coupled with the state of alertness constantly demanded of everyone, was tiring despite the short duration of the race. No doubt seafarers in square-riggers blundering around the oceans would smile at the thought, but there is no doubt that the racing crews worked hard at refined sailing. At midday, during a run downwind, they ate a quick sandwich passed around by the cook and his mate, and the owner's party might manage a hot meal in the saloon.

When the racer had crossed the finishing line, sails were gradually lowered and the yacht brought to anchor. Then all hands were busy coiling down and making a neat and seamanlike stow of the sails; the mainsail (the foresail of a schooner or the mizzen of a yawl) was carefully flaked across the top of the boom with outhaul slacked and battens drawn. The mate saw that the leech was well pulled out aft and that the long canvas tyers were lying ready, passed under the footrope of the sail and over the boom. Then, when the sail was settled, the tyers were passed around it and knotted. A detail, but typical of the routine care on board these craft. Meanwhile, other hands were flaking and bagging headsails and spinnakers for stowage in the sail locker in the counter or, if the owner and his party were not staying on board, perhaps temporarily in the saloon, the floor of which was carefully covered with protective canvas. The cook and his mate would be preparing a meal for the crew and, if the owner and guests were to remain, an evening dinner; the steward would be fussing between the fo'c'sle stove and his pantry and laying out the silver and linen. In later years many owners lived on board their attendant steam or, later, motor yachts, which were better equipped for accommodating them and their guests, who might number as many as eight. Such a yacht could also act as tender to the racer, carrying spare sails and providing a tow if the racer was becalmed on passage or in a hurry to get to the next regatta. Some of her hands would be experienced racing men and these could supplement the racing crew, if required, as 'extra hands'.

In Decline

The period 1920 to 1936 saw a new flowering of big-class yacht racing with big cutters, sloops and schooners thrashing to windward in clouds of spray or surging along under enormous spinnakers, their crews of nineteen to thirty-five men driving them hard. The 12 Metre class emerged as the secondary racing yachts; they were miniatures of the big class in many ways and at that time also demonstrated useful seaworthiness and speed, following the large class around much of the coastal regatta circuit. The British big class enjoyed an unparalleled season in 1935 with up to seven yachts racing, and included the visiting American *Yankee*. But during the 1930s changing social attitudes in sailing were strongly reflected in the tremendous growth of ocean racing in Britain, America, Germany. Holland and Belgium.

The collapse of big-class racing after 1935 has often been attributed to excess and to ever more ambitious design, with particular regard to the height and complexity of a rig for sailing in light or moderate winds and relatively smooth water, the best conditions for yacht racing. This lead to the occasional failure. Although several large yachts lost their masts and sometimes would not risk them by racing, this was a matter of seamanship rather than design, as the mast could stand moderate canvas even in strong winds. Had the owners of the large racers encouraged designers to think in terms of providing a smaller mainsail to be set in strong winds, perhaps also with two reefs in it, these undoubtedly seaworthy hulls would have confidently faced anything encountered in summer racing.

In many ways the heart went out of the British big class with the death of King George V in 1936 and the subsequent scuttling of the *Britannia* in accordance with his wishes. The two succeeding monarchs were not interested in yacht racing and the big class survived the 1936 season in reduced numbers. *Endeavour II*'s challenge for the America's Cup prolonged interest into 1937 but thereafter the large racers were almost all converted to cruisers or laid up. In America they were gradually broken up. The *Cambria*, *Shamrock V*, *Westward*, *Candida* and *Lulworth* had become cruisers. *Endeavour*, *Endeavour II* and *Velsheda* were laid up at Gosport; *Astra* became a tender to her owner's 12 Metre yacht until 1939.

When British large-class racing ended, in 1937, the 12 Metre became the largest class making the traditional round of the British coastal regattas, but they were usually confined to the east and south coast events and a short foray across the Channel to Le Havre and other regattas. Despite the high quality of their racing and the visit of the successful American 12 Metre *Vim* in 1939, they did not attract the same public interest as the grander spectacle of the big-class yachts.

The end of the long tradition of racing in the regattas around the British coast ended at Dartmouth in August 1939, under the shadow of a war which irrevocably changed the old order.

In America the big-class racers enjoyed a final flurry of racing glory during the 1937 season, culminating in the decisive defeat of *Endeavour II* by *Ranger* in the last America's Cup series to be sailed by large yachts. As in Britain, the 12 Metre then became the largest competitive class from 1938 until 1941. By 1942 all the surviving American large-class racers had been broken up.

Several British large racers survived the war, but *Westward* was deliberately sunk in 1947 in accordance with her owner's will and the *Endeavour II* was broken up in 1957. *Lulworth*, *Velsheda* and *Endeavour* survive, unrigged, and their futures remain uncertain. *Astra*, *Candida*, *Cambria* and *Shamrock V* continue to sail in the Mediterranean under cruising rigs and with auxiliary engines, as reminders of the big-class glory.

This book is concerned with the large racing yachts at the peak of their long evolution. I hope it expresses the aspirations and abilities of their designers, builders, captains and crews, and the pride of their owners – all of whom strove to achieve perfection in every way with these fine craft.

PART ONE

1893–1900

The mighty *Satanita* in 1893, reaching towards the next mark at speed and preparing to set her spinnaker. Captain Tom Jay of Rowhedge stands to leeward of the long iron tiller and two hands stand by the mainsheet and the weather shifting backstay purchase. The yacht is close to her maximum speed in this smooth water: the fastest cutter ever built, she once achieved over 16 knots on a timed course off the Isle of Wight. She also averaged 13.7 knots during a race from Gravesend, on the lower Thames, around the Mouse light vessel and back, on a broad and a close reach.

Satanita's dimensions were 131 ft 6 in overall, 93 ft 6 in waterline length, 24 ft 6 in beam, 14 ft 6 in draft. She displaced 126 tons. Her sail plan was the tallest of the splendid quartet of big racers which were completed that spring. The newly permitted forward overhang shortened the bowsprit and enabled the forestay to be set further forward, reducing the foot of the jib and improving its aspect. However, the total hoist compared to the waterline length was still only 1.2:1 compared with 1.14:1 of the *Vanduara* of 1882. *Satanita*'s total sail area was 10,094 sq ft, comprising mainsail 5264, headsails 3360 and topsail 1470 sq ft. The boom shown was 91 ft long and the height from the deck to the topmast shoulder was 114 ft. Her first boom was replaced before she had raced, by a stronger one. In her second season the sailplan was altered; boom length was reduced to 88 ft, 5 ft was cut from the bowsprit and 5 ft added to the gaff.

The increased sail area and speed of these cutters resulted in many broken topmasts and bowsprits, and several sprung masts, for staying was lagging behind the rapid development of the hulls. Their deeper and more concentrated ballast keels and greater beam, allowed by the rules, improved their power to carry sail and made designers contemplate taller sailplans.

The cut of her sails is interesting as an example of the best British practice of the time. The mainsail cloths are parallel to the leech, which does not have battens but stands well. The staysail has cloths from luff to leech, the jib and jib topsail have a mitre seam, and the yard topsail with its cloths parallel to the leech sets badly.

BELOW

The royal racing cutter *Britannia* in 1894, fetching for a mark under her large reaching staysail and long-roper 'Yankee' jib topsail. The sails set perfectly and all hands of her crew of twenty-seven, with perhaps five 'extra hands', are busy on the broad deck. She was sailed by Captain John Carter, an experienced racing skipper who, like most of his contemporaries, was a polished personality.

In this picture *Britannia*'s quarter wave suggests that she is probably sailing at about 11–12 knots. The topsail yard and jackyard are both bending with the strain from halyard and sheet; the running and shifting backstays hang slack on the lee side. A hand works on the bowsprit, tending the smaller jib topsail which is neatly stopped along it ready to hoist.

PAGE 29, ABOVE

Captain John Carter of Rowhedge was a brilliant racing skipper, and sailed the royal racing cutter *Britannia* for the Prince of Wales, later King Edward VII, from her launch in 1893 until his death in 1910. He was born at Wivenhoe, Essex in 1850 and with his family later moved across the River Colne to the similar fishing, yachting and shipbuilding village of Rowhedge. Like all the Colne skippers and hands he began his seafaring by sailing in fishing smacks out of Rowhedge, Wivenhoe and Brightlingsea, working in the sprat and trawl fisheries and at dredging oysters and scallops in Essex waters and beyond, in the North Sea, English Channel, Irish Sea and off Scotland and the Dutch and French coasts. The smacks were a hard but fine school for handling fore-and-aft rigged craft and those with an aptitude for helmsmanship could gain much experience in the fast and weatherly cutters and the few ketches in the fleet of several hundred vessels fishing from the Colne and the nearby River Blackwater until the 1920s.

John Carter became skipper of a small yacht when he was twenty-two, and in 1875 his ability at the helm led to the offer of command of the Clyde 10 ton racer *Lancer*, and subsequently *Gondola*, *Merle* and *Sayonara*. He jumped up to the 110 ton cutter *Moina* and then to skipper the America's Cup challenger *Genesta* in the 1885 challenge when, although he did not win the trophy, he did win the Cape May and the Brenton Reef Cups in races in America. During her voyage home across the Atlantic the *Genesta*, under ordinary canvas, made a fast passage, logging 240 and 238 nautical miles in two consecutive days. She also won the long-distance yacht race around the British Isles which celebrated the Jubilee of Queen Victoria in 1887.

In the winter of 1892–3 Captain Carter was asked to become skipper of the new big cutter *Britannia*, then building on the Clyde. At the same time he was offered the new and similar sized, Fife-designed cutter *Calluna*. Perhaps naturally, he chose to sail the royal cutter and with her established a tremendous reputation, backed by a well trained crew from the Colne.

Like his contemporaries, Captain Carter rose from humble origins to command spectacular racing yachts for men of culture, wealth and the highest social standing. Despite brief formal education, these captains became polished but modest men, aware of the wide social differences between themselves, their owners and their guests, when on board; yet able to adapt to this paradox and to behave and converse in a relaxed manner and deport themselves in any company. The first personal aim of such captains was usually to own their own home in their native village or town, where they also probably already possessed a fishing smack. If successful, they often invested in other property and sometimes in shares and bonds. They became the most respected men in their seafaring communities, and a successful racing skipper of a large yacht hardly needed to continue fishing in winter unless by choice; often he retained his smack but she was worked by others. Sometimes he sailed in her for old time's sake, but all enjoyed smack racing in the village regattas which were held in autumn when the yachts had laid up. The skippers spent much of the winter attending to the business of refitting and any alterations in the yard, and in consultation with their owner and designers.

The Prince of Wales valued John Carter's skill as a helmsman and his ability in tuning and commanding a large racer and he conferred on him the membership of the Victorian Order, for personal service. He continued as captain of *Britannia* throughout the Prince's ownership.

After five seasons of successful first class racing, *Britannia* retired. She had sailed in 219 races, had won 122 of them, and was second or third in 25 others. She had won £10,172 in prize money. Due to the admission of the smaller racing yachts *Isolde*, *Caress* and *Bona* to the big class to maintain its numbers, the handicaps became widely varying and favoured the smaller yachts. This displeased owners and skippers and the British large class almost collapsed for a few years. In December 1897 *Britannia* was sold for about £4000, passing through two owners without fitting out. John Carter was appointed to command the large racing schooner *Rainbow*, then building on the Clyde, but serious illness prevented his taking up the appointment, which was passed to Captain Tom Jay.

In 1899 the America's Cup challenge by the first *Shamrock* again brought *Britannia* back to the Prince's ownership to race in trials and Captain Carter was again appointed her skipper. He also enjoyed a few races against *Meteor II*, *Bona* and *Rainbow*. In 1900 the Prince again sold the *Britannia*, to Sir Richard Williams-Bulkely who appointed Captain John R. 'Jack' Carter, son of John Carter, as skipper. He had served on board the *Britannia* as ordinary seaman, able seaman and mate, before going deep sea to obtain his square-rigged Master's certificate. Under him *Britannia* spent much time cruising in the Irish Sea for her owner.

However, the Prince still loved his old yacht and chartered her for Cowes Week in 1901 and repurchased her the following year. By then big class racing had reached a low ebb and for the next eight years *Britannia*, with the elder Captain Carter again in command, was generally cruising leisurely about the Solent and south coast of England with King Edward and Queen Alexandra on board, often accompanied by foreign royalty and other guests.

In 1910 *Britannia*'s skipper and owner both

died. However, it heralded a new beginning for King George V took over his father's yacht and re-appointed Captain Jack Carter. Her racing days appeared to be over as the big class was again poorly supported. With her long tiller replaced by a wheel, bulwarks raised and a sunk deckhouse fitted, the yacht seemed destined to end her days cruising about the Solent and South Coast with the royal family quietly enjoying themselves on board for a few weeks each year. In 1913, however, the King decided to enter her for the large handicap class and Carter started putting her through her paces (see jacket painting). A new owner's representative was appointed – Major Philip Hunloke, a close friend of the King, and an enthusiastic amateur helmsman in the Solent small classes. After learning something of the handling of a big cutter from Captain Carter, he began to hold strong views on the duties of an owner's representative, which normally consisted of checking the starting time and signing racing declarations, and began to insist on handling the yacht while racing. It took unusual skill, nerve and judgement to handle a big class racer at close quarters, but he persevered and with the captain's guidance acquired sufficient ability to sail her in the large handicap class, by then a varied collection of yachts keeping alive a semblance of big class sport.

Captain Carter left *Britannia* at the outbreak of the war in 1914, when she was laid up; her subsequent career is related below in this book.

BELOW
Captain Aubrey Crocker was one of the most distinguished skippers of large American racing yachts. He was born at Provincetown, Massachusetts in 1847 and went to sea in fishing schooners when twelve years old. He afterwards served as a hand in several yachts and desplayed an aptitude for racing. In 1876 he was took charge of the new Herreshoff-designed centreboard sloop *Shadow* in the 35 ft class. In over 150 races she won 126 first prizes, and maintained her reputation for several years with him at the tiller. In October 1882 *Shadow* met the Fife-designed cutter *Madge* off Newport in a breeze and sea and beat her soundly, but lost the next day. However, Captain Crocker proved that a well designed centreboarder could match the deep cutter type in American coastal racing.

He was appointed skipper in 1885 of the Boston sloop *Puritan*, which defeated the British cutter *Genesta* under Captain John Carter in a hard-fought series. For several years he then skippered

racers in the 40 ft class, there being little interest in larger racing sloops unless it was an America's Cup season. He also raced *Beatrix*, a Burgess designed 46-footer which came a close second to the Herreshoff *Gloriana*. By then Captain Crocker had moved to a snug home at Cohasset, Massachusetts, in sight and sound of the sea.

In 1893 he was asked to go to England and take command of the large-class sloop *Navahoe*, launched earlier that year by the Herreshoff Manufacturing Co. for American Royal P. Carroll. She had started her first season under Captain Charles Barr, who had sailed her across the Atlantic to race with *Britannia, Valkyrie II, Satanita, Calluna* and *Iverna*. However, she had not done well and possibly at the suggestion of Nathanael Herreshoff, Captain Crocker was asked to sail her. He had changes made in the rig and in her trim and she improved.

Captain Crocker's finest race in *Navahoe* was against *Britannia* for the Brenton Reef Cup, which had been won by Captain John Carter with *Genesta* during her American racing in 1885. Regaining this cup was perhaps the principal reason that Carroll had sent *Navahoe* to England. Appropriately, the two yachts were again sailed by the same helmsmen. They were driven hard through a strong northeast wind and considerable sea. Captain Crocker expected the mast to go in *Navahoe*, but as *Britannia* continued to sail hard he was obliged to carry on. After racing 106 miles across the English Channel and back, *Navahoe* won by seconds.

OPPOSITE PAGE

The hull lines and accommodation arrangement of *Britannia*, designed in 1892 by G. L. Watson & Co. of Glasgow and built there by D. & W. Henderson, a shipyard which constructed some distinguished racing yachts. Both *Britannia* and her near sister *Valkyrie II* were built during the winter of 1892–3 to rival the similar sized *Calluna* which was built at A. & J. Inglis's yard lower down the Clyde; another rival was the larger cutter *Satanita*, built by J. & G. Fay of Southampton to the design of Joseph Soper. The yachts by Watson and Soper established a classic hull form, which though modified has lasted into the late twentieth century. Unfortunately Fife's *Calluna* was a failure for various reasons, including probably more wetted surface and wavemaking resistance from her hull and her young captain's inexperience with large crews, though she was attractive and well built. She lost her rig overboard in an early race and suffered from other rig problems.

When commissioning Watson to design *Britannia* the Prince of Wales (later King Edward VII) requested an ideal large racing yacht within the limits of the Length and Sail Area Rule of rating then current. His one stipulation was that he should be able to enjoy a hot lunch on board when racing. *Britannia*'s dimensions were 121 ft 6 in length overall, 86 ft 10 in waterline length, 23 ft 8 in beam, 15 ft 1½ in draft. Displacement was 154 tons. She was launched from the Partick yard by Mrs Henderson, who christened her *Britannia* as the sleek black hull slid into the narrow Clyde. Essentially a relatively beamy and flat-sheered yacht with freeboard typical of her time and type, her hull form was graceful in every way, though when the quartet of new racers of which she was part appeared they were criticized for their 'ugly' bows. Conservative yachtsmen, conditioned by a century of straight, plumb stems and 'clipper' bows, could not at first accept the overhang. The body sections are typical and the bow allowed her to go to windward well and kept her decks reasonably dry. The flat sections of the counter conferred added stability under sail but kept everyone awake at anchor with the wind from astern over the tide, when it slapped down violently. *Britannia* was to become known as a boat that liked a breeze. She was one of the most successful racing yachts in history.

Below deck the royal yacht provided plain but comfortable accommodation for owner and guests, though it was seldom used except for day racing. The dark mahogany and white enamelled saloon had a piano, and the royal cabin had a bathroom attached – then an unheard-of luxury in a racer. The ladies had a separate cabin aft and all lighting was by oil lamps or candles. The crew had the usual accommodation in the foc's'le: cots and hammocks for thirty men were crammed into a bow area 30 ft long, and sometimes overflowed into the sail locker aft. Only the captain had a cabin. Such conditions were then an inevitable part of a racing man's life, though what it was like below after a few days' hard racing, with everyone's clothing drying

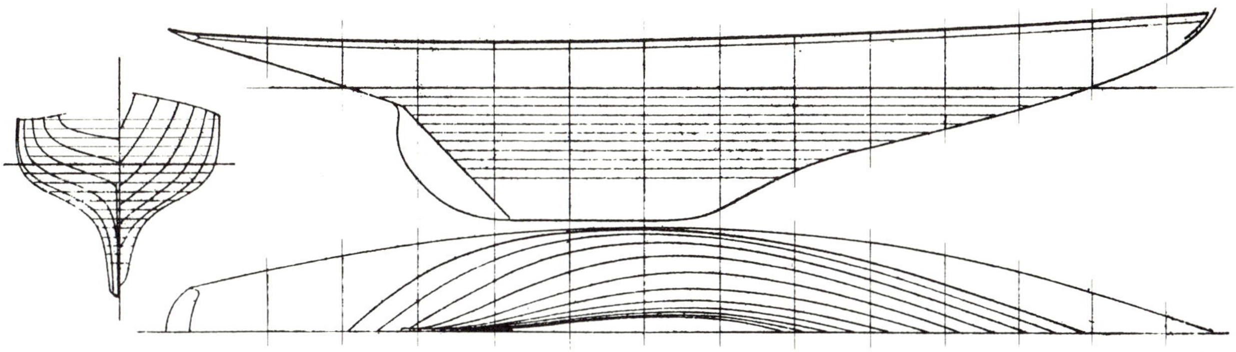

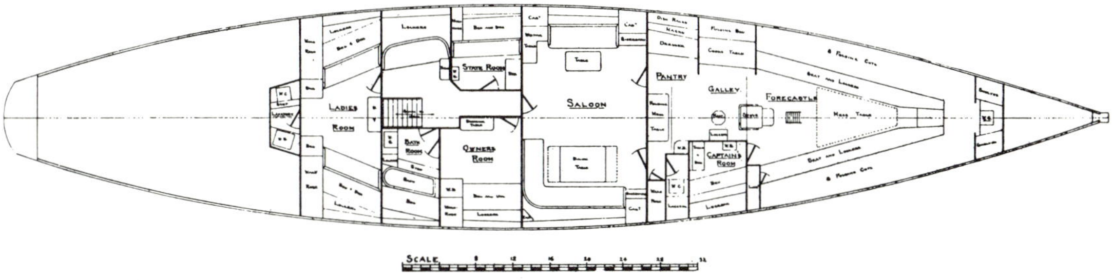

around the single cooking and heating stove, is not hard to imagine. The mast heel came down in the foc's'le and Captain Carter would ask visitors, 'How would you like to be shipmates with that chap? Four tons if he's a pound.' But, despite its size, the yacht's hard driving was to spring three of them before her first season ended.

FOLLOWING PAGE
Valkyrie II racing in 1893. Her captain, William W. Cranfield of Rowhedge, sits on a fender with his hands on the tiller and its lines. His brother, Lemon Cranfield, acting as 'racing pilot', is on board to assist the skipper with his special knowledge of the local tides and wind conditions. Both men were among the small band of leading racing captains, and Lemon was regarded by his fellows as the greatest racing genius of them all, though his restless personality led to his being captain of only two large racers – the *Neva*, and the *Galatea* when she was new. Immediately behind William is Mr Wadley, who had been first mate at the beginning of the season but who became a hand at his own request because he felt too old for the drive and bustle of a mate's duties although he had carried them out well. Instead, William Cranfield chose young William Taylor, seen here at the extreme right in his cheesecutter cap. A few of her crew of thirty-five are lying on the weather deck.

The low stanchions and guardwires in way of the tiller were the only concession to safety on deck, and they were only there because the helmsman's attention could not be diverted in any way from handling the yacht, watching his opponents and working out tactics. Many skippers also preferred or needed to stand to leeward of the long tiller, particularly in light weather or to see clearly ahead when going to windward. The well-scrubbed white pine deck, varnished teak skylights and companion hatch, sparkling sunshine and a fair wind added to the smart and pleasant atmosphere of a large racer – in some ways similar to that of a man-of-war.

When this photograph was taken William Cranfield was thirty-seven years old, Lemon about fifty. Their beards, cheesecutters and style of dress make them appear much older. William was then at the pinnacle of a thirty year career as a brilliant racing skipper. He died in 1914 aged fifty-eight. Lemon, who frequently acted as a racing pilot into the early 1900s, also commanded the 40-rater *Corsair* and the 20-rater *Stephanie* for a season each. His later years were spent fishing and sailing his smart cutter smack *Neva* from Rowhedge. She was the fastest of the large fleet of smacks working from the Essex coast and she and her owner became a legend in

the autumn regattas on the Colne, where the helmsmen tended to settle old scores from the past racing season.

RIGHT, BELOW
Satanita at full speed. The cutter is reaching in smooth water with the bow wave tumbling on board by the lee rigging and the quarter wave hissing up by the tiller. Captain Tom Jay stands at the lee tiller lines, foot braced in the surge, feeling his mighty cutter roaring along at about 13 knots, sails drawing as though cut from card and all hands 'lively' and anticipating the next mark.

The spinnaker boom is topped up the mast out of the way. The patches and tabling at the clew of the jib topsail testify to the strain which could come on its sheet. She appears to have a multiple martingale to the bobstay but there is no other evidence of this fitting in other photos of her and it may have been experimental. The jackyard topsail has a mitre seam, which is an improvement on the earlier cut which had cloths parallel to the leech.

The Clydeside hills rise in the misty background of a summer morning. One of the great yachts of history at her best.

RIGHT, ABOVE
Britannia's crew in 1894. John Carter stands in the centre by the binnacle, one hand on the tiller, and the first and second mates stand to port and starboard in jackets and cheesecutters. Twenty-one deck hands, two stewards and the cook complete the muster of twenty-seven crack professionals which was augmented as necessary by extra hands for racing days. There were often a total of thirty-seven on board, besides the owner and his guests, who contributed nothing to the yacht's handling.

The photograph emphasizes the breadth of deck of these first-class racers and their ship-like feel. The heavy boom and the stowed mainsail have been swung out to starboard, clear of the group. End-of-season photographs such as this were cherished in the living rooms of the crews for decades, until death and indifferent descendants lead to their being discarded.

FOLLOWING PAGE
Britannia running in a fresh wind with a jib-headed topsail set above an unreefed mainsail. She also carries a balloon foresail, a large jib and 'long-roper' jib topsail. The spinnaker was set inside the forestay in accordance with a long-

standing rule and it would be many years before racers were allowed to improve the set of spinnakers by setting them before it, a change which brought in the 'parachute' type of sail.

RIGHT
Setting *Britannia*'s spinnaker, 1894. Four men are hauling on the halyard purchase at the foot of the mast. The 90 ft spinnaker boom is being lowered to starboard and is visible between the clew of the jib and the sausage-like soft cotton spinnaker which is rising from the forehatch. The staysail is set in stops, ready to break out when needed. Two hands forward overhaul the spinnaker boom foreguy and the spinnaker sheet.

The shroud ratlines show clearly in this photograph and the comparatively slack rigging, particularly the topmast shrouds, is noticeable. The boom is low in this first phase of her cutter rig, and the lightness of the wind can be gauged from the wrinkles in the mainsail running from tack to head. The bowsprit staying had been improved since *Britannia*'s debut in 1893 by the fitting of a martingale to spread the rod and wire bobstay. This was braced transversely to a pair of bowsprit shroud spreaders, which the hands called 'whiskers'.

The spinnaker then had an area of about 5500 sq ft. British yachts crews always set the spinnaker flying, until the visit of the American racing sloop *Vigilant* in 1894, when they saw how her crew sent the sail up in stops, as the British crews had done with racing headsails for generations. *Vigilant*'s crew had it up and broken out in a few seconds and were all the time in more certain control than by the method shown here, which in strong winds was difficult and often dangerous.

FOLLOWING PAGE
The Herreshoff Manufacturing Co. of Bristol, Rhode Island, designed and built the racing sloop *Vigilant* in 1893 for a syndicate headed by C. O. Iselin. She was chosen to defend the America's Cup against the British *Valkyrie II* that year and visited England in 1894 to race around the coast with the first-class yachts.

Her hull sections show the characteristics of Herreshoff hull form, with a relatively slack bilge. In contrast, the profile is conservative and the draft shallow, in the contemporary American style and because of launching depth limitations at the Herreshoff yard. A large bronze centreplate was fitted and caused considerable trouble during her visit to England. *Vigilant* was 124 ft long overall, 86 ft $2\frac{1}{2}$ in on the waterline, with 26 ft 3 in beam and drawing 13 ft 6 in without the centreboard lowered. Her sail area was 11,272 sq ft rigged as a sloop.

She was sailed in England by Captain Henry C. 'Hank' Haff, an accomplished racing skipper from the oystering village of Islip on the south shore of Long Island, home of many men who sailed in American racing yachts in summer and sailed their graceful oyster sloops to dredge on the grounds at other seasons.

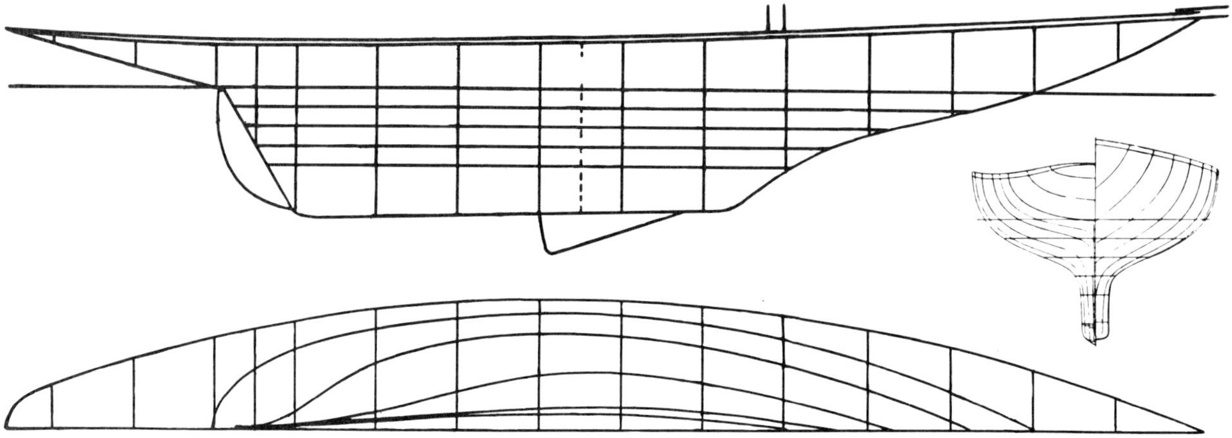

RIGHT
The American sloop *Vigilant* slides along with Captain Haff at the wheel. She sailed to England early in the summer of 1894 to spend the season racing around the coastal regattas with the British large class. Nathanael Herreshoff came over by liner to superintend her fitting out, and the owner's steam yacht *Atalanta* arrived to act as her tender. The English captains and crews of the large cutters *Britannia*, *Satanita* and *Valkyrie II*, her rival for the America's Cup the preceding year, were keen to show they could beat her.

Vigilant's first appearance racing in Britain was on the Clyde at the regatta of the quaintly named Mudhook Yacht Club on July 5, 1894. This was the one fixture of the year in which amateur helmsmen were allowed to steer the large-class yachts. While all four were manoeuvring for the start a small sailing boat appeared in the course of the fast-moving *Valkyrie II*. To avoid a fatal collision, her amateur helmsman, quickly aided by Captain Cranfield, took avoiding action with the result that she was run into by the *Satanita*. The two yachts were locked together for a few minutes, then the sinking *Valkyrie II* drifted away to foul a steam yacht. One of her smartest hands, William Brown of Rowhedge, was crushed between them and later died. *Valkyrie II* then sank and *Satanita* lay in the water disabled. *Vigilant* and *Britannia* were unaware of all this, and during the first of a series of engagements and in a fine race the American yacht was beaten by only 36 seconds. With *Valkyrie II* sunk and *Satanita* towed away for repair, *Britannia* alone was left to race *Vigilant* again at the Royal Clyde Yacht Club regatta two days later. *Britannia* won by 1 minute 7 seconds after 50 miles of sailing. Two days later the yachts met again and when the race was stopped due to lack of wind she was 9 minutes 33 seconds ahead of *Vigilant*. Next day *Britannia* won again and *Vigilant*'s crew were becoming disheartened, despite a good showing against a well-tuned and manned racer in her home waters. *Vigilant*'s great fault was her slowness in stays compared with the British yachts, and her badly setting sails.

Before leaving the Clyde to race in Northern Ireland, *Vigilant* had her spars slightly shortened and her sail area reduced accordingly. She was towed to Bangor, County Down by her tender *Atalanta*. At the Royal Ulster Yacht Club regatta in Belfast Lough *Vigilant* showed improved form and led *Britannia* for part of the first race in squally weather with jackyard topsails though *Britannia* won by 1 minute 31 seconds over the 50 mile course. Afterwards, at anchor, Captain Carter called over to Captain Haff wishing him a pleasant day's racing next morning, and the American replied, 'Yeah, so long as we don't get none of them goddamned squalls!'

In the second day's racing *Britannia* broke her gaff jaws and had to return to anchor. *Vigilant* took things easy and sailed over to win. *Britannia* won again at the Royal St George Yacht Club regatta on July 20, in Dublin Bay, but *Vigilant* beat her the next day. At Queenstown *Britannia* won again but lost to *Vigilant* at Cork on July 24.

By July 28 *Vigilant*, *Britannia* and the 40-rater *Corsair* were at the Penzance and Mount's Bay regatta in Cornwall, one of those pleasing coastal fixtures offering classes for everything from the largest yachts to local fishing craft and attended by thousands, afloat and ashore. *Britannia* beat *Vigilant* by 5 minutes 14 seconds

and the still disabled *Satanita* did not start. By then the American's sails were misshapen and in poor condition, to the despair of her crew.

There was continued good feeling between the skippers and crews of the British and American racers. *Britannia*'s win was 'the signal for the most enthusiastic cheering from thousands of throats, the noise of yachts' whistles and sirens adding to the excitement which prevailed. *Vigilant* also came in for an ovation. After rounding the committee boat the two cracks came close together and the crew of the *Vigilant* gave hearty cheers for the *Britannia*, whose crew vigorously returned the compliment.'

Two days later, at the Royal Cornwall Yacht Club regatta at Falmouth, the three big yachts were preparing to race when *Vigilant* suddenly lowered her mainsail and withdrew from the race, to the disappointment of the vast crowds of spectators. She had strained her bobstay and Hank Haff thought that the headgear would come down if they raced in a freshening wind. With her races at Plymouth cancelled, *Vigilant* then sailed for the Solent, to refit for Cowes Week and a private match which was being arranged with *Britannia*.

PAGES 38–9

Valkyrie III, almost ready to be launched at the Glasgow yard of her builders D. & W. Henderson in 1895. The big racer has been 'struck over' transversely from the berth where she was built, close to the shed in the background, and rests on a slipway carriage supported by a built-up cradle of blocks, planks and wedges. She remains shored up as no chances could be taken with such a deep and long-ended hull.

LEFT

Vigilant surging towards the finish line at Cowes on August 4, 1894, in the lead during her private match with the Prince of Wales's cutter *Britannia*. After her defeats by *Britannia* on the Clyde and at Penzance regatta, where the yachts raced in an annual fixture on the way from the Clyde to the Solent, there was tremendous interest in this match race, especially as it was a prelude to Cowes Week.

Englishmen hoped for a hard breeze with plenty of windward work, which would suit *Britannia*. By the time *Vigilant* reached the Solent she had been tuned up and had her sail area slightly reduced. Her owner approached Ratsey & Lapthorn for an English suit of sails to replace the ill-fitting ones she had carried on the Clyde. The firm felt that they could not supply them and instead *Vigilant*'s big mainsail was sent by rail from Penzance to Southampton, together with some of her headsails, where it was practically rebuilt by Tilling & Son.

The two yachts were docked for bottom cleaning and were remeasured at Southampton the day before the race, when the *Vigilant*'s crew turned everything possible out of her, even food and drinking water. As a result of the measurement *Vigilant* had to allow *Britannia* 2 minutes 4 seconds over the course. The prize was a £100 (cost) silver cup to be given by the owner of the losing yacht to the owner of the winner. They started over the Royal Yacht Squadron line, westward to round the East Lepe buoy and then to the Warner light vessel off the east end of the Isle of Wight, then back to Cowes, twice round – in all about 42 miles. Hundreds of steam and sailing yachts crowded Cowes Roads to see the start of this international contest. The westerly wind was fresh and they made the East Lepe buoy in three tacks over the foul tide, the only windward work all day, with *Vigilant* leading by 50 seconds in the gybe round the mark to sail eastward, and setting a large jib topsail (such a sail was afterwards called a 'Yankee jib topsail' by English crews), compared to the British yacht's ordinary sized one. *Vigilant* continued to draw away and a spectator wrote: 'As the yachts threaded the fleet at anchor in Cowes Roads they were heartily cheered. The crews of HMS *Dreadnought*, the German corvette *Stosch* and the *Osborne*, royal yacht, being particularly demonstrative.'

Off Seaview the breeze freshened, and at the Warner the *Vigilant* was 2 minutes 44 seconds ahead. They reached back through Spithead and into the Solent, around the East Lepe and again back to the Warner, the jib topsails being taken in as the breeze freshened. On the reach back to the finish at Cowes the German Emperor's cutter *Meteor* was pacing *Vigilant*, which was also followed by her owner's large steam yacht *Atalanta*. *Vigilant* won by 4 minutes 29 seconds, a few minutes after this photograph was taken. She is travelling at her maximum speed, perhaps 12 knots, in the smooth water and will get some fresher puffs when she clears the high land at East Cowes. She carries her jib-headed topsail, and the large light weather jib topsail is stowed on the bowsprit end ready to be re-set if needed. Someone, probably the mate, checks the lee rigging and all hands are low on the broad deck as Hank Haff drives his Yankee 'sloop' to victory.

RIGHT, ABOVE

The mighty *Valkyrie III* beats down the Clyde in 1895. Captain William Cranfield is to weather of her long tiller and Captain Edward Sycamore of Brightlingsea is at the lee side; both are distinguished by their blue suits from the crew of thirty-five in white duck jumpers and trousers.

She is setting her full sail area of 13,028 sq ft, which was increased to about 20,000 sq ft when the spinnaker was set. The jib and mainsail are not setting well, despite careful trimming of the new sails. In contrast, the jib topsail and the yard topsail stand beautifully. The size of her individual sails is emphasized by the three rows of reef eyelets across the big mainsail, instead of the two which were customary in contemporary yachts. The staysail, which appears of modest size but is actually 1530 sq ft could have two reefs tucked in when racing in conditions when it might be preferable to reef rather than lose more time changing down to a smaller one. The big boom is supported by two topping lifts and has necessarily elaborate sheeting. The bowsprit, 33 ft outboard, was proportionally longer than in Watson's earlier cutters of this type, and is bending upwards despite the bobstay and martingale. The first mate, in a dark jacket, is out along it, probably to observe the set of the headsails, which were his responsibility. The topsail soars above the head of the topmast, 137 ft above deck. One of her mastheadsmen is at his lonely perch aloft on the jumper strut, below the crosstrees.

Valkyrie III is probably sailing at 13–14 knots and though her bow makes little fuss she leaves a curling, breaking quarter wave. During one of her trial races, in a strong wind, she came down the Clyde on a reach and her surging wake capsized a small ferry boat, though fortunately none of its passengers were drowned.

A great yacht and crew, with high hopes of winning the America's Cup races later that year.

RIGHT, BELOW

The crew of *Valkyrie III* in 1895. She needed forty men to race her and here they are grouped on the foredeck for the camera. Captain William Cranfield is seated in the centre, before the mast in the second row. Edward Sycamore, the yacht's second captain, is seated third from left in the second row. The first and second mates are wearing cheesecutters and pilot jackets, and the cook has on his white jacket. The thirty-six hands were the pick of Rowhedge, Wivenhoe and Brightlingsea racing men, with a few from the Clyde and Tollesbury: this was one of the ablest racing crews in history. The hand seated at extreme left in the first row is John Fale, who painted the picture of *Valkyrie III* which is in the Nottage Institute, Wivenhoe.

The appointment of a second captain was confined to yachts racing for the America's Cup and originated in the U.S. during the 1880s. It was also the practice in a few British challengers, and in a very few instances on both sides there were three captains though one was in overall command. The second captain was there to assist when yachts became so complex as to be beyond one man's capacity to manage the steering, tactics, observation of competitors, direct the mates for sail changes and crew disposition, decide the best course and keep track of changing depths, wind shifts and tidal streams.

FOLLOWING PAGE

A view of *Valkyrie III* becalmed emphasizes her vast sail area and its proportions. The housing topmast rig was preferred by English and American large racers until the early 1900s, as the topmast could be housed underway in bad weather if this were necessary when sailing a long course. However, this was rarely done and usually the topmast was brought snugly down before the start. All hands are quiet as she ghosts through the water with a ripple at the forefoot. William Cranfield coaxes her along at the tiller lines, keeping the headsails full in an apparent calm. He had a reputation for exceptional ability in light weather, besides being a first-rate hard weather helmsman and seaman.

Tiller lines were rigged much of the time in large yachts when racing and often on passage. They took the form of purchases on each side, shackled to a band on the tiller and to eyebolts on

the covering boards. The falls led outboard, enabling the skipper to stand in any position across the deck and maintain full control of the helm. The forces on the rudders of these large yachts could be considerable. The advantage in strong winds is obvious and in calms, with the hull affected by any swell and transferring movement to the rudder, the lines kept control when there was even greater need to sail the fastest course possible. Also the breeze might freshen or a squall blow up and the helmsman would need the lines even more.

RIGHT
Valkyrie III on the Clyde on her return from racing for the America's Cup in 1896. The low ketch rig almost disguises the long hull. Until the first 12 Metre challenge in 1958, all challengers for the America's Cup had to sail across the Atlantic, and by the time of the Earl of Dunraven's attempt in 1895, the racing rig had become so large that it became necessary to rig the yachts as ketches for the passages out and home. There is little unusual in the ocean rig shown except that the short bowsprit seems unnecessary – though without it, it would not have been easy to connect the topmast forestay to the stemhead, or successfully to transmit forces from it into the bow. The ocean passage from New York to the Clyde took twenty-nine days and the racer had to be sailed carefully to avoid damage at sea.

PAGE 46, ABOVE
Valkyrie III in drydock in New York before the 1896 races for the America's Cup, showing her

106 ft long boom and the four stout strops attaching the mainsheet blocks. *Valkyrie III* was among the most extreme racing yachts built, but in her hull Watson had embodied some American features: greater beam than earlier British racers of comparable size, a broader counter and a fuller bow. Her 20 ft draft and large ballast keel bring her deck almost level with the top of the dock, and this was one good reason why these craft were placed in a ship dock instead of being hauled out on a slipway carriage at a yacht yard. Considerable care was necessary to dock such a comparatively deep, narrow and slender vessel successfully, and trouble was taken over dropping the shores in as she settled on the blocks.

Her crew of forty are busy fitting out for the Cup races. A hand in a bosun's stool is cleaning the mast. Others are working on the foredeck and more are amidships, dwarfed by the boom. Six shipwrights are working on the counter, probably recaulking and paying the deck.

Even in dock, yacht customs are observed and the canvas deck bucket is in its proper place, upside down on top of the stock of the anchor, which is stowed on deck in chocks. Other men, probably painters from the yard, will be working on her sides from the slung stagings. Access across the abyss of the drydock is by a plank catwalk (left). The crowds of spectators at the dock edges hardly diminished during daylight and the crew were regarded with the same public interest now accorded to a visiting international football or cricket team.

FOLLOWING PAGE, BELOW
Nathanael Herreshoff giving directions to the skipper of a tug at the Herreshoff Manufacturing Co. yard during attempts to launch the big racing sloop *Defender* in June 1895. Herreshoff could often be impatient and brusque: an accident such as a large racer sticking on the launching ways must have made him almost unapproachable.

ABOVE, RIGHT
The launch of the America's Cup sloop *Defender*. Due to the lack of sufficiently deep water at the ends of the ways, there was trouble with launching several yachts built at the Herreshoff yard. Although this was regarded as an ill omen by many sailors, the yachts were usually remarkably successful.

PAGE 49, BELOW
Captain Henry 'Hank' Clayton Haff of the big American sloop *Defender* at Newport, Rhode Island before his successful defence of the America's Cup against the challenge of *Valkyrie III* in 1895; he was then at the peak of his career as a racing skipper. His beard, dry wit and shrewd racing skill made him a popular American hero during his three defences of the America's Cup. Haff was also well liked by British yachtsmen and, perhaps more important to him, by the professional skippers and hands against whom he sailed.

Hank Haff had an unusual start to his career. He was born in Brooklyn in 1838, of Dutch descent; his father was a sailor who was lost at sea four years later. Henry started work on a farm when seven years old and left ten years later to become a section hand on the Long Island Railroad, afterwards becoming a foreman. When he was twenty the family moved to Islip, New York on the south shore of Long Island by the Great South Bay, then a delightfully rural area. For some time he worked afloat in oyster sloops and other fishing craft and in winter as a hand in coasting schooners. During the American Civil War he sailed in a government schooner. About 1868 he became 'bosun' of a sailing and sporting club, where he looked after members' yachts and the clubhouse. He gradually became noted for his fast sailing of centreboard boats in the locality and in 1876 took charge of the centreboard sloop yacht *Onward*, racing her successfully. During the 1881 season Captain Haff was released by his owner to sail in the sloop *Mischief* which under his old friend Captain Nathan Clock defended the America's Cup against the challenge of the Canadian sloop *Atalanta*. This was his first taste of the wrangles and problems associated with that trophy. In 1882 he became skipper of the larger sloop *Fanny*, a fast centreboard yacht with a reputation that was enhanced by his expert handling. In 1886 he was again released, to sail the America's Cup defender *Mayflower* against the challenging *Galatea*. This was at the request of Major General Charles J. Paine, a wealthy lawyer who had large interests in western railroads and was a member of the Eastern Yacht Club and New York Yacht Club. He was an able organizer and protagonist of Boston racing interests, and had been principal member of the syndicate behind the Cup defender *Puritan* in 1885 and sole owner of *Mayflower* and *Volunteer* for their defences. When the *Volunteer* was built in the following year Haff was given command of her and beat the British cutter *Thistle*. After two seasons in Paine's *Volunteer* he took charge of the 70 ft sloop *Titania* for C. O. Iselin, a particularly wealthy American owner of racing yachts. In 1890 he returned to *Volunteer*, which was perhaps his favourite command. During 1892, with large yachts temporarily out of fashion in America, Captain Haff became skipper of the *Alborak* in the keenly contested 46 ft class. She was designed by General Paine's son John B. Paine, an amateur who produced several designs, and was not a successful racer.

With the burst of building large-class racers during the winter of 1892–3, Captain Haff was appointed to sail the big sloop *Colonia*, owned by Archibald Rogers, as a contender to defend the America's Cup against the *Valkyrie II*. *Colonia* raced in trials against *Vigilant*, *Pilgrim* and *Jubilee*, and *Vigilant* was selected. In 1894 Haff skippered *Vigilant* for George J. Gould during her season spent racing in Britain against the big class. In 1895 he sailed *Defender* against the America's Cup challenger *Valkyrie III*, and afterwards spent a couple of years ashore. In 1898 he returned to sailing to skipper *Volunteer*, by then long out of competition, for J. Malcolm Forbes who delighted in fast cruising and following the racing fleet. In 1901 Captain Hank was put in charge of the giant sloop *Independence*, the Boston contender for selection as America's Cup defender against *Shamrock II*. However, the combination of a radical design, an ageing skipper and a feverishly partisan Boston owner led to his most disappointing command. After that he did not go afloat but continued to take keen interest in yacht racing.

Three of his sons became yacht skippers: Captain Harry P. Haff distinguished himself in the schooner *Quissette* and the sloop *Weetamoe*. Captain Henry Haff was the most famous resident of the little town of Islip – perhaps he best enjoyed his informal office as commodore of the Islip scooter races, a winter sport for sailing iceboats which achieved tremendous speeds over the frozen creek and bay.

Captain Haff's health declined and he died in July 1906. A fine tribute came from Archibald C. Smith, the successful American designer of many large yachts who had sailed with Captain Hank over many years.

> The captain was one of the select few that the country could turn to when the America's Cup was to be sailed for. He was one of the still fewer few who had inspirations at a critical time in a race. During one of the Cup races the boats had been gone nearly two hours and neither had the advantage. Captain Hank Haff, after much discussion, ordered the outhaul of the mainsail slackened and at once the American boat took the lead, and added to it every foot of the way home. While the New York Yacht Club flag flies, all will remember Captain Hank.

One wonders if that is still true.

RIGHT, ABOVE

The crew of the American sloop *Defender*. The bearded man in the centre, second row, is Captain Hank Haff, who was highly thought of by his crew. They were all from Deer Isle on the northeast side of beautiful Penobscot Bay in Maine. Many were from the village of Stonington at the island's southeast tip and most were accustomed to sailing sloops of about 28–40 ft in the lobster and other fisheries. Their background and skills were thus similar to their contemporaries manning the large British racers and these men from the small fore-and-aft rigged fishing vessels always made the smartest yacht sailors. The Deer Isle tradition of manning racing yachts extended back to at least the 1880s. In 1886 the island supplied half the crew of the Cup defender *Mayflower* and repeated this for *Volunteer* in 1887.

The crew comprised the following men, though the list sequence bears no relation to their position on the photograph: G. Conant, second mate; quartermasters I. G. Barbour, Bentley Barbour, John E. Billings, John T. Staples; seamen Winslow C. Pickering, Forrest B. McCauley, Ross L. Fifield, Walter Eaton, Gardiner K. Green, George W. Stinson, Elmer E. Hamblen, Joseph

Robbins, Ernest C. Haskell, Samuel Bray, Elmer Hardy, Roland Staples, Charles H. Scott, John T. Marshall, Harry W. Gray, William Scott, Herbert Bray, Leslie Stinson, W. W. Horton, Thomas Horton, Roland Small, H. P. Davis, Everett H. Haskell, Stephen Sellers, Warren Bray, Charles Barter, Thomas Robbins and Willard G. Haskell.

Defender's crew were selected on Town Meeting Day at Deer Isle in 1895 and included men from Green's Landing (Stonington). Local Captain Fred Weed made the selection from the many who applied, on behalf of Captain Haff. Many were young, and the last living member of the *Defender*'s crew was Edmund C. Wood of Oceanville who died there in 1974 aged 96. He had also sailed in *Columbia* in 1899 and was a lobster fisherman besides occasionally finding work at the island's stone quarries. When he heard that Captain Weed was signing on men for *Defender* he jumped on his bicycle and made twenty miles an hour to Green's Landing.

The crew lived mostly on board the steam tender *St Michaels* and each morning rowed over to the yacht to start the day by washing down deck and sides, polishing brass and putting in stops the headsails and spinnakers for the day's racing. If

there was a breeze the yacht got under way, if not she would wait for one. It was not considered worth towing the large American racers out if there was no chance of wind. On non-racing days the mainsail was unfurled and the dew or rain was dried off on the mooring. Headsails and spinnakers were, if necessary, taken ashore to be spread out for drying. At Newport, where these yachts spent much time, this was done on Goat Island. At New Rochelle, New York, the Iselins' home, they were dried on the lawn of their house.

Head of the millionaire syndicate of owners was C. C. Iselin who with his young wife spent most of their time on board while racing in sitting by the companionway hatch. As the principal, his main task was to provide the money for the yacht's construction, outfitting, crew and maintenance.

ABOVE, LEFT
The American sloop *Defender* before the start of a Cup race. The most extreme racing yacht then built in America, she was owned by a syndicate headed by C. Oliver Iselin, who with W. K. Vanderbilt and E. D. Morgan commissioned the Herreshoff Manufacturing Co. to design and build her. The hull had mild steel frames with manga-

nese bronze keel and bottom plating; side plating was aluminium, then little understood in marine work. The subsequent reaction between the dissimilar metals in salt water caused rapid deterioration. *Defender* also suffered structural weakness from the strains of her rig but was stiffened sufficiently to see the series through successfully and survived to participate in the trial races against the next defender *Columbia* in 1899. She was scrapped in 1901.

Defender was the first American fin-keel yacht in Cup racing, all the previous defenders having had centreboards working through their ballast keels, and was similar in dimensions to her opponent, being 123 ft overall length, 88 ft 6 in waterline length, 23 ft 4 in beam, 19 ft 8 in draft. She carried 12,602 sq ft in the sails shown here, 426 sq ft less than on *Valkyrie III*.

The American yacht won the first race. Afterwards the Earl of Dunraven complained that it was thought that she had taken on additional ballast from her tender the night before; also that the course was being seriously obstructed and the racers harassed by wash from the numbers of large spectator steamers. Investigation proved that *Defender*'s crew had shifted and restowed some

internal ballast but the yacht was remeasured satisfactorily and the matter was temporarily dropped.

PREVIOUS PAGE
Defender, immediately after being fouled by the boom of *Valkyrie III* before the start of the second race of the America's Cup series on September 10, 1895.

Both yachts were approaching the line closehauled, just before the starting gun, with *Valkyrie III* on *Defender*'s weather, when the large passenger steamer *Yorktown* blundered across their course and separated the yachts for a few seconds. When they emerged *Valkyrie III* was still on *Defender*'s weather but had drawn slightly ahead. Just before they reached the weather end of the line and a few seconds before the gun, Captain Edward Sycamore who was at the time steering *Valkyrie III* under Captain Cranfield bore away slightly towards *Defender* under his lee, to keep clear of the line. The official explanation was that, realizing he could not draw clear across the *Defender*'s bow and that if Hank Haff held his course the yachts would collide, Sycamore was then forced to luff sharply. The end of *Valkyrie III*'s 106 ft boom swept the deck of *Defender*, touching her lee rigging as the British yacht turned. *Defender*'s shifting backstay broke and her topmast sagged to leeward under the large yard topsail. Hank Haff shot her up into the wind and hands swarmed aloft to attempt to repair the topmast, which had cracked 5 ft above the lower mast head. *Defender* hoisted a protest flag. As the topmast did not come down, though

it sagged to leeward on the starboard tack, the jib topsail was taken in and a temporary topmast stay rigged as the yacht pursued *Valkyrie*, which was 3 minutes ahead at the weather mark. The next leg was a reach and Captain Haff took a chance and ordered a small jib topsail set. The crippled *Defender* did not lose further ground and on the last leg her topmast stood at its best, so a large jib topsail was set and she began to close the British lead, but *Valkyrie III* crossed the line 2 minutes 18 seconds ahead.

As a result of this incident *Valkyrie III* was disqualified. In return the Earl of Dunraven complained strongly of the crowding at the start and on the course by spectator steamers. It was this that caused a breakdown of relations between the owners of the two yachts and between the New York Yacht Club and the Earl. There was worse to come in the third race.

The photograph shows the damaged topmast sagging to leeward, the jib topsail being hurriedly taken in, and a number of hands and the mate working by the weather shrouds preparing a temporary stay. The club at the clew of the jib and the topsail cut with cloths parallel to the leech are interesting details.

OPPOSITE PAGE
Valkyrie III crossing the line to win the disputed second race for the America's Cup against *Defender*, on September 10, 1895. She is reaching at speed, having sailed the 30 mile course in 3 hours, 55 minutes and 22 seconds in light winds. Her sails set perfectly and the jib topsail and reaching foresail are pulling well. All hands are

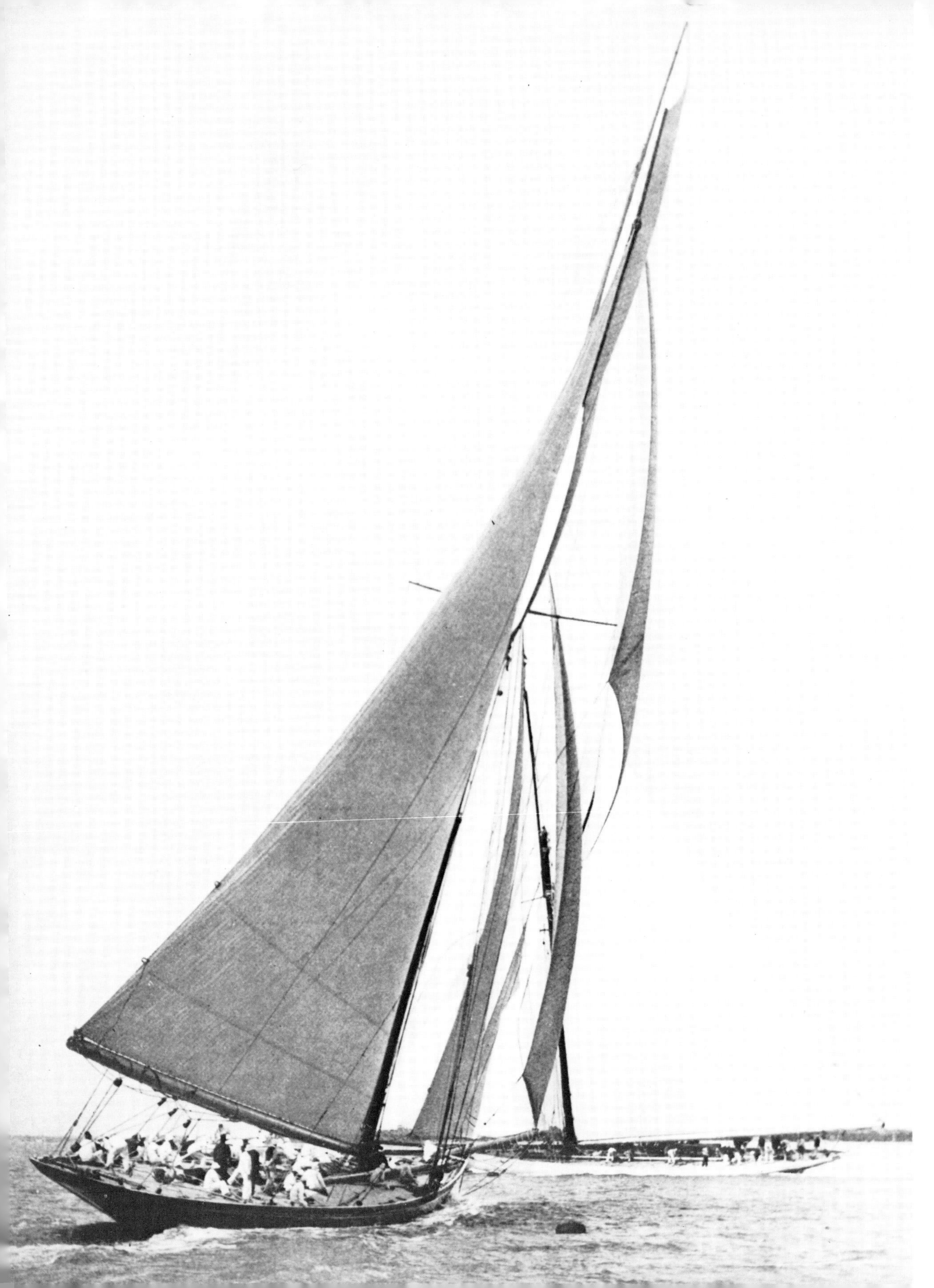

jubilant but she was to be disqualified for the foul at the start and would not race again for the Cup. After recriminations over lack of American control over large spectator steamers obstructing the course, her owner, the Earl of Dunraven, ordered *Valkyrie* to come to the start in the third race. Captain William Cranfield took her across the line in racing trim, then had her blue and gold racing flag lowered as she swept round and sailed back to the anchorage, leaving *Defender* to sail the course alone and claim the Cup – an English snub which took the New York Yacht Club by surprise and inflamed an already delicate situation. This decision by their owner caused disappointment to the captain and crew of *Valkyrie III*, who were sure they could have beaten *Defender* had the series continued. Certainly she was the fastest and finest yacht to challenge up to that time.

PAGE 53
The Kaiser's *Meteor II* stands down the Firth of Clyde on her maiden passage south to join the racing fleet for the opening of the 1896 British season, at the River Thames matches. This was the other side of large-yacht racing and one in which the owners rarely participated. The topmast remains 'on end' but the big racing mainsail is stowed securely in its crutch and is secured by breeching tackles to the quarters. The sail was much too large for passage making except in light winds and it was the practice that the set of its canvas must be preserved only for racing, so it remained carefully flaked, stowed and canvas coated on passage. Instead, the trysail was set, sheeted by a pair of tackles to the yacht's quarters. *Meteor*'s trysail has what appears to be a detachable laced bonnet rather than a reef at its foot and has one deep or 'storm' reef halfway up the sail; this and the storm jib would be the canvas she would set in gales, which were sometimes met on passage.

In this photograph she has just got under weigh and eight hands forward are rousing the anchor cable home under the eye of the mate. Others of her thirty-five man crew work about the deck and a mastheadsman dangles in the port topmast shrouds, looking for chafe. Captain Robert Gomes of Gosport crouches on the weather side, his hand on the tiller tackle and a keen eye on the anchor party forward. The spinnaker boom and boat are on deck and a boat tows astern, ready for the pilot when he leaves the racer, lower down the Firth.

LEFT
The British cutter *Ailsa* crosses tacks ahead of the German Emperor's *Meteor II*, 1896. The latter yacht was designed by George Watson of Glasgow and was built there by D. & W. Henderson of Meadowside, who had constructed many of her contemporaries, though their principal work was steel merchant steamships. She was a powerful and graceful yacht, sailed by Captain Robert Gomes of Gosport, Hampshire with an English crew, to which a few German hands were progressively added to be taught the ways of yacht racing in a first-class cutter. Her sails are well set and the angles they make, the variation of sheeting and the boom hove in hard with the powerful mainsheet are all worthy of study. *Meteor II* has the graceful Watson sheer and the broad deck of the Length and Sail Area Rule.

Naturally she had to race in several German Baltic regattas, which complicated her engagements with the British big class. In 1896 she concluded her Baltic visit by racing at Lübeck and on June 26 was towed as fast as a large torpedo-gunboat could take her, down the North Sea with a brief call at Dover, then down Channel, around Land's End and up the Irish Sea to the Clyde, arriving at Gourock on July 6 to proceed upriver and prepare to join the British racing fleet for the rest of the season.

Meteor II was involved in a collision while racing in the regatta of the Royal Albert Yacht Club at Southsea, on August 18, 1896. Others in the big class that day included *Ailsa*, *Britannia* and *Satanita*. Six of the much smaller 52 ft Linear Rating class were started forty-five minutes after them and included the American *Niagara* and the German *Isolde*, which was sailed by Captain William Miles of Itchen with an English crew. The courses of these two classes and the conditions of wind and tide brought them together near the committee boat by the Spit Fort. In the ensuing close quarters *Isolde* found herself running with the big *Britannia* to windward, *Meteor II* to leeward and the British *The Saint* (52 ft rating) running hard at her stern. *Isolde* luffed slightly to avoid fouling *Britannia*,

which would have meant disqualification according to the current strict interpretation of the yacht racing rules. At that instant the topmast stay of *The Saint* fouled her boom end, forcing *Isolde* round to leeward and out of control. She went under the bow of the onrushing *Meteor*: her bowsprit was broken off and she was pinned under the lee bow of the giant racer. The shock of the impact did not slow the Kaiser's yacht but her 100 ft boom gybed and swept *Isolde*'s deck from aft to forward, carrying away her mast and throwing the crew overboard. All the racers brought to at once, boats were lowered and lifebuoys thrown. Every member of the crew of the *Isolde* was rescued from the water, but her owner Baron von Zedtwitz was severely injured in the head by *Isolde*'s boom and he died on board a steam yacht on the way to Ryde for medical attention. The regatta was closed in gloom and *Britannia* and *Meteor II* were immediately laid up for the remainder of the season. Captain Gomes, through no fault of his, was later relieved of command of *Meteor II*. He does not appear to have subsequently obtained a berth as skipper of a British or German racer – such was prejudice.

PAGES 56–7
The River Dart, crowded with yachts for Regatta Week in 1896. This event was typical of the gatherings at the many regattas held around the British coast from May until September

during the yacht racing season. A first-class racing cutter, probably *Ailsa*, lies anchored in the foreground and close by the town, and dwarfs a 40-rater ahead of her.

Dartmouth regatta was one of the end-of-season fixtures and very enjoyable for the racing men. Its events included craft from the large class to dinghies, and included a popular rowing race for yachts' gigs which was hotly contested with some exceptionally fine rowing.

LEFT, ABOVE
Meteor II in drydock for bottom cleaning, 1896. It was easier to dock a large racing yacht than to haul her out on a slipway carriage, which required elaborate preparation of sliding cod blocks and forward cradling, with after shores as she emerged from the water, and this could rarely be done with the mast stepped. Drydocking allowed the deep keel to settle on the blocks as the dock was pumped out and for the side shores to be slipped into place as soon as possible to prevent the long-ended and short-keeled yacht pitching forward or aft and drawing the side shores in a calamitous falling over. Here the Kaiser's racer is safe in dock, and her copper sheathed bottom appears to have been scrubbed and burnished to a smooth surface for the next series of races. Even in dock the racer was kept smart. The spinnaker boom is topped up and down the mast, the stowed mainsail is carefully coated, and the headsails are unbent and folded

and stowed in the sail locker in the long counter. The white painted chain cable leads from the hawsepipe aft to an anchor stowed at the rail. The jib traveller is run in along the bowsprit to the stemhead and is well served with white hide.

Captain Gomes and the first and second mates discuss a point with the yard foremen. Aft, the German Imperial Yacht Club ensign stirs above the counter.

When in dock, the large racers were usually painted by small specialist firms of 'yacht decorators'. One such was Scrutton & Sons of Rowhedge, which in 1894 obtained the contract to repaint *Britannia*, *Valkyrie II* and *Ailsa* in drydock at Tilbury, on the River Thames. Chartering the old yacht *Antelope*, they filled her with casks of paint and equipment and, shipping the staff, the lot was sailed round to Tilbury where the painters lived on board.

PREVIOUS PAGE
Ailsa and *Britannia* at their best. The two gracious Watson-designed cutters are going to windward in ideal conditions – smooth water with sufficient breeze. *Ailsa* heels to a puff that reaches her just before *Britannia*. Sunlight dapples her scrubbed white pine deck. The graceful sweep of the bows, sheers and counters of the cutters is typical of the period. There is little to choose between the yachts, their crews or handling. Captains Tom Jay at the tiller of *Ailsa* and John Carter in *Britannia* were old rivals and near neighbours at their home village.

The sails set well, and endless care was lavished on these finely made wings of creamy cotton canvas. The jib and jib topsail have a mitre seam; the other sails are cut with cloths parallel to the leech. Both topsails are standing well to windward and each has a vertical batten at the centre of the leech. The topsail yards are bending slightly at the head and the jackyards curve to the strain of the sheet drawing them towards the peak of the gaff. Both yachts have large steel-shelled blocks for the peak halyards, and the strain on these, the halyards and the wire gaff spans was immense.

RIGHT
After *Ailsa*'s success at the Riviera regattas during the winter season of 1896, Captain Tom Jay stands by two enormous silver cups with his owner, A. D. Walker, and his wife. For several years during the 1890s two or three British first-class racers, and sometimes several 40- and 20-raters, sailed out to the Mediterranean coast of France for two months' keen winter racing.

Here *Ailsa* seems to be ready for a sea passage; perhaps she was going back to refit at Fay's Northam yard, while her crew went home to enjoy a short holiday before rejoining to prepare for the British summer season. The clew of the strong flax trysail lies stowed on top of the boom, which is bound with protective canvas at that point. Purchases for the trysail sheets lead to port and starboard – short breeching tackles securing the boom are made fast to bollards on each side of the deck and the weight of the 90 ft spar is settled on a standing gantry aft for the passage home. The only concession to passage making comfort was the low stanchions and guardwire on each side on the rail in way of the tiller, with dodgers rigged on them. The brass-capped head of the wooden rudder stock is hidden by the captain's knee and the 14 ft long forged iron tiller with its wooden handgrip curves forward.

Cups and sometimes other trophies, often also with substantial money prizes, were usually offered for the racing of large-class yachts and those of moderate size from the end of the eighteenth century until 1937. Until the mid-nineteenth century only the first prize winner usually received money; afterwards prize money was usually also offered for second and third places, particularly in the large classes. Cups varied from the smaller and usually more tasteful to the large and almost vulgarly ornate. Most were of silver, a few of gold. Many were given by clubs sponsoring the racing, paid for from their prize funds. These might be offered to be won outright, as was usual, but sometimes were 'challenge cups', which usually had to be won three times by the same yacht or owner before retention. These were not popular with owners, captains or crews. Some cups and the associated prize money were given by club members, by yachtsmen interested in the racing in some way, and occasionally by royalty or a head of state. Infrequently, large yachts sailed a match race for a money prize which might be put up by one of the owners or an independent 'sport' wishing to see a race.

The value of cups offered for large class racers varied considerably from perhaps the £40 silver

cup put up by the annual regatta committee of a seaside town, hoping to attract the first-class racers to perform off their locality and attract attention and trade to the town, to an ostentatious trophy such as the one worth £2000 given by King Edward VII for the A Class schooners at Kiel in 1904. More usually a cup for the first-class racers around 1900 would be of £100 value and would be won outright. Some clubs, such as the Royal London, offered a money prize of perhaps £100 for the first-class yachts and recognized the skill of the men who sailed them by awarding a silver medal to the captain. Typical prize money in the regattas around the British coast where the large class raced during their season was that put up by the Royal Cinque Ports Yacht Club at Dover where in 1895 the first prize was £50 and the second £20.

In 1895, which was not a particularly exciting season for the large class with often only *Britannia* and the new *Ailsa* racing, the former started 50 times, won 38 races and 2 other prizes for which her owner received £3039 10s. in prize money. Her rival *Ailsa* started 41 times, won 12 first prizes and 3 seconds, value £2363. These were considerable sums in contemporary value and assisted towards the considerable outlay on maintaining the yacht. However, by custom a proportion of the prize money was paid to the captain and crew; generally the captain received 5 per cent of the total, a practice prevailing for many years and in the case of a successful man considerably augmenting his wages, which as skipper of a first-class racer were generous by contemporary standards. From *Britannia*'s prize money in 1895 it is probable that Captain John Carter received a share of £152, a sum then equal to twice the wages of a skilled shipwright for one

year. This was usually supplemented by a handsome gratuity for a skipper having a successful season and at times by presents from an appreciative owner. The crew also received their share of the prize money; around 1900 each man received £1 for a first prize and 15s. for a second. A custom also grew of owners paying 10s. 'starting money', win or lose. It must be remembered that the crews were not highly paid men, despite their skills. A racing yacht hand received 26s. per week, generally, during the period 1893–1910, those having additional responsibility receiving slightly more; for instance the mastheadsmen received an additional 5s. and bowspritendsmen 2s. 6d. They also received 2s. 6d. per day when racing as dinner could not prepared on board with all hands at racing duties. This can be contrasted with a skilled shipwright's wages of 28–30s. per week.

Immediately after the First World War the wages of racing yacht hands increased to £3 10s. for skilled men and £3 for youths and stewards. The high rate did not last long, added to which the prize money was drastically reduced from its pre-war level and never regained it. Increasingly cups and trophies, without prize money, were offered. By 1933, at the depth of the Depression, the wages were £2 14s. per week and the prize money remained at £1 for a win, 15s. for a second prize and 5s. for a start, win or lose. 'Grub money' on race days remained at 2s. 6d.

Crews of yachts challenging for the America's Cup usually received rather higher wages than others, and in 1937 a hand in *Endeavour II* was receiving £3 4s. per week, with £1 extra for each week he was away from England for the Cup series. These men also knew that should their yacht win the Cup they would receive a handsome gratuity from a delighted owner.

The dress of the group represents the best of contemporary fashion and quality afloat. The captain's pilot cloth jacket is crumpled from

active wear but his weskit and watchchain, collar and tie, cheesecutter cap, cuffs and trousers are smart. The owner's more elegant garb emphasizes his position as a wealthy sailing man who delighted in having a fine yacht and in the success of a skipper and crew sailing under his colours. The lady's long full skirt and straw boater with club badge were equally fashionable. Everyone is careful not to look at the camera.

PAGE 62
The men who won the trophies. *Ailsa*'s crew of thirty gather around Captain Tom Jay, seated in the centre with his hand on the large cup. By 1894 the number of large racing yachts had so increased that it was not possible to man them fully from the traditional localities. About half of Tom Jay's crew were from his village of Rowhedge with some from Wivenhoe and others from Newlyn, Penzance, Mevagissey and Port Isaac in Cornwall. West Country fishermen accustomed to mackerel driving and long-lining on luggers made capable hands when taught yachting customs. Many captains of racers who sailed around the coast from Harwich to the Clyde each summer came to prefer a crew with varied home ports since they did not all ask for shore leave at once, which could happen when crews were almost totally drawn from one area near which the yacht happened to race during the season. A racing crew such as *Ailsa*'s would leave their homes in late April to fit out and did not return until the yacht laid up five months later, unless she was within a few miles of home.

These men were a very fine racing crew of a notably successful yacht sailed by a consistently successful skipper of great experience. Tom Jay was a resolute captain who achieved a fine record

in many yachts from 20-raters to the giant schooner *Rainbow*. Their racing season still glowed in the minds of two of them many years afterwards and Bill Wadley (sixth from left in the third row) was able to recollect their voyagings accurately for the author fifty years later.

PAGE 63
Ailsa setting a yard topsail. The 126 ft cutter is preparing for the day's racing. The topsail has been hoisted and the hands clustered at the mast are sheeting the jackyard home to the gaff end. When the tack tackle is set up, the topsail luff and the topsail yard will stand taut, up and down the topmast, to give a firm leading edge to this 1500 sq ft sail. The first and second mastheadsmen are aloft; one is standing on the starboard cap shrouds by the masthead, the other climbing aloft in the lee rigging. *Ailsa* is under easy canvas, the mainsheet slacked and the jib backed over the forestay; the staysail is ready to be hoisted on the foredeck. She can be kept slowly jilling around while the topsail is set and to ease the motion for the mastheadsmen. Tom Jay stands at her long tiller, one eye aloft and the other on his competitors who are doubtless preparing nearby.

LEFT
Ailsa running in the Firth of Clyde under mainsail, yard topsail, balloon staysail, long-roper jib topsail and spinnaker. The total sail area set here is about 20,000 sq ft, possibly slightly more. Captain Tom Jay is standing to leeward with the tiller line and the mate and several hands are sending up a jib which has been stopped along the bowsprit. The dimension from the end of the spinnaker boom to the end of the main boom would be slightly over 195 ft.

PREVIOUS PAGE

The American racing schooner *Colonia* preparing for the day's racing off Larchmont, New York in 1896. She was designed and built by the Herreshoff Manufacturing Co. at Bristol, Rhode Island during the winter of 1892–3 for a syndicate of New York Yacht Club members as a contender for the defence of the America's Cup that year against *Valkyrie II*. A Boston designed, built and owned rival sloop was named *Jubilee*, and a second Boston syndicate had the *Pilgrim* built for the trials. At the same time another New York Yacht Club syndicate ordered *Vigilant* from Herreshoffs. *Vigilant* and *Colonia* were the best of the four during the trial races and although the latter was well sailed by Captain Hank Haff the selection committee chose *Vigilant*, under Captain William Hansen.

Colonia was an interesting racer, built of steel with 'in and out' strakes of shell plating in the contemporary shipbuilding fashion. She was 122 ft overall, 86 ft waterline length, with 22 ft beam and 15 ft 4 in draft; the ballast keel carried 80 tons of lead and had been hastily added during construction after the poor stability of the similar sloop *Navahoe*. 'In and out' plating was a normal method of plating a steel vessel at the time and for many years afterwards, and one of several methods used in shipbuilding. However, large racing yachts usually, if steel or bronze, had flush shell plating having strapped butts and seams. These methods remained in use until the end of riveted construction in shipbuilding in the early 1960s. Electric welding did not become general in shipbuilding until the 1940s, although it was used in certain aspects of ship and engine construction from about 1916.

In the following season *Colonia* proved to be fast and in 1896 she was bought by Clarence L. Postley who converted her to schooner rig with a centreboard fitted through the lead keel. She was then sailed by Captain Charles Barr and raced in the schooner class with success against the principal rivals *Amorita* and *Emerald*.

Foredeck hands are preparing to set the staysail; the mate and other hands amidships and aft stand by. Barr is at the wheel, used on American racers for some years though British contemporaries still favoured the tiller. Three battens of varied length stiffen the mainsail leech. The foresail (as the forward gaff sail in a schooner is called) has a boom for the length of the foot which will pass between the fore and main masts. The sail's clew is extended abaft the mainmast when sheeted with a lug sheet purchase, set up at each tack. The topsails are sent aloft in stops, ready to be broken out and sheeted home shortly before the start. The portlights along her sides are a reminder that at that period the larger American yachts were designed for accommodation comfort as well as speed.

Colonia was subsequently renamed *Corona* and won many races including the Astor Cup in 1900 and 1904. She was the flagship of the New York Yacht Club from 1900 to 1902 and remained in use for some years, ending her days as tender to the America's Cup defender *Enterprise* in 1930.

RIGHT

The beautiful schooner *Rainbow* was one of the largest yachts to race in the coastal regattas. She was designed by George Watson & Co. and built in 1898 by Hendersons of Glasgow for C. L. Orr Ewing. Principal dimensions were 132 ft 8 in overall length, 116 ft 3 in waterline length, 23 ft 11 in beam, 17 ft draft. Her hull was planked over steel frames and deck beams, with keel plate, bilge and sheerstrakes, floors and deck tieplates also of steel. This view of her at anchor on the Clyde soon after completion shows the grace of her black hull and its outreaching clipper stem. An impression of *Rainbow*'s size can be gained by looking at the hand working at the bowsprit end and others aft and by the foremast.

Particularly interesting is the contemporary interpretation of the racing schooner's rig: the mainmast amidships had a very large mainsail, and the foremast was stepped as far aft as possible to keep weight 'out of the eyes of her'. This resulted in a tall narrow foresail which was difficult to set well, although the experienced crews usually managed it. The sailplan of 13,400 sq ft in mainsail, foresail, staysail, ordinary jib and fore and main topsails had almost the power of a cutter, and the mighty *Rainbow* was the fastest displacement yacht ever built. Like all racing schooners she could set a spinnaker from each mast. The spinnaker boom on the mainmast is topped up and its lift is led from the strut of the jump stay. Ratlines on the shrouds were usual at the time to enable hands to swarm aloft and 'string down' on the halyards of gaff sails, adding their

hanging weight to the pull of those on deck. In American yachts the fall of the halyards was led through a deck block by the mast, enabling all hands to heave on the fall along the deck in an efficient pull, a practice which British yachts later adopted.

Rainbow was to be commanded by Captain John Carter but her construction lagged, and the hull swarmed with two hundred workmen rushing to complete the big black schooner. John Carter brought many of his *Britannia* crew with him to *Rainbow*; seven officers and stewards and twenty-three hands joined as she fitted out at Partick. To handle the powerful rig they were picked for strength as well as skill and none was less than 40 inches around the chest. Unfortunately Captain Carter was taken ill and sent home to Rowhedge while Captain Tom Jay superintended the fitting out. Captain Carter was unfit for a long period and command passed to Tom Jay, who found her extremely fast, making her maiden passage down from Gourock to Southampton in 50 hours.

Rainbow had the fastest timed speed of any displacement yacht. In the English Channel she sailed 60 miles in four hours, the log twice registering $16\frac{1}{2}$ knots; during this performance her helm balance was perfect and the yacht steady. Her principal opponents were *Satanita* and *Ailsa*, re-rigged as yawls, and the newer cutters *Bona* and *Aurora*. Although *Rainbow* finished first in many races she did not win on handicap, which made the sport dull.

Few large yachts raced during 1899, but on the Clyde *Rainbow* and *Bona* sailed against the gigantic three-masted schooner *Gleniffer* which George Watson had developed from the *Rainbow* as the largest schooner yacht which ever raced inshore. She was 141 ft on the waterline with 180 ft overall hull length and built in steel for James Coats of Glasgow. This 496-tonner proved too cumbersome for racing and was well beaten by *Rainbow*, which as usual lost on time to the smaller *Bona*.

Rainbow was Tom Jay's last racing command

and he left her in 1900 for the less strenuous life as master of the 141 ft steam yacht *Kempion*. The schooner was later sold to a German owner and was renamed *Hamburg*. She raced in the Transatlantic Race of 1905 for the German Emperor's Cup, from Sandy Hook to the Lizard; the first to finish being the winner, without time allowance. Eleven yachts entered, from a full-rigged ship to cutters, yawls and schooners. The American three-masted schooner *Atlantic* was the favourite and the winner, setting a record for the passage that was not broken until 1981. *Hamburg* finished second in 14 days. Captain Peters, her German skipper, wrote in his log of her speed in ocean conditions: 'May 26th . . . Miles covered from noon to noon, 272. 3.30 a.m. set square sail; 7 a.m. put one reef out of foresail. 9 a.m. lowered close-reefed mainsail 4 ft to keep the yacht before the sea during the heavy squalls; plenty of water on deck; a terrible high sea running; used oil to prevent the sea from breaking. 8 p.m. stowed foresail. 10 p.m. took in square sail . . .'. The average speed for the 24 hours was 11.3 knots. Peters had been trained in the *Meteors* under English skippers and was highly regarded by his owner while in the *Hamburg*. Adolph Tietjens appeared as her nominal owner but the registered owners were the Hamburgischer Verein 'Seefahrt'.

Hamburg, again renamed *Rainbow*, ended her days as a cargo schooner sailing to the Cocos Keeling Islands in the Indian Ocean during the First World War.

RIGHT
The Deer Isle, Maine crew of the America's Cup defender *Columbia* in 1899. They were selected by Captain Fred Weed, who had done so well picking men for *Defender* and earlier Cup yachts. The hands received \$45 a month and the officers \$60; for each race sailed, including trial races, each man on board received an additional \$5. Their dress of white canvas trousers and 'jumpers', sun hats and deck shoes is almost identical with that of their English rivals. The complete crew list is not known but it included Philip Haskell, John E. Goss, Charles Gray, Leslie Gray, Edmund Wood, Cyrus Thompson, Ed Carman and Will Young. There are twenty-four hands in this photograph; the skipper, mates and stewards are absent.

The Scottish-American Charles Barr skippered *Columbia* to beat Sir Thomas Lipton's *Shamrock*, which was sailed by Captain Archie Hogarth and Captain Robert Wringe, with a crew from the River Colne, the lower Clyde and the Solent area. At Deer Isle the population eagerly followed reports of the Cup races, and each time *Columbia* won an old cannon was fired in celebration. On one of these firings the ancient piece exploded on reloading and injured a gunner.

Charles Barr was almost lost overboard from *Columbia* when standing on the lee side of the wheel, racing in a fresh wind. A larger than usual wave swept up the lee deck and carried him away to leeward. Ed Wood leapt from his station at the mainsheet fall and grabbed the skipper by his coat as he was going over.

The crew of *Columbia*, like all sailors, were fond of a run ashore and at City Island, New York one of them fought five policemen after a saloon argument. The police station sergeant asked him where he came from and, at the proud reply 'Deer Isle' told him, 'Well, don't let any more Deer Islanders come here.' 'There are forty of them just across the street at Nevins Yard, on board the *Columbia*,' replied the islander. The law did not press charges.

The Deer Isle yacht hands' racing connections were weakened in 1901 when Thomas W. Lawson, a Boston stockbroker, ordered the huge *Independence* to compete for the defence of the America's Cup against *Shamrock II*. Captain Henry Haff was appointed skipper and favoured a Deer Isle crew, as he had in the *Defender* and earlier yachts, and as before he had the help of Captain Fred Weed in obtaining island men. Meanwhile, in February 1901 Captain Uriah Rhodes of the new *Constitution*, building at Herreshoff's and already favourite for Cup-defence selection, arrived at Deer Isle with a list of forty-five racing hands he wished to interview, from which twenty men would be selected. Rhodes was a distinguished racing skipper but his proposed screening upset many islanders and this, coupled with his ignoring Weed, resulted in his leaving without obtaining a single man from the two hundred potentially suitable, the cream of American racing hands. These all quickly pledged to Captain Weed not to sign papers until Captain Haff had picked his crew of about forty men. The unforeseen results of this action were that, as

Captain Haff was to sail no other potential Cup defender after *Independence*, the Deer Isle men lost their racing connections and lost favour with other skippers and yacht owners.

Moreover, Captain Rhodes, who was an excellent racing skipper, had to make do with an inferior crew, a fact apparently lost to America's Cup historians. It was this, rather than deficiency in design or a magical superiority of Captain Charles Barr, that resulted in the older *Columbia*'s being selected for the second time as Cup defender in 1901. This situation contributed substantially to the antagonism of the New York Yacht Club towards Thomas Lawson and his 'outside' Cup defender and the unfortunate *Independence* was barred by the club from competing in the trials for the selection of a defender. However, a group of Rhode Island yachtsmen organized a series of races for all potential Cup defenders and the *Independence* raced in these – unsuccessfully, to the great disappointment of her keen crew.

For the America's Cup defender *Reliance* of 1903 Captain Charles Barr shipped Norwegian hands to make up her crew of forty-five; the Norwegians were willing to accept lower pay than the American yacht sailors. Captain Barr and some other American racing skippers continued this practice, to the disgust of the 'down east' yacht hands. However, there were several hundred men from Deer Isle who went yachting for many years in other craft, both sailing and steam yachts, during the early twentieth century.

FOLLOWING PAGE
Shamrock thrashes to windward under 13,492 sq ft of canvas. In 1899 Sir Thomas Lipton began his five challenges for the America's Cup with his first yacht of this name, designed by William Fife Jr and built on the Thames by John I. Thornycroft & Co., noted as builders of steel torpedo boats, destroyers and special light craft. She was 128 ft overall length, 89 ft 8 in on the waterline, 25 ft in beam and drew 20 ft 3 in. The hull was flat-sheered and beamy with long ends, and the keel was a deep fin with considerable rake to the rudder stock at its after end. The younger Fife had designed many successful smaller yachts but had previously drawn only two large racers, neither particularly successful. *Shamrock*'s bottom was plated in manganese bronze, with side plating of aluminium. Her mast, boom and gaff were of steel. The mast gave constant trouble by bending in a breeze, impairing the set of her sails,

of which she had six suits that season. She was commanded by Captain Archie Hogarth from Portincross, Ayrshire and also had Captain Robert Wringe of Brightlingsea to sail her in conditions favouring his most outstanding ability. The practice of having two captains in Cup challengers was a feature of the period 1895–1903, when the yachts grew so large and intricate that the experience of two men was considered necessary, and the possibility of one of them falling ill during the series or the working-up period also made it desirable. Her crew were principally Essex men from the Colne, with others from the Clyde and the Solent.

Shamrock was beaten by the similar sized *Columbia*, designed and built by Herreshoff and sailed by Captain Charles Barr. The crew were in part from Deer Isle, Maine.

The races were held at the then usual venue off Sandy Hook, at the approaches to New York, in October. *Shamrock* lost the first race, which was marred by fog, by 10 minutes 8 seconds. She lost her 56 ft topmast during the second race and had to retire. After repeated postponements because of fog, the third race was sailed in a fresh wind but *Columbia* won by 6 minutes 34 seconds. In 1901 *Shamrock* raced in the British season and as trial horse for tuning up Lipton's next challenger, *Shamrock II*.

RIGHT
Shamrock starts to show her form, displaying all the grace and power of a large racing yacht. Five hands prepare to set the jib topsail from the bowsprit end, supervised by the first mate on the foredeck. Several others are trying gear by the lee rigging, with the second mate farther aft. Captains Archie Hogarth and Robert Wringe, at the tiller, have discarded their pilot jackets.

She is setting 13,492 sq ft of canvas in this 1899 photograph. The jackyard is unusually far away from the gaff but the diagonal-cut topsail is setting beautifully and spreads almost 3000 sq ft – considerably more than the total sail area of a present-day 12 Metre. Despite the elaborate rig, her designer still considered a fidded topmast necessary and it was not until *Shamrock II*, designed by Watson in 1901, that the lower mast and topmast were brought into line.

PART TWO

1900–1914

RIGHT, ABOVE

The German Emperor's *Meteor II* racing for the King's Cup at Cowes in 1901. In the fresh breeze she is not carrying a topsail and the mizzen, fitted on her conversion to yawl rig to take advantage of the rating rules, has carried away. The mizzen mast, spars and sail trail over the stern, where they have been secured for the remainder of the race. Captain Ben Parker continues to drive her hard and she is travelling at near maximum speed.

The quarter waves, particularly on the lee side, are considerable and were the result of the usual after hull form of most British designed racing yachts, which were narrower than their American contemporaries. The after buttock lines rose more steeply resulting in finer and more veed sections in the counter, which stimulated wave-making aft. Most of the American yachts had less steep buttocks and a flatter counter which reduced this aspect of resistance and appeared to be faster, within the same rating rules. The two trends were characteristic of hull form of the two nations' racers for a long period.

RIGHT, BELOW

The officers and crew of the America's Cup challenger *Shamrock II* pose with her owner and designer in 1901.

Front row, left to right: Aldous (Brightlingsea), F. Banks, Captain Edward Sycamore (Brightlingsea), Sir Thomas Lipton (owner), George L. Watson (designer), C. Biffin (Brightlingsea), W. Poole (Brightlingsea).

Second row: R. Cotton, O. Springett (Rowhedge), B. Chaplin (Brightlingsea), J. Fale (Rowhedge), G. Major (Brightlingsea), J. Diaper, F. Longley (Brightlingsea), G. Percival (Wivenhoe), C. Osborne (Brightlingsea), P. Higgins.

Third row: H. Matthews, Pettican (Tollesbury), A. Watkins, R. Ruffell (Brightlingsea), A. Scarfe (Rowhedge), R. South (Wivenhoe), W. Wadley (Rowhedge).

Fourth row: Aldous (Brightlingsea), W. White (Brightlingsea), T. Godfrey (Rowhedge), C. T. Nettleingham, A. Lay (Rowhedge), A. Richardson (Brightlingsea), W. Clark (Rowhedge).

Fifth row: Heard (Tollesbury), C. Crane, A. Polter, J. Finch, F. Farman, W. Allen (Rowhedge), W. Dent (Brightlingsea).

They were a typically smart and experienced racing crew, principally from the River Colne in Essex. Most of these men spent their winters fishing in the Essex smacks.

Sir Thomas Lipton had been created a knight in 1898, one year before his first challenge for the America's Cup in 1899. He had never previously owned or sailed in a yacht when as a successful businessman he was suddenly keen to challenge for the Cup with 'a green yacht named *Shamrock*'. He had risen from poor circumstances to own a chain of grocery shops and large associated businesses in several countries; many considered his sudden interest in yachting to be connected with promotion of Lipton's Tea. Some saw it as a new interest for a wealthy batchelor seeking recognition in society. As a 'man of the people' he achieved public acclaim, became a friend of King Edward VII and many other influential men, and commissioned the designing, building and racing of six large cutters, besides owning two steam yachts. His *Shamrock*s were America's Cup challengers five times between 1899 and 1930. At his death in 1931 he was planning to make a sixth challenge.

PAGE 74

Lines and a structural section of the American sloop yacht *Independence*, designed by B. B. Crowninshield and built in 1901 by George Lawley of Boston, Massachusetts for Thomas W. Lawson. At 140 ft 10½ in overall, she was the longest yacht then built for America's Cup racing. Waterline length was 90 ft, beam 23 ft 11½ in and draft 20 ft. Although her body sections appear fair, the waterlines and buttocks show the flat bottom forward and aft which gave her a scow-like hull form and caused pounding in even

a small chop. The finely formed fin of the keel swelled at the bottom to provide adequate space for the lead ballast inside it. Transverse hull bracing was provided to distribute strains from the deck edge, floors and frames.

A committee of Boston yachtsmen decided to raise funds for a '90 ft Sloop' as a contender for Cup defence against Sir Thomas Lipton in 1901. They reckoned on needing $100,000 to design, construct and equip the yacht, compared to the sums of $4–500,000 expended on the building and maintenance of *Columbia* which had defeated *Shamrock I* in 1899. This target was not reached and the costs were shouldered by Thomas W. Lawson, a wealthy Boston businessman who stipulated that the yacht participate in the trials to be held between the new *Constitution* and the two year old *Columbia*, both Herreshoff designed and built. He wanted the sloop to be managed by a committee of Massachusetts yachtsmen and sailed by the best available American captain and crew. Bostonian General Charles J. Paine, prominent in Cup defence and a member of the New York Yacht Club committee that had drafted the new deed of gift for the Cup, was of the opinion that *Independence* would be eligible for the trial races even though her owner was not a member of the N.Y.Y.C. On this assurance Lawson instructed Crowninshield and Lawley & Son, both Boston firms, to start work. She first hoisted sail on June 3, 1901 and lowered her sails for the last time on September 3, to be broken up later that month.

Lawson's troubles commenced with his attempt to enter *Independence* for selection. The New York Yacht Club were willing to admit her to the trial races providing Lawson temporarily transferred ownership to a member of the club. This he refused to do and commenced a furious battle of words with the N.Y.Y.C., much of it in the press.

It was the newly formed Newport Yacht Racing Association which enabled her to compete. Many of its members were also in the N.Y.Y.C. The Association invited *Independence*'s owner to enter her against *Constitution* and *Columbia*, off Brenton's Reef. During June she underwent sailing trials in Massachusetts Bay against the large schooner *Hildegarde* and the 70 ft sloop *Athene*: neither were a match for her. Lawson contemplated buying the old *Defender* as a more suitable trial horse but examination of her hull revealed that interaction between its mixed metals had rendered her unfit to float.

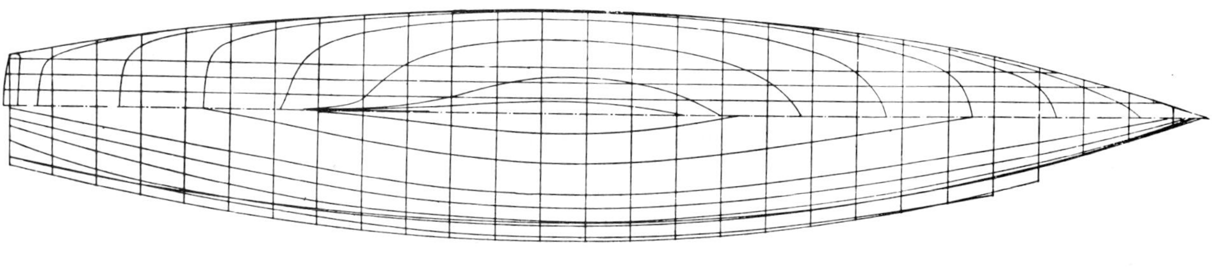

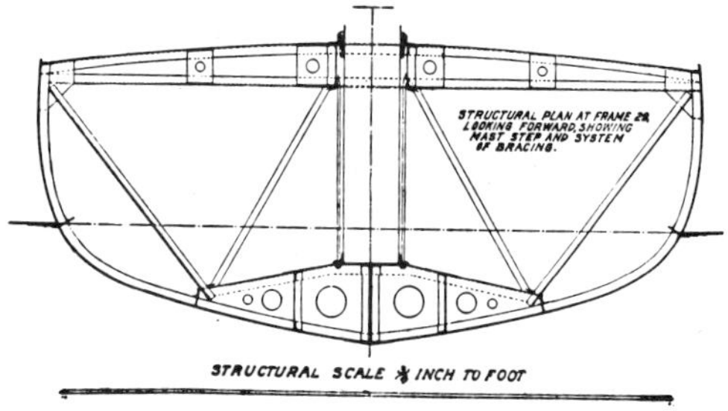

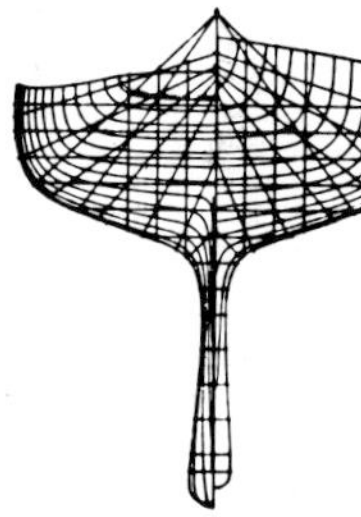

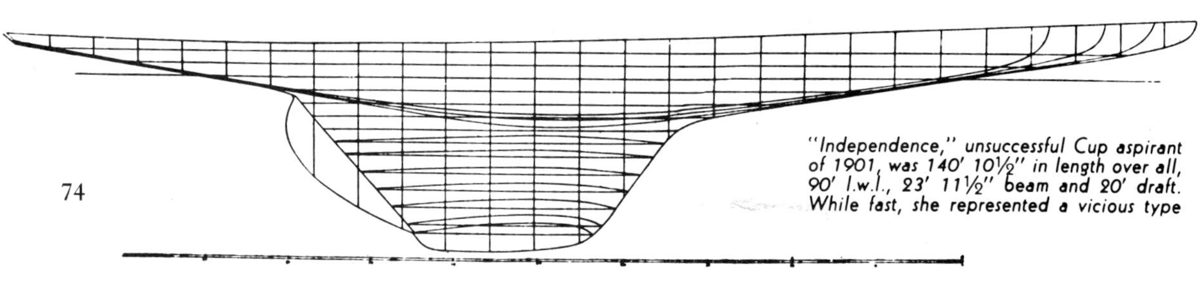

"Independence," unsuccessful Cup aspirant of 1901, was 140′ 10½″ in length over all, 90′ l.w.l., 23′ 11½″ beam and 20′ draft. While fast, she represented a vicious type

Defects showed early in *Independence*'s trials. The fin keel was too far aft for good balance and the long and flat sectioned overhangs were inadequately supported by the transverse framing and longitudinal structure. However, her modified scow hull form achieved speed with the wind abeam and at times she astounded all with her bursts of speed, giving rise to hopes that when worked up she might surprise everybody.

The trip around Cape Cod was made on a day of wind and seas which made her pound badly. Her deck showed signs of wracking and buckling. Some deck seams started but she entered the Thames River to New London under her own sail. On arrival on June 30, Captain Hank Haff reported that the yacht could not be prepared in time to meet her rivals off Newport on July 6. Lawson, however, insisted that she be brought to the line even if she sank immediately afterwards and he gave orders for rectification work to proceed night and day, regardless of expense.

Independence appeared at the start of the first trial race with the fin of her keel filled with water and some of her hull seams working in the swell. In the light air she made a slow start and continued to fall well astern of *Columbia* and *Constitution*. She took nine hours to return to moorings and was untimed. The hull continued to leak badly but her crew had orders not to pump when near other craft, to conceal the defect as much as possible. Yachtsmen and the press were mystified by her poor performance as her trials had been kept as secret as possible since launch. Captain Haff and his excellent Deer Isle crew were dismayed. The second race was sailed in a light southerly breeze and *Independence* still lagged, being beaten by more than 60 minutes over a 30 mile triangular course by *Columbia*. All Captain Haff's considerable skill could not make her respond. Afterwards 2 tons of ballast was removed before the third race, sailed in a lively southwest wind over a course of 15 miles to windward and 15 to leeward. She was improved but was still beaten by 5 minutes by *Columbia* and 3 minutes by *Constitution*.

The following day the sloops started with a brisk 12 knot northeast wind. *Columbia* and *Constitution* took the lead but the great *Independence* was coming up fast when her topmast carried away. She was delayed several minutes while the wreckage was cleared by her smart crew, then resumed chase of the others. Despite losing her topsail she came on again and even with this handicap finished only 10 minutes astern of *Columbia* and not quite 9 minutes behind *Constitution*. The supporters of the *Independence* felt that with some further alteration she might show a further gain in speed and took heart at her dry-docking at New London for this purpose.

However, on August 1 she raced against *Columbia*, *Constitution* not entering, and was beaten by over 5 minutes. Two days later she showed her truest form and Captain Haff and his boys brought her across the line only 1 minute 11 seconds after *Columbia* in an 18 knot wind over a triangular course. On the first leg she had lagged by over 3 minutes but on the other two she continuously gained, looming like doom over the flying *Columbia*, and had it been a longer course she would certainly have overtaken the Herreshoff boat. However, that was her last race. *Columbia* was again nominated Cup defender and Lawson ordered *Independence* to be broken up soon afterwards. She had cost him $205,034.05 in her short career – for three months' sport.

The power and speed shown by *Independence* in the August 3 race impressed many, including her rivals. It inspired Nathanael Herreshoff, who realized the great potential speed of such a hull in match sailing conditions. But her wild steering and unpredictable performance in most conditions was largely caused by the hull and rig being out of balance, and the steering and rudder failed several times. Crowninshield was a clever and innovative designer and had he had experience in designing first-class racers she would have been a formidable opponent. The *Independence* concept and her gradually improving performance caused Herreshoff to use a 'scow' hull for the even larger sloop *Reliance*, the Cup defender in 1903.

Few large racers were as disappointing as *Independence* and she and the British racing schooner *Waterwitch* of 1911 shared the dubious distinction of being broken up shortly after completion.

B. B. Crowninshield did not design another first-class racer but sensibly produced large numbers of fishing schooners, commercial craft of other types and many cruising and small racing yachts. In a way he was a pioneer with *Independence*. He made his point and Herreshoff picked it up and perfected the concept in *Reliance*.

CONSTITUTION
NYYC

LEFT, ABOVE

The crew of the unselected America's Cup defence contender *Constitution*, 1901. *Front row, seated, from right to left in peaked caps:* first mate Howell, Captain Uriah Rhodes and second mate Nelson.

Captain Rhodes was born at Bay Shore, Long Island in 1862, the son of a captain of coasting vessels, in which he went to sea. Afterwards he took to yachting and served in the large schooners *Atlantic, Volunteer, Sea Fox, Lasca, Montauk, Ariel* and the yawls *Sybarita* and *Ailsa*, when they were in America; also the auxiliary *Hussar*. Captain Rhodes died in 1942. He was not the most dashing of the big class skippers but was an excellent seaman.

LEFT, BELOW

Independence, *Constitution* and *Columbia* racing in one of the trials to select a defender for the America's Cup races of 1901. *Independence* (left) was considerably larger than her opponents.

An American observer of the trials wrote, of *Independence* leaving Boston for the races,

> As the big ninety-footer of which Boston hopes and expects so much slipped out from between the piers where she had been lying, the big Nantasket boat *Mayflower* passed and gave three rousing blasts of her powerful whistle, making a demonstration as a salute, and this was a signal for almost every boat in the harbour to let loose its steam whistle, making a demonstration scarcely less enthusiastic than that which greeted the fleet of United States warships when they first entered the harbour after the late war.

Another observer described her racing performance.

> I was rather surprised and a bit pleased to note the kindly manner in which the Boston craft banged into the sea. She neither splashed nor pounded anything like I was led to believe she did. Just before the start, when she warped off to wear, she gave an exhibition of heeling such as we had never before witnessed, going clean over 45 degrees or better; in fact it knocked out the heeling gauge on board, going far beyond the scale. But getting down on her side did not seem to stop her in the least, and except for evident hard steering she paced up to the starting line like a winner.

The trial races were hard fought by the *Columbia*.

> Barr, as usual, went to windward and preferred to make one of his eagle swoop starts – and he did, the result being a very close approach to a bad foul. He drove close down on *Independence*'s weather and as they circled round for the line the clew of *Columbia*'s mainsail swept across the Boston boat's headstays. It is a very pretty method of starting, as it is bound to carry with it the weather position, but some day there will be a grand smash up if the practice is continued. Luckily for *Columbia* Captain Haff very good naturedly gave way, and as the Boston people are too full of the true sporting feeling to bother with protests, all went merrily on. This encounter forced *Independence* well to the leeward side of the line and gave Barr a big advantage at the outset. But I would advise the skipper who sails the Cup defender not to try the Barr game with the *Shamrock*.

He quickly appreciated the failings of the mighty *Independence*.

> If the *Columbia* under Barr's skilled hand was doing her duty, *Independence* was by no means out of the running. But she was going like a huge, unruly beast. A half-wild horse with the bit in its teeth was nothing to this great leaping, rushing scow. One could not but help feeling sorry for her crew in their desperate effort to master the monster and keep her on the course. The difference of the action of the two boats at this time was most marked. *Columbia*, trained to perfection, was utilising every ounce of her power without fret or fuss. . . . Turn from her to the other. *Independence* was rushing at the wind, diving first into it, then hurling herself away from it. She filled, took a mad rush forward, luffed, shivered, rolled up, then heeled, filled and went off again. There was a continual waste of power. To look at the two was like looking at a contest between a trained athlete and an untrained muscular giant. At times her crew seemed to have the mastery of the brute and she moved grandly to windward, but it was only for a short spell; then she made one of her mad breaks from the course and what she had gained was speedily lost. But all the time, although losing the weather gauge, she was forging ahead at steamship speed and the first mark not in sight.

FOLLOWING PAGE

Meteor III leaves for her sailing trials at New York in 1902. The excitement of the first sail in a new large racer on trials was well caught by an American observer at New York.

> All her sails seemed to sit first rate when the wind came freshly, and the captain of the *Patrol* [an escorting police launch] began to open his eyes when he found that his steamer, which is credited

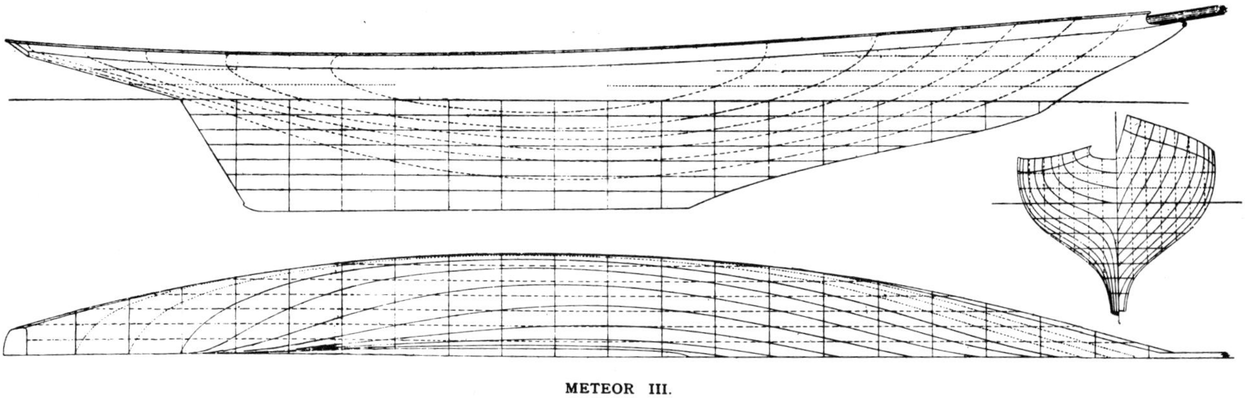

METEOR III.

with 16 knots an hour, could not hold the big two-sticker. At 2.28 the wheel was put hard over . . . and it was then seen that the Emperor's boat was exceedingly active during her spin. The way she carried was great, and she spun round into the port tack like a 90-footer racing for the America's Cup. But this new direction she only held for two minutes, when she went about to the starboard tack again and payed away to gybe. While she wore ship she gave another unmistakeable proof of activity, and she was going like a steam engine when she swung down to take the flap over. Here the wind increased very much, and before the *Patrol* could get on the same course the *Meteor* headed up about north on the west wind and smoked off at a terrible rate. While following in this wind, which was now blowing wicked as the sailors say, it was seen that the spray was so great off her bows and side that the craft had all the appearance of being on fire. There was no blaze seen, but the smoke of spray swept off from her fully 40 feet, and it was an inspiring sight to see the new craft, with all her gear perfect in its first trial, lie down and take the gale most ably. Her rails were under water and the crew were working at the loose dories, apparently trying to lash them in place on the decks. . . . In the run back to the anchorage the *Patrol* was shoved to every pound of steam she could produce, but she was getting left about two miles in ten. Of course her people told wonderful stories of her speed, but she was probably going a full 12 knots an hour, which would mean that the *Meteor* was travelling at 14 knots. There is no reason why she should not do her 14 knots as she is over 30 feet longer on the waterline than the *Columbia* and *Shamrock II*, both of which can do better than 13 knots.

LEFT, BELOW

Lines of the German Kaiser's schooner *Meteor III* of 1902. She was designed by Archibald C. Smith & Barbey and was built by the Townsend-Downey Shipbuilding Co. in New York. The firm closed shortly after her completion.

Her principal dimensions were 130 ft between perpendiculars, 118 ft waterline length by 27 ft 6 in beam. The lines are typical of the many beautiful and fast schooner yachts produced by Archibald Cary Smith and his partners. The long, sweeping buttock and waterlines make for speed on a reach and off the wind. The schooner rig and large area of immersed lateral plane would make her slower in stays than cutters, sloops or yawls,

but the sections promise speed to windward, with perhaps a suggestion of tenderness from the high and slack bilges.

Meteor III was not a thorough success as a racer, despite skilled handling by Captain Ben Parker and a carefully selected English crew with a number of German yacht hands. However, as she was ordered as a 'fast cruiser' which would also be capable of winning a race against others of her type – at the time this was likely to replace the pure racer in the large class – her designer and owner were well satisfied with her performance, though the skipper and crew were not.

PREVIOUS PAGE

Dining saloon of *Meteor III*, 1902. Although designed and built in America, the Kaiser's third racer was completely overhauled and completed on arrival in England to fit out for racing under Captain Ben Parker. Several firms contributed to her cabin furnishing, and the owner's cabin and bathroom were by Warings, who specialized in interiors for ships and yachts. The style and detail is typical of the times.

> The treatment throughout [of the owner's cabin and bathroom] is white, highly enamelled, and relieved with a colour note of pale green; the style employed being known as Colonial Adams, which is distinguished by the extreme delicacy and refinement of its detail. In the owner's cabin is a dressing table made of oak from the *Foudroyant*, Nelson's old flagship; the curtains and carpets are green, the former being ornamented with a silver coloured embroidery. All the metal work is silver plated, including the bedstead which is of the swing pattern. His Majesty's bath is sunk below the level of the deck for economy of space. All the fittings here again are of silver plate, and the wash stand is of the purest marble.
>
> The ladies' cabins have satinwood fitments including at the aft end a writing table and wash stand; comfortable lounges are arranged on either side, and at the forward end two satinwood tables and a finely inlaid and decorated satinwood piano form attractive features. The dining saloon, which is an apartment of about 25 by 18 ft, is panelled all round in white, and the ship's sides are constructed as cupboards, arranged to display the racing trophies which have been won by his Imperial Majesty with the old *Meteor*. There is also a finely inlaid bookcase and writing table of the same design. Below are very comfortable seats. The chairs are of mahogany with fine satin inlay, and their leather backs are embossed with the Imperial monogram. The sideboard is semi-circular in shape, and finished in the same way with fine gold metal work. The yacht's piano, which is placed in this room, is specially designed to match the sideboard. The inside, however, is lined with holly, giving the appearance of ivory. This saloon is lighted with thirty silver candles and candlelabra, and it may be pointed out that the whole vessel is lighted with candles, as the Emperor will not have oil used for lighting.
>
> The deckhouse and stairway leading to the Imperial apartments are constructed of inland Spanish mahogany, and fitted with a seat and table for writing, etc so as to insure the minimum of inconvenience in wet weather. The ceiling is of tulip wood, with fine bands of mahogany, inlaid with satinwood.

RIGHT

Sailplan and accommodation arrangement of the racing schooner *Cicely* which was designed by William Fife and built by J. & G. Fay & Co. at Southampton in 1902 for Cecil Quentin. Her dimensions were 113 ft 6 in between perpendiculars, 90 ft 2 in waterline length by 23 ft 4 in beam by 14 ft 4 in draft. The frames and beams were of steel, with the remainder of the construction of wood. Her launch was typical of those of most large racers.

> The owner and a large party of guests were present at the ceremony, which, owing to the careful arrangements made to ensure success, passed off without a hitch, notwithstanding that the tide was a very poor one for floating such a big vessel. Mrs Quentin performed the christening ceremony, naming the boat *Cicely* as she left the ways, and accompanying her on the temporary staging erected under the bow of the vessel was her young daughter, after whom the vessel is named. Handsome bouquets were presented to Mrs Quentin and her daughter by Mrs Moore, wife of the general manager of Fay & Co., and Miss Ena Moore, and the bows of the vessel were gaily decorated with flowers. She glided very easily into the water to the accompaniment of cheers from a very large crowd assembled on the jetty, and at all points of vantage whence a view of the launch could be obtained. There were general expressions of admiration of her appearance afloat, and she is an undoubtedly powerful looking craft. As soon as she was free of the cradle a steam tug took her in tow to the docks, where her masts were stepped, after which she returned to the yard to complete her fittings.

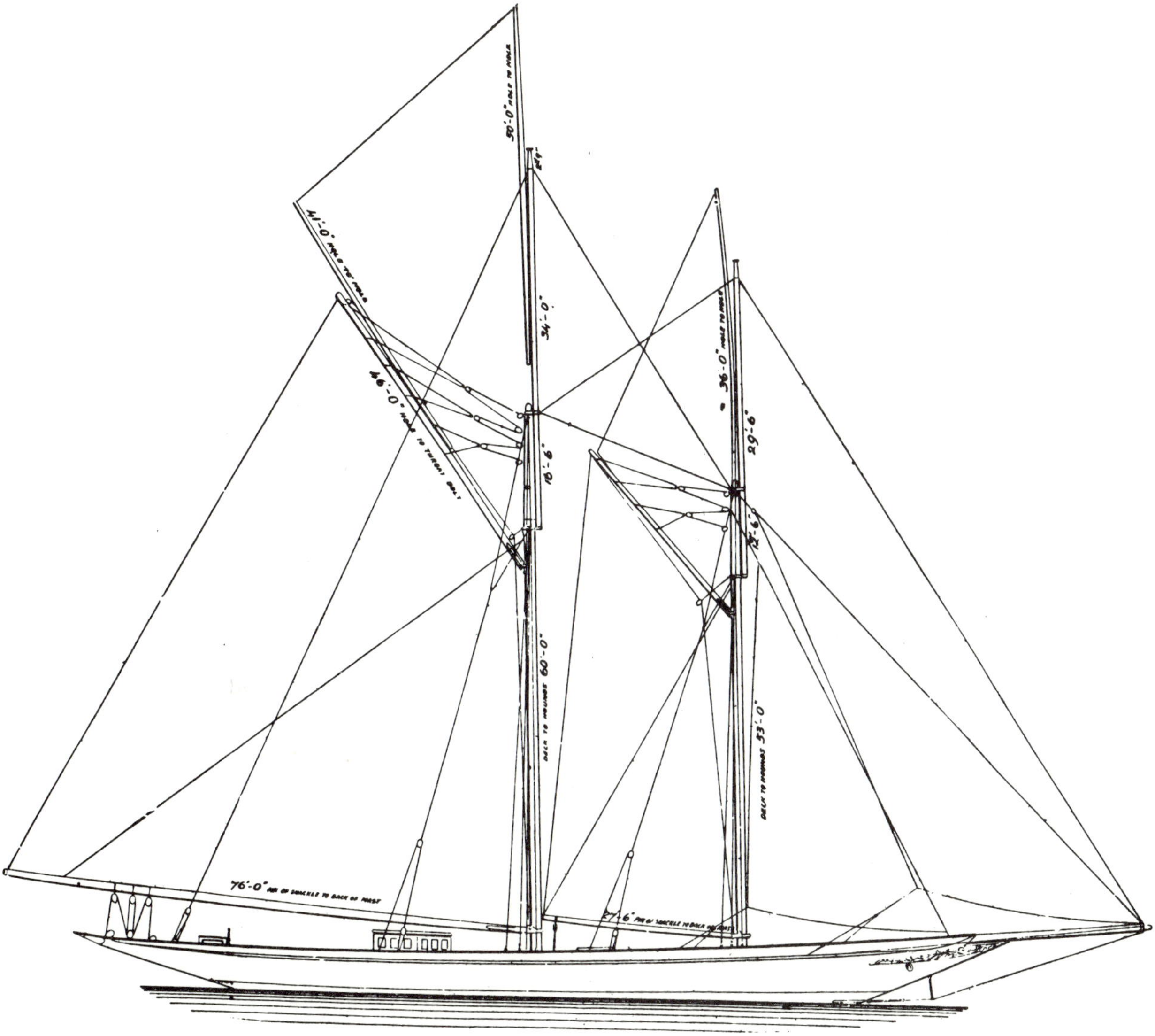

SAIL PLAN, SCHOONER *CICELY.*

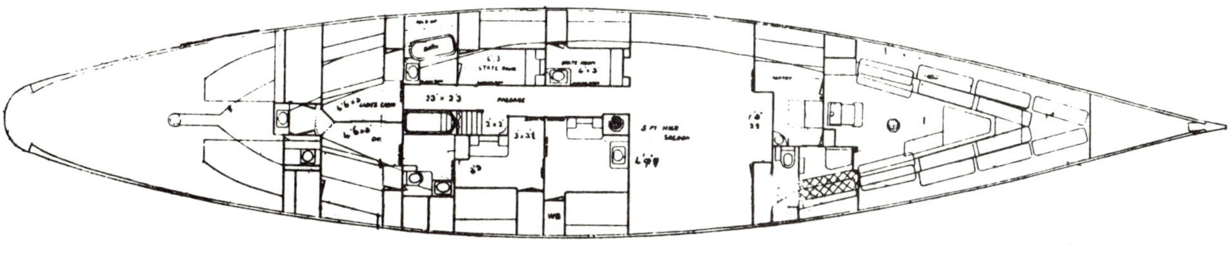

ACCOMMODATION PLAN, SCHOONER *CICELY.*

Quentin spared no efforts to ensure that her debut in racing was successful. Captain Lemon Cranfield (older brother of Captain William of the *Valkyries* and one of six distinguished racing brothers) was in command and had with him Captain Robert Wringe with a fine racing crew. Although then elderly, Lemon Cranfield had great experience of schooner racing and was probably most successful of all the captains.

Cicely's long raking stem was typical of many Fife designs of the period, and the sailplan shows the usual arrangements of the racing schooner rig: the mainmast is stepped almost amidships, resulting in a powerful mainsail and a narrow foresail and fore topsail. A large yard topsail is shown, but she also set smaller triangular topsails, with and without a jackyard at the foot to extend the clew well beyond the gaff. The spar dimensions are interesting though not exceptional in a racing schooner of this size. The mainmast was 78 ft 6 in from deck to masthead, the main topmast was 55 ft 3 in long; the main boom 76 ft, the main gaff 46 ft, the topsail yard was 50 ft, the jackyard 41 ft, the foremast was 65 ft 6 in from deck to masthead, the foresail boom 27 ft 6 in, the fore topmast 42 ft and the fore topsail yard 36 ft.

The accommodation from forward was arranged with a foc's'le with pipe berths for fourteen men and a small cabin for the skipper. A galley and lavatory divided this from the saloon, across the full breadth of the yacht. Abaft this was a passageway leading to the main companion stairway. On each side were two staterooms and bathrooms; a ladies' cabin was at the end of the passageway to port and another stateroom to starboard. The counter was a sail locker for the large number of topsails and headsails needed by a racer, and the trysail used for passage making or bad weather.

Cicely was a fast and successful schooner but unfortunately she was built at a time when large-yacht racing was at a low ebb and the yachts she raced against were a mixed assortment of cutters, yawls, schooners and occasionally ketches. The best sport was when a number of these large schooners raced together, when she proved fast and weatherly. Later she was renamed *Lamorna* and was fitted with an auxiliary engine. After being laid up for many years she was hauled out and had her lead keel removed for scrap. During the early 1950s she was refitted by some enthusiasts who intended to sail her on an ocean cruise and a concrete keel was made and fitted to her. The unfortunate yacht drove ashore on the Dorset coast on her outward voyage and was wrecked – a sad end for a magnificent racing schooner.

LEFT
Sailmakers in the Cowes loft of Ratsey & Lapthorn spread out as much as possible of the mainsail of *Shamrock III* in 1903. This sail was 103 ft on the boom; 69 ft in the luff; 65 ft 6 in on the gaff and 130 ft on the leech. Because of its size, such a sail could not be fully spread in any sail loft and the cut and fullness of its shape and set were conceived on the floor from the design plan by the foreman sailmaker, and in such an important sail with the agreement and advice of Mr Ratsey, possibly other principals of the firm and perhaps the yacht's designer.

These sails were made from cloth woven from flax or cotton fibres and varied in dimensions with changes in humidity and temperature. Considerable experience is necessary to achieve a good set and keep within stretched dimensions which do not contravene sail area rules, and good sailmaking has always been a mixture of art and science. English yacht sails were notably fine in the period from the 1880s to 1914 and maintained a high standard through the 1919–39 period. The problems of cutting a large sail were considerable, but stitching it presented even more difficulties. No machine could sew the seams of this broad and heavy canvas assembly and all the stitching was done by hand, with rows of men and boys plying palms and needles on their benches, working along the seams. There were standards for spacing of stitch: five per inch was usual for such seams. The watchful eyes of the foreman and chargehands maintained the standard.

Thomas Ratsey, head of the firm, stands at the extreme left and the foreman sailmaker is next to him. There are forty-nine sailmakers including apprentices in this picture, probably the whole staff at the time. They wear the white canvas trousers, and some the jackets, of their trade. An early task given to an apprentice was to make himself a pair of trousers from duck canvas, to cope with the considerable kneeling required in a sail loft.

BELOW
A giant ready to launch. *Reliance*, America's Cup defender of 1903 against *Shamrock III*, on the slip after bottom cleaning and before measurement for rating. There are thirty men on deck, including her skipper Captain Charles Barr. When racing there were sixty-four professionals on board, besides the four or five amateurs who were owners, representatives or guests.

Reliance was designed and built by Herreshoff in 1903 for a syndicate of the New York Yacht Club and cost about $175,000, then a huge sum. Her hull form had the shallow bodied, full-ended characteristics then common in many American racing yachts. Principal dimensions were 149 ft

8 in overall length, 89 ft 8 in waterline length, 25 ft 10 in beam, 19 ft 6½ in draft; sail area 16,159 sq ft. The gaff was 72 ft long, the boom 115 ft and the spinnaker boom 83 ft 9 in; from the bowsprit end to the end of the main boom was 201 ft 9 in. Her rival, *Shamrock III*, was slightly smaller. Herreshoff decided the form of his sailing craft by carving a scale half-model from which the preliminary lines were lifted by a machine. This unorthodox method appeared to serve his purpose well and it is recorded that the model for *Reliance* was shaped during two evenings.

Reliance had a lightly constructed rig and Herreshoff had testing machines to evaluate strengths of materials and fittings. She was equipped with many winches, then unknown in British racing yachts. These handled the headsail sheets, backstay falls and the topmast heelrope. Many were two-speed and self-reeling, for wire sheets and backstay falls, winding on drums and with worm gearing and disc clutches. Many of these winches were subsequently used in other America's Cup defenders from *Resolute* to *Ranger*, and duplicates were made for other large American racers. *Reliance* had other unusual features, including a rudder which could be filled with water to ease steering in some conditions and emptied by a pump while racing.

LEFT
Bow view of *Reliance* on the slip in 1903, showing her full bow sections and deep fin keel. Footropes are spread between the bowsprit shrouds and bobstay to collect jibs during sail handling. The stocked anchor was of a type designed and manufactured for yachts by the Herreshoff Manufacturing Co.

The small number of shores supporting this very large racer with her mast standing is a tribute to the skill and care of the shipwrights who slipped her.

RIGHT
Reliance carried the largest measured sail area of any single masted vessel – 16,160 sq ft. The head of her topsail yard was 193 ft above deck and the boom was 115 ft long; from the bowsprit end to the main boom end was 201 ft 9 in.

In this drawing *Reliance* is to scale in comparison with the American clipper ship

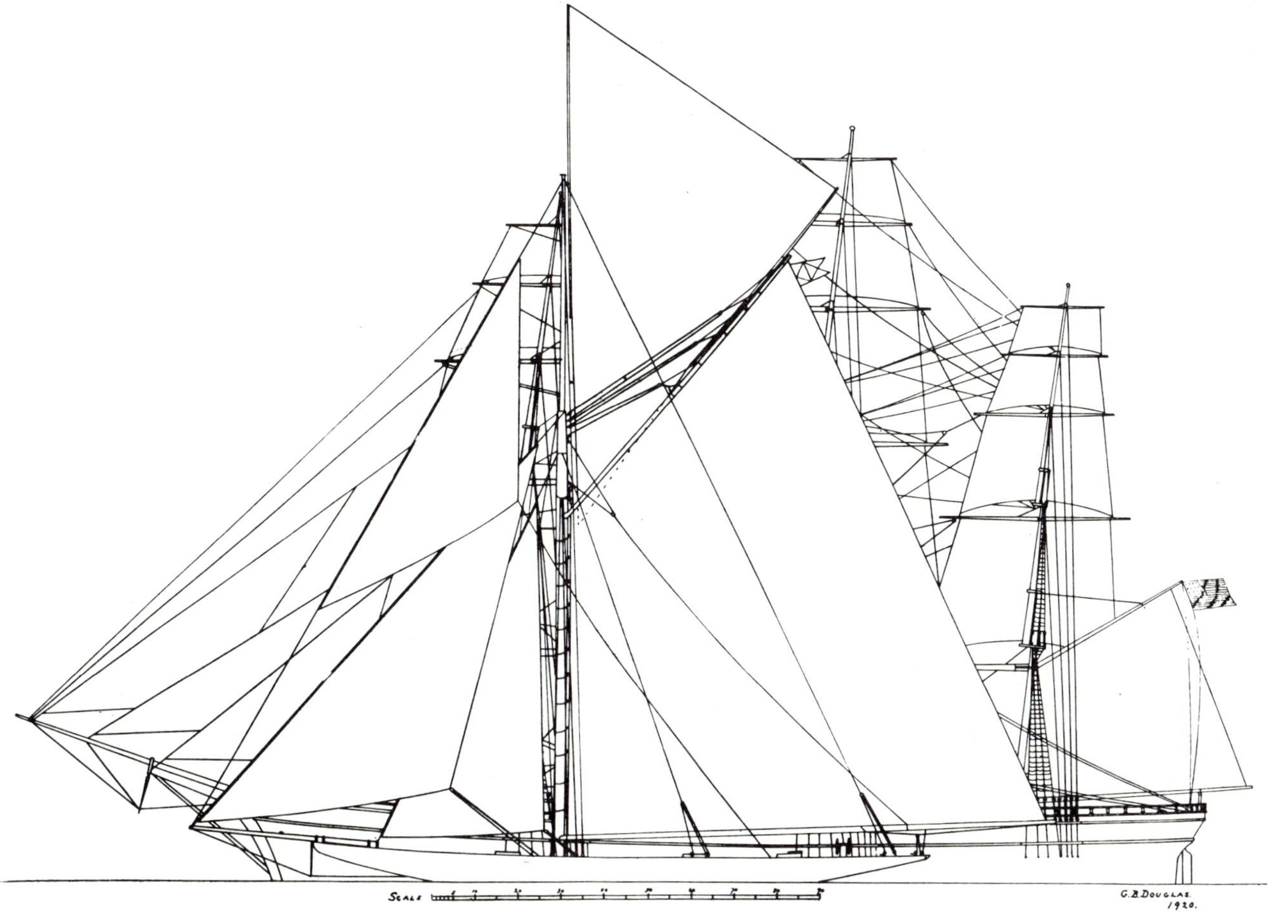

Flying Cloud which set 22,000 sq ft on three masts, or 18,586 sq ft without her staysails.

FOLLOWING PAGE

Captain Charles Barr was a successful skipper of a number of American racing yachts, mostly designed by Nathanael G. Herreshoff. He originated from Gourock and on leaving school became a grocery clerk in Greenock. He left this to ship as a hand with his half-brother Captain John Barr in the cutter *Clara* and was one of the crew which sailed her across the Atlantic when she was bought by an American yachtsman. In America, Charles Barr was put in charge of the cutter *Shona*, and attended navigation classes.

The owner of *Shona* had the larger cutter-style *Minerva* built and Charles Barr became her captain. Her success established him as a rising racing skipper and he advanced to the American 46-footer *Oweene* and had further success; then to the Herreshoff-designed 46 footer *Wasp*. In 1893 he was captain of the American sloop *Navahoe* during part of her visit to England; by early August he had been replaced by Captain Aubrey Crocker. In 1895 Barr took charge of the American *Vigilant* for the trial races against *Defender*, and was afterwards captain of the schooner *Colonia*, the Cup defenders *Columbia* and *Reliance*, and the famous schooners *Ingomar, Atlantic* and *Westward*. The photo shows him on *Westward*, and it is probably her owner Alexander S. Cochran who has the helm, on his left.

Charles Barr was a competent yachtmaster who studied navigation to be able to fully command yachts on ocean passages – in contrast to many able racing skippers in America and in Britain who had no knowledge of other than coastal navigation and made the ocean passages with a navigating master on board, though they were in command and responsible for sailing the yacht. Captain Barr's great chance came in 1899 when he was offered command of the America's Cup defender *Columbia*. This was because the ageing Captain Hank Haff, America's most experienced racing skipper, did not wish to continue active

racing, preferring to skipper a fast cruiser, where the responsibility and pace were less for the same wages and a more comfortable life. Although Barr was absolutely loyal to his owners and was a distinguished racing helmsman, his British origins caused concern and considerable criticism among American yachtsmen and the American press, who questioned whether a British helmsman should defend the America's Cup against a British challenger. However, his ability swayed opinion, though he did eventually become a naturalized U.S. citizen.

In January 1911 Barr died suddenly in Southampton, England when skipper of the schooner *Westward*. Despite his untypical beginning, he was among the greatest of the professional racing captains.

RIGHT
The schooner *Adela* reaching at her maximum speed in a handicap race, about 1904. When first-class yacht racing in Britain slumped during the early years of the century, some owners of large cruising yachts entered suitable handicap events at the coastal regattas. *Adela* was a powerful schooner, 224 tons Thames Measurement, designed by W. C. Storey, who was well known at the time for similar cruisers. She was built in 1903 by J. & G. Fay & Co. for Claud T. Cayley and was not intended for racing, but slipped along well particularly in fresh breezes. She only entered a few races and with little success against large cutters and yawls. Her composite hull was planked over steel frames, sheer, bilge and keel plates, diagonal straps, deck beams and knees. Dimensions were 131 ft 9 in overall, 21 ft 11½ in beam and 13 ft 3 in draft. Sail area was 8874 sq ft excluding the long-roper jib topsail and small main topmast staysail carried here. This photograph also shows the long-footed 'reaching foresail' that large yachts carried after the 1880s in light-weather racing. This sail was later 'invented' by amateur yachtsmen in the 1920s and renamed a 'Genoa', a term still in use.

This fine schooner was later renamed *Heartsease* and given an auxiliary engine, and during the 1930s she was well known under the ownership of Sir Bolton Eyres Monsell. After 1939 she became a houseboat at Tollesbury in Essex, gracing the mud berths for many years as a reminder of that village's involvement with yachting on the grand scale. She has recently been restored to use as a yacht and is refitting for ocean sailing.

FOLLOWING PAGE
The yawl rigged *Navahoe* beating up Kiel Fiord during regatta week in 1904. Her mizzen would today be reckoned a good sized gaff mainsail and the mitre-cut yard topsail is as large as a 12 Metre's mainsail. The low bulwarks and wheel steering were original features. *Navahoe* was designed and built by the Herreshoff Manufacturing Co. in 1893, for Royal P. Carroll. Her dimensions were 87 ft 8 in waterline length and 23 ft 4 in beam, with only 12 ft 6 in draft and a large steel centreboard that extended it to 20 ft. The shallow hull form was dictated by the owner and, lacking stability, she was overpowered by her rig in strong winds. She floated 3 in deep above her designed waterline and 20 tons of lead ballast was removed from the bilge and placed outside on the garboard plating to stiffen her.

During the spring of 1893 she sailed for England to race under Captain Barr for the season with the large class, then comprising *Britannia*, *Valkyrie II*, *Satanita*, *Calluna* and *Ivernia*. She was frequently beaten by the British cutters, until a spectacular match race against *Britannia* for the Brenton Reef Cup, one of the last races during her visit. The cup had been won by the English yacht *Genesta* in 1885, in America, and Carroll had challenged for it prior to his visit. *Navahoe* rated 157 and was consistently beaten by *Britannia*, rating 151, in British waters; *Navahoe* could not match her to

windward but could equal her otherwise, particularly reaching and running. As the race was for an American cup it was sailed under the rules of the New York Yacht Club and no time allowance was given, whereas under Y.R.A. rules *Navahoe* would have allowed her rival 2 minutes 17 seconds over the distance.

The course was across the English Channel, around Cherbourg breakwater and return, starting and finishing off the Needles at the entrance to the Solent. The strong easterly made it a reach both ways, and the heavy seas were a severe test of hulls, spars and gear. The masts of both yachts buckled ominously, but everything held and both finished, *Britannia* 2½ seconds ahead after 10 hours 36 minutes and 29 seconds of racing, an average speed of 11.3 knots *Navahoe* protested that the club steamer acting as mark boat had been moved (she had gone away after dark but returned and re-anchored well in time for the finish), and though *Britannia*'s crew felt they had won fairly the Royal Yacht Squadron awarded the visitor the cup, so ensuring that her season ended with goodwill.

Navahoe remained in Carroll's ownership until 1897, with Captain Crocker in command though she seldom raced. She was then bought by a German, George W. Watjen, who had her converted to yawl rig. Like most German yachts of the time, *Navahoe* had an English captain and crew; Edward Sycamore was her skipper and his crew were almost all from Rowhedge, Wivenhoe and Brightlingsea. She was most successful in German and British waters at a time when first-class racing was principally among schooners and yawls. She featured in a famous incident at Kiel Week in 1904 when the American schooner *Ingomar* struck her side bow-on at about 9 knots, fortunately without serious damage except to the pride of the two captains, who were involved in an iron-nerved test of the right of way rules. Barr was sailing *Ingomar* and met his match in Sycamore: both were experienced racing skippers attempting to take the most out of the racing rules. Barr held on and expected Sycamore to give way, possibly because Barr was racing in the large schooner class against *Meteor* and *Hamburg* while Sycamore was in the 'cruisers over 21 and under 26 Rating' class. However, the latter was equally sure of his ground and held his course. Both yacht hulls were steel and the collision would have been partly absorbed by the bowsprit and headstays; no doubt Barr attempted to ease it when it became inevitable. In the same Kiel Week regatta *Meteor* held on when sailing on port tack against *Ingomar*, which protested and both withdrew.

By 1914 *Navahoe* had a French owner, and she was broken up for scrap during the First World War.

FOLLOWING PAGE
Captain Robert Wringe was a well known racing skipper before the First World War. Born at Brightlingsea in 1861, he first went to sea in fishing smacks as a boy in 1875 and shipped in yachts during the summer. He quickly rose to command some of the largest of the Brightlingsea smacks and several from Grimsby, where a branch of his family owned them; working all over the North Sea and around the British coasts. He served in the 40-rater *Velzie* (about 70 ft long) under Captain Edward Gould, also of Brightlingsea, during 1890 and left her to captain the 39 ton cutter *Alceste* before joining the 40-rater *Carina* as mate when she came out in 1894 under Captain Sycamore. This was a champion boat, and when Sycamore left at the end of the season Robert Wringe was appointed her skipper. He was a man of few words but of lightning and iron-nerved decisions, a temperament which suited bluff old Admiral Montague, his owner. Wringe's splendid sailing of the *Carina* established him as a great racing captain.

By 1898 he was skipper of the new 52 ft Linear Rating Class racer *Eldred* which was battling in a class of five boats, all evenly matched. The closeness of the competition which took them around the coasts can be gauged by the finish of their race at Campbeltown Regatta in Scotland, where only 57 seconds separated the first and last of the class after a 50 mile course. At the end of 1895 Wringe was appointed skipper of the large racing cutter *Ailsa*, a command just relinquished by Tom Jay. He sailed her out to the Mediterranean to race against the royal cutter *Britannia* for the Riviera season. A hand was lost from the *Ailsa* on passage in bad weather, but on arrival the big cutters had some spirited races.

In 1899 Sir Thomas Lipton made his first challenge for the America's Cup with *Shamrock*,

commanded by Archie Hogarth from the Clyde but sailed in the races by Wringe. After the series Wringe was approached to sail the American racing yacht *Mineola*, built by Herreshoff as one of four sisters which were gigantic one-designs, 106 ft long over all and 70 ft on the waterline.

Cornelius Vanderbilt's *Rainbow* also had an English crew, skippered by George Parker of Itchen, Hampshire. W. K. Vanderbilt Jr owned *Virginia*, under Captain Hansen with a Norwegian crew, and Harry Whitney owned *Yankee*, also with Norwegians. The crews of *Mineola* and *Rainbow* were meant to be Americans but they would not sail under an English master so Captains Wringe and Parker were, to their relief, able to bring out picked English crews in the spring. *Mineola* was best to windward and *Rainbow* off the wind, and these two dominated the class. Their superiority and English crews caused jealousy among the other yachts which was expressed by many protests and charges which probably would not have arisen if all boats had had American crews and skippers. Great rivalry also arose between the Essex crew of *Mineola* and the Solent-manned *Rainbow*, aggravated when Wringe once forced *Rainbow* about on the starboard tack. During one series of races off Newport *Mineola* averaged 11 knots over the 30 mile course, winning by 34 seconds from *Rainbow*, but in a strong breeze the hulls of the yachts were badly wrung and had to be repaired. They were fast boats, approaching large-class characteristics in handling, and set 7000 sq ft of working canvas. The owners spared no expense to ensure good racing and each ordered an 80 ft steam yacht to act as tender for that season.

In 1901 Wringe joined Edward Sycamore as joint racing skipper of *Shamrock II* in another unsuccessful attempt to win back the America's Cup. In 1903 he skippered the Cup challenger *Shamrock III* with Captain Charles Bevis, when they were beaten by *Reliance*. Then in 1904 he took command of the new Fife-designed racing schooner *Susanne* then building at Inglis's Clydeside shipyard for German owner Herr Huldschinsky. Her great rival was the German schooner *Clara*, sailed by Wringe's old skipper Edward Gould, and both competed against neighbour Edward Sycamore in the then German yawl *Navahoe*.

In 1912 Wringe commanded the 19 Metre cutter *Mariquita*, one of four particularly lovely yachts built as an intermediate class below the big cutters and schooners, the others being *Octavia*, *Norada* and *Corona*. *Mariquita* was top of the class and was his last racing command.

FOLLOWING PAGE
Captain Edward Sycamore at the wheel of Sir Thomas Lipton's 23 Metre cutter *Shamrock*, racing on the Clyde in 1908. The owner sits immediately before it with his amateur 'representative', Colonel Duncan Neill. The hands wear the white canvas sun hats and racing suits of the time. In the right foreground Herbert Springett of Rowhedge and the second mate stand by a sheet. The cutter close astern is probably the similar *White Heather*, sailed by Charles Bevis with a predominantly Solent crew. She was *Shamrock*'s closest rival in several seasons of brilliant racing.

The 23 Metre cutters were the first large yachts built under the International Yacht Racing Union rules, established in 1906 to encourage a revival of racing yacht building after several years of stagnation. It was hoped to encourage yachts that combined speed with reasonable accommodation and could later be useful as cruisers, though this did not result. The 23 Metres were successful, fast but wet boats and had crews of twenty-two. They cost around £12,000 fitted out, a considerable sum at the time, and a season's racing cost an owner about £5,000. Three were built: *Shamrock*, *White Heather* and *Brynhild II*; the last was owned by Sir James Pender and sailed by Captain Steven Barbrook of Tollesbury, Essex as his first large command, with a crew from the Blackwater and the Colne. *Brynhild II* and *White Heather* were the first to be built, in 1907, and *Shamrock* followed the next season. *Brynhild II* sank as a result of failure of her mast off Harwich in 1910.

This 23 Metre *Shamrock* was designed by William Fife and built at his yard at Fairlie in Scotland as a light weather boat; her finest point of sailing was turning to windward in light or moderate breezes. Waterline length was 81 ft 4 in and beam 20 ft 10 in. In one of the Nore to Dover races the 23 Metre yachts carried whole mainsails through a heavy sea at the back of the Goodwins: this shook them, straining them from stem to stern as they battled to windward through

green seas for three hours in clouds of spray. Although beautifully built and handled, the racers' design had become extreme, even under the Metre rule, and the owners preferred more comfortable quarters than could be provided on board. Sir Thomas Lipton and his guests lived on board the large steam yacht *Erin* and Miles Kennedy, owner of *White Heather*, chartered an ocean tug as her tender.

RIGHT

Preparing to set a spinnaker on the 23 Metre *Shamrock*. She is hard on the wind, which is fresh bordering on strong, and all hands are alert on the streaming deck. The spinnaker boom is run forward and supported by its lift, ready to be swung out when the yacht comes off the wind at the next mark. First mate William Wadley of Rowhedge and two hands at the forehatch are probably shackling on the headboard swivel of the immense sail which will emerge, gathered sausage-like in stops, from the hatch. A reaching staysail curves away above but the main boom is sheeted in hard, almost to the centreline. The reaching staysail was probably set for an earlier leg of the course and kept because she will shortly be off the wind again with the spinnaker also set. The weather shrouds and backstays and the lee sheets are bar-taut, while the lee shrouds and backstays are slack. The weather headsail sheets trail on deck in lazy curves. The small capstan on the foredeck was used to make taut the headsail tack downhauls and for other purchases. Foam sweeps the lee deck as Captain Sycamore drives her hard.

PAGE 94, ABOVE

The first and second mastheadsmen lacing the topsail luff on *Shamrock III* before a start, 1903.

Ben Chaplin of Brightlingsea is above, settling the lacing which commenced from a cringle in the luff, just below the heel of the topsail yard. The lower man, William Wadley, is passing the lacing around the topmast and working his way down towards the lancewood spreaders. Between them they drew the luff in along the topmast in a taut leading edge for efficient windward sailing. They are about 130 ft above the deck and the yacht is being prepared for the start. All racers of consequence carried at least one hand who specialized in this task and the larger ones had two, the first and second mastheadsmen.

Noted among this daring breed were Jack 'Pups' Cranfield of Rowhedge, mastheadsman of the *Valkyries* and 'Monkey' Byford of Colchester, for many years mastheadsman of *Britannia* and in later years her mate. William Wadley was second mastheadsman of *Valkyrie II* at the time of the fatal collision between her and *Satanita* on the Clyde and he witnessed this most spectacular of yachting disasters from aloft. Jack Cranfield, the first mastheadsman, seeing the inevitable, had shouted for him to make the deck and as they slid down the shrouds they were flung clear into the water by the shock of impact as the flying *Satanita*, desperately attempting to avoid a small yacht, crunched a gaping hole in the side of *Valkyrie II*.

William Wadley was later mate of *Shamrock* (23 Metre) and was eventually skipper of several 12 Metre yachts. Ben Chaplin became skipper of the renovated 40 ton racing cutter *Bloodhound* from 1908 to 1914, winning 126 prizes in 218 starts in the large handicap class. He was killed in a mine explosion three days before the end of the First World War while in command of H.M. Drifter *Rhiannon*, when he was Lt Chaplin, DSC, Croix de Guerre, RNR.

FOLLOWING PAGE, BELOW
The hulk of the 23 Metre *Brynhild II*, beached in Brightlingsea Creek in Essex for breaking up after her disastrous sinking at Harwich regatta in

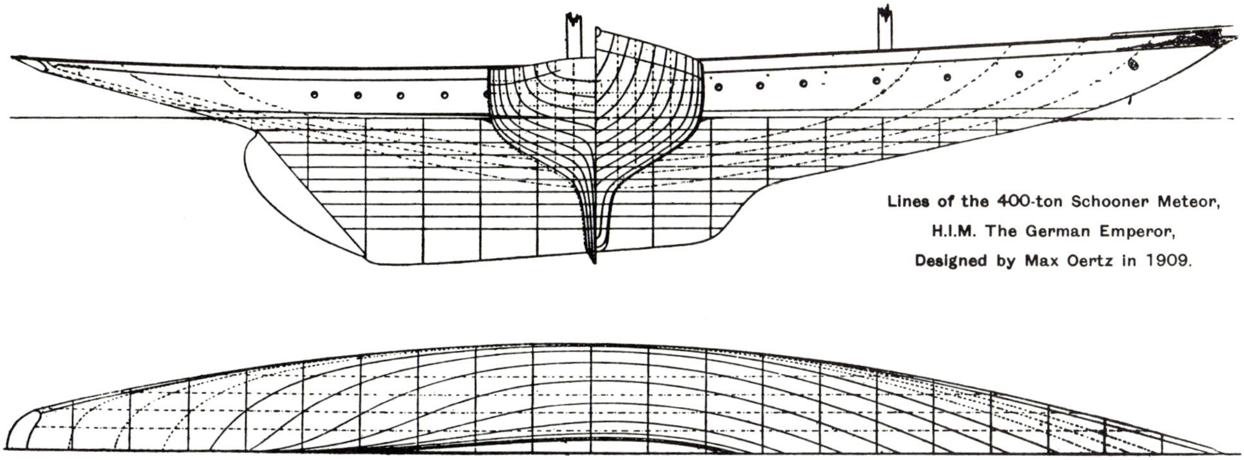

1910. This fast cutter was designed and built by Camper & Nicholson at Gosport in 1908 and was the largest racing yacht they had built. She was dogged by bad luck. At her launching the cradle killed a shipwright and during her first race, in the Thames, her mastheadsman fell from aloft and was killed. A hand was lost from her in the Solent and there were other mishaps which made sailors growl that she was ill fated. Captain Steven Barbrook of Tollesbury took *Brynhild II* over from her previous skipper knowing this background of tragedy and set about improving her performance against the slightly smaller *Nyria*, sailed by Captain Stephen Ray of Gosport, and the 23 Metre *White Heather II*, built by Fife in 1907 and sailed by Captain Charles Bevis with a crew predominantly from the Solent. They had a formidable competitor in the newly launched 23 Metre *Shamrock* under Captain Sycamore. Until well into the season, *Shamrock* and *White Heather II* were the most successful, but in a spurt during Cowes Week and in the subsequent west country regattas Barbrook brought *Brynhild II*'s first prizes up to eight against *Shamrock*'s twelve and *White Heather II*'s five. Sir James Pender was delighted. Always an enthusiastic owner, he wore a specially knitted striped guernsey for racing that was in *Brynhild II*'s racing colours of red and black.

Brynhild II remained laid up during 1909 but the next year Barbrook and his crew fitted her out. Camper & Nicholson had carried out alterations to the heel of her mast to increase the height of the sailplan. At the Orwell Corinthian Yacht Club regatta off Harwich on May 23 *Shamrock*, *White Heather II* and *Brynhild II* started and, near the weather mark – the North Cutler buoy – the mast failed below deck, drove down through her bottom and sank her in fourteen minutes. *Brynhild II* was leading at the time; the dinghy was quickly launched, her complement of twenty-five clinging to it until her competitors launched theirs and a torpedo boat steamed up to assist. The yacht filled slowly at first, then lay over on her side until her mast was lying on the surface. Sir James Pender insisted on being rowed over to her to cut the racing flag from the masthead, and a few minutes later his fine racer sank. Her wreck was subsequently run into and suffered more damage before being raised and taken into Harwich to be temporarily patched and then towed round to Brightlingsea.

ABOVE
Lines of the 400 ton racing schooner *Meteor IV*, designed by Max Oertz and built in 1909 by Krupp's Germania Werft for the Kaiser. The lines are easy and the underwater body promises speed. Her principal dimensions are: overall length 154 ft 10 in, length on the waterline 104 ft 11 in, beam 27 ft 2 in, draft 18 ft, sail area 13,719 sq ft.

PAGE 97
Kaiser Wilhelm II owned successively the ex-British racing cutter *Thistle* of 1889 (later renamed *Meteor*), the British designed, built and manned first-class cutter *Meteor II* of 1896, and a schooner designed and built in America in 1903 named *Meteor III*. All had English captains and crews of the best racing men, though the crews of the second and third *Meteor* contained a small number of Germans whom the English were ordered to train in racing so that an efficient nucleus of German yacht-racing men would be established.

During the first decade of the century first-class racing cutters were in decline and schooners and yawls became fashionable for a time, particularly in Germany where the Kaiser wished to attract the goodwill of American notables, many of whom were yacht owners. The European visits of the American schooners *Ingomar* in 1904 and *Westward* in 1910 encouraged this schooner racing revival.

In 1908 the Kaiser ordered Germany's leading yacht designer, Max Oertz of Hamburg, to design for him a large racing schooner, to be built by Krupps at their Germania Werft in Kiel. This was the largest yacht Oertz had then designed – a 400 ton Thames Measurement racer. He was an able naval architect and a shrewd observer of the work of other yacht designers, particularly the British, but he had an innovative streak of his own. This fourth *Meteor* was built of steel and was to some extent a development of Dr Krupp's own schooner *Germania* (107 ft waterline length) which Oertz had designed in 1907–8. The new yacht was 104 ft 11 in waterline length by 27 ft 2 in beam. Her sail area was moderate at 12,487 sq ft but could be considerably increased by a large main topmast staysail, shown here, and with large headsails and spinnakers.

Meteor IV was launched in 1909 and was the pride of the German yachting fleet; she had a German skipper, Captain Peters, German mates and a crew keen to prove to 'the Englanders' and the Americans that German skill in yacht racing was equal to theirs. In 1909 she sailed well against Krupp's *Germania*, the British *Cicely* and the German *Susanne*, but she was frequently outsailed by the American *Westward* which came over for the 1910 season. At Cowes Week in 1912 *Meteor IV* raced for the King's Cup on August 6 against the British *White Heather II*, *Waterwitch*, *Lamorna*, *Cetonia*, *Julnar*, *Cariad II*, *Valdora*, *Susanne* and *The Lady Anne*. All started in a strong wind and all except the ketch *Cariad II* were reefed. *Meteor IV* had one reef in her mainsail but kept the whole foresail. The first leg from Cowes to the Warner light vessel east of the Isle of Wight was a broad reach which only the well-reefed yachts could stand. *Meteor IV* was leading and she heeled to an amazing angle in a hard squall and would not answer her helm. Then she bore away across other competitors to become unmanageable, her hands frantically trying to release the foresail and jib sheets. They succeeded and she carried on racing, but shortly afterwards she was struck by a more severe squall and repeated the performance, paying off before the wind with the mainsheet fast under the tons of water on deck and pouring down hatches and skylights, her rudder ineffective at the extreme angle of heel. At last she was brought under control and ran back to Cowes with seven feet of water in the bilge.

In 1913 the Kaiser sold *Meteor IV*, which was re-christened *Aar* and fitted with a Daimler auxiliary motor. After the First World War she was sold to a syndicate of Dutch yachtsmen and then to Madame Heriot, a well-known French yacht owner who renamed her *Ailee*. When Madame Heriot had a new schooner built in 1929 the yacht was sold to Camper & Nicholson who in turn re-sold her to a Spanish owner, whereupon the boat became *Maria del Carmen Ana*. In 1930 she won the race from Plymouth to Santander in Spain, and was presented with a cup given by the King of Spain.

PAGE 98, ABOVE

Westward was a notable design by Nathanael Herreshoff, built in 1910 by his yard for Alexander S. Cochran who ordered her as a racing schooner fit to beat the Kaiser's *Meteor IV* The steel hull had little sheer but a well shaped stern. She was 135 ft long overall, 96 ft 1 in on the waterline, of 27 ft 1 in beam and drew 16 ft 11 in. The attractive gaff schooner rig set 15,498 sq ft and she carried a crew of thirty-five. During her first season she won eleven first prizes in eleven starts, sailed by Captain Charles Barr. She was afterwards bought by the Verein Seefahrt of Hamburg, who renamed her *Hamburg II*, and raced in European waters against similar large schooners.

After the war she fitted out at Brightlingsea in 1920 for Clarence Hatry, the financier, and in 1924 was sold to Warwick Brookes and the following year to T. B. F. Davis, then living in his native Guernsey, and commenced many years of racing with the British big class, in which she was the largest yacht. Davis, who had been a professional mariner, was unusual among owners of large racing yachts in that he not only took her wheel during much of a race but had forceful opinions on tactics and racing manoeuvres. Her

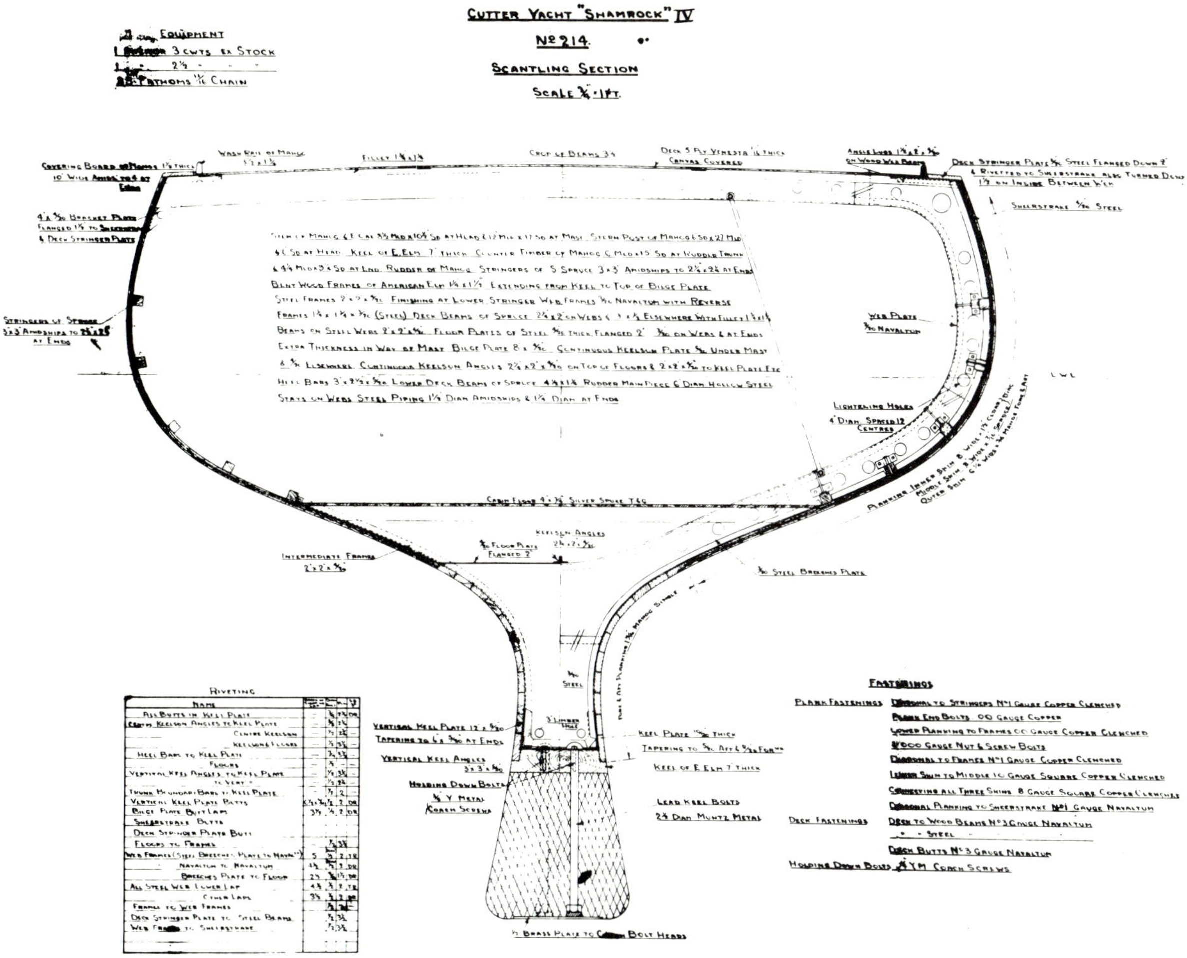

captain, Alfred Diaper of Itchen, combined diplomacy with a fine record. Although *Westward* frequently finished first she rarely won, because of her size and consequent handicap. If the course had much reaching she could romp ahead and perhaps save her time, but like all schooners she was slower to windward than the cutters.

In 1931 her sail area was reduced to 13,455 sq ft to improve her rating, and in 1934 she won the King's Cup against the big-class cutters. But the next season was her last, against the glorious competition of *Britannia*, *Velsheda*, *Endeavour*, *Candida*, *Astra* and *Shamrock V*; all matched against the American sloop *Yankee*, sportingly sailed across to race under the ownership of G. B. Lambert. By 1937 *Westward* had become a cruiser with two auxiliary diesel engines, but she retained her majestic rig until she was destroyed in 1948 under the terms of her owner's will, which decreed that unless she could be sold to an owner who would maintain her in good sailing condition she must be taken into the Channel and sunk. In postwar shortages of materials and skilled craftsmen this was not possible, and a last duty was carried out under the supervision of two of her old racing crew.

Westward is going well in this photograph. Besides mainsail, foresail, staysail and jib, she sets a yard topsail and jib topsail, and a small but efficient main topmast staysail to suit the weight of wind and to enable it to be carried to windward without having to overhaul the sheets each time she tacked, as would be required for a larger sail where the clew had to be handed over the stay between the mastheads. *Westward* had ample accommodation in her roomy hull and the row of sidelights was typical of many large American racing schooners of the time.

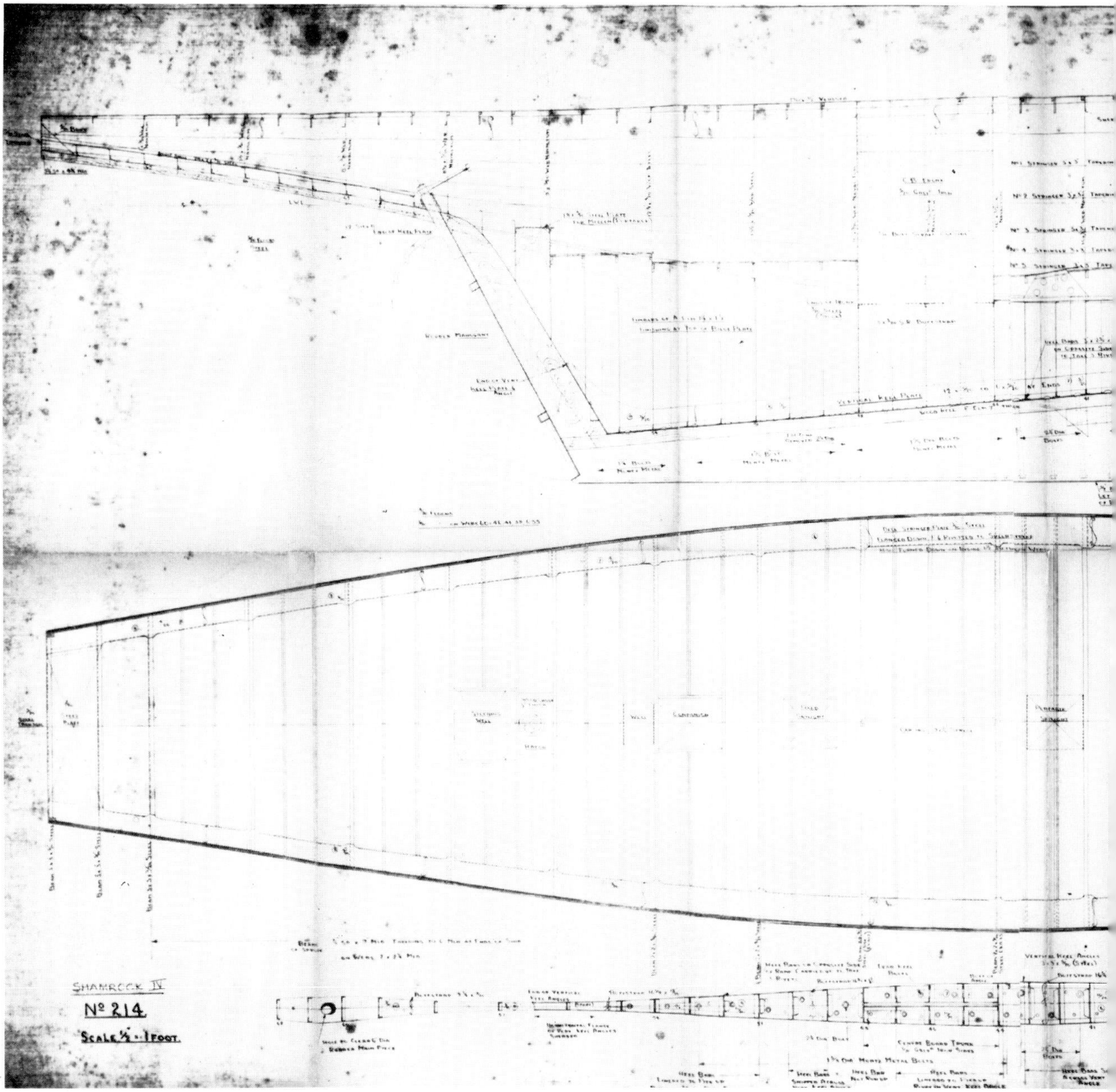

PAGE 98, BELOW
Meteor V racing in a strong wind in 1914. The largest of the German emperor's racing schooners, she was also designed by Max Oertz and built by the Germania Werft, in 1914. There was a strong wind, bordering on a gale, when this photograph was taken; she is down to an unreefed mainsail, foresail and jib. The sails set well and she is storming along for the next mark, probably at about 14–15 knots.

The lug sheet foresail seen here was fitted to a number of large racing schooners in Britain, Germany and America between about 1893 and 1914. The foot was spread by a boom to just clear of the forward side of the mainmast, which the clew overlapped. The boom sheeted to a traveller on a deck horse and did not require tending in stays. The lug sheet had to be handled on each tack or gybe and this was difficult and sometimes dangerous in strong winds. The object was to gain some additional area in the racing rig and to make the rather narrow foresail of the racing

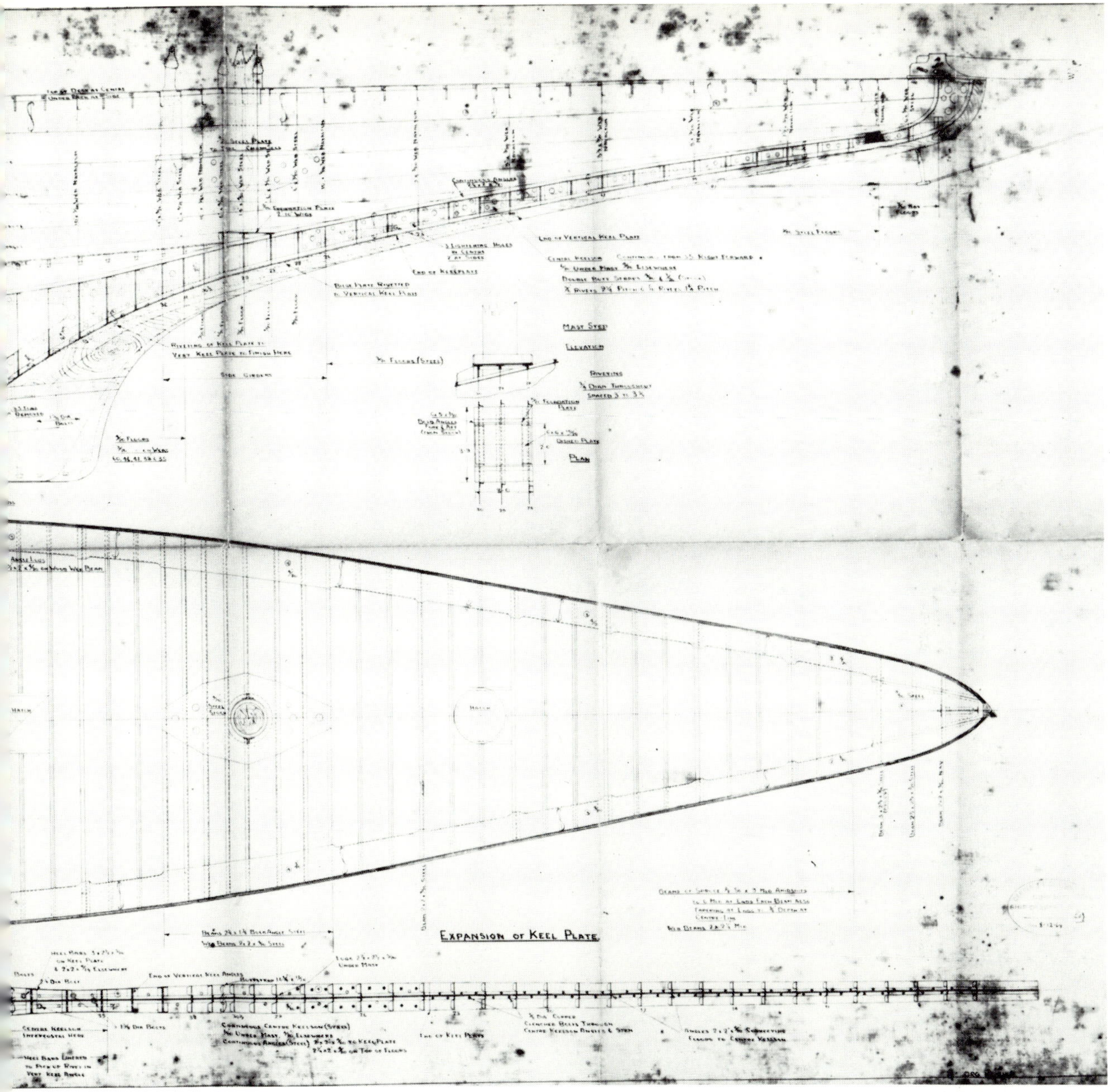

schooner type stand better when going to windward by means of the additional sheeting.

The outbreak of war in 1914 stopped all racing and afterwards *Meteor V* was sold to an Egyptian prince. She was taken out to Alexandria by an English crew, who soon tired of swinging around the mooring instead of sailing and left.

PAGE 99
Structural midship section of the America's Cup challenger *Shamrock IV*, designed and built in 1914 by Camper & Nicholson for Sir Thomas Lipton and the smallest of his racers at 110 ft overall. Other dimensions were 75 ft waterline length, 22 ft 4 in beam, 13 ft 8 in draft; sail area was 9860 sq ft rigged first as a sloop with a single headsail but soon changed to the conventional cutter rig.

This section drawing illustrates her peculiar form, showing the sides heavily tumbled-in to cheat the deck measurement rule and the splaying of her ballast keel to place weight as low

as possible. The construction was interesting: spruce longitudinals were supported by transverses, the web plates of which were made from the seawater resistant alloy Navaltum. Side and bottom planking was three skins, two laid diagonally and the outer longitudinally; the inner skin was of cedar, the centre one spruce and the outer mahogany. Bottom planking was single-skin mahogany. The sheerstrake, deck stringer and lower frames were steel. The deck was plywood covered with canvas.

Shamrock IV was the first British yacht designed to the American Universal Rule of Measurement.

PAGES 100–1
The structural profile and deck plan of *Shamrock IV*, 1914. The snubbed bow, flat stern, cut off counter and the pronounced toe on the keel profile were distinctive features of this innovative yacht. The step for her mizzen mast, stepped for the ocean crossing, is shown.

ABOVE
Launch of the racing schooner *Margherita* from Camper & Nicholson's yard at Gosport in May 1913.

When the large Metre Rating classes were established in 1907, larger yachts raced in the A Class for schooners, yawls and ketches exceeding 23 Metres rating. The British schooner *Cicely*, then owned by G. Cecil Whitaker and sailed by Captain Jesse Cranfield of Rowhedge, did well in this class until the American schooner *Westward* came over in 1910 and won most of the prizes. To meet *Westward* on more even terms, Whitaker commissioned William Fife to design the finest racing schooner he could devise – *Waterwitch* – but as *Westward* had left England before she was launched at Troon in 1911 they never met. Although one of the most handsome racing schooners, *Waterwitch* was a hopeless failure and no match for the German *Meteor* and *Germania*. That winter she was extensively altered and came out in 1912 with more sail area, but was beaten worse than before. Dismayed, Whitaker ordered her to be dismantled and the hull broken up; the rig and fittings were removed to be fitted in her successor, a new racing schooner to be designed by Charles Nicholson.

Margherita was the largest racing yacht built in the south of England, 162 ft long overall, 100 ft waterline, 25 ft 10 in beam and with the moderate draft of 18 ft. She was a fast yacht, with long overhangs and tumblehome in her sides, ending in a flat sheer. The steel hull was a fine plating job and the whole concept, allied to clever handling by a smart skipper and crew, was as successful as the unfortunate *Waterwitch* had been a failure.

The problem of adequately supporting large

deep-keeled sailing yachts out of the water is demonstrated by the wooden cradles built up above the sliding ways on each side, to support the lower bilges and keep the yacht safely upright and moving true on the ways during the few seconds of travel from her building berth to the water. The provision of a hawsepipe facilitated anchor work for such a long-bowed yacht.

PREVIOUS PAGE
Margherita on her sailing trials against the 23 Metre cutter *White Heather II* in May 1913. She is sliding up Spithead under 14,000 sq ft of sail, with notably little fuss from her bow and quarter waves. Captain Alfred Embling at the wheel knows he has a fine racer and all hands can sense it too. The jib topsail inevitably sags a little on its stay as she whispers to windward.

By 1913 *Westward* had been bought by a syndicate of German yachtsmen and was renamed *Hamburg II*. *Germania* was sailed by Captain Loveless of Brightlingsea with a crew of German mates and hands, and *Meteor* was under Captain Begas with an all-German crew. The class was joined by the smaller racing schooner *Susanne*, then in French ownership. Despite this opposition, the new *Margherita*, sailed by Captain Alfred Embling of Gosport with a crew from the south and east coasts, was tremendously successful, from her first races at Kiel regatta. She dominated the big schooner class until the outbreak of war in 1914.

LEFT, ABOVE

Owner and some of the crew of the America's Cup challenger *Shamrock IV* at Gosport in 1914. Sir Thomas Lipton stands at the centre with a white-topped cheesecutter cap and on his right is Captain Albert Turner of Wivenhoe. To Lipton's left is Edward Heard of Tollesbury, first mate. Most of her crew were from the Colne, and those still recalled on this photograph were (*second from left, front*) Bert Pearman, (*third from left*) 'Chubby' Cranfield and (*left, behind owner*) Bob Fisk – all from Rowhedge. This was a very experienced racing crew, snapped just before sailing for America under an ocean-going yawl rig and escorted by the owner's steam yacht *Erin*. While on passage *Shamrock IV* and her escort received a wireless message of the outbreak of war and they were diverted. *Shamrock IV* eventually arrived at City Island, in then-neutral New York, where she was hastily laid up, remaining there until relaunched in 1919 to prepare for the delayed Cup races. Most of her crew were Royal Naval Reserve men and were quickly transferred to the Canadian cruiser *Niobe* at Halifax to commence their war service.

LEFT, BELOW

Captain William F. Dennis was one of the outstanding American professional racing skippers of the first two decades of the twentieth century. Born at Greenport, Long Island, an oyster port, he started his seafaring as a hand on board an oyster dredging sloop, like many another good racing man. From deckhand he became a mate and then a skipper. He was an unusually clever helmsman and had great daring at close quarters, like most of his kind. His first large command was the schooner *Elmina*, designed by A. Cary Smith for Frederick F. Brewster, in which Bill Dennis won two Astor Cups. In 1905 Brewster had a second *Elmina* designed by Smith and sailed by Dennis, who afterwards won five Astor Cups and several Squadron runs of the New York Yacht Club.

Elmina's performance at sea in the New York Yacht Club cruise to Maine in 1909 was well described by L. Perry. The yachts, large racers and cruisers, sloops, schooners and steam yachts, set out from Vineyard Haven, Massachusetts with the racing classes in competition. They encountered gale force winds overnight on passage, which battered and scattered most of the fleet. The larger racers held on and *Elmina* stormed through the night, her captain anxious to beat their great rival the Herreshoff designed schooner *Queen*.

> After the start, in fine weather, there was great racing until early evening, *Queen* a bit in the lead; but then came increased winds, and the tall beautiful schooner, that was designed to live her life in a more quiet environment, began to find conditions unsuitable. She began to fall off in speed. In the meantime Dennis was nursing *Elmina* along, like the fine skipper he is. He had doused his topsails early in the evening and guided his craft carefully over the rough seas. By midnight not only *Queen* but *Vigilant*, which had been doing well, were lost [left behind]. Then, with all competitors astern, Captain Dennis took in his foresail and forestaysail and the schooner went on her course under mainsail and jib only. In the course of the gale which began at 9 o'clock, reached its greatest force at midnight and finally died out at 5 o'clock in the morning, *Elmina* ran through thunder storms, black squalls and cross-seas, without the slightest damage to hull or spar and without the loss of even a belaying pin. She tacked past Cape Elizabeth lightship outside of Portland harbour at 9.30 o'clock on Wednesday morning and two hours later Captain Dennis had his craft off the Portland Yacht Club anchorage and was enjoying a well earned sleep.
>
> *Elmina* sailed the 154 miles in under 25 hours. She had been tried by the winds and the waves and out of the test she had come with every spar intact and with not even a ripped sail. Her decks were littered with gear and other mess accumulated throughout a night of windward work. Her canvas was wet, heavy and distorted and her rigging coated with brine. On the deck stood her crew in oilskins, as sturdy a crew as ever drank salt spray, their matted hair straggling from under the brims of their sou'westers. . . . they just stormed along on that staunch fore-and-after, dousing canvas when the wind hit up 40 miles an hour, breaking it out when it diminished, working here and there cheerfully, with the deck canted to a 35 degree angle and Captain Dennis, lashed to the wheel, often standing up to his waist in water. This was sport with a vengeance.
>
> But, you see, *Elmina* was out to beat that fair-weather wonder, *Queen*. Herreshoff, who built *Queen*, knows how to impart speed to his products,

but it is not always that he combines with this quality any great amount of weatherly ability. Cary Smith can do both, and on that tumultuous night Dennis had his chance to 'show up' the Maxwell flyer. And he did.

In 1911 Morton F. Plant was having the big racing schooner *Elena* built and talked Brewster into releasing Captain Dennis to sail her. She won the Astor Cup in 1912 and 1913 and also won the Clark Gold Cup for three races from New London, Connecticut to Marblehead in Massachusetts.

In 1914 Captain Dennis was chosen to skipper the new bronze-hulled sloop *Vanitie* owned by Alexander Smith Cochran, a contender with *Resolute* and *Defiance* in the selection trials for Cup defender against the British *Shamrock IV*. *Vanitie* was unsuccessful and *Resolute* was selected, sailed by amateur Robert W. Emmons with a number of other amateurs in his crew, reinforced by Scandinavian professionals under Captain John Christiansen. The unlucky *Defiance* was sailed by amateur George M. Pynchon. As the United States was then neutral the tuning-up and racing of the large-class yachts continued until 1917, and in 1916 Captain Dennis returned to *Elena*, which was his most successful command.

ABOVE
After deck of the American racing schooner *Elena* in 1913. Captain William Dennis is at the wheel and the yacht appears to be preparing to tack. Three hands aft on the counter are standing by the mainsheet compressor gear. The owner, in a dark suit and cloth cap, and a steward in a white coat are immediately forward of this group. Three hands and two guests in cloth caps are coiling down the fall of a sheet, while two mates and a hand are working at a rope leading along the main boom, which may be a boom stay. The sidelights are typical of these large American racers and the sight edge of one of her shell plates is visible.

Elena's owner Morton F. Plant had been owner of a large steamship company which he sold in about 1902 for forty million dollars. He took up 'yachting' and ordered a large steel-hulled racing schooner from the Herreshoff Manufacturing Co., which was launched in 1903 as the *Ingomar*, the first of five yachts to be built for him by the company. She cost $115,000.

Although enthusiastic, Plant had no knowledge of yacht sailing, unlike one of his rivals, J. Rogers Maxwell, owner of the Herreshoff racing schooner *Queen*, who was a keen sailor and able to design a yacht. *Ingomar* was sailed by Captain

Charles Barr in her first season. In 1911 Plant ordered from Herreshoff the large racing schooner *Elena* which was similar in size and characteristics to Alexander Cochran's *Westward*, against which she raced. *Elena* had considerable success in 1912 and 1913. Mr Plant died soon afterwards.

BELOW
Defiance was a contender for the defence of the America's Cup against *Shamrock IV* in 1914 and is shown here under her knockabout rig. She was designed by George Owen for a syndicate of yachtsmen from New York and Philadelphia, headed by George M. Pynchon (her amateur helmsman) and E. W. Clarke, and was built at the Bath Ironworks in Bath, Maine in 1914. She was 115 ft long overall, 74 ft 9 in on the waterline, with 22 ft 6 in beam and 13 ft 9 in hull draft extended by a centreboard to 22 ft. Sail area was 9400 sq ft. The hull was of composite construction with steel frames and double-skin fir and mahogany planking, fitted by Hogdon Bros. of East Boothbay, Maine.

Defiance was an unlucky yacht and did not come out until six weeks after her competitors. The original rig was too much for her and the 150 ft steel mast was removed and a shorter, wooden one substituted. George Owen was a thorough naval architect and had considerable success with smaller racers, but the *Defiance* never seemed to settle down. Her average speed per mile was 10 minutes 12 seconds; *Resolute* and *Vanitie* were equal at 9 minutes 12 seconds.

Resolute was designed and built by Herreshoff, and *Vanitie* was designed by William Gardner and was built by George Lawley & Son for Alexander Cochran, who had earlier owned the racing schooner *Westward* and was also having the very large, fast, three-masted schooner *Sea Call* designed and built by the same firms. (The cost of *Vanitie* and *Sea Call* exceeded half a million dollars – a tremendous sum at that time.)

Defiance had a short bowsprit and single headsail, as on the other four yachts built for the series. When she was found to be tender the bowsprit was removed and she became a stemhead 'knockabout' style sloop for a time, until it was replaced. All of this did little to improve her speed and she was not able to beat *Resolute*, and only once beat *Vanitie* for a second place: she was a disappointment – not least to her brilliant designer. Although well built, she was only sailed for the season of 1914 and then broken up.

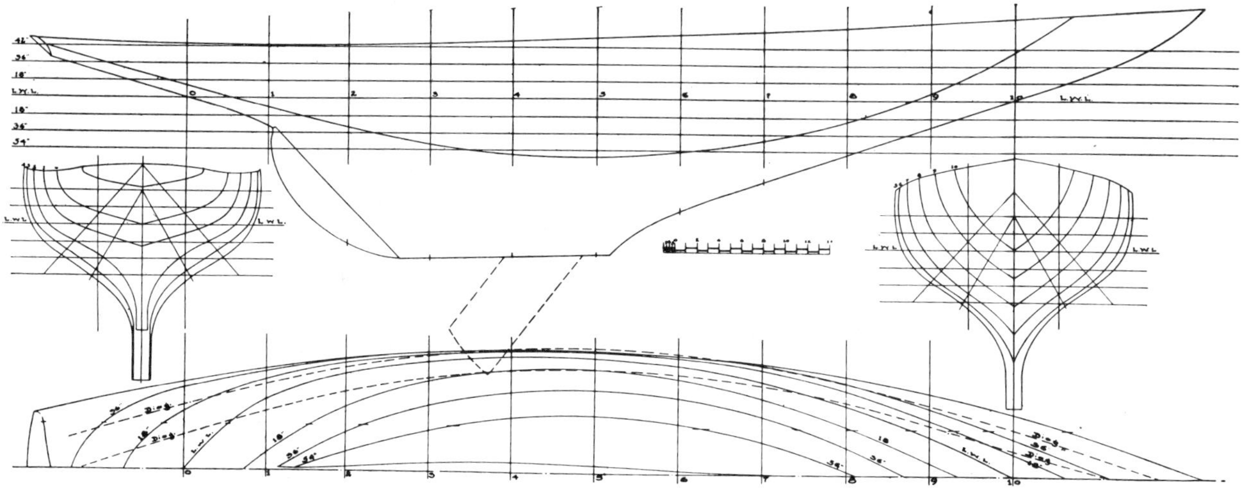

ABOVE
Lines of the American sloop *Resolute*, 1914. This N. G. Herreshoff design was built at his Bristol yard to compete with the new *Vanitie* and *Defiance* to be Cup defender against *Shamrock IV*. These comparatively small first-class yachts were designed to the American Universal Rule. *Resolute*'s principal dimensions were 100 ft length overall, 75 ft waterline, 21 ft $1\frac{1}{2}$ in beam and 13 ft hull draft extended by a centreboard. The hull form is typical of Herreshoff's work, with high slack bilges which resulted in her being tender; she heeled quickly even in light winds. When sailing she was not very fast on a reach, and pulled up a big wave forward of the mast and another off the lee quarter. The hull was constructed in steel and bronze and was a very light, weak structure. She worked a great deal and was several times returned to the builder's yard for repairs and strengthening, though she lasted well enough to defend the Cup in 1920 and to be re-rigged for schooner racing in 1926.

Like most of the American Cup defenders, *Resolute* was owned by a syndicate. She flew the racing flag of Robert W. Emmons Jr and the other members were George E. Nichols, George A. Cormack, Charles Francis Adams Jr and John Parkinson. During the 1914 trials *Resolute* was not the popular favourite and her designer, builders and amateur afterguard were for a time criticized in yachting circles. Most yachtsmen wanted *Vanitie* to be selected. She was first sailed by Captain William Dennis and after he resigned by Captain Henry P. Haff. However, the trials and preparations were nullified by the outbreak of war between Britain and Germany, which lead to *Shamrock IV* being hurriedly laid up on her arrival in America.

In 1915 the two American sloops remaining in commission met for a further series. *Resolute* won most of the races during the New York Yacht Club cruise and thereafter was laid up until the war ended and the challenge could be revived.

PART THREE

1919–1930

FOLLOWING PAGE

The postwar launch of Sir Thomas Lipton's America's Cup challenger *Shamrock IV* at City Island, New York in 1920. Captain Albert Turner and first mate Edward Heard stand amidships. When the yacht was examined in her cradle after being laid up in America throughout the First World War her builders and crew were dismayed to find that the cradle had buckled and her long ends, left partly unsupported, had sagged and distorted. Little could be done about this and she was made ready to race against the American sloop *Resolute*, which had had the advantage of tuning up until 1915.

In 1920 the two yachts raced for the Cup and *Shamrock IV* was in the charge of Sir William Burton of Ipswich, Suffolk, with Captain Turner to relieve him at the wheel. Captain Alfred Diaper of Itchen, who had been sailing Lipton's 23 Metre *Shamrock* against the challenger in trials, was also on board. Sir William Burton was a member of the Royal Harwich Yacht Club and a formidable owner of racing yachts up to the 19 Metre class. He was the best available British amateur helmsman in large racing yachts; until then, only professionals had sailed challengers for the America's Cup.

Despite troubles of many kinds, *Shamrock IV* came closer to winning the Cup than any of her predecessors of the same name. She was the first British attempt to design to the American Universal Rule of Measurement, which American designers had been using for eight years. Accordingly, Charles E. Nicholson concentrated on producing the fastest yacht he could, but as a result she attracted a penalty in rating which gave *Resolute* a 7 minute 1 second advantage. Nevertheless, she could sail faster than the American boat and was a more ingenious yacht in hull design, construction and rig.

The rigs of both yachts were approaching the shape, and had if anything exceeded the height, of the contemporary bermuda rigs. Though similar in hull size, *Shamrock IV*'s 10,450 sq ft measured sail area towered over *Resolute*'s 8775 sq ft, as a difference in rating between the competitors was then allowed under the rules of the contest. Both yachts had sails made by Ratsey, in England and America, and they set perfectly.

Some idea of the height of these gaff rigs is given by the topmast head on *Shamrock IV* being 146 ft above the deck and the topsail yard extending to 176 ft above deck. All possible weight aloft was saved, the steel housing socket for the hollow spruce topmast having many lightening holes carefully calculated to retain strength of metal between them. Her housing topsail yard, another innovation, was not allowed in the Cup races, however. The throat halyard led through a dumb (non-revolving) sheave in the mast, which was strengthened locally by a forged iron band. Although this saved weight and windage it meant that considerable force had to be used to hoist the mainsail. To resist the forward thrust of the gaff four jump stays were fitted, led over struts which were socketed in place after the mainsail had been hoisted. The two outer struts spread the shrouds from the masthead to the deck outriggers; the next two carried stays from the masthead to the deck at the mast. The centre strut carried the throat halyard, which was a single part leading aloft through the dumb sheave in the mast. When the mainsail was half-hoisted the halyard was led over the strut by the mastheadsman and hoisting was completed. Getting the main up was heavy work for all hands and afterwards the crew were tired – a bad thing before the start of a race.

Shamrock IV was provided with two hollow spruce masts and one steel one. The wooden masts were 26 in diameter at the deck. She had very light weight topsail and jack yards and spinnaker boom, all made by the McGruer Hollow Spar Co. of Gosport from steam-bent wound veneers; the spinnaker boom was so light that only two men were needed to lift it. These

were the envy of the Americans, as was her light and strong five-ply plywood deck, afterwards copied in *Vanitie*. Almost all her original light spars and rigging were burned in a fire at Jacob's yacht yard in 1919 and replaced with new ones made in England.

Other innovations in *Shamrock IV*'s rig included a light weather headsail set from a lug on the mast below the forestay with the tack on the jibstay. It filled the space below the jib topsail and although odd-looking was efficient. The Americans had not previously seen such a sail. When combined with the largest jib topsail it enabled her to sail well in light wind and swell. Charles Nicholson nicknamed it a 'fiddler's jib'. In the first race a canvas sleeve around the mast faired off the gap between the luff of the mainsail and the spar; it was counted as measured sail area. Both yachts laced their mainsails to the masts, though originally they had hoops. *Shamrock IV* also had a speedometer, the first America's Cup yacht to use one. It was a Sail-Log operated by water pressure on a small Pitot tube under the hull with a dial for the helmsman.

The greatest feature of *Shamrock IV* that amazed the Americans was the lightness of her hull construction while it was also adequately strong. The unusual hull form to take full advantage of the rules, and the lightweight mast and spars and efficient sailplan, contributed to her challenge and to some extent unnerved the Americans in 1914.

FOLLOWING PAGE
Resolute in a light wind. A jib is set in stops and a balloon jib draws her along over an almost glassy sea – conditions typical of the New England summer.

During the preparations for Cup defence in 1920 *Resolute* was skippered by Captain Chris Christiansen, a Norwegian-American, with a professional crew of twenty-eight. Her helmsman was the amateur Charles F. Adams. By then *Vanitie* had been presented to the New York Yacht Club and in these trials was sailed by amateur George Nichols. She came very close to the performance of *Resolute* and the selection committee had a difficult choice but, possibly out of prudence, chose the Herreshoff boat.

The lapse of six years (1914–20) between their design and building and the Cup races allowed *Resolute* and *Shamrock IV* ample time to alter their rigs. *Resolute* was of course particularly fortunate as the U.S. did not enter the war until 1917 and she had raced against *Vanitie* in 1915 and also against *Defiance* in 1914. These trials and races showed that she could be improved and the rig was the principal area in which this could be done. Sail area was increased for the 1920 Cup series and the rig heightened and extended; N. Herreshoff designed a new sail and spar plan. The boom was lengthened by 2 ft to 77 ft 6 in, the bowsprit was made longer outboard, and the mast length increased by 4 ft giving the mainsail greater hoist. The topsail had a shorter jackyard spreading it little beyond the gaff end, but the topsail yard was lengthened by several feet and the combined mainsail and topsail profile had the appearance of the contemporary bermudian rig mainsails. These alterations increased her rating to 80.9 ft. She had a new one-piece wooden mast, which collapsed in its first race, breaking about 9 ft above the deck, and new hollow topsail yard and jackyard. There was trouble with her new tubular aluminium gaff, which broke its jaws in a gybe, and she also broke a topsail yard. *Resolute* had a better peak halyard arrangement, which *Shamrock IV* copied for the last race. A wire bridle from the topmast head to the lowermast head had on it a block through which the peak halyards were rove, helping to keep the gaff well inboard when going to windward.

In the first Cup race *Resolute*'s throat halyard parted at the drum of the hand winch and the mainsail slid down the mast, bending the jaws of the gaff and then breaking the gaff. The jackyard was ripped from the topsail which thrashed aloft. She was crippled and had to retire. After doubts on the part of her helmsman as to whether it was sportsmanlike to continue the race, *Shamrock IV* finished to win. In the second race she again won, by 2½ minutes on corrected time. She had only to win once more to return to Britain with the America's Cup but unfortunately only crossed the line 19 seconds ahead, thus losing on time allowance. The fourth race was *Resolute*'s. The fifth was tremendously exciting as each had won twice and no challenger had previously come as close to taking the coveted Cup. On the day, a southwesterly of about 28 knots forced the amateur helmsmen to decide whether to risk their rigs. Burton and Adams decided to start and sailed for the line, but both yachts were unhappy in the strong wind which kicked up a steep lively sea and their masts were particularly vulnerable. *Shamrock IV* had a reef in the main and set a small jib topsail and a jib; *Resolute* carried a full main and a jib. The wind gradually increased to 35 knots and the committee asked each yacht if they would agree to a postponment. They concurred and sailed back to their moorings. Both pounded badly and it is very doubtful whether either could have sailed the course without serious accident and possible loss of life. When the postponed race was sailed, *Resolute* won by 19 minutes in light winds and retained the Cup.

These Cup racers were built for average American East Coast summer conditions and not for steep seas. However Lipton, who hardly knew a topsail sheet from a spinnaker guy, was furious. Scorn for this sensible decision was also voiced by the press, many yachtsmen and others who knew little of the risks of sailing such extreme craft as these Universal Rule designs in strong winds and a small sea. There was much criticism of the racers and the racing rules; many thought that the America's Cup should be sailed for by schooners such as *Elena*, *Westward* and *Queen*. An American observer compared these sloops with the contemporary British 23 Metre racers:

> *Shamrock IV* was built for American racing and not for racing in home waters. The 23 Metre yacht *Shamrock* is a fair example of what the British rules develop. She is rather heavy in construction, perhaps too heavy for our waters and for all practical

H 2

purposes, but she is staunch. She is completely furnished and fitted and races in home waters with all her equipment on board. When a race is finished she can anchor and all hands can turn in if they wish to do so. The mast must be a solid spar. *Shamrock* would have sailed over the course on the day of the postponement and beaten the two Cup yachts. In the other races the Cup yachts would have sailed away from the 23 Metre yacht.

Shamrock IV was broken up in 1924 at the yard of Robert Jacob at City Island, New York where Lipton's challengers since *Shamrock II* had been cared for while in America. Her wooden mast was presented to New York University for a flagpole.

In 1926 *Resolute* and *Vanitie* were re-rigged as staysail schooners with bermudian mainsails; they were then owned by E. Walter Clarke and Robert E. Tod respectively. *Vanitie* was sold to Harry P. Whitney before the season opened, and up to seventeen similar large schooners were for a time competing in northeastern races. In 1929 the two yachts were again re-rigged, as bermudian sloops with two headsails (cutters in British terms), but were outsailed by the new J Class yachts which appeared in 1930.

FOLLOWING PAGE

White Heather II storms away on a reach in a good breeze in 1926. She is at maximum speed with the jib topsail and jib-headed topsail pulling well. The bow and quarter waves show how fast she is moving, and Captain Charles Bevis at her wheel must be feeling well pleased with his cutter's performance nineteen years after her launch. *White Heather II* was a most successful 23 Metre yacht, like her near-sister and lifelong rival in the same class, *Shamrock*.

Her fine counter and gentle sheer were typical of the draughtmanship of William Fife. She was built at his yard at Fairlie on the lower Clyde in 1907 and was launched from a pontoon in the deeper water off that shallow shore. Her original sail area was 9576 sq ft, reduced to 8048 sq ft in the 1920s and further reduced on her conversion to bermudian rig, when she set 7600 sq ft but retained her speed and windward ability. Her hull form and scantlings were surpassed by newer competitors but in 1925 she raced around the Isle of Wight in the record time of 4 hours 45 minutes 1 second.

White Heather II remained in first-class racing as a gaff cutter until the 1931 season. From her launch until the late 1920s her skipper was Charles Bevis of Bursledon, Hampshire with a crew drawn mainly from the Solent ports. She was a consistent prizewinner until 1929, as was the 23 Metre *Shamrock*, but thereafter rarely successful, despite excellent handling by Captain Charles Mountifield, an Essexman then living in Gosport. In 1932 she was bought by W. L. Stephenson, a newcomer to big-class racing, and was re-rigged as a bermudian cutter with a steel mast. She picked up a few prizes in the class but really served to test her owner's liking for large-yacht racing before he ordered the new *Velsheda* from Camper & Nicholson in the autumn. The fine old racer was broken up soon afterwards.

PAGE 115, ABOVE

Big-class racing as it is usually recalled: a sunny summer day with sea smooth and sparkling, and a light but firm breeze bunching the class at the mark. This photograph was taken from the large schooner *Westward* in 1928. Male guests in cheesecutter caps and white flannels and ladies in cloche hats watch the bermudian-rigged *Cambria* coming up on the wind after rounding the buoy and sheeting home her newly set jib. The black-hulled *Britannia* is approaching the buoy and prepares to gybe as a jib is being sent up. The class has recently been kedged and the stocked anchors are still hanging from a snatchblock at the bowsprit end on *Britannia* and the bermudian cutter *Astra*, next astern, which appears to be luffing the larger gaff cutter *Lulworth*, while *Shamrock* (23 Metre) comes down on both of them. A few tense moments and all will go clear to round the buoy within touch of each other, booms slumping over in the gybes, shaking the rigging slightly and with the patter of reef points as the mainsail settles down on the windward leg and sheets are trimmed. *Yachting*!

PAGE 115, BELOW

The crew of the royal cutter *Britannia* pose on deck during a break in fitting out at Marvin's yard at East Cowes in 1928. By then the large racing yachts were manned by a more varied selection of hands. No longer did a skipper strive to select most of his crew from his native village or town, or even from the same district, but took on men from other places providing they were

smart yacht racing hands. During the 1920s King George V, mindful that *Britannia* had since her launch been manned predominantly by crews from northeast Essex, requested that in those times of severe unemployment her men be drawn from several small ports then providing racing men on the east and south coasts of England.

From left to right:
B. Blackwood, foc's'le steward (Wivenhoe); E. Friend, bosun (Brixham); E. Ives, second mate (Brightlingsea); G. Stringer, seaman – always known as a 'hand' other than on articles (Portsmouth); A. 'Monkey' Byford, first mate (Colchester); T. Harvey, seaman (Wivenhoe); A. Turner, captain (Wivenhoe); J. Holland, foc's'le cook (Brightlingsea); J. Turner, mastheadsman (Wivenhoe); W. Bailey, chef (Clacton-on-Sea); F. Simonds, seaman (Wivenhoe); D. Mason, messroom steward (Wivenhoe); F. Batchelor, signalman – Royal Naval rating seconded to the royal racer (Portsmouth); P. Cundy, seaman (Looe); P. Martin, seaman (Looe); J. Vaughan, seaman (Cowes); R. Ager, seaman (Pin Mill); A. Pengelly, seaman (Looe); T. Francis, mastheadsman (Brightlingsea); L. Fletcher, caterer (Plymouth); A. Clements, seaman (Looe); L. Lamberton, seaman (Brixham); E. Percival, seaman (Wivenhoe).

RIGHT
The magnificent new cutter *Astra* sweeps past the battleship *Rodney* during Cowes Week, 1928. The 115 ft *Astra* was designed and built by Camper & Nicholson to rival the similar-sized cutter *Cambria*, designed by William Fife and built at Fairlie by W. & R. B. Fife. Both were 75 ft on the waterline and the style, size and rig were followed by the Nicholson designed and built *Candida* the following year. These yachts were built to the International Yacht Racing Union Rule of measurement, *Astria* and *Cambria* rating at 23.2 Metres. In many ways they were more attractive than those built from 1930 onwards under the American-inspired J Class Rule, adopted by Britain at the end of 1929 to promote racing between the two countries, particularly for the America's Cup.

Astra was of composite construction with steel keel plate, sheerstrakes, bilge plates, transverse floors, frames, beams, knees, tieplates and bracings. Her principal dimensions were 115 ft overall, 75 ft waterline length, 20 ft 2½ in beam, 13 ft 9½ in draft, displacement 140 tons; sail area 7500 sq ft in mainsail, staysail and ordinary jib. Here she runs under spinnaker, still the triangular type and tacked down inside the forestay, with the luffs of staysail, jib and long-roper jib topsail distorting its creamy canvas.

Astra's 164 ft mast was lower than that fitted to the re-rigged *Nyria* in 1921, and her original sail plan was moderate in hoist compared to boom length, particularly when compared to those of smaller racers. The staying is interesting: two sets of crosstrees or 'spreaders' with small intermediate spreaders between the upper pair and the deck. An additional pair of diamond shrouds led from about midway between the masthead and the upper crosstrees, through leads on the latter, and down to the mast at the lower crosstrees. A jump stay led over a strut at the jib halyard position, at the upper crosstree. The solid spruce mast was of rectangular cross-section and despite careful design and construction its weight was considerable and its staying gave anxiety to all in a breeze.

There were several mishaps with *Astra*'s early rig: she carried away all the slides on the mainsail luff in one race, and lost her mast in the first match of the Clyde Fortnight. In many races in which the two new bermudian cutters participated, the old 23 Metre *Shamrock* and *White Heather II* were successful. In contrast, *Cambria* could and did sail in wind strengths which made the older 23 Metres give up, or prevented their starting. However, at the end of the season there was a surprising result. Top of the class was the twenty year old *Shamrock* (23 Metre) under Captain Sycamore, with thirteen first, seven second and one third prize in thirty-five starts, followed by *Britannia* and *White Heather II*: all gaff cutters. Then came *Astra* with five, two and five in twenty-six starts, then *Cambria* with two, six and five in thirty-five starts, with *Westward* and *Lulworth* in the rear. There was much discussion about this order. Some attributed it to the larger sail area and greater height of sailplan of the gaff-rigged cutters; others to the greater weight of scantlings of the new boats, which had been built to Lloyd's Register of Shipping ordinary yacht scantlings instead of to their R Class Rules.

In this photograph the scupper slots show

prominently in the low bulwarks. The relatively high, glass-windowed deckhouse combined a companion hatch to the accommodation with useful seating space for ladies and other guests in breezy weather or during particularly hectic moments.

The skipper crouches by the wheel, and crew and owner and guests enjoy this brief spell 'off the wind', slicing eastward through Cowes Roads. Some of the crew of the battleship eye this skimming butterfly with mild interest, but they are probably thinking more of the good times they will shortly enjoy ashore in Cowes, when the liberty boat is ready to leave the booms.

FOLLOWING PAGE

The big racers sailed hundreds of miles each season on passage between regattas. Sometimes there were long coastwise stretches such as from the Solent to the Clyde, or Northern Ireland to Falmouth – an inevitable part of the racing year. This photograph was taken on board *Lulworth*, on passage under trysail in 1926. The boom is settled in its gallows and secured by two breeching tackles set up to ringbolts in the covering boards. The trysail is set above it with its gaff aloft out of sight. The lee trysail sheet leads down in the foreground to the powerful purchase sheeting it to the quarter; the weather sheet and its purchase hangs slack. The trysail had two or possibly three reefs and was a sail which could be carried in the worst weather. The davits are swung outboard to port, and five hands gather in the lee of the deckhouse to yarn away part of their watch. They are dressed in the cloth caps and workaday clothes of the sailor, in contrast to their smart rig

when racing or when the owner or his guests were on board. The mate stands by the lee runner and with a dry deck the big racer rumbles along down the Channel past the Cornish coast, bound round Land's End for the Clyde regattas.

A guest on board a racer during the 1920s vividly recorded the atmosphere on passage.

> Somewhere off Land's End. An inky black night – starless, moonless. A huge sea is running, an angry following sea from which there is no escape. The great waves pursue as like demons in a mightmare – menacingly, appallingly near they seem. The wind whistles in the rigging, the rain rattles against the sodden flapping trysail. We have rolled, rolled, rolled for an eternity, climbing up and tumbling down the seas. The red and green of our navigation lights are reflected in wet deck, the skipper is at the wheel – a huge indefinite figure in his black oilskins. By the glow of the binnacle lamp I can see the rain dripping from the end of his nose. Every now and again he spits over the side with infallible accuracy. Beside him crouches Bill, smoking his pipe and mopping his face with a shammy.
>
> Passage . . . Tomorrow we are due at Kingstown [Cork, in Southern Ireland]. The next day will see us spick and span in racing trim. Bill and the rest of them in their whites, the skipper in his pilot boat, and in that cockpit now half full of water a party of pretty girls will sit asking charmingly silly questions. So we go on around the coast on our lawful occasions without fuss or talk or boast.
>
> I leave the companion and stagger aft along the lurching deck. 'Well, skipper, how goes it?' 'All right, sir, dirty night. I reckon this 'ere'll blow itself out by the morning.' He looks aloft. 'Them clouds ain't travellin' as fast as they was,' he says. I try to penetrate the darkness: I can see no clouds – nothing but blackness. 'Reckon we'll beat that there *White 'Eather* into Kingstown.' This from Bill, who is optimistically wringing out his shammy. 'You're right, Bill,' the skipper agrees, spitting emphatically.

Crews made little fuss about passage making, other than perhaps a passing remark about bad weather. It was part of the season's round: the interest was in what happened when you arrived!

BELOW AND FRONTISPIECE
H. F. Paul's *Astra* leading *Candida* at Harwich regatta in 1934. Both yachts were built as bermudian cutters and both were designed and built by Camper & Nicholson at Gosport in 1928 and 1929 respectively. Herman Andreae,

Candida's owner, is at the lee side of her wheel and Captain Joe Gilbey of Bosham, Sussex stands to windward. The sheer and beam of her hull and lift of her ends exemplify the grace of these last large racers built under the International Rule. The mate squats to leeward of the mast, watching the headsails. The round, hollow wooden boom has its single strut and bracing wire lifted on the lee side. She is hard on the wind in smooth water, chasing her rival.

In 1938 the *Candida* was converted to a ketch for cruising and she is still sailing in the Mediterranean as *Norlanda*.

PREVIOUS PAGE
Astra preparing to set her spinnaker as she rounds the Guard buoy off Harwich. While she is travelling at speed the spinnaker boom is already being guyed out to port, where two of the hands hauling on the purchase can be seen at the left. The mate, in whites, is rushing aft. Two hands on the foredeck prepare for the sail to be hoisted in stops and three others on the lee side seem to be clearing gear. In a few seconds about twelve men will rouse the long bundle of spinnaker aloft and it will be broken out from the soft yarn stops to fill and be sheeted home as she storms along.

RIGHT
Candida slides along in one of her first races, in 1929. She was designed and built by Camper & Nicholson for Herman Andreae, an owner who had previously raced various yachts, including the smaller cutter *Candida* (ex *June*) and the 19 Metre *Corona*, in the handicap classes.

Candida's hull dimensions of 117 ft 2 in overall, 79 ft 5 in waterline, 20 ft 6 in beam and 14 ft 5 in draft were typical of her type. Sail area was 7500 sq ft in this rig, which had the low aspect ratio of 1.77. The wooden mast, long bowsprit and long low boom were then usual, but the height of the jib halyard block is interesting. The long battens are poking into the pockets up the leech of the mainsail, which does not appear to be fully stretched and all the sails seem new. A high-cut jib topsail is set and a smaller jib is stopped along the bowsprit and up the lower part of the forestay with rotten yarn, ready to be broken out when the jib topsail is lowered. Most of her crew of nineteen are sitting quietly on the lee deck amidships, concentrating their weight to keep the sails full in the light air. Those aft are standing by the mainsheet and backstay falls. The skipper, mates and guests are aft where the owner is at the wheel, proud of his new yacht, with an eye on his rival to windward and on his red and white racing flag.

Candida's skipper was J. Gilbey of Bosham and many of his crew were from Emsworth and other villages on Chichester Harbour, from where they fished in smacks during the winter, dredging scallops and oysters in the English Channel. Captain Gilbey was one of the best-liked racing skippers, and though his owner tended to take the wheel for much of the race he maintained, 'As long as my gentleman has a good race I feel well pleased.'

When *Yankee* visited England to race against the British big class in 1935 one of her opponents was *Candida*. As she crossed the line after her first race against the American sloop, Captain Gilbey stepped to the rail to lead the crew in the traditional British custom of cheering the winner. Waving his cap, he began, 'Come on boys, three cheers for . . .' and suddenly scratched his head and turned to the owner with, 'What's the name of this 'ere Yank, Sir?'.

PAGE 124
Yacht owner and yachting journalist. Herman Andreae (left), owner of *Candida*, is interviewed by Major Brooke Heckstall-Smith (right), known among yachtsmen as 'Bookstall' Smith. His yachting experience stretched back into the 1880s, and from the early 'nineties he reported British yacht racing from the season's regattas and various fixtures around the coast; he sailed in many of the yachts and knew the owners, their guests, captains and crews. He moved with facility between the different social levels of the owners and guests and the crews. He was on the same friendly basis with the Commodore of the Royal Yacht Squadron or the *Shamrock*'s cook. Heckstall-Smith wrote actively until 1943, just before his death, and recorded in detail much of that era of yachting.

Herman Andreae was a keen racing helmsman who owned several large handicap class yachts before *Candida*. When she was sold, to be converted to a cruising ketch, he took to cruising and by the 1950s owned the motor yacht *Idalia* on which he cruised extensively in the

K 8

Mediterranean. He often had on board his young grandson David Mallet, who has inherited his grandfather's liking for the sea and particularly for the Solent, where he carries on the tradition in sailing and motor yachts of advanced design.

RIGHT

Hugh Paul's *Astra* reaching along for the next mark at near maximum speed off Harwich. Her bermudian cutter rig seems slender after the greater sail areas of the older gaff-rigged racers. The spruce mast towered 153 ft above deck and needed three sets of spreaders. It was supported by lower, upper and topmast shrouds, led to channels on each side at the sheer, a forestay and topmast forestay, running backstays and shifting backstays (the weather ones being set up in this photograph). Standing backstays were not used in these large racing yachts. The boom was supported by spreaders and bracing wires.

In this photograph *Astra* is carrying a whole mainsail, a small staysail, a jib to suit the wind strength and a 'baby' jib topsail: a sail area of 7500 sq ft, little more than half that set by the big racing cutters of the 1890s. However, with improvements in rig and hull form she is sailing almost as fast – by bow and quarter waves, about 12 knots. The mate by the forestay keeps a wary eye on any craft ahead and is in charge of the foredeck. Her owner is at the wheel and Captain Edward Heard of Tollesbury stands on the quarter in whites.

Astra was the smallest of the large racing yachts of the period 1919 to 1937, and in 1930 she was altered to conform to the adopted J Class rules. Her hull was particularly well formed and she was potentially a good sea boat, restricted like her contemporaries by an extremely tall rig suitable only for day sailing. The destroyer anchored in the background is HMS *Scout* (H.51), 1075 tons, built in 1918 as one of the numerous S Class; she survived to fight in the Second World War and was scrapped in 1948.

PAGE 126

Storming through Cowes Roads in 1930 are (*left to right*): *Astra*, *Britannia*, *Candida* and *Lulworth*. The gaff-rigged boats are fighting gamely, but the efficiency of the bermudian cutter rig is conspicuous. The new *Candida* has a fine lead and *Astra* is well to windward, covering the King's *Britannia*. There is 'a strong hard wind' and although the Solent is relatively smooth under the lee of the Island one can sense the surging power of the puffs and almost hear the windsong in the tall rigs. When the racers fetch into the more exposed waters of Spithead the reefs will be needed.

This picture illustrates particularly well the racing efficiency of the bermudian sail. *Britannia* and *Lulworth* have about 80 ft of exposed mast and rigging which is doing no work and creates undesirable windage. In contrast, *Astra* and *Candida* are using all but about 20 ft of their masts and the mainsails are setting flatter than on the older cutters, whose gaffs are inevitably sagging to leeward with the long drift of peak halyard caused by the reefed sails.

RIGHT
The Fife designed and built *Cambria* stemming the tide past Cowes in 1930. She had been built in 1928 for Sir William Berry as a rival to *Astra*. However, although well sailed *Cambria* never seemed to distinguish herself, winning only two firsts, six seconds and five thirds in thirty-five starts during her first season against *Astra*'s 5, 2, 5 and the champion *Shamrock*'s (23 Metres) 13, 7, 1; she placed fifth in the seven-boat prize list. The following year *Cambria* was fifth with 6, 3 and 6 in forty-one starts, beating *Astra* but well behind the champion *Shamrock*'s 9, 10, 1.

The new bermudian cutters were built in accordance with ordinary yacht scantlings of Lloyd's Register of Shipping, rather than the R Class scantling rules previously applied to racers of this size since 1906, though the increase in hull weight seemed acceptable. The hull shows the typical Fife sheer and stem profile, but her rig is interesting as it represents early thinking on a large bermudian mast and the length of crosstrees (spreaders) and bowsprit is noticeable. She also has a swinging lower spreader, visible under the lower crosstree, set up to distribute forces from the jib halyard. Her sail area of 7600 sq ft needed a crew of seventeen compared with the twenty-nine or thirty manning a gaff cutter such as *Britannia*. Racing hands' wages were then £3 per week and a saving of up to £36 per week on crew wages for the April to September season was attractive to owners, wealthy though they were. This, and the comparable performance of the smaller, more easily handled sail area, advanced bermudian rig in the big class. Since the yachts were of various sizes and several were designed under different rules of measurement, time allowances were given. These related to

K
4

performance, dimensions and in some cases age.

During 1924–6 the British large class had been allowed to carry whatever spars and sail area they pleased, and the heights of sailplans and areas of spinnakers increased, leading to some loss of spars and occasionally of masts with these gaff rigs. In one race a large cutter suddenly set a spinnaker from the top of her 'marconi' topmast, to the astonishment of the handicappers. For 1927 it was decided that all the British big class be rated under the I.Y.R.U. rules. The large-class cutters then ranged from 21 to 24 Metres rating; *Cambria* rating 23.2. By 1929 all raced without time allowances, except for the old *Britannia* which received 8 seconds a mile. It is interesting that the calculated time for *Cambria* to sail one mile in average racing conditions was 4 minutes 40.1 seconds.

PREVIOUS PAGE
The last season in which gaff-rigged cutters challenged the new bermudian racers in the British large class was 1930. Shown in light weather are (left to right) *Astra*, *Lulworth* and immediately beyond her *Britannia*, *Candida*, the new *Shamrock V* and the old 23 Metre *White Heather*.

Lulworth was the last first-class racing cutter launched with gaff rig. She was designed by Herbert White and, like *Terpsichore*, built at Itchen by White Bros. (Southampton) Ltd. She always appeared to have more freeboard and a bolder hull than most of her predecessors in the class and was a frequent prizewinner. When this photograph was taken her captain was Archie Hogarth of Portincross, Scotland, with a crew from Essex, the Clyde and the Solent.

In 1926 *Lulworth* raced against the schooner *Westward* in a private match around the Isle of Wight. After 60 miles *Westward* won by 4 feet.

LEFT
On August 2, 1930 the big class started in a strong southeast wind which brought a jobble of sea in the Solent. *Lulworth* (6) and *Britannia* have just crossed the Royal Yacht Squadron line at Cowes, with the bermudian-rigged *Shamrock V* beyond to windward. The gaff cutters carry a double reefed mainsail and a moderate sized staysail and jib, but their decks are already wet with spray. The standing and running rigging can be seen in detail and the elaborate staying of the mast, with its 'Marconi' topmast above, indicates the complexity of strains imposed on the rigs of these last large gaff-rigged racers. *Lulworth*'s mast has a single pair of principal spreaders at the hounds and a secondary pair midway between them and the deck, socketed in place after the mainsail was hoisted; there is a jumper strut on the forward side to counteract the pull of the halyards and thrust of the gaff. The peak halyards lead from the gaff spans to blocks positioned to oppose the pull of the staysail and jib halyards, which are also partially supported by the upper leg of a span at the head of the running backstay. The tall topmast, with its head about 150 ft above deck, has a small pair of spreaders supporting a diamond stay and is further supported by the two legs of a span at the top of the shifting backstay.

Britannia has a small topsail set in stops, above the peak halyards, with its sheet rove through the block at the end of the gaff, ready to be broken out on a reach or run. Her gaff is bending in the strong wind which sends these big racers surging eastward towards the first mark, in Spithead.

BELOW
Shamrock V rounding the Cork light vessel off Felixstowe, Suffolk during her first race, June 1930. Her three-headsail rig without a bowsprit was reckoned to be advanced for a large British yacht, but unfortunately the hollow spruce mast

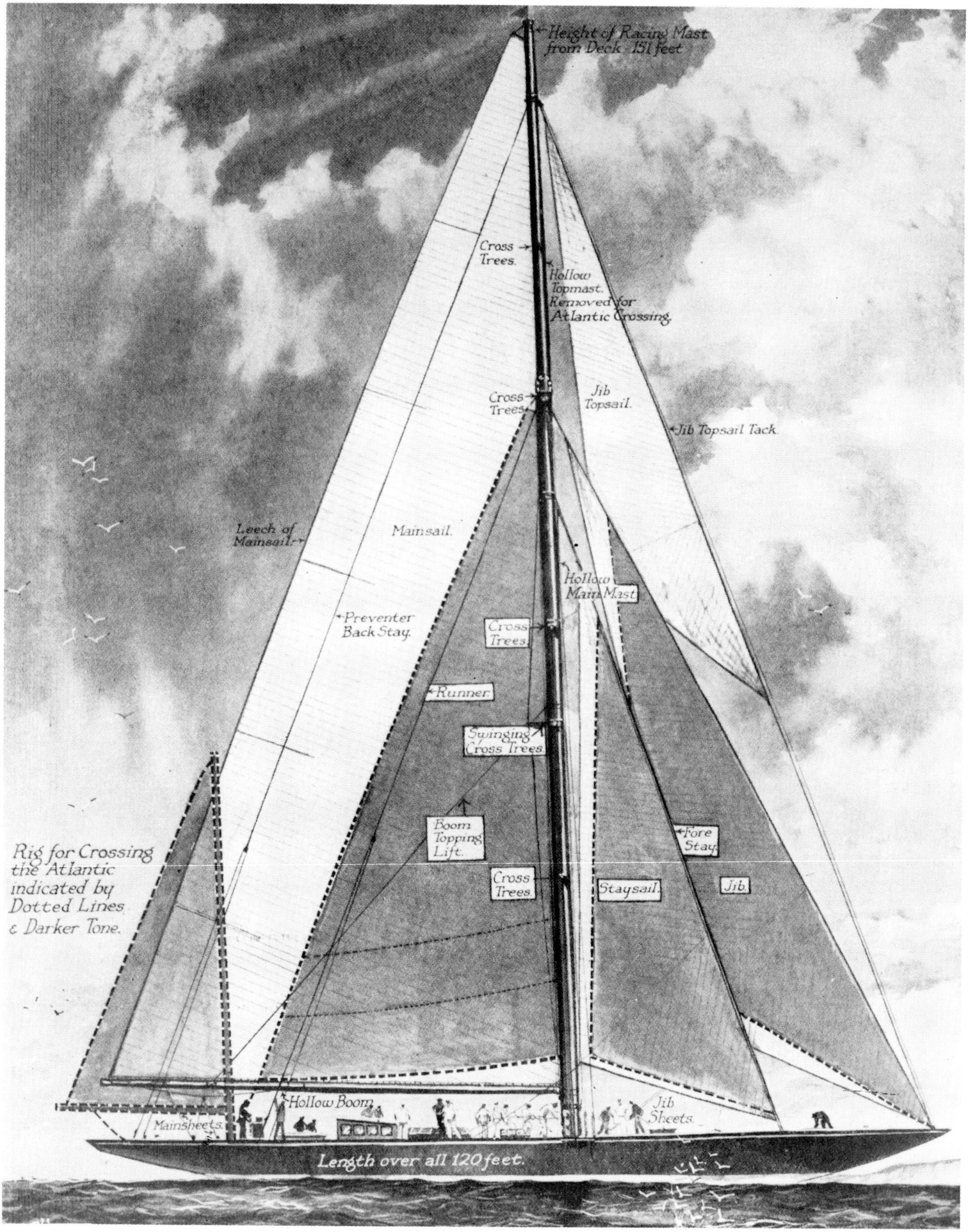
Height of Racing Mast from Deck - 151 feet
Cross Trees.
Hollow Topmast. Removed for Atlantic Crossing.
Cross Trees.
Jib Topsail.
Jib Topsail Tack.
Leech of Mainsail.
Mainsail.
Hollow Main Mast.
Preventer Back Stay.
Cross Trees.
Runner.
Swinging Cross Trees.
Boom Topping Lift.
Fore Stay.
Rig for Crossing the Atlantic indicated by Dotted Lines & Darker Tone.
Cross Trees.
Staysail.
Jib.
Hollow Boom
Jib Sheets.
Mainsheets.
Length over all 120 feet.

was heavy and stilted her performance against the American *Enterprise* in the races for the America's Cup which were sailed that September.

The photograph shows Harwich regatta in full flow and all hands are full of hope and keenness, but Captain Heard at the wheel already feels the weight of her mast and knows that, although the beautiful green *Shamrock V* is leading the British big class, she will have to make superhuman efforts to beat the Americans.

LEFT
Shamrock V's racing cutter rig (*white*) contrasted with the ketch rig fitted for ocean passage making (*shaded*); a snug and seamanlike sail plan compared to the racing mast, which was 151 ft above deck and needed four sets of fixed crosstrees (spreaders) and one set of swinging crosstrees to support the shrouds. The hollow spruce 'topmast' was removed as far as the second crosstree position for ocean sailing. The boomless trysail with two rows of reef points was sheeted by powerful tackles to the quarters.

Shamrock V was the first British large-class racer to hoist and lower her mainsail on a reel winch, fitted below deck. However, this innovation paled before the numerous winches on the American *Enterprise*. These were worked by eight hands who remained at their stations below deck throughout the races, keeping the deck clearer, saving windage and lowering the yacht's centre of gravity in racing trim.

Shamrock V did indeed meet bad weather on her transatlantic crossings. The outward voyage was typical, taking twenty-four days from Brixham in Devon to New London, Connecticut.

Lipton's steam yacht *Erin* escorted her and towed whenever conditions permitted, which, to the crew's relief, was not often, as the racer was much easier under her double reefed trysail and storm jib than when corkscrewing along through long steep Atlantic seas on a towline. Sometimes she lost touch with *Erin* for days and was becalmed in mid-ocean, with the crew working in vain to get her along with a big headsail and squaresail. They boxed about for a time before the western horizon darkened again with shrieking squalls, and days of big seas and wind forced them to crawl about the heaving deck at the change of watches, or to tend the badly chafing running rigging. The foc's'le became almost uninhabitable in the pounding seas and some hands shifted their berths to the sail locker in the long flat counter, where the slamming was as noisy as in the long, overhanging bow but it was drier. Often, the saloon skylight would darken with a green sea and cascades of water would pour down over the watch at their meal below. On deck they clustered around the wheel in streaming oilskins and soggy sea boots, swaying to the pitch and roll of the lean racer. This was the other side of the America's Cup races.

PAGE 133

The crew of *Shamrock V*, at anchor before her transatlantic passage in 1930. Mate Lemon Cranfield stands by the guardwires at the extreme left. Pride of place is taken by the gramophone, obviously the joy of the younger hands who have plenty of records spread out on the foc's'le hatch.

The guardwires and stanchions were shipped soley for ocean passages, being regarded as unnecessary and totally unacceptable for racing or coastal sailing. The large stocked anchor carried on the starboard bow for passage making was of a type much favoured in the larger yachts, where quick holding on a short scope might be required; the severe windage of a tall mast and its considerable rigging added to the problems of a vessel with a deep draft which tended to 'sail' around her anchor.

LEFT

The newly launched *Shamrock V* slides past in one of her early races, before sailing to challenge for the America's Cup in 1930. The bow wave glistens on her bottle-smooth bow planking. She

retains the shroud channels of earlier large racers. Twelve of the crew of nineteen are visible; the others are out of sight on the counter, trimming their weight aft while she is before the wind. The first mate, Lemon Cranfield, is emerging from the foc's'le hatch, probably checking stowage for the spinnaker when it is brought down in a few seconds at the next mark. The boom is broad off and the mainsail is girt across the after shroud. Captain Edward Heard is at the wheel as she runs for the lee mark. The second mate stands by the skipper and a party of guests clusters by the deckhouse. The weather running backstay is set up but here the shifting backstay is invisible aloft.

ABOVE
Captain and crew of the America's Cup challenger *Shamrock V* in 1930. *From left to right:*

Back row: Charlie Dan, cook (Wivenhoe); Tom Cudmore, steward (Rowhedge); Sidney Stroud (Whitstable); Lemon Cranfield, first mate (Rowhedge); Captain Edward Heard (Tollesbury); Bert French, second mate (West Mersea); Alfred Stroud (Whitstable); Cyril Heard (Tollesbury); Chris Hilliard, cook (Wivenhoe).

Centre row: Jack Sargeant (Looe); Joe Uglow (Looe); Bill Bradock (Brixham); Jack Gempton (Brixham); Billy Wilkinson (Tollesbury); Harry Harman (Whitstable).

Front row: Dick Howard (West Mersea); Edward Heard, son of the captain (Tollesbury); Alfred Pengelly (Looe); Harry German (Brixham); Frank Paddy (Plymouth).

This is a typical photograph of a racing crew, taken while their yacht was fitting out, with all hands wearing the peaked caps which were reserved for shoregoing, fitting-out and laying-up.

The deck shows the marine glue still unscraped from its seams and has doubtless received several coats of varnish for protection during fitting out, which will be scraped off before she sails.

RIGHT, ABOVE
Structural midship section of the America's Cup defender *Enterprise*, built in 1930.

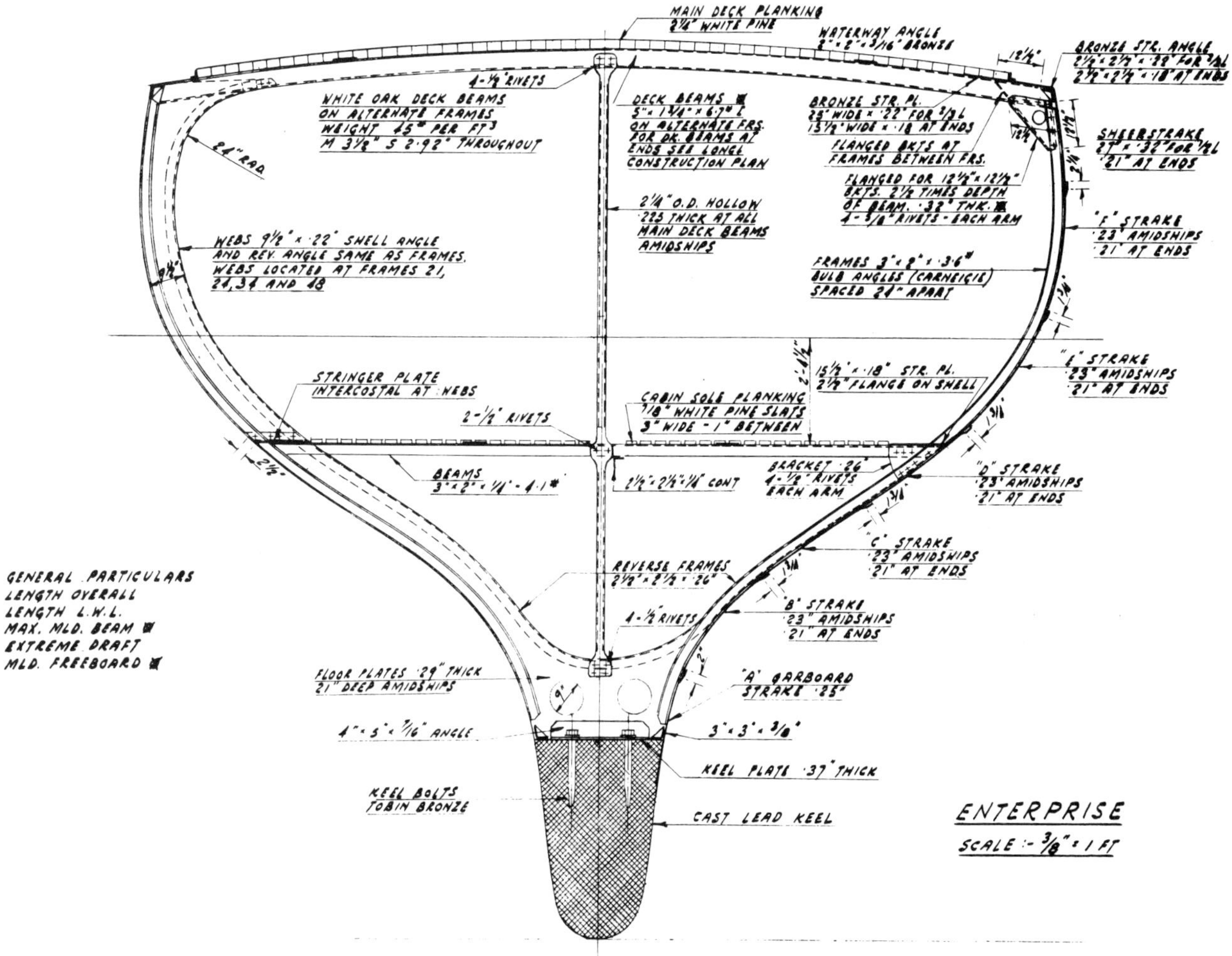
MAIN DECK PLANKING
2¼" WHITE PINE
WATERWAY ANGLE
3" × 3" × 3/16" BRONZE
12½"
BRONZE STR. ANGLE
2½ × 2½ × .38 FOR ½L
2½ × 2½ × .18 AT ENDS
4-½" RIVETS
WHITE OAK DECK BEAMS
ON ALTERNATE FRAMES
WEIGHT 45# PER FT³
M 3½" S 2.92" THROUGHOUT
DECK BEAMS
5" × 1¾" × 6.7# L
ON ALTERNATE FRS.
FOR DK. BEAMS AT
ENDS SEE LONGL
CONSTRUCTION PLAN
BRONZE STR. PL.
25" WIDE × .22" FOR ½L
13½" WIDE × .18 AT ENDS
FLANGED BKTS AT
FRAMES BETWEEN FRS.
FLANGED FOR 12½" × 12½"
BKTS. 2½ TIMES DEPTH
OF BEAM. .32" THK.
4-⅝" RIVETS - EACH ARM
SHEERSTRAKE
.27" × .32" FOR ½L
.21" AT ENDS
24" RAD.
2¼" O.D. HOLLOW
.225 THICK AT ALL
MAIN DECK BEAMS
AMIDSHIPS
"F" STRAKE
.23" AMIDSHIPS
.21" AT ENDS
WEBS 9½" × .22" SHELL ANGLE
AND REV. ANGLE SAME AS FRAMES.
WEBS LOCATED AT FRAMES 21,
24, 34 AND 48
FRAMES 3" × 2" × 3.6#
BULB ANGLES (CARNEGIE)
SPACED 24" APART
"E" STRAKE
.23" AMIDSHIPS
.21" AT ENDS
15½" × .18" STR. PL.
2½" FLANGE ON SHELL
STRINGER PLATE
INTERCOSTAL AT WEBS
CABIN SOLE PLANKING
⅞" WHITE PINE SLATS
3" WIDE - 1" BETWEEN
2-½" RIVETS
BEAMS
3" × 2" × ¼" - 4.1#
2½" × 2½" × ¼" CONT
BRACKET .26"
4-½" RIVETS
EACH ARM
"D" STRAKE
.23" AMIDSHIPS
.21" AT ENDS
"C" STRAKE
.23" AMIDSHIPS
.21" AT ENDS
GENERAL PARTICULARS
LENGTH OVERALL
LENGTH L.W.L.
MAX. MLD. BEAM
EXTREME DRAFT
MLD. FREEBOARD
REVERSE FRAMES
2½" × 2½" × .26"
"B" STRAKE
.23" AMIDSHIPS
.21" AT ENDS
4-½ RIVETS
FLOOR PLATES .29" THICK
21" DEEP AMIDSHIPS
"A" GARBOARD
STRAKE .25"
4" × 5" × 7/16" ANGLE
3" × 3" × 3/8"
KEEL PLATE .37" THICK
KEEL BOLTS
TOBIN BRONZE
CAST LEAD KEEL
ENTERPRISE
SCALE :- 3/8" = 1 FT

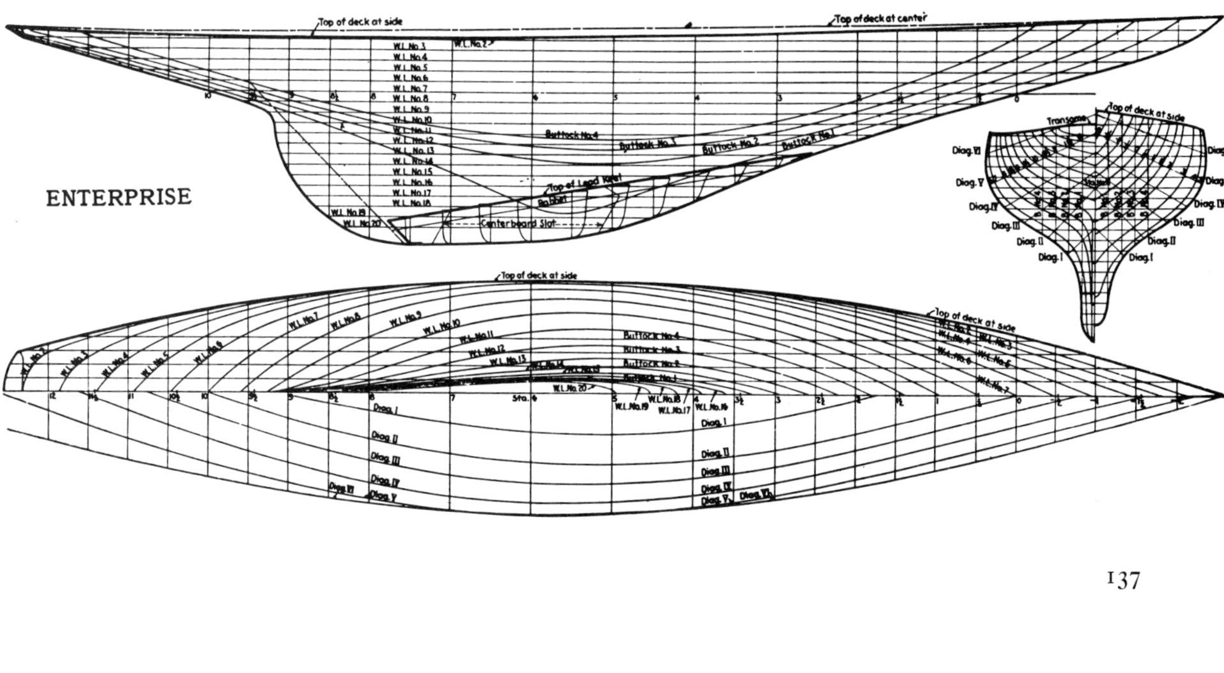
Top of deck at side
Top of deck at center
ENTERPRISE
W.L. No. 2
W.L. No. 3
W.L. No. 4
W.L. No. 5
W.L. No. 6
W.L. No. 7
W.L. No. 8
W.L. No. 9
W.L. No. 10
W.L. No. 11
W.L. No. 12
W.L. No. 13
W.L. No. 14
W.L. No. 15
W.L. No. 16
W.L. No. 17
W.L. No. 18
W.L. No. 19
W.L. No. 20
Buttock No. 4
Buttock No. 3
Buttock No. 2
Buttock No. 1
Top of Lead Keel
Rabbet
Centerboard Slot
Transome
Diag. I
Diag. II
Diag. III
Diag. IV
Diag. V
Diag. VI
Sta. 6

PREVIOUS PAGE, BELOW

Lines of the American J Class sloop *Enterprise*, 1930, built for Harold S. Vanderbilt of the New York Yacht Club and that year's defender of the America's Cup. Her sections show the characteristic hull form designed by W. Starling Burgess. *Enterprise*'s lines make interesting comparison with those of *Shamrock V*, which followed British racing yacht tradition. Both have the swollen mid-body and relatively fine ends engendered by the new rating rule for the J Class. The Cup races were for the first time to be without time allowance for differences in rating. Principal dimensions of *Enterprise* were 120 ft 11 in overall length, 80 ft waterline, 22 ft $1\frac{1}{2}$ in beam, 14 ft 7 in draft. Displacement was 128 tons.

ABOVE

Making port under the ocean rig, *Shamrock V* enters the harbour of Fayal in the Azores, on passage to America for the 1930 America's Cup races. A boomless trysail is set on the shortened mast and, as with most ketches, the mizzen is stowed, the boom being lashed to the quarter. Her crew are preparing to anchor, glad to see port after many days of ocean sailing. Under this rig she resembled a large offshore racer and it is interesting to speculate on the kind of sport which would have resulted if transocean races in yachts of this size and rig had been fashionable.

PART FOUR

1933–1937

FOLLOWING PAGE
Britannia's bermudian mast. The royal cutter is being warped into drydock at Southampton for bottom cleaning in 1932. During the winter of 1930–31 she had been converted from gaff to bermudian rig, not without misgivings as to the hull's ability to stand the strains from the new rig. Looking at this photograph, one sympathizes with this view. Charles Nicholson is credited with this towering rig, typical of the others of the class at that time. The 175 ft hollow mast was scarphed up from selected spruce, glued with casein adhesive, shaped by adze and hand planes, then dummy scraped, glasspapered and varnished to a gleaming butter-coloured finish. It was stayed by three principal pairs of spreaders, and the masthead further supported transversely by a pair of small spreaders and their diamond stays. Two light spreaders helped to brace the lower mast below the lower crosstrees. Forward, the spar was supported by a forestay, an inner forestay and a topmast forestay. The usual pairs of running and shifting backstays were fitted aft. The rig dwarfs the hull end-on and looks daunting enough in the calm water of the docks. What it was like on passage in a strong wind and lumpy sea only the crew could describe.

As neither the King nor his representative are on board the yacht wears the red rather than the white ensign. The mainsail is stowed and coated on the boom and the staysail and a jib are set in stops. Her varnished cutter is hoisted aboard on the port side. One of the hands follows the yacht in the dinghy, after running off another warp to the men who will walk her into the huge graving dock, built to accommodate the largest liners of the day but also used for painting the bottoms of the large racers. The tug which moved her to the dock stands by until the caisson is in place.

PAGE 141
Stepping *Britannia*'s bermudian mast, in April 1932. The tenoned heel of the hollow spar dangles above her deck from a large crane at Portsmouth Naval Dockyard, across the harbour from Camper & Nicholson's Gosport yard.

During the 1920s and 1930s the masts of most large British racers were stepped and unstepped there. The standing and running rigging is dressed on the mast, held by temporary stops. Some of her crew and three riggers from C & N are on deck to steady it down and align the heel through the hole in the deck, under the eye of Captain Albert Turner (third from left). Below, others are ready to guide the tenon safely into the step and set the wedges, while the deck party set up the shrouds and the forestay to secure the mast for towing back to the trots off Gosport, where the rigging could be set up properly.

PAGE 142
Britannia running hard under a full-cut triangular spinnaker off Harwich. Her slow roll can almost be felt and all hands who can be spared are aft to trim her.

Britannia's entries for 1932 were typical of the season's series of racing fixtures for the big class during the 1930s. July 1 and 2, Harwich; July 9, Harwich to Southend passage race; July 11, Royal Thames Yacht Club at Southend; July 12, Southend Regatta; July 16 and 18, Lymington; July 19, Bournemouth; July 23 and 25, Ryde, I.o.W., Royal Thames Yacht Club; July 28–29, Southsea, Royal Albert Yacht Club; July 30, Royal Southampton Yacht Club; August 1, Cowes, Royal London Yacht Club; August 2–5, Cowes, Royal Yacht Squadron; August 6, Cowes, Royal Southern Yacht Club; August 8–9, Ryde, Royal Victoria Yacht Club; then, leaving the Solent and going westward, August 12–13, Weymouth; August 15, Babbacombe; August 17, Paignton; August 19–20, Brixham; August 21–24, Torbay; August 26–27, Plymouth; Dartmouth; August 30, Plymouth; September 1–2, Plymouth; September 3, Falmouth.

H60

K
-1

Throughout the season the royal yacht was escorted by a Hunt Class minesweeper; a different ship for each season after 1920. For 1932 it was HMS *Tiverton*. The 'sweeper provided the general facilities of a mother ship, occasional extra hands on racing days, and a welcome tow in calms when on passage. *Britannia*'s crew most appreciated her ability to dry their soaked sailing clothes.

ABOVE
Britannia reefed down and driving hard on a close fetch. It is a grey, cloudy day and the wind is coming hard in squalls. The crew work about the streaming deck checking gear, ropes and fittings. Philip Hunloke is at the wheel as the King's sailing representative; Captain Albert Turner stands by with a keen eye for a lifting headsail luff and ready with, 'A little too near, Sir.' The second mate and a hand are riding the boom, securing the clew of the mainsail with a lashing to back up the earring. The reefed mainsail sets badly: the second reef had probably been put in during the race, which was unusual. The first reef was undoubtedly put in neatly at anchor before the start and its lacing line lies evenly around the sail with an even tension on the boom lacings. The second reef has been laced around the first and this has led to unevenness and distortion of the sail.

Three hands are working at the sheet by the mast and several are hauling on the weather deck, probably setting up the jib halyard.

FOLLOWING PAGE
Candida slashes towards the next mark during Harwich regatta of 1935, leading *Astra*. *Candida* is setting a double clewed or 'quadrilateral' jib while her rival still has the three-headsail rig. In 1931 the large class had dropped the time allowance for older yachts such as *Astra*, *Candida* and *Britannia* and the sail areas of these cutters had to be reduced in relation to the displacement and other factors in the rating formula. The new sail area had to be redistributed in the most efficient way and as the sailplan height was to be increased, hollow masts had to be fitted to replace the solid spruce ones. *Britannia* was converted from gaff rig to bermudian at this change of rule.

The quadrilateral jib was developed in wind tunnel tests for T. O. M. Sopwith who conceived the sail while having experiments carried out with two baby jib topsails set one above the other. It was first set by *Endeavour* at Southend-on-Sea, Essex regatta in 1934. The sail combined the

functions of a jib and jib topsail but was much more efficient. Its luff was of great length, $82\frac{1}{2}$ per cent of the total height of sail plan in *Endeavour*. The luff was parallel to the leech and there were two clews and consequently two sets of sheets, which needed careful handling and trimming. The object was to obtain a jib with a luff parallel to that of the staysail, which would stand to windward better than the old jib and long-roper jib topsail combination and would not backwind the staysail in windward work. The double-clewed jib, or quadrilateral jib as it also became known, was spotted by American observers in England and a description was cabled to American owners. By the time *Endeavour* arrived there to tune up for the Cup races, *Rainbow* and *Yankee* were practising with similar sails.

The area of *Endeavour*'s No. 1 double clewed jib was 1715 sq ft and it was usually set in combination with a staysail of 945 sq ft and the mainsail of 4860 sq ft, a total of 7520 sq ft. This compares with the combination of mainsail and genoa which was a total of 8570 sq ft.

Apparently a double-clewed jib had been proposed in 1926 by L. F. Herreshoff for an M Class yacht, but it was not adopted. L. F. Herreshoff designed a two-headsail rig for the J Class sloop *Whirlwind* of 1930, having a large jib and a very small staysail. The two-headsail rigs in both *Whirlwind* and *Endeavour* were a development towards the single headsail rig then set by the 12 Metre I.R. class yachts. Another step towards this in *Endeavour* was a shifting forestay which could be released and cleared away in light weather, allowing the genoa to be tacked more readily and converting her temporarily to a single headsail racer. The American J Class *Vanitie* had been given a two-headsail rig, setting a jib of conventional form, in 1932 and in 1937 *Yankee* was re-rigged with a single headsail but it was not a success due to mast staying problems.

J
K3

PREVIOUS PAGE
Shamrock V running fast before a freshening afternoon breeze and sparkling sea. The curling bow wave betrays her speed but the hull leaves a smooth wake. The sail combination set is ideal for the conditions, with the 'baby' jib topsail doing good work in the gap between the mast and the spinnaker head. The staysail is also filling but the jib inevitably lacks wind. The head of the spinnaker luff has caught over the topmast forestay – undoubtedly to the joy of the crew as it is helping to keep the sail drawing to maximum effect, although the tack is still inside the forestay in accordance with the rules. She is going well for the next mark and the racing flag flies broadside with her speed.

The scene epitomises the legendary fine summer days of big-yacht racing.

ABOVE
Making the pattern for casting the lead keel for *Velsheda* in 1933. Keel patterns were usually large and had to be accurately made in wood; white pine was used, finished to the designer's detailed plans with a tolerance for contraction of the metal when it cooled in the mould. Here, Camper & Nicholson shipwrights have erected the plumbed and shored transverse wooden shapes on a levelled base and are fitting the centreline strake of 'planking' that will cover these to make the mould surface. After planing, glasspapering smooth and checking with outside templates, the pattern is coated with size and core prints are fitted to indicate the position of boltholes. Then it is laid carefully in a large, open casting box and black casting sand is tamped and rammed carefully around it, after which it is lifted out and perhaps the bolt cores are fitted in the smooth keel-shaped cavity thus created. The lead pigs, about 70 tons in this case, are stacked on top of the five iron melting coppers visible in the photograph, each supported by pigs of iron ballast. With the keel formed in the mould sand and casting ready to begin, wood fires are lit under each copper. Pigs of lead stacked in them melt as heat increases and eventually the eight or ten coppers needed are brimming in turn with molten lead. Several men with long-handled ladles dip the lead

J
K7

from several coppers at the same time, carefully pouring it into the bottom of the mould, where steel plates are set in to take the impact of the initial pouring. The ladling has to be done quickly and without pause. Heat, grime, sweat, aching arms, danger from splashing lead, concern if it is a rainy day as drips from the roof could fall into the molten lead and send it flying to burn hands and faces. The foreman watches for any sign of the lead cooling in the mould, as this could lead to layers of partially cooled lead forming and hardening against the hot lead poured over them. (Such 'lamination' in a lead keel would lead to cracking and possible rupture.) Then all hands pause for a well earned cup of tea and a sandwich. Foreman, chargehand and yard manager watch the slow cooling of the radiant metal, whose grey-brown dross forms a scum on the surface.

When the lead has cooled the sand is broken away from the casting, which because of its weight is then struck over (moved on ways) to the keel blocks on which the yacht will be built. It is aligned, wedged and shored to its correct position, and with its upper surface planed true, ready to receive the wood keel and floors and the keel bolts, it stands in the shed as the first visible member of the new yacht.

PREVIOUS PAGE

A happy yacht in perfect racing weather. The *Velsheda* of 1933 was one of the most consistent racers in the mid-1930s big class. She was designed and built to the J Class Rule by Camper & Nicholson for W. L. Stephenson who had previously briefly owned the old 23 Metre cutter *White Heather II*, which was re-rigged as a bermudian cutter and sailed by Captain C. Mountifield. 'Mounty' was a bluff figure, with a white walrus moustache. He was a well liked racing helmsman and transferred to the new *Velsheda* to begin her successful career. Her hull was of rivetted steel with joggled shell seams, a practice followed in the two subsequent *Endeavours*. Here she fetches along at a good clip in a breeze which nicely suits the three-headsail rig.

Her crew seemed to enjoy sailing *Velsheda* and her owner, his wife and their three daughters, after whose combined names the yacht was christened, were usually on board when racing. They followed the racing fleet around to the coastal regattas in the motor yacht *Bystander*, which acted as tender.

The crew of twenty-one included men from the Solent area, Essex, Devon and Cornwall. Curiously, the coming of bermudian rig in the big class did not abolish the old post of mastheadsman, which persisted because of the need for a hand to work aloft to check and maintain the rigging, and in many yachts to go aloft to release the masthead hook which locked the mainsail aloft when hoisted and so relieved the forces on the halyard. Any work aloft can be dangerous, but with these 160 ft bermudian masts it was particularly so as the mastheadsman usually had to be hoisted aloft in a bosun's stool, rather than going up the mast hoops or the ample rigging of the earlier gaff-rigged racers. William 'Cush' Cole of Rowhedge was *Velsheda*'s mastheadsman and his spry figure was often seen about her lofty rig.

The *Velsheda* is still afloat after being laid up from 1937 until 1945 and then spending thirty years as a houseboat in the Hamble River. The beauty of her lines remains but the graceful rig is long gone.

RIGHT

Velsheda bears away around the Beach End buoy during Harwich regatta, followed by Herman Andreae's *Candida* in typical close racing (1933). *Velsheda*'s long bow is foreshortened by the camera, which has caught the height and power of the cutter rigs. One can almost hear the strumming, muted roar of wind in the wire and the myriad creaks and surges of the gear. Taking shots such as this was close work for the photographer's launch. One old hand amusingly recalled a breezy day at a Cowes start which was being photographed by a noted cameraman in a launch. Several times he dodged in close among the large racers before the start. At the gun, three of the big boats were bunched together hard on the wind when there was a shout from forward and the mate and a hand ran to the bow. Another came running aft to the skipper, shouting 'There's a gent, all wet, a'coming up the bobstay with a camera!'

PAGE 150

Velsheda gybing. The helmsman is putting the wheel down slowly in the light air. In the

K 8

foreground the running and shifting backstays are being set up for the new gybe. A hand overhauls the runner purchase (far right) and others (left) slack away the purchase of the starboard 'shifter' while one reaches to release the hook of its span so it can be shifted forward, clear of the boom. On the counter the second mate tails on to the fall of the port shifting backstay tackle, and further forward the port runner span is being set up.

All these men are working at top speed, in contrast to the correctly attired guest who sits on a skylight, sensibly out of the way but in conversational reach of the helmsman, who, unusually for *Velsheda*, appears to be an amateur (she was usually sailed by Captain Charles Mountifield).

The large-sectioned triangular 'Park Avenue' boom was adopted by British large-class yachts in the early 1930s to allow the foot of the sail to move transversely on slides across tracks set on its top surface, to take up a fair curve. Many of the skippers considered that such booms justified themselves. They were never prohibited by the rules and remained in use in many boats until the end of the large class.

A joggled seam of the riveted steel side plating shows clearly. Although slightly less efficient hydrodynamically than a flush-plated hull, the joggles did not seem to make any appreciable difference to the speed of *Velsheda*, *Endeavour* or *Endeavour II*; they were then common in shipbuilding and less weighty than flush-strapped seams and butts.

RIGHT
Captain C. Mountfield at the wheel of *Velsheda* in a strong breeze, 1934.

FOLLOWING PAGE
The mighty *Westward* storming away on a reach at maximum speed with all sails set and the long-roper jib topsail and a small main topmast staysail pulling well. She carries jib-headed topsails to suit the breezy day. The fore-topsail sheet has been slacked to ease weather helm and gain lift.

When in the ownership of T. B. F. Davis *Westward* laid up for the winter in Guernsey, where he then lived. There she was stood on a hard and many of her crew were retained for winter work on the yacht. Besides cleaning and repainting, minor structural alterations were carried out by a few skilled shipwrights in her crew, who sometimes made new spars. One winter they built a fine launch as a tender to the yacht. By the early 1930s several of *Westward*'s sails were made in Jersey by two of her crew who had been trained and had worked as sailmakers. In 1932 they made her a new racing mainsail which stood well and attracted favourable comment, but caused some dismay at the sailmaking establishments at Cowes and Gosport.

In 1929 and 1930 the old tradition of a spring racing season on the Riviera was revived at Cannes by Le Union des Yachtsmen. Typically there

were races for the large class, 8 and 6 Metre yachts, and smaller handicap and one-design classes. In 1930 the large class comprised *Westward*, the large French cruising schooner *Aile* owned by Madame Heriot and the ex-19 Metre racing cutter *Corona* then altered to yawl rig. *Westward*, not unexpectedly, dominated this class which was not joined by any other British yachts.

A reporter wrote, 'The sea front was literally black with spectators, many of whom anxiously enquired why the *Westward* still had men up at the crosstrees and when they were coming down, and seemed astonished when told that they stayed up there for the whole race.'

FOLLOWING PAGE
Shamrock V in 1933. Her rig has been lightened and altered since the Cup challenge of 1930 and a stump bowsprit with an unsightly bobstay and martingale to spread it has been added. She was then owned by Thomas Sopwith and the hull has been painted white instead of the 'Shamrock green' of Sir Thomas Lipton's days. She is going well to windward over the foul Solent tide with another of the class to windward. The dinghy is carried amidships, inverted over the saloon skylights. The mast section has been reduced but the boom appears as heavy as ever. The set of the seams of the mainsail is interesting, showing the sail shape on the wind, and the lower pocket has a much shorter batten than it provides for.

The yacht is standing out into the worst of a fierce tide and the crew are alert to tack when their rival does: the helmsman will then come round to cover her. It appears that *Shamrock V* is being sailed by an amateur helmsman and the skipper (in whites) is standing to leeward of the wheel. There are twenty-one professionals on deck, the full complement allowed by the J Class rules. The strong tabling and patches at the clew and leech of the mainsail in way of the clew reef cringles and eyelets are clearly shown.

PAGE 156
Velsheda's broken boom: the crumpled hollow spruce spar failed at Harwich regatta. The creamy cotton mainsail has been run off the mast and boom tracks and lies on deck awaiting an opportunity to get it ashore for a fuller examination and probably minor repairs to its foot. Boom breakages were uncommon and most often occurred while gybing in strong winds when the boom might hit one of the backstays if it had not been let go in time on the new lee side.

The photograph also shows the swelling topsides shape of these yachts and the pairs of outriggers to which the lower shrouds were consequently set up. These extended the shroud spread to what would have been the junction of side and deck if the section were not distorted by the rating rules. The starboard runner is set up, its span hooked into an eye in the covering board (invisible left foreground). The other part of the span is shackled to the upper block of the treble and double purchase, which was slacked away to allow the hook to be disengaged and then further slacked allowing the unhooked span and the running backstay to be run forward to the after shroud, to which it was temporarily made fast with a lanyard. The setting up and slacking off of the pairs of running and shifting backstays was critical in a large yacht, even in ordinary winds. In strong breezes split-second timing was necessary. The power of the stout tackle and its blocks contrasts with the diameter of the shackle pin connecting it to the span.

Staying of booms in racing yachts was used at various times after about 1902 for a number of different reasons. Until the appreciation of correct camber in the bermudian mainsail, which subject attracted interest in the early 1930s, the long booms of many gaff-rigged and some early bermudian rigged racing yachts were sometimes stiffened by a wire stay on each side of the boom set up with a strut at about half its length on the windward side. (Also seen in the earlier photos of *Elena* and *Britannia*.)

In 1933 *Velsheda* experimented with a 'flexible' hollow boom of narrow and deep section, made of spruce and supported by two sets of tubular spreaders over which a wire stay ran on each side and was connected to a small winch at the forward end, which could tauten the weather stay to bend the boom to the camber of the mainsail foot when going to windward or close-reaching. This type of boom had earlier been tried in the 12 Metre *Iyruna*. *Velsheda*'s boom broke when racing in Belfast Lough but the following season she came out with a similar boom and at Harwich regatta this also broke. The problem with booms of this type was that the downward component of

the mainsheet when sailing close to the wind tended to break them, there being insufficient sectional modulus to resist this. Later in 1934 *Endeavour* also experimented with a similar boom, which the Yacht Racing Association allowed on classes above $14\frac{1}{2}$ metres rating.

The objective of the flexible boom was better achieved by the triangular sectioned 'Park Avenue' type with its upper surface curved to an approximate optimum camber of the mainsail foot, which worked across it on transverse slides, although it was heavier.

OPPOSITE PAGE
Looking forward from the starboard side up the mast of a J Class racer, with a mastheadsman working aloft at the main halyard sheave. The comparatively slender crosstrees (spreaders) with tapered ends contrast with the stout mast sections which taper to the masthead. The mast, of finest quality spruce, had galvanized steel bands with lugs to which the crosstrees were attached. The upper crosstrees supported the 'topmast' shrouds. The second pair (intermediate shrouds) took strain principally from the jib halyard. The third and

lower crosstrees supported further intermediate shrouds, while the 'main' or lower shrouds led down from the masthead band of this crosstree. Standing lifts of wire rope were rigged to each crosstree to prevent sagging.

The jump strut stands forward at the upper crosstree position, taking compressive thrust from the jump stay, which leads from the masthead to the mastband at the jib halyard block (second crosstree); this kept the upper mast straight when the mainsail was set and helped prevent the masthead from whipping when pitching in a seaway. The jib and spinnaker halyards can be seen leading down from blocks near the jumper strut; the staysail halyard is visible below the second crosstree.

The pendants of the running backstays lead down from the second crosstree, and the two legs of the pendants of the shifting backstays lead down from the masthead and upper crosstree band.

The rigging appears complicated, but everything was there for a purpose and was as light and strong as possible, within the technical knowledge and materials available at the time. The mainsail track appears to be a brass or bronze flat bar, screw-fastened to a batten on the aft side of the mast to provide a T-shaped male track on which the C-shaped slides gripped.

FOLLOWING PAGE

The after deck of *Astra*, travelling fast in 1933. The owner H. F. Paul is at her wheel and Captain Edward Heard stands (in whites) immediately forward of him. The second mate is going aft, just beyond the wheelbox, possibly to check the port shifting backstay tackle. James Mussett of West Mersea tends the mainsheet and four other hands are squaring up the falls of the lee shifter tackle and probably a spinnaker guy, as *Astra* has not long come on the wind after a spinnaker run. Three guests sit in the shallow cockpit and a hand crouches ready by the port running backstay tackle. Two hands to leeward are clearing up the fall of the lee running backstay tackle. *Astra* is moving at speed, with her lee rail down in a smooth sea. The sheet capstans and their levers are comparatively small. The size of the varnished spruce boom with the reefing tackles along it is perhaps the most impressive thing in this photograph.

PAGE 159

Britannia's spinnaker, set on her new, tall rig in light airs. The mainsail of 4600 sq ft and the full-cut spinnaker 5500 sq ft. The circular holes were introduced in spinnakers about 1930 in an attempt to gain lift in light winds by allowing air to flow from the after to the forward side of the sail. Opinion on this theory was divided but it was in vogue for a few years. The spinnaker has a centreline seam, with the cloths diverging from it parallel to the leech and luff. Methods of spinnaker setting had changed little for forty

years, though spinnakers had increased in hoist with the bermudian rig. Here the hollow spruce spinnaker boom is set in its cup on the mastband and supported by the lift with its purchase, to top up the boom. It was trimmed by an after guy to the quarter and with a foreguy, which is lifting the foot of the sail in this photograph.

The mainsail has two rows of reef points and the foot lacing to the round-sectioned boom has been carefully adjusted before getting under weigh, to get the best set from the sail when on the wind. The wire boom stay and strut are triced up out of the way and to help support the weight of the boom end when off the wind.

The old yacht slides easily through the water with Captain Albert Turner of Wivenhoe at the wheel and Sir Philip Hunloke taking a spell. Most of the crew are aft and to leeward. This view emphasizes *Britannia*'s shapely hull and the fine finish maintained on it to the end.

PAGES 160–1

Endeavour surges by, following *Velsheda* out of Harwich in 1934. Despite the light wind she moves swiftly in the calm water under a large Genoa jib and mainsail. The mate stands by the lee rigging, where the steel bar shrouds connect to channels on the tumbled-in sides. Mr Sopwith is at the wheel, with Captain Williams standing by. The second mate sits on deck by the winch for the starboard shifting backstay and all hands aft appear to be watching an opponent to windward. The stocky, rather incongruous, figure in navy blue suit and cloth cap standing behind the helmsman is Mr Good, a well known Harwich fisherman; he is on board for the day to act as local pilot and provide his extensive knowledge of the tidal sets and eddies, depths of water and local winds so that the most could be gained from conditions. Most of the other competitors in the big class when racing around the British coast took the advice of similar local men, usually fishermen, who were well respected for their special knowledge. They took no physical part in handling the yacht.

The subtly hollow shape of the counter and the triangular section of the 'Park Avenue' boom are shown clearly.

K
1

J
US 2

A lifebelt has been lightly stopped at the extreme end of the counter, ready to be flung or dropped to anyone unwise enough to fall overboard and risk the skipper's wrath in losing the yacht her 'chance of a flag'.

LEFT

Yankee storms towards the mark boat to finish the first race of her summer spent in English waters to compete with the British J Class around the coast, and dispelling the myth that the Js only raced in light airs. On June 6, 1935 the racing fleet lay off Southend, on the Essex shore at the mouth of the River Thames, for Southend's annual regatta. However, *Shamrock V* would not start because of repairs needed to her boom and *Candida* refused because of a new and unstretched mainsail which she did not wish to pull out of shape in the continually freshening wind, then blowing at about 17 miles per hour. *Endeavour* led over the line off Southend pier end, followed by *Velsheda*, *Yankee* and *Astra*.

The course was to the Nore light vessel, then the West Oaze buoy, round the Mouse light vessel and back to the mark boat off Southend, twice round. The four J Class yachts roared away in the southwest wind, which quickly freshened to half a gale. Disaster struck at the Mouse when *Astra* lost a steward, George Lewis of Brightlingsea, overboard while attempting to control a wildly thrashing spinnaker sheet: he was drowned. *Endeavour* lost her mast and *Velsheda* broke her boom in the gybe. As there were vessels nearby, *Yankee* carried on to finish as winner of the shortened course without mishap and displaying good seamanship. In that season she was to win eight of the thirty-two races she entered on the east and south coasts, as well as four second and two third prizes.

FOLLOWING PAGE

Mast staying arrangements compared. *Yankee*'s rig in 1930 had only two spreaders and the long masthead stood with its topmast shrouds but without an upper spreader or jump strut. The L. Francis Herreshoff designed *Whirlwind*, also of 1930, has both, besides diamond stays. *Endeavour* (1934) had distinctive shrouds of solid rod fitting into specially made connectors, all giving a heavy look to her rigging, which was strong and reduced windage considerably. The distinctive wide crosstrees contributed to her staying. In contrast, *Istalena*, one of the few M Class yachts built, is dwarfed and dainty, though at 87 ft overall she was larger than the 12 Metre class boats, which averaged 65–70 ft.

PAGE 165, ABOVE

The afterdeck of *Endeavour*. The fall of the port running backstay purchase is lead to a capstan (now termed a winch); these were of special, geared design at a time when all such items were individually made. The barrel was rotated by 'rowing' the tubular bars, up to four men sitting on deck and bracing their feet against the white-painted wood cleats, seen close to the wheel by the covering board. Considerable power could be exerted by this means, though they were slower than the modern 'coffee grinder' winch and the long levers got in the way on a deck often filled with quickly moving ropes and men. The eye of the after leg of the running backstay is engaged in a hook which is chained to a plate at the covering board. The shifting backstay, further aft, is similarly set up, with the purchase fall led to one of the two capstans on the after deck. The coil of light line made fast to the lower end of the runner and shifter are to carry them forward to the shrouds when that side is to leeward.

One end of the mainsheet leads forward from the deck block, and the powerful tackle, which could be clapped on to the sheet fall with a mechanical stopper in strong winds, lies flaked out in the foreground. The mainsheet is taut to keep the triangular boom in the gallows when at anchor. The deck track for the mainsheet lower block slider traverses the deck abaft the open hatch.

The sweeping, well scrubbed deck, planked with white pine, polished brass wheel pedestal and other brasswork are typical of the racer in early morning, with the deck work done and all the varnish 'shammied' down with the dew, the mainsail coat off and all hands below at breakfast before preparations begin for the day's sailing.

PAGE 165, BELOW

For some reason, the American J Class yacht *Rainbow* attracted less attention than the earlier *Enterprise* or the later *Ranger*, despite her contretemps with the challenging *Endeavour* in the 1934 America's Cup races. Like *Enterprise*,

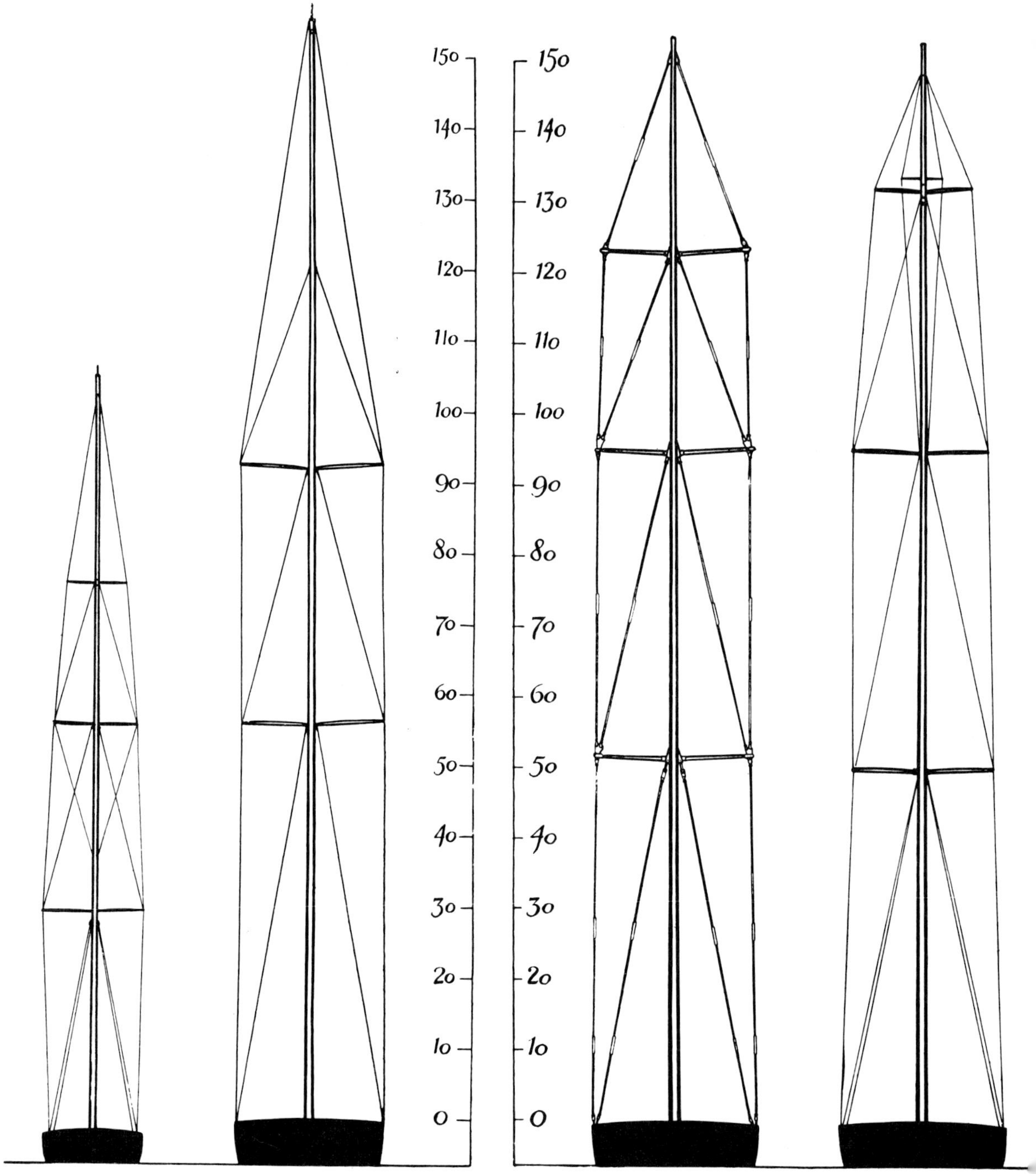

ISTALENA M CLASS (Herreshoff)

YANKEE J CLASS (Paine)

ENDEAVOUR J CLASS (Nicholson)

WHIRLWIND J CLASS (Herreshoff)

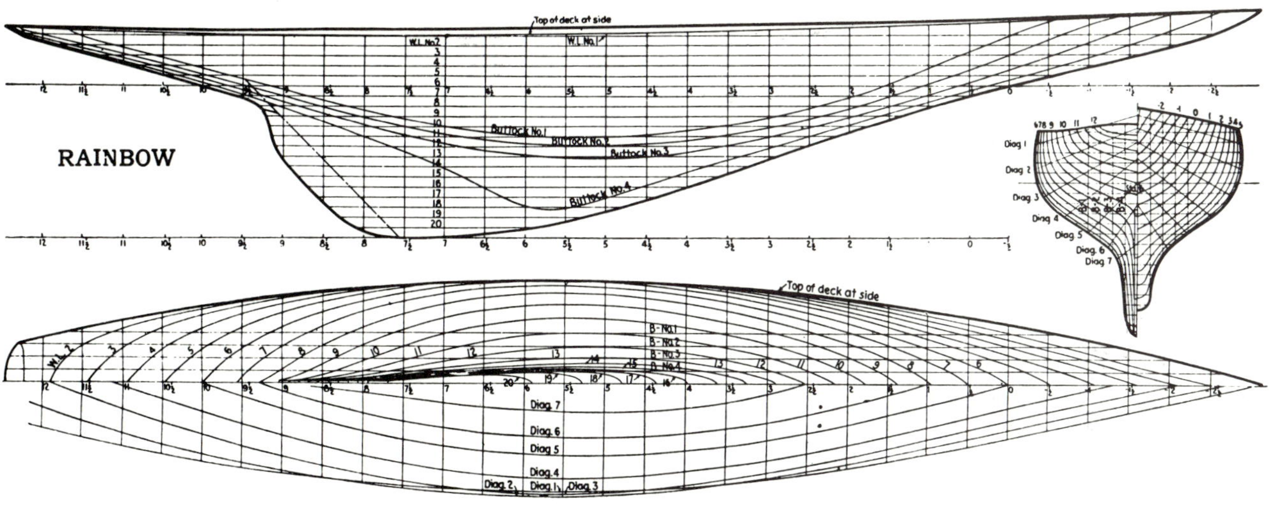
Top of deck at side
W.L. No.2
W.L. No.1
Buttock No.1
Buttock No.2
Buttock No.3
Buttock No.4
Diag 1
Diag 2
Diag 3
Diag 4
Diag 5
Diag 6
Diag 7
Top of deck at side
B-No.1
B-No.2
B-No.3
B-No.4
Diag. 7
Diag. 6
Diag. 5
Diag. 4
Diag. 2
Diag. 1
Diag. 3

RAINBOW

Rainbow was designed by W. Starling Burgess, but had fairer bilges and a fuller bow; and also a more restrained forward profile. Although a notably fast yacht, she was outsailed by *Endeavour* which lost the series after a remarkable incident resulting in a protest, and a decision which disgusted and demoralized the crew of the British yacht.

Endeavour's challenge was dogged by unusual events. Eight days before sailing for America some of her professional crew struck for increased pay, to bring their wages and prize money up to that which their American counterparts in the *Rainbow* were receiving. This was resisted by her owner, T. O. M. Sopwith, who discharged all those who were protesting. The captain, mates and many of the hands remained loyal to the yacht and, as experienced professional replacements could not be obtained at such short notice in mid-season, selected amateurs were shipped instead and in general proved themselves good racing hands, making up with keenness and and attention for their inevitable lack of experience in large-yacht practice. Their stout efforts were stiffened by the professionals remaining in the crew. *Rainbow*'s crew also struck at about the same time for more pay, but that dispute was settled amicably. Both incidents were almost unique in yacht racing and it is almost certain that, if *Endeavour* had carried her full and original professional crew, she would have won the America's Cup – but yacht racing is full of 'ifs'.

As usual, *Endeavour* was sailed by her owner, with Captain Williams standing by with advice, sometimes taking the wheel and always in charge of the crew. Sopwith never spoke to any of his professional crew except through the skipper and accordingly they considered him aloof.

Endeavour proved a faster yacht than *Rainbow*,

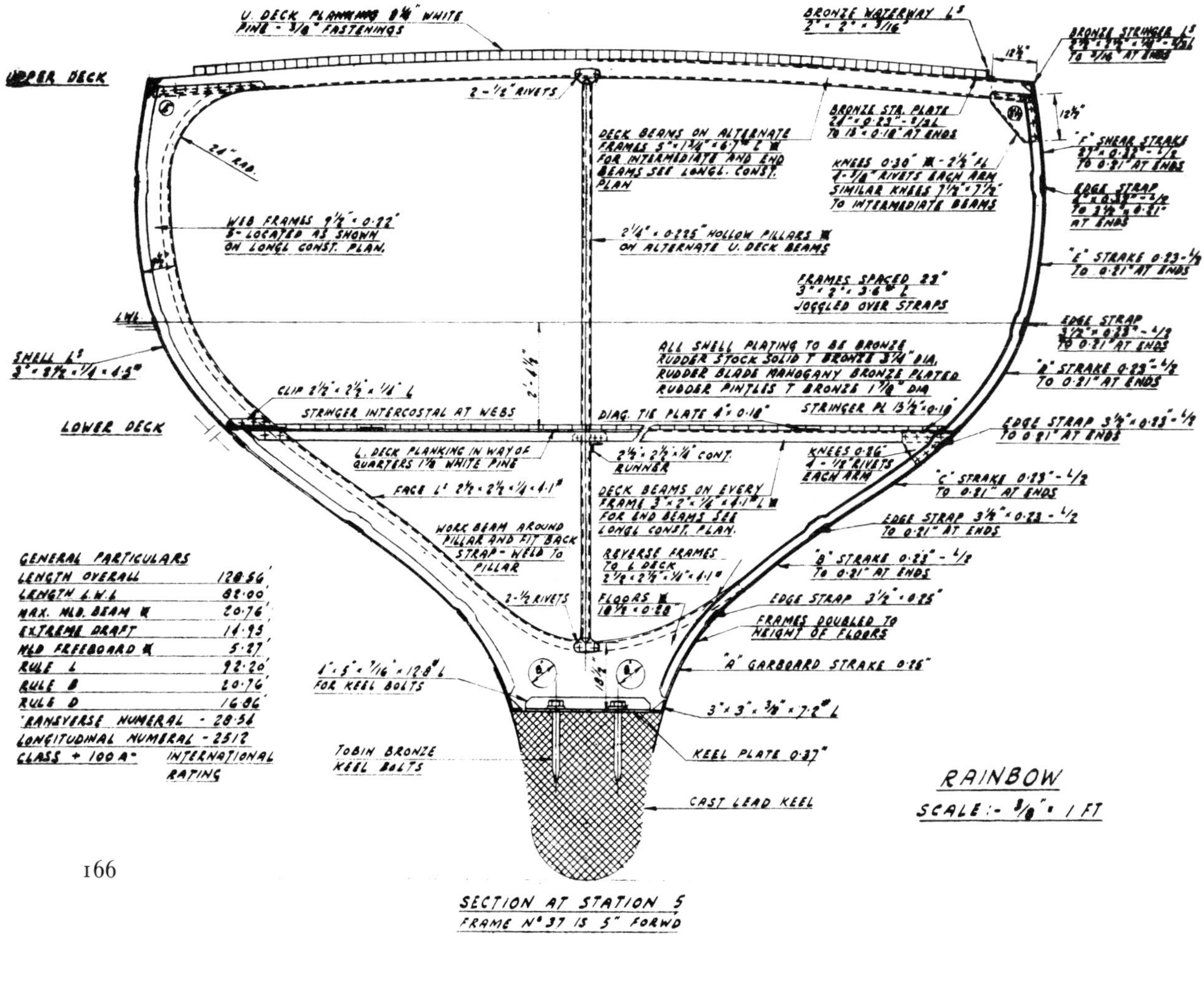

which was also sailed by her owner, Harold Vanderbilt. Before the start of the first race *Endeavour*'s mastheadsman was injured while attaching the masthead hook to the head of the mainsail, a method of relieving the compression on the mast. Fortunately the start was postponed by the race committee. *Endeavour* won this race by 2 minutes and the second race by 51 seconds. By then the Americans were faced with the probable loss of the America's Cup – an unthinkable blow to national prestige. In the third race *Endeavour* was leading by 6 minutes and on *Rainbow* Vanderbilt turned the helm over to Sherman Hoyt, another amateur who had sailed against Sopwith before and knew of his sensible habit of covering an opponent in match racing. Hoyt used this knowledge to bluff *Endeavour* into standing between *Rainbow* and the finishing line. The British yacht ran into a calm and in the local haze and flukey conditions *Rainbow* found the line first and won.

This unexpected defeat unsettled *Endeavour*'s crew, but an incident in the fourth race almost caused the withdrawal of the British yacht from the series. The yachts were luffing each other before the start, causing *Endeavour* to start after the American, but by the first mark *Endeavour* was 24 seconds ahead. Immediately after Vanderbilt had rounded the mark, to weather of *Endeavour*, Sopwith luffed hard, as he had the right to do under the racing rules. The long sharp stem of *Endeavour* came slicing to within 10 ft of *Rainbow*'s side forward of her mast, but Vanderbilt desperately held to his course and did not respond, despite shouted appeals to do so from his crew. Faced with ramming his opponent, probably bringing down her mast and possibly killing several men, Sopwith bore away and consulted with the American observer on board as to the correct time when he should hoist a protest flag under American practice. This was done when *Endeavour* was closer to the committee boat, but the protest was disallowed on the grounds that the protest flag should have been hoisted immediately after the incident, under the racing rules.

Vanderbilt's holding on and the committee's decision demoralized the crew of *Endeavour*, which lost the fifth race. However, the sixth race went badly for *Rainbow* and *Endeavour* was abeam and beginning to take her wind. Defeat was again imminent, but Vanderbilt bore away to leeward of the finish and again Sopwith followed to cover, sailing by the lee and therefore slowing, allowing the American boat to run away ahead and then luff up towards the finish and victory in one of the closest Cup series, but one which left much bitterness among the British.

LEFT
Structural midship section of the America's Cup defender *Rainbow*, 1934.

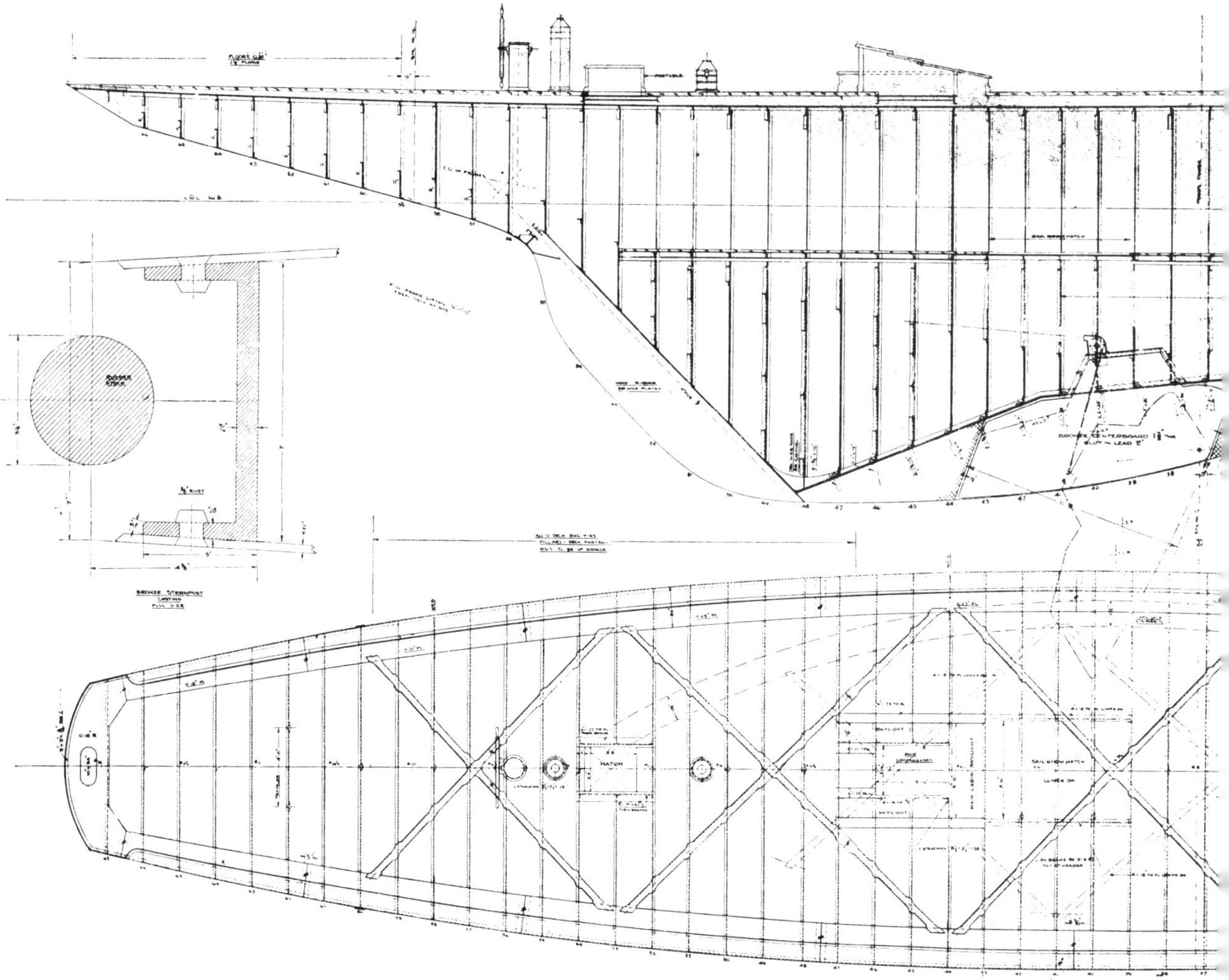

PREVIOUS PAGE

T. O. M. Sopwith at the wheel of *Endeavour*, with (left) Mrs Sopwith looking anxiously ahead, 1934. Three hands are alert by the lee shifting and running backstays. The mainsheet is in and the great yacht is smoking along to windward and well ahead of what is probably *Velsheda* (right). The exceptionally long-handled spokes of *Endeavour*'s wheel were probably requested by her owner, who took close interest in her conception, design, construction, rigging and handling. He seemed often to prefer wearing simple, comfortable racing clothing, in contrast to the more orthodox dress of many other owners in the class.

This photograph was probably taken in Stokes Bay, at the northern shore of Spithead, with the class standing towards the entrance to Portsmouth Harbour, and *Endeavour* will soon tack as she nears the spit.

The angle of heel shows that it was but a short step or stumble over the lee side: such a slip was a disgrace in those hotly contested races, where it meant certain loss of the chance of a prize, and in some cases probably death, as many of the racing skippers and hands could not swim, though they were outstanding seamen.

ABOVE

The structural profile and deck plan of *Rainbow*, designed in 1933–4 by Burgess & Donaldson and built by the Herreshoff Manufacturing Co. This transversely framed sloop was, like the other J

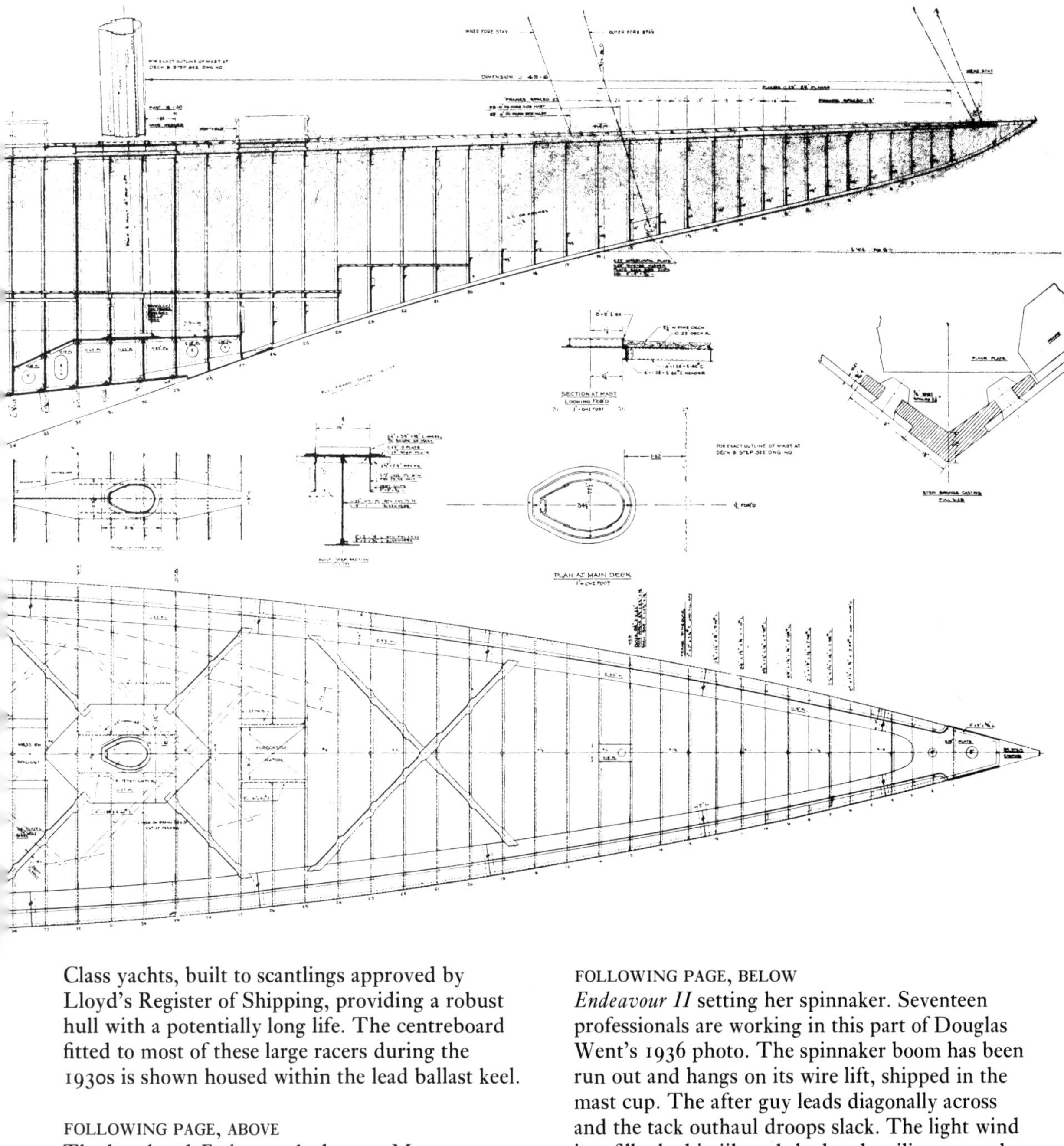

Class yachts, built to scantlings approved by Lloyd's Register of Shipping, providing a robust hull with a potentially long life. The centreboard fitted to most of these large racers during the 1930s is shown housed within the lead ballast keel.

FOLLOWING PAGE, ABOVE
The becalmed *Endeavour* kedges on May 9, 1934. She has just anchored with her long blue hull swung to the tide. Sixteen hands and the first and second mates are on deck. Captain Williams stands by the forestay and the owner is amidships. Her canvas hangs in folds, waiting as the tide thrums past her taut cable and all hands look for catspaws of wind.

FOLLOWING PAGE, BELOW
Endeavour II setting her spinnaker. Seventeen professionals are working in this part of Douglas Went's 1936 photo. The spinnaker boom has been run out and hangs on its wire lift, shipped in the mast cup. The after guy leads diagonally across and the tack outhaul droops slack. The light wind just fills the big jib and the hands tailing on to the spinnaker halyard are starting to raise its several thousand square feet of fine cotton, steadied upwards by the mate. The huge sail had a wide headboard with many lightening holes. It needed skilful handling in strong winds, when such sails had awesome power.

RIGHT
On board *Britannia* in 1935. Her owner, King George V, chats with retired Admiral of the Fleet Sir John Jellicoe, who commanded the Grand Fleet from 1914 to 1916 and was afterwards First Sea Lord. He was a frequent guest on the larger British racing yachts of the time, and during his governorship of New Zealand he inspired much sailing activity there. Queen Mary, in a dark hat, stands beyond him and the Duchess of York, later Queen Elizabeth and now the Queen Mother, stands by the skylight.

Dress and attitudes are typical of owners and their guests during the period 1919 to 1939. Male attire was usually white flannel trousers, blue reefer jacket, white deck shoes with blue or black socks, white shirt and the club or a plain navy blue tie. Ladies were allowed choice, but plain white for everything including the hat, as the Duchess wears here, was fashionable, and of course Queen Mary was never without her distinctive toque. The wives and daughters of many owners who raced on board regularly preferred the more practical tam-o'shanter or beret. All ladies wore skirts, as trousers for women were not accepted in sailing until after 1945.

FOLLOWING PAGE
Four of the big class laid up for the winter at the Gosport yard of Camper & Nicholson, 1934–5: from left to right, *Velsheda*, *Candida*, *Astra* and *Endeavour*. Each autumn these large yachts were hauled up on ground ways laid on the hard foreshore, carefully cradled and then well shored against winter winds and tides. Canvas covers, often called 'hullets', were rigged over the sacred white pine decks, supported by wooden A-frame spreaders and a ridge. Long ladders enabled the skipper and mates and the yard workmen to go on board to attend to the winter's alterations and repairs on deck and below. In spring the covers were removed and with shipwrights, painters and hands from her newly joined crew working on deck and on the hull, the pristine yacht finish was achieved before re-launch. Then the yachts were towed across to Portsmouth Dockyard to have masts stepped under a big crane.

PAGE 173, ABOVE LEFT
The American *Yankee* sets her genoa on a close reach during one of her first races. Her mast appears to be slightly further aft and the counter is fuller than her British J Class rivals *Shamrock V*, *Velsheda* and *Endeavour*, developed under the same rule.

Yankee was designed by Frank C. Paine and built by George Lawley & Sons (in which Paine had financial interests) in 1930 as a potential Cup defender against the challenge of *Shamrock V* that autumn. Though the selection trials were won by Harold Vanderbilt's *Enterprise*, *Yankee* went on to enjoy a successful eight year racing career, after 1934 in the ownership of Gerard B. Lambert.

Her principal dimensions were 125 ft 6 in overall length, 84 ft waterline, 22 ft 5 in beam and 15 ft draft, displacement 148 tons. The sail area was 7550 sq ft without spinnaker. Her skipper was Captain John Christensen and her crew were almost all Norwegians, many of whom had become accustomed to yacht racing in the

several large, ex-British racing yachts sold to neutral Norway during the First World War. Afterwards, when the wartime shipping boom burst, many of these yachts were sold back to British owners and their Norwegian crews found berths in American racing yachts, where some had sailed before 1917.

With her owner at the helm we may be sure she is being sailed as well as possible, for Lambert was a keen yachtsman, well liked by the English captains and crews against whom he raced. He brought *Yankee* to England in 1935 to race with the large class around the coast, commencing the season in the Thames at Southend and participating in the round of regattas on the east and south coasts, finishing at Dartmouth. Mr Lambert recounted his experiences in the facinating book *Yankee in England*.

When large-yacht racing ended in America, and during the close of the 1937 season, *Yankee* and her contemporaries were laid up, never to race again. In 1940 Gerard Lambert, like many in then neutral America, warmed to Britain's lone fight so he had *Yankee* broken up and the scrap sold. He sent the proceeds to Queen Mary for use in nursing charities of which she was patron.

OPPOSITE, ABOVE RIGHT
Endeavour (K4) leading *Yankee* (US 2) in a relatively smooth sea but with a freshening wind which has caused a reef to be taken in the mainsails. Both set the double-clewed jib and are sailing at near maximum speed, judging by the bow and quarter waves. The shape of these is interesting: the bow wave of each yacht is almost identical in form, as is the following hollow as the water eddies around the lower bilge amidships. The quarter waves rise and follow the counter in a similar way, but *Endeavour* appears to be 'pulling' her wake along after her whereas *Yankee*'s broader, American style counter and differing afterbody seems to be allowing it to break away up the centreline. American designers seemed to have long had the ability to create sterns which flattened the wake of sailing craft and minimized the effect of the quarter waves, which can considerably slow a racing yacht. The photograph was taken in England in 1935.

OPPOSITE, BELOW
Yankee racing during a gale off Southend in 1935. This photograph by Douglas Went strongly expresses the speed and power of a large racing yacht in a strong wind. *Yankee* has one reef in her mainsail and only a small staysail set forward. It is almost possible to hear the surge, hum and whistle of the rig above the crash of small seas tramped under the long, out-reaching bow, and one can almost feel the vibrating thrum of the weather shifting backstay whose runner block is visible just above the leech of the mainsail. The lee shifter and runner hang slack.

The owner stands at the wheel giving her a spoke this way or that. The deck is swept and saturated with spray and all hands are probably glad that the day's racing is almost over, even though she will subsequently have to anchor in the rough, exposed tideway off Southend Pier, with the rest of the class, the 12 Metres and attending sailing and motor yachts.

Yankee sailed to England under a yawl rig and stepped her racing mast at Portsmouth, then tuned up for the season. It was to be the last summer in which a full fleet of large racing

J
US2

J
US 2

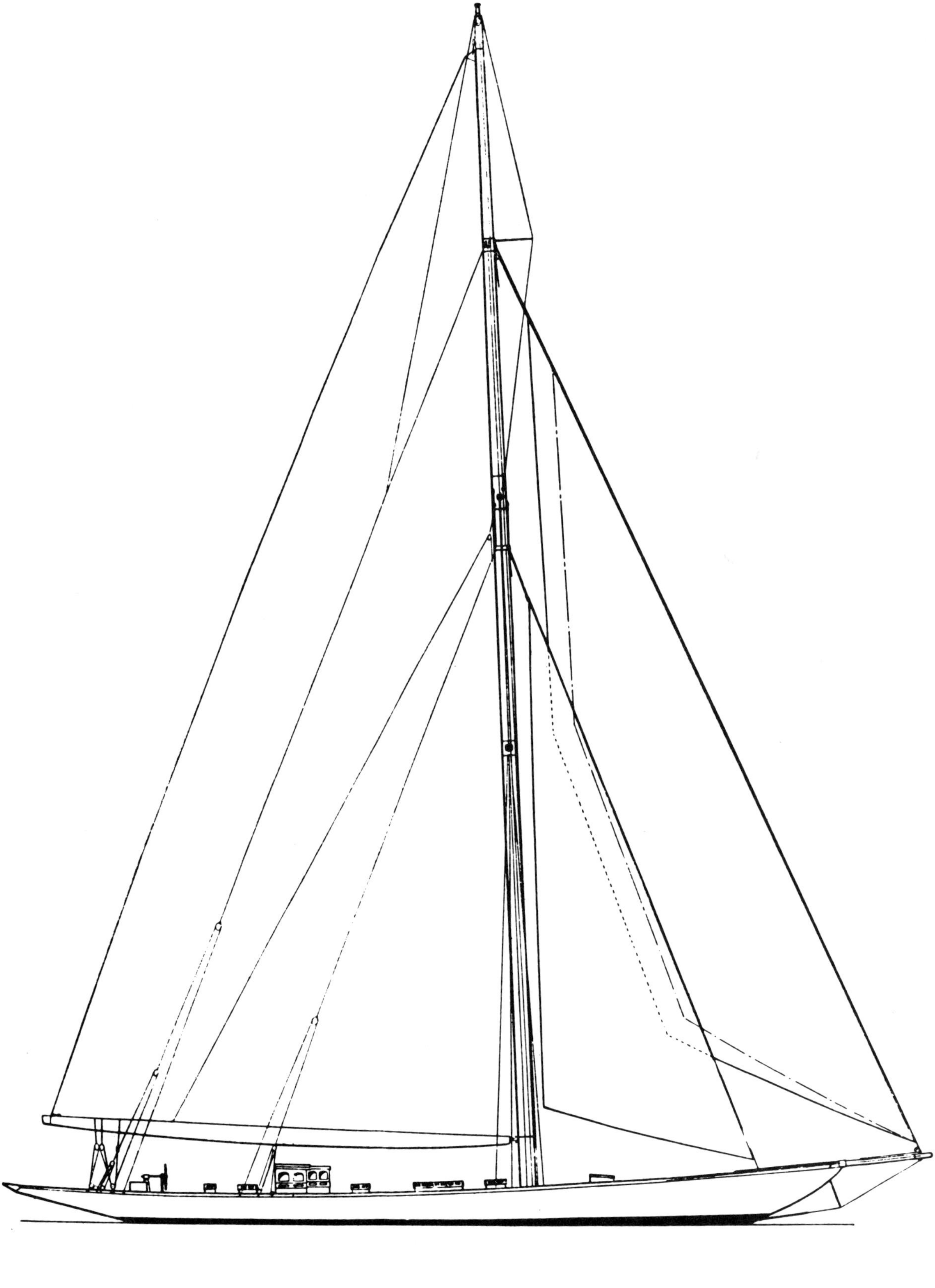

yachts would make this voyage around the coast fixtures, ending a century-old tradition in English yachting.

Comparatively few men were lost from these yachts, but an hour or two before this photograph was taken *Astra* had lost a man overboard while gybing at the Mouse light vessel. The big racers carried a wooden dinghy in gripes on deck amidships over the saloon skylights and it could be launched very quickly. A pair of lifebelts was also usually placed on the counter, ready to throw if anyone went overboard from the wet, slippery deck which had only a low toerail to provide a grip at its edge.

Sheet capstans were an early feature of American large racers and *Yankee*'s can be seen as gleaming polished chrome around her deck, with the anchor cable capstan forward.

PAGES 174–5
The big class running. *Candida* leads the green-hulled *Shamrock V* in the foreground and *Astra* is beyond. The bow wave of *Shamrock V* is surging, indicating she is closing the land in a fresher puff which has yet to reach *Candida*. *Shamrock V* is setting a double-clewed jib, the upper clew of which is visible above the forestay. *Astra* seems to be relying on her spinnaker and has no staysail set, but the jib is ready to be broken out.

The elaborate staying of the 165 ft wooden masts is well shown here. Three sets of spreaders are supplemented by a jumper strut on the upper set. The running backstay leads to the forestay position at the second spreader and the shifting backstays, which are set up from the counter, have a tail leading to the jib halyard position at the upper spreader and to the masthead. Although the rigs seem excessively high, they are little taller than those of the marconi rigged gaff cutters preceding them in the 1920s.

LEFT
During the winter of 1934–5 the old *Britannia* was given yet another rig, which was to be her last. It was designed by Camper & Nicholson and included a quadrilateral jib and Park Avenue boom, but it did not seem to suit the aged hull and she had no success with it during her last season.

ABOVE
The lee deck of *Britannia*, 1935. In the foreground the mainsheet leads through a lever-operated compressor which locks it while the fall is belayed around the large bronze bollard, at which a hand stands by. Compressors were introduced during

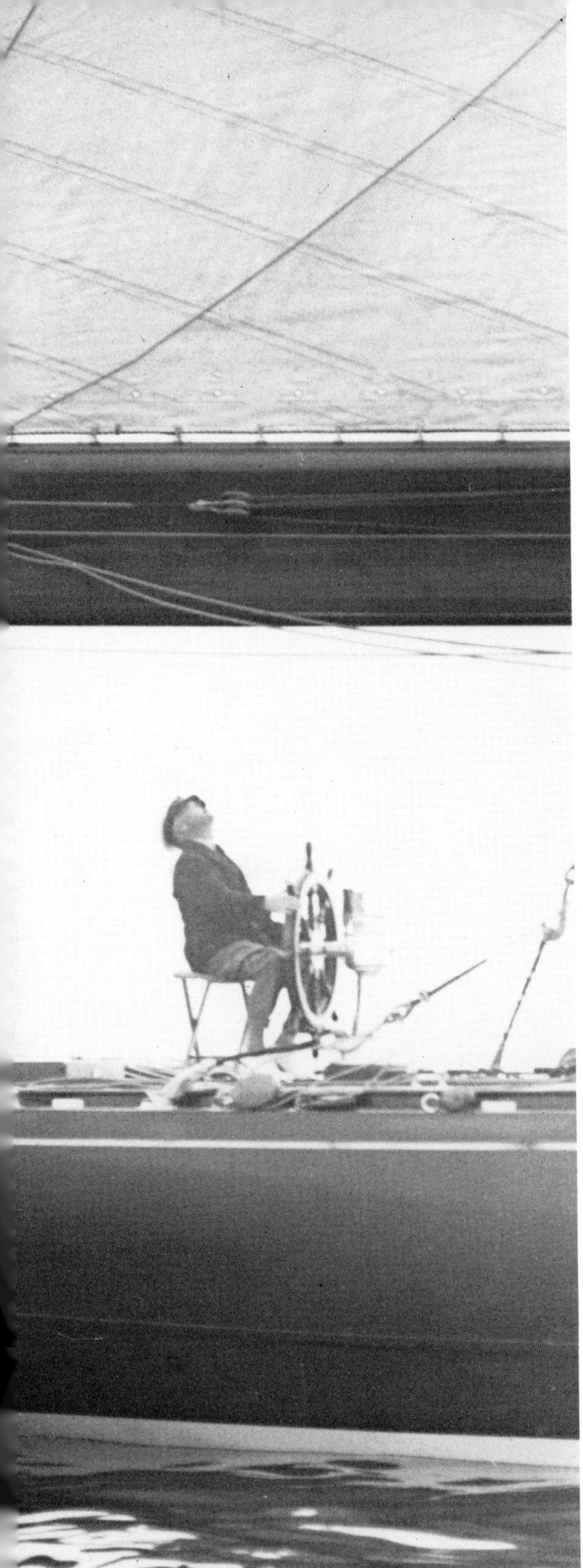

the 1930s to speed the work of sheeting in or easing out the mainsail. The order 'All hands on the mainsheet' brought every available man tailing on to its fall in a long line stretching almost to the mast; they pulled with all their strength, feet braced on the heeling deck, getting it in with those short, jerking heaves of the professional yachtsman, to the informal, gasping chorus timing each pull 'Ah hay, hey yo, ah ho . . .'

The sheet capstan was another innovation, but the circular hatch to the aft peak sail store and the teak skylights are relics of the old yacht's origins, forty-three years before.

LEFT
This photograph of the stern of *Endeavour* gives a good impression of the size of a large racer. Her freeboard aft was 5 ft 6 in and five or six men could comfortably stand and move about on the end of the counter, clear of the shifting backstays and mainsheet. The second mate is engrossed on the port quarter and a guest stands by the mainsheet. The helmsman watches the upper luffs of the headsails for a breeze and sits, uncharacteristically, on a folding stool; this suggests it is probably the owner, Mr Sopwith, who sometimes used a large fender as a seat in calms or quiet weather.

FOLLOWING PAGE, BELOW
Five of the large class in light airs, 1935: from right to left, *Endeavour* (K4), *Astra* (K2), *Velsheda* (K7), *Shamrock V* (K3) and *Yankee* (US2). They are standing slowly down Spithead. The long, lean hull of *Endeavour* contrasts with the shorter and fuller-bodied *Astra*. *Velsheda* shows a form transitional between the two. *Endeavour*, *Velsheda* and *Yankee* set large, single headsails but the others have the old jib and staysail foretriangle. *Astra*'s mast was painted black, a most unusual colour in racing yachts of the time. (The photograph is from a damaged negative.)

FOLLOWING PAGE, ABOVE
On board *Britannia*, 1935. Major Philip Hunloke, the King's representative, sits with hand on the wheel, accompanied by the then Duke and Duchess of York (later King George VI and Queen Elizabeth). A guest who is probably an

equerry stands at the right by the mainsheet. A leg of the runner from the shifting backstay leads down in the foreground. The Duke appears to be adjusting his movie camera. (One wonders if the films survive as they would now be of considerable interest.) Although trained as a naval officer, the Duke was not a yachtsman and his appearances on board *Britannia* were rare. His sons' lack of enthusiasm for yachting must have been disappointing for King George V, to whom a good race, particularly in a fresh wind, was a delight, and the old *Britannia* an institution.

BELOW
Launch of *Endeavour II* from Camper & Nicholson's yard, 1936. Her skipper, mates, crew, and shipwrights and riggers from the yard are on deck to handle the lines and help release the cradles from under her deep bottom when she leaves the ways and is well afloat. Among them is the owner's son, 3½ year old Tommy Sopwith, with one of the hands keeping a special eye on him.

The launch of an America's Cup challenger was then a considerable event and attracted large crowds of spectators, both yachtsmen and the general public. Steam and motor yachts lying off the yard are dressed to greet the blue-hulled racer, whose long bow brought new grace to the big class. She is moving down the greased ways at good speed and a second or so later will be waterborne for the first time. Camper & Nicholson's chief draughtsman and his staff will be particularly anxious, watching her waterline when she comes to rest. Months of work in calculations and on the drawing boards culminate here, and it is essential that a yacht floats to her 'launching condition' waterline and is not 'deep' or over draft at this stage in construction and completion, which would ruin her racing chances.

FOLLOWING PAGE
Endeavour II going well before a start with a double-clewed jib set. She was designed under the supervision of Charles E. Nicholson and was built at Camper & Nicholson for T. O. M. Sopwith as the ultimate British concept of the large racing yacht, the last of a line stretching back 150 years. Surprisingly, she was little photographed in English waters. Here she stands to windward on a fine summer morning with only the feathering bow wave to suggest speed. She is probably sailing at 9 or 10 knots. Her mast towers above deck but the sailplan appears trim

J
K6

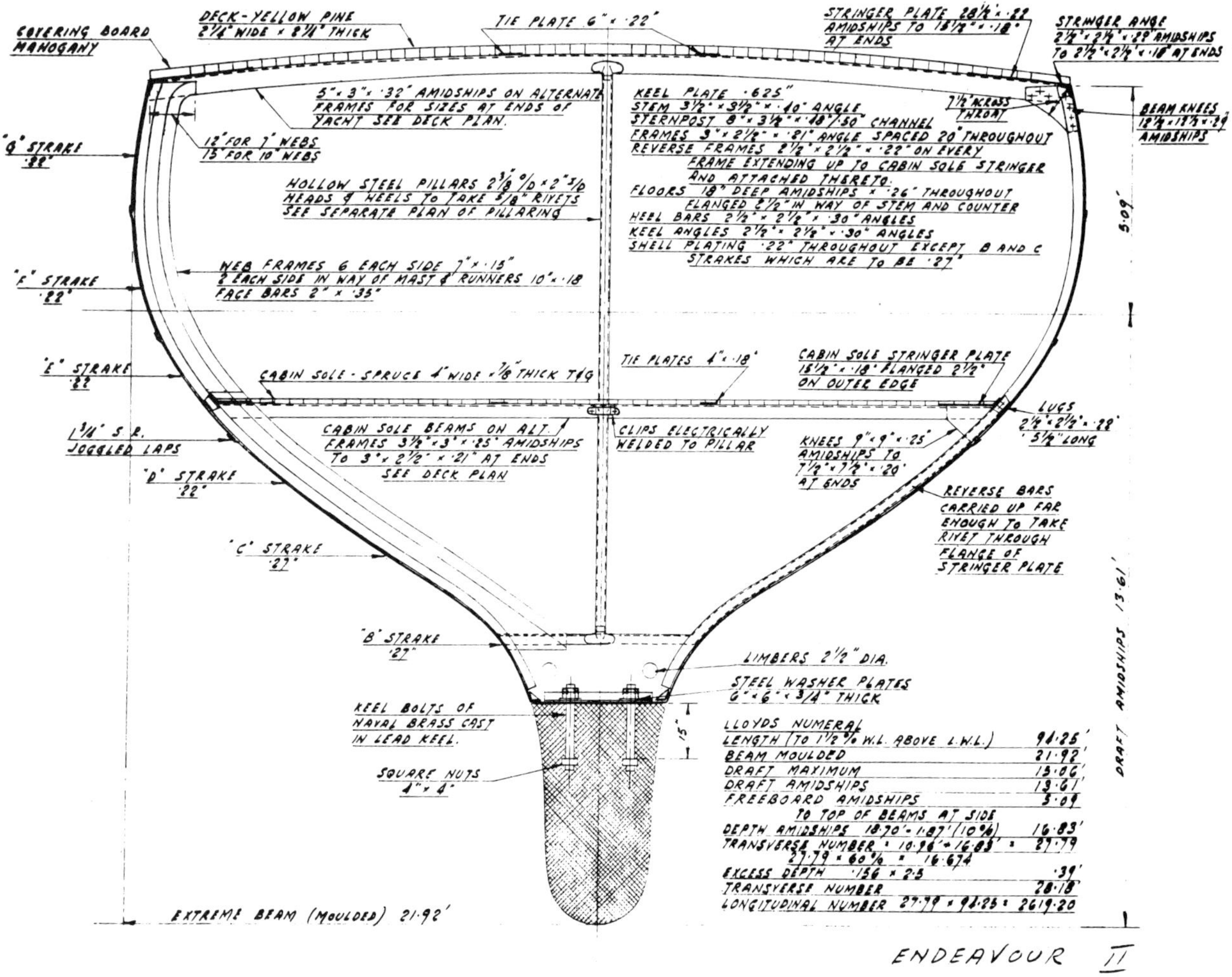
COVERING BOARD MAHOGANY
DECK - YELLOW PINE 2¼" WIDE × 3¼" THICK
TIE PLATE 6" × ·22"
STRINGER PLATE 28¼" × ·22 AMIDSHIPS TO 15½" × ·18" AT ENDS
STRINGER ANGLE 2½" × 2½" × ·22 AMIDSHIPS TO 2½" × 2½" × ·18 AT ENDS
5" × 3" × ·32" AMIDSHIPS ON ALTERNATE FRAMES FOR SIZES AT ENDS OF YACHT SEE DECK PLAN
KEEL PLATE ·625"
STEM 3½" × 3½" × ·40" ANGLE
STERNPOST 8" × 3½" × ·48"/50" CHANNEL
FRAMES 3" × 2½" × ·21" ANGLE SPACED 20" THROUGHOUT
REVERSE FRAMES 2½" × 2½" × ·22" ON EVERY FRAME EXTENDING UP TO CABIN SOLE STRINGER AND ATTACHED THERETO.
FLOORS 18" DEEP AMIDSHIPS × ·26" THROUGHOUT FLANGED 2½" IN WAY OF STEM AND COUNTER
HEEL BARS 2½" × 2½" × ·30" ANGLES
KEEL ANGLES 2½" × 2½" × ·30" ANGLES
SHELL PLATING ·22" THROUGHOUT EXCEPT B AND C STRAKES WHICH ARE TO BE ·27"
7½" ACROSS THROAT
BEAM KNEES 18½" × 18½" × ·29 AMIDSHIPS
"G" STRAKE ·22"
12" FOR 7" WEBS
15" FOR 10" WEBS
HOLLOW STEEL PILLARS 2⅜" O/D × 2" I/D HEADS & HEELS TO TAKE ⅝" RIVETS SEE SEPARATE PLAN OF PILLARING
5·09'
WEB FRAMES 6 EACH SIDE 7" × ·15" 2 EACH SIDE IN WAY OF MAST & RUNNERS 10" × ·18 FACE BARS 2" × ·35"
"F" STRAKE ·22"
"E" STRAKE ·22"
CABIN SOLE - SPRUCE 4" WIDE × ⅞" THICK T&G
TIE PLATES 4" × ·18"
CABIN SOLE STRINGER PLATE 15½" × ·18" FLANGED 2½" ON OUTER EDGE
1¼" S.R. JOGGLED LAPS
CABIN SOLE BEAMS ON ALT. FRAMES 3½" × 3" × ·25" AMIDSHIPS TO 3" × 2½" × ·21" AT ENDS SEE DECK PLAN
CLIPS ELECTRICALLY WELDED TO PILLAR
KNEES 9" × 9" × ·25" AMIDSHIPS TO 7½" × 7½" × ·20" AT ENDS
LUGS 2¼" × 2½" × ·28" 5½" LONG
"D" STRAKE ·22"
REVERSE BARS CARRIED UP FAR ENOUGH TO TAKE RIVET THROUGH FLANGE OF STRINGER PLATE
"C" STRAKE ·27"
DRAFT AMIDSHIPS 13·61'
"B" STRAKE ·27"
LIMBERS 2½" DIA.
STEEL WASHER PLATES 6" × 6" × ¾" THICK
KEEL BOLTS OF NAVAL BRASS CAST IN LEAD KEEL.
·5"
SQUARE NUTS 4" × 4"
LLOYDS NUMERAL
LENGTH (TO 1½% W.L. ABOVE L.W.L.) 94·25'
BEAM MOULDED 21·92'
DRAFT MAXIMUM 13·06'
DRAFT AMIDSHIPS 13·61'
FREEBOARD AMIDSHIPS 5·09
TO TOP OF BEAMS AT SIDE
DEPTH AMIDSHIPS 18·70' – 1·87' (10%) 16·83'
TRANSVERSE NUMBER = 10·96' + 16·83' = 27·79
27·79 × 60% = 16·674
EXCESS DEPTH ·156 × 2·5 ·39'
TRANSVERSE NUMBER 28·18'
LONGITUDINAL NUMBER 27·79 × 94·25 = 2619·20
EXTREME BEAM (MOULDED) 21·92'
ENDEAVOUR II

compared with, say, that of *Valkyrie III*. Her dimensions were 132 ft overall length, 87 ft waterline, 22 ft 6 in beam, 15 ft draft. Displacement was 164 tons and sail area 7500 sq ft. With her outreaching bow, ample freeboard and well-setting sails, she seems the ideal of the large racing yacht.

Endeavour II had only a short career. Launched in 1936, she participated in the last summer of large-yacht racing in England and in 1937 was towed across to America to refit for the America's Cup races in September against the American sloop *Ranger*. She lost the challenge and was broken up in 1956.

PAGE 183
Velsheda leading *Endeavour*, 1936. She has set a double-clewed jib and *Endeavour* appears to be just setting hers. Both are sailing much faster than this smooth-water photograph suggests – probably at about 11 knots – but the hulls make little fuss and there is an absence of hollow in the wave formation on the windward side. *Velsheda*'s crew are concentrated to windward amidships. Captain Mountifield is at the wheel and the mate forward keeps a lookout for small craft eager to get a close view of the racers.

LEFT, ABOVE
Structural midship section of the British America's Cup challenger *Endeavour II*, 1936.

LEFT, BELOW
Launch of the American J Class racer *Ranger* from her building berth at the Bath Ironworks at Bath, Maine on May 11, 1937. She is coming down the ways fast, with the aluminium alloy mast laid on deck and cradled carefully. *Ranger* is generally regarded as the fastest J Class yacht built and was probably also faster on a reach than the earlier and larger racers such as *Reliance* or *Valkyrie III*. She easily defeated the America's Cup challenger *Endeavour II* in the 1937 series, the last in which the big class sailed.

The design of *Ranger* was worked on by the then ageing W. Starling Burgess, who had designed the earlier defenders *Enterprise* and *Rainbow*, and collaborating with him was the youthful Olin Stevens Jr. Several designs were produced and the model which was chosen as giving the best performance was ugly, but the boat was built from that set of lines. However, which of them conceived the design remains a secret, known only now to Olin Stevens and perhaps some surviving tank staff. Some model testing had been carried out for the American yachts built for the America's Cup defence in 1930 and for *Rainbow* four years later, while *Shamrock* had been tested in a ship-testing tank in 1899. Using methods developed during the early 1930s by Professor K. Davidson, models of the American racers *Weetamoe*, *Rainbow* and the first British *Endeavour* (whose lines had sportingly been presented to the Americans by Camper & Nicholson) were towed against four proposed new hull shapes. The model selected, from the lines of which *Ranger* would be built, was so unusual that it was said both designers were apprehensive of her appearance and its effect on owner, crew and public. *Ranger*'s principal dimensions were 135 ft 1 in overall length, 87 ft waterline, 20 ft 11 in beam, 15 ft draft. Displacement was 166.5 tons and sail area 7546 sq ft.

FOLLOWING PAGE, ABOVE
Structural midship section of the American J Class yacht *Ranger*, built 1937.

FOLLOWING PAGE, BELOW
Comparison of the J Class racing sloop *Ranger* (1937) with a contemporary 12 Metre International Rating Class racing yacht (*in black*). Nowadays the 12 Metres, which retain the same principal dimensions and sail areas, are regarded by many as 'big yachts' (though smaller than the recent 'maxi' racers). Here we can appreciate why the professional crews of the older large yachts referred kindly to the 12 Metres as 'Fine little boats – just right for a gentleman what wants an afternoon's sail in comfort.' *Ranger*'s staysail would make the 12 Metre a mainsail.

The dinghy, shown dotted and inverted on *Ranger*'s counter, is stowed in the position usual on board American racers of this class, whereas British yachts carried them amidships over the saloon skylight, clear of hands working backstays and spinnaker guys at the quarters.

Direct comparison of rigs is difficult but the load on the mast of a J Class yacht was approximately five and a half times that on the mast of a 12 Metre. The frequent rig failures of

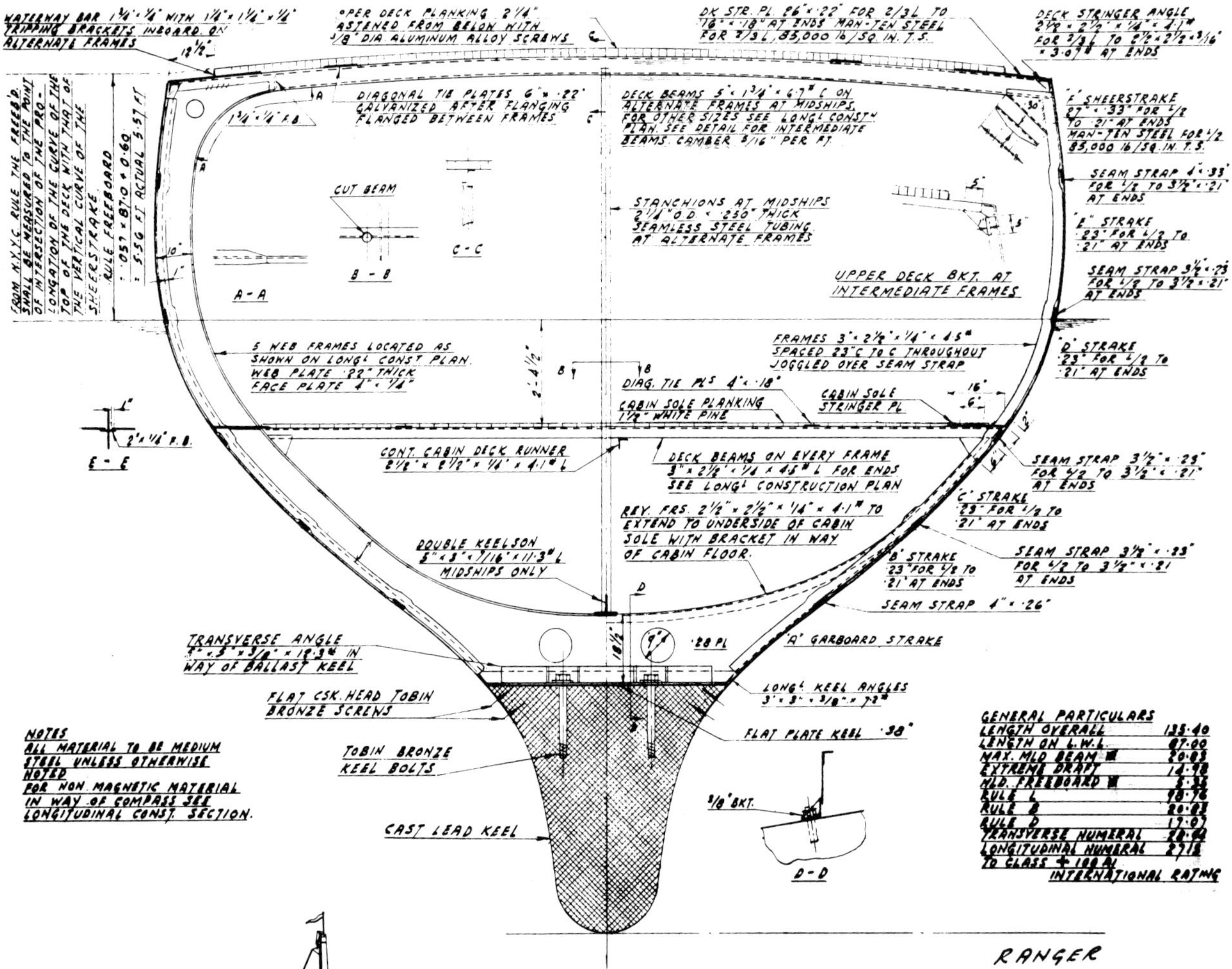

the large racers after the adoption of the J Class rule in 1930 were partially due to the mast weights permitted by the rules being based on the cube of size, which resulted in masts lighter than those of the earlier International Rule.

In any racing yacht the aim of the designer is to achieve a rig which is light yet with sufficient strength to stand in any conditions and to be within the rating rules. The large racers of the 1920s and 1930s were increasingly sailed on inshore courses in well established patterns of events in Britain and on the American northeast coast. The increasing height of sailplans in this period led to masts in both the gaff and bermudian rig which became weak if reasonable weight aloft was to be maintained, consequently large yachts of both rigs were unreliable in strong winds on inshore courses and masts were occasionally lost in the gaff-rigged racers of the 1920s.

In 1928 the two American large racing yachts *Vanitie* and *Resolute* were again re-rigged as bermudian sloops, having been schooners for several years. In 1930 the four contenders to defend the America's Cup against *Shamrock V* were bermudian cutters having three headsails (staysail, jib and jib topsail) as did the challenger. The American yachts could set a genoa jib going to windward in light airs; however, as wind increased to about 7 m.p.h. its luff sagged and the sail lost efficiency due to mast bend. The material of the masts and their design were then incapable of withstanding the considerable compression load from this sail set high on the mast.

The masts of the potential Cup defenders *Weetamoe*, *Vanitie* and *Whirlwind* were of spruce, with a hollow core and not of unusual construction, and weighed about 5000 lbs. The similar mast of *Shamrock V* was much heavier at 6350 lbs: this factor alone was primarily responsible for her poor showing in the races.

Enterprise, chosen to defend the Cup, had a mast designed by C. P. Burgess, the brother of her designer W. S. Burgess, who was employed in the Navy Department. It was made of Duralumin, an aluminium alloy, and weighed only 4000 lbs. Its section and longitudinal form created less wind resistance and eddying than the wooden spars of the yachts against which she raced. As there was then no minimum mast weight in the class rules this light mast was permitted. *Enterprise*'s was the first made of Duralumin. It was 162 ft long by 18 in diameter at heel tapered to 9 in at head, and fabricated of two thickness of plate, shaped 12-sided and with over 80,000 rivets. It was very flexible longitudinally and had to be carefully used. The spreaders were also metal, and there were mechanically connected stay end fittings. This mast was discarded after the races. *Enterprise* also introduced the triangular sectioned 'Park Avenue' boom. This was adopted by other yachts in the class in both America and Britain, though it was for a time later superseded by various types of 'bending boom', then was again used by some large racers.

The combination of this rig's lightness and advanced details with the excellent hull design and a determined crew ensured that the much heavier and more crudely rigged *Shamrock V* had no chance, despite her well trained and very experienced helmsman and crew. After the 1930 races it was known that British yachtsmen would not challenge again for the America's Cup unless minimum mast requirements were laid down. The New York Yacht Club eventually agreed to the weight of masts, excluding fittings, to be at least 5500 lbs. A minimum diameter of 18 in was required, and the height of the foretriangle was limited to 82½ per cent of the measured mast height above deck. This was based on use of a fabricated steel mast. At the same time requirements for minimum accommodation were instituted, and the working of sheets or backstays below deck was prohibited.

The transverse support of these high masts of the period was relatively easy to arrange as the trusses of spreaders and shrouds could be disposed into as many panels as thought necessary, consistent with minimal windage. However, fore-and-aft support of such a mast is much more difficult as the backstays have to be adjustable. The mast of *Enterprise* was supported by the jib-topsail stay, the luff wire of the working jib, which was set flying, the fixed forestay and an auxiliary stay led from the deck 10 ft before the mast to the top of the lower shroud panel. There were three sets of backstays, the lower two worked from winches below deck and the upper pair, the shifters, by wire rope purchases. There were also winches below deck to set up the forestay, the auxiliary forestay, and to handle the jib and staysail sheets. The genoa and other big jibs were sheeted via a winch drum on deck which was driven by four men on crank handles below deck.

In 1932 *Vanitie* was fitted with a new wooden mast and rig designed by W. S. Burgess. It had a two-headsail arrangement in place of the three then usual, and the shifting or upper backstays became the principal backstays. The result was that in 1934 the America's Cup yachts *Endeavour* and *Rainbow* also appeared with two-headsail rigs as did *Yankee* and *Weetamoe*. The use of two headsails conferred much greater driving power and increased heeling forces compared with the earlier three-headsail rig, and encouraged new yachts to have a greater waterline length to improve stability and motion in a seaway. The mast of *Endeavour* was of steel, fabricated with electric welding. It was of circular section, 20 in diameter at the heel, and more aerodynamically efficient than a pear-shaped mast but comparatively less stiff fore and aft. After experimenting with a bending boom she shipped a Park Avenue boom which was able to rotate about its long axis, unlike those used in *Enterprise* and *Rainbow* the upper surfaces of which were held horizontal. *Weetamoe* had pear-sectioned Duralumin masts designed by W. S. Burgess and intended to stand in moderate winds with only one forestay and the shifting (upper) backstay to support them longitudinally. This was reasonably successful. The mast of *Rainbow* was 18 in wide and 30 in fore-and-aft dimension for most of its length, and had about $\frac{1}{3}$ in wall thickness at the base to about $\frac{1}{6}$ in at the head. The three sets of spreaders of length equal to the yacht's beam at the mast allowed the genoa to be carried to windward. Steel rod standing rigging set up with turnbuckles was used, designed to a factor of safety of 2. It stretched about 5 in from deck to masthead when she was heeled on the wind and in that condition the mast compressed about 1.5 in: it was not possible to keep such masts straight throughout their length when sailing and the direct load on such a mast was sometimes about 126 tons. To relieve the compressive strain of a halyard they had a masthead hook on which the mainsail head rested when hoisted. In many yachts this had to be released by the mastheadsman before the main could be lowered. *Endeavour* had a similar but lighter and improved system of steel rod standing rigging. Rod was also used instead of wire rope, which was not available in sizes suitable to absorb the loads of the rigs without unacceptable windage, in *Weetamoe*. The Duralumin masts on *Rainbow* and *Weetamoe* were only used for one season. They were not made of the most corrosion resistant aluminium alloy, but showed no sign of corrosion or fatigue.

Rainbow also had an effective bending boom, of a type tried in Britain for several years with varying success. *Endeavour* used a triangular Park Avenue boom which was heavier as a type but more reliable and its flat upper surface directed air over the leech of the mainsail. The Cup yachts of 1934 were the first large racers to set a parachute spinnaker. These averaged 17,000 sq ft in area – over twice the measured sail area. When set they imposed great strain on the rig in most conditions.

In 1936 *Rainbow* and *Yankee* were fitted with new masts of electric-welded steel and designed by Frank C. Paine. They were of smaller longitudinal section than the earlier Duralumin masts and reduced wind eddies. Larger quadrilateral jibs, which had been introduced by *Endeavour* in 1934, were used by these two yachts in 1936 and single sheeted jibs were generally discarded in the class that year. *Rainbow* also experimented with a loose-footed mainsail, which as would be expected was most efficient in light airs but induced weather helm in stronger winds. This arrangement was banned for the 1937 America's Cup races.

In 1934 *Endeavour* had been rigged with a forestay which could be released to allow the genoa jib to be used when tacking in light winds. In 1937 *Yankee* was re-rigged with a single headsail, which required the mast to be stepped 6 ft farther forward and alterations had to be made to her forebody as a result. It was not a successful rig. That year larger and more efficient quadrilateral jibs were used and the parachute spinnakers, which had been introduced in the class by *Vanitie* and *Weetamoe*, soon followed on the others. Genoa jibs were by then little used in these yachts. *Ranger* (1937) had the final development in the large-class rigs with her mast, bending boom and two spinnaker booms of Duralumin.

The losses of masts in the J Class racing yachts during the 1930s aroused much comment and criticism. Given that the masts, which stood on average 152 ft above the deck, had to be stayed on a base of the beam that averaged only 20 ft at the shrouds, this is not surprising though the two *Endeavours* had additional spread with channels. The bury of these masts below deck was about 10 ft. For mast losses and rig damage. 1935 was a good example of a contemporary racing season. Seven and occasionally eight large racers competed in the English regattas and briefly across the Channel at Le Harve, in a total of 35 races. *Endeavour* was dismasted in the Thames estuary on June 6, when *Velsheda* broke her boom and *Astra* lost a man overboard. The next day's racing was abandoned because of a gale and strong winds also caused cancellation of the Southend to Dover race. At Dover bad weather allowed only one of two races to be sailed. *Endeavour* rejoined the fleet in the Solent with a new welded steel mast, and there were no more dismastings that season until the last race at Dartmouth when the American sloop *Yankee*, which had raced for most of that season with the British large class, lost hers.

The day was squally with winds up to about 30 m.p.h. and a choppy sea. *Yankee* had then won eight races and *Endeavour* nine so her owner was keen to start and had his racing flag hoisted, which challenge was followed by *Endeavour*, *Velsheda* and *Shamrock V*, but *Candida* and *Astra* remained at anchor. It is thought that the British boats would not have started in the conditions, particularly at the end of a season, had the American not intended to race. *Yankee* set a reefed main and a staysail, her usual hard weather racing rig; the others set a reefed mainsail, staysail and a jib. Towards the end of the first leg of the course *Yankee* broke out her double-clewed jib (a similar sail was carried by *Endeavour*) and her owner, at the wheel, bore away slightly in preparation for the gybe at the mark. The mast then buckled and collapsed, falling to leeward with shrouds and spreaders intact. All the yachts abandoned the race as a gesture to the crippled visitor, but it is thought also with relief for their masts. *Yankee*'s mast had been sent over in three pieces and assembled and welded together at the yard of Camper & Nicholson. These connections apparently did not contribute to its failure.

The use of electrically welded steel masts was advantageous for repair. *Endeavour II* and *Velsheda* lost masts at Plymouth in 1936. There were squalls and the *Endeavour II* mast broke in four places. It was re-welded and strengthened and soon restepped. On the first day of Cowes Week she luffed up to trim sheets and as she bore away the mast again went overboard.

The failure of the masts of the bermudian rigged large-class yachts, as with their predecessors with gaff rigs, was almost always due to the imposition of a sudden increase in load on the mast due to a sudden change in wind strength, to 'filling away' on the boat after trimming sheets or to a sudden squall. The cause of failure may often have been the incorrect tensioning of the backstays, remembering that the transverse and the head staying was relatively rigid but the backstays had to be let go and set up very quickly when racing, leading to error in the tension applied despite the care taken. The considerable loads imposed on these masts have been described and in view of their extreme height, small staying base and construction their loss is not remarkable. However, the acceptance by owners of such a rig for eight years is truly remarkable in view of the potential danger of dismasting and the cost of replacement.

ABOVE
The long bows of the J Class racers posed problems in handling headsails and spinnakers below decks. These were stored in the foc's'le when racing and sent up on deck as required, and had to be as quickly sent below to be refolded and ready again for possible use. The Cup defender *Ranger* was fitted with this metal sail chute, a giant forerunner of today's spinnaker chutes. One of the crew's cots is stowed up out of the way.

This photograph shows the careful construction of these yachts. *Ranger* was framed and plated in steel, the side plating being of a special grade. The frames are joggled over the strapped and riveted seams of the flush shell plating. The flush butts of the plating are strapped and have double-riveted connections. The heads of frames connect by knees welded to the frames and beams. A deck of selected white pine is laid on deck beams braced with stringer and tie plates; pillars connect the deck to keelson angles on top of the floors. *Ranger* was built under the special survey of Lloyd's Register of Shipping, who since 1907 have provided scantling rules, survey and classification of the construction of most international racing yachts of the IYRU and J classes. *Ranger* was classed +100A International Rating.

The hulls of the big-class yachts were strong and seaworthy and would potentially have lasted many years, though they were mostly broken up by 1941. *Endeavour* and *Velsheda* alone linger as the last metal hulled J Class racers and the composite hulled *Shamrock V* (now *Quadrifoglio*) still sails as a cruiser in the Mediterranean, where the older IYRU Metre Class racers *Cambria*, *Candida* and *Astra* are also usefully extending their long careers under reduced rigs.

They will never race again.